25,95

Promises
to Keep

D0068140

Social Theory, Education, and Cultural Change

Series Editors: Carlos Alberto Torres and Raymond Allen Morrow

Promises to Keep

CULTURAL STUDIES, DEMOCRATIC EDUCATION, AND PUBLIC LIFE

EDITED BY

Greg Dimitriadis
AND **Dennis Carlson**

RoutledgeFalmer
NEW YORK AND LONDON

Published in 2003 by
RoutledgeFalmer
29 West 35th Street
New York, NY 10001
www.routledge-ny.com

Published in Great Britain by
RoutledgeFalmer
11 New Fetter Lane
London EC4P 4EE
www.routledgefalmer.com

Copyright © 2003 by RoutledgeFalmer

RoutledgeFalmer is an imprint of Taylor & Francis Group.
Printed in the United States of America on acid-free paper.
Design and typography: Jack Donner

All rights reserved. No part of this book may be reprinted or reproduced or utilized in any
form or by any electronic, mechanical, or other means, now known or hereafter invented,
including photocopying and recording or in any information storage or retrieval system,
without permission in writing from the publishers.

Earlier versions of the chapters by Crichlow, Denzin, Carlson, Henke, and Freedman appeared
in *Cultural Studies/Critical Methodologies*, 3(1), (2003).

"Extraordinary Conversations in Public Schools," by Lois Weis and Michelle Fine, from *INternational Journal of Qualitative Studies in Education*, 14(4), (2001) 497–523. Reprinted by permission of Taylor & Francis, Inc. © 2001 by Taylor & Francis, Inc. www.tandf.co.uk

Chapter 2 was adapted from "Civil Society as a Site for Building Educational Publics: Possibilities and Limitations," by Kathleen Knight Abowitz, from *Educational Studies*, 31(4), (Winter 2000) 375–393.

10 9 8 7 6 5 4 3 2 1

Library of Congress Cataloging-in-Publication Data

Promises to keep: cultural studies, democratic education, and public life / co-edited
by Greg Dimitriadis and Dennis Carlson.
    p. cm. — (Social theory, education, and cultural change)
    Includes bibliographical references and index.
    ISBN 0-415-94474-0 — ISBN 0-415-94475-9 (pbk.)
        1. Critical pedagogy—United States. 2. Democracy—Study and teaching—United States.
    I. Dimitriadis, Greg, 1969–   II. Carlson, Dennis. III. Social theory, education & cultural
change.

    LC196.5.U6 P75 2003
    370.11'5—dc21

                                                                    2002036706

Contents

Acknowledgments

This volume grew out of several AERA panels on cultural studies and education, held between 1999 and 2002 in Montreal and New Orleans. We would like to thank all participants on these panels as well as the contributors to this volume. We've learned much from you all. Dennis would like to thank those faculty and graduate students affiliated with the Center for Education and Cultural Studies at Miami University and the Miami Initiative for Leadership, Culture, and Schooling. Greg would like to thank his colleagues and students in the Graduate School of Education at the State University of New York at Buffalo. In particular, he would like to thank all those in the Social Foundations of Education program in the Department of Educational Leadership and Policy for their unwavering support and encouragement. We would also like to thank our series editors Carlos Alberto Torres and Raymond Allen Morrow as well as Joe Miranda, Paul Johnson, and Ben McCanna at RoutledgeFalmer for encouraging us in this project and helping us see it through to completion.

We would like to note that this project has been collaborative in every way. Because Dennis was the introduction's primary author, Greg is listed as the volume's first editor. In alternating these designations, we have tried to signal the wonderfully balanced effort this volume has been all along the way.

Between Unthinking Modernism and Rethinking Postmodernism

Raymond Allen Morrow and Carlos Alberto Torres

"We live in perilous times." This book, telling us about the promises we need to keep in public education, is an excellent reminder of this biblical aphorism. The hysterical fears evoked by threats of terrorism should not be used to distract us from the unfinished and fragile character of the democratic experiment in education in the United States and elsewhere. *Promises to Keep* is theoretically distinctive in its weaving together of insights drawn from theories of cultural reproduction, cultural studies, the theory of the democratic public sphere (engaged in the spirit of Dewey's pragmatism), and postmodern sensibilities. These questions are addressed through a nuanced appropriation of themes drawn from the Marxian and critical theory traditions, critiques of Eurocentrism, the limits of theories of identity based on subordination of others, and the necessary focus on communities as the space for organizing change.

Though mostly focusing on North American case studies, this collection should be of methodological and theoretical interest elsewhere for those concerned with breaking through the rhetorical slogans and false oppositions that has plagued much critical scholarship. Particularly instructive is capacity of authors—as articulated synthetically in the editors' introduction—to move beyond the more abstract call for a "language of possibilities" to confront the messy realities of identity politics and their difficult articulation with the renewal of democracy. The authors do not shy away from confronting the complex issues flowing from the inability of classic modern models of normalization and social integration based on strategies of governmentality (as described by Foucault) to deal effectively with the crises at the community level. In the process the authors develop a reflexive attitude toward their postmodern commitments, acknowledging the practical dilemmas arising from deconstructive modes of theorizing: the general questioning truth claims; demystification of the disciplinary and anti-democratic effects of governmentality; valorization of the fluidity and instability of identity; and embracing popular culture as a resource for transformative imagination.

As necessary reactions against the limits of modernity, these responses also beg the question of the pragmatic, reconstructive alternatives. Challenging dogmatic ideological and positivist truth claims is not sufficient to deal with how, in local contexts, empirical knowledge can be brought to bear upon persuading people about the implications of the "facts of the matter." Repudiating of the insidious effects of governmentality does not adequately deal with the practical implications of Foucault's simultaneous stress on the productive potential of power.

The pragmatic reference to democratic public spheres—in search of forms of democracy that are neither "exclusionary" nor "disciplinary"—takes a step toward how to recognize such constructive uses of state power, a theme that otherwise gets lost in standard, blanket condemnations of the state. Similar dilemmas are evident in the clash between how individuals and groups become obsessed by essentializing identity claims in an epoch where, supposedly, fluidity, hybridity and incessant change offer new forms of autonomy and freedom. Nor does the often-elusive search for the emancipatory potential of popular culture resolve the questions posed by colonizing effects of transnational culture industries. Nor does the postmodern questioning of the pretensions of "universalistic" intellectuals deal with the need for a constructive dialogue between creative and oppositional forms of popular culture and some form of inevitably elitist (academic) "moral-intellectual leadership," to use Gramsci's term in another context. Without claiming to resolve such issues, the authors do provide sensitive explorations of their implications in case studies that demonstrate the empirical richness of cultural studies and qualitative methods.

Paradoxically, as Dennis Carlson and Greg Dimitriadis stress in the introduction, their strategy involves the use of postmodernism as the basis of a negation of modernity, for "unthinking modernity," without falling into the illusion of leaping outside of or beyond modernity. Whether one calls this a form of "critical modernism," a rethinking of the modern, or a postmodern unthinking of modernity, does not matter a great deal. What is of more decisive importance is that it may open the way for a "new progressivism" attuned to the realities of the 21st century. The vision embraced in this collection is on the possibility of keeping the promise of public education as the construction of a new set of social relationships that are built on collaboration, solidarity, social justice, and equity for all. From this perspective, education is not only as a means of social mobility, creation of knowledge, or transmission of culture but as also inevitably as a site of political-economic contestation and identity formation.

In a low-keyed, non-explicit form, this anthology provides evidence of the shifting terrain of the politics of knowledge and the volatile status of "postmodernism" as a buzzword for signaling, however confusingly, methodological and theoretical positions. Regrettably, careers have been made and lost, for better and worse, on the capacity of charged terms to obscure the deeper issues and longer history of scholarly debates. One can only hope this sensible and selective invocation of a postmodern sensibility can provide a model for avoiding the confusions created by sectarian oppositions that unwittingly contribute to the reproduction of the system that is overtly opposed.

Finally, this book offers also a powerful and historically nuanced critique of neoconservative and neoliberal educational reforms. While the authors of this book probe the futility of many of these reforms in the United States and elsewhere, they show the ironies of neoliberal and neoconservative educational reforms, considering the many border crossings that we are experimenting, and the progressive blurring of the lines between fiction and reality (or as the editors say in their introduction, between reality and hyper-reality).

Promises to Keep: Cultural Studies, Democratic Education, and Public Life, opens up new ground by reminding us that the question is not to search for untested solutions or to strive in achieving the kind of ideological answers that the Right is portraying as the return to a safer past, but to keep the promises of public education in the construction of an autonomous democratic public sphere and revitalized political system.

Introduction

Dennis Carlson and Greg Dimitriadis

The year is 2019, and the place is Los Angeles, an environmentally degraded, postnuclear war space of ominous dark rain that never seems to stop. Those few who still inhabit LA (most have fled to the "off world," a human colony on Mars) live in a chaotic, violent, inhumane world. The poor and the homeless roam the streets, fearful of others and of the all-seeing, all-pervasive police in their hovercrafts, while other people make homes for themselves in abandoned, run-down buildings. The workforce, meanwhile, has become more racialized, with Chinese assigned the role of street vendors. This is the dystopian future represented in one of the most written-about film of the past two decades, *Blade Runner* (1982). Re-released in 1990 in a somewhat reedited form, director Ridley Scott's film adaptation of Philip K. Dick's science fiction novel, *Do Androids Dream of Electric Sheep?* raises troubling questions about where we are headed as a culture, and about the very real possibility that the promises of democratic public life may become hollow and meaningless in the decades ahead if certain tendencies continue. The film, to this extent, reflects the growing sentiment among many that the promise of democracy, of a better, more humane, equitable, and freer future that lies ahead, always has been a false promise.

In *Blade Runner*, global corporate capital, along with what is left of a crumbling state infrastructure, reigns supreme—along with the police. Douglas Kellner, Flo Leibowitz, and Michael Ryan observe that the film "projects a future city which perpetuates corporate capitalism's distinguishing features—urban decay, commodification, overcrowding, highly skewed disparities of wealth and poverty, and authoritarian policing" (1984, p. 100). As the infrastructure of society deteriorates, and as the fragile fabric of community life breaks down, order depends more and more upon a police force. The inner city is virtually an occupied zone, and its citizens kept, as much as they can be, under the gaze of surveillance cameras and bands of roving police. Meanwhile, the final dream of those with power is being realized. People are both figuratively and literally being "produced," "programmed," and dehumanized so that they can be efficient slaves and servants of power. On a literal, although also metaphoric, level, the Tyrell Corporation is involved in producing and marketing "replicants," androids or human-like robots that are advertised to be "more human than human," virtually identical to humans in every way. Replicants have become the working class on the off-world, forced to labor under oppressive conditions as slaves, and some replicants stage a revolt and escape to earth. The story revolves around the efforts by one police android hunter named Rick Deckard to kill the escaped androids.

A central question raised by the film, like a number of other science fiction movies about androids and artificial intelligence, is "What makes us human?" Are we, in modern, advanced capitalist society, being programmed by educational institutions and the popular media so that we are becoming virtually indistinquishable from robots? *Blade Runner* represents a postmodern sensibility in its antiutopianism, its rejection of the grand master narratives of progress through science and industry. The postmodern cultural terrain is one in which people are less hopeful and idealistic about progress—and for some very good reasons. At the same time, this is not a moment, we believe, when the democratic imagination has completely dimmed or the democratic project has completely exhausted. For *Blade Runner* is, at its core, a story of resistance and rebellion, of the struggle by those who have been oppressed to claim control over their own lives and begin reclaiming the democratic promise. In the film, it is the androids who are becoming human through their struggles for freedom, even as the "real" humans become increasingly dehumanized, objectified, and programmed to serve and kill. The film holds out some hope, for it ends with one of the replicants, a woman named Rachel, fleeing the city along with Deckard—who has become more self-conscious of his own programming, and also of the possibility that he has been a replicant all along without knowing it. The two flee north to an ecologically safe zone, a symbolic space of relative autonomy and freedom where they can engage in their own re-programming and self-production along new lines. The film thus affirms the capacity of humans to become more self-reflexive or self-aware of how they have been programmed by both the "official knowledge" (Apple, 1992) they have learned in school and the "hidden curriculum" of popular culture and the mass media that increasingly surrounds us every waking hour of the day. It also holds out the hope that we can resist being "programmed," resist becoming androids produced by educational institutions and global capital to be docile citizens and consumers. Finally, *Blade Runner* suggests that there is an "outside" space within culture that is not determined, that has some relative autonomy, a free space, or more accurately a counterspace, from which it may be possible to construct empowering and affirming identities and engage in our own self-production with others. Of course, such a space can never be a space apart, some "blessed isle," to borrow Nietzsche's term. It is, in the end, a space that takes on meaning only out of the battle between democratic and non-democratic narratives of public education and public life.

This book is about the promise of democratic education and public life in an unsettling new age, in which the future represented in *Blade Runner* must now be considered a very real possibility, a future in which education and programming have become one and the same, indistinguishable aspects of the production of docile citizens and consumers. In such a context it is all the more important for progressives to articulate persuasive new counternarratives of public education and public life, that give new meaning to the democratic language of "freedom," "equity," "social justice," and "community," and that provide the basis for building a different kind of future than the one represented in *Blade Runner*. We begin with the premise that the current system of schooling, along with the way we think about curriculum and pedagogy, are inadequate to the task at hand. Public education, wittingly or not, has become inextricably involved in the process of reproducing and legitimating class, race, gender, and other inequalities. At the same time, public education (including college education) risks becoming irrelevant in young people's lives as the power of popular culture programming is increasing dramatically, as the information age further undermines public education's claim to a monopoly on useful knowledge, and as the idea of a unified public is disappearing and is being replaced by the idea of communities of identity and affinity. In the face of these conditions, we affirm the importance of the idea of public education, while also recognizing that this idea has to be thoroughly recast or reformed rather than merely reformed.

In what follows we want to explore the promise and the possibility of democratic education and public life at this historical juncture, a promise and possibility we associate with a new progressivism. Our basic argument is that out of the ashes of modern forms of education and public life, something like a new progressivism is beginning to emerge and test its wings. Or perhaps we should say new progressivisms, for we can no longer speak of progressivism in any unified sense. It exists only as a loose coalition of interrelated discourses in the public and in the academy that are engaged in re-thinking the organization of educational institutions, giving new meaning to the curriculum, and reorienting pedagogy. Yet, a key, perhaps overarching discourse here is that of cultural studies. As it has ruptured the borders that separate traditional academic disciplines and has emphasized the important role of popular culture in identity formation, cultural studies has begun to establish an intellectual and political space for rethinking education and public life that is potentially quite important. It might serve as a starting point for cobbling together something like a strategically unified progressive vision of what education can and should be—one that emerges out of dialogue among and between various movements and discourses of democratic education and public life.

Promises to Keep

In order to give new meaning to the promise of democratic education and public life, we need to have some idea of how this promise historically has been represented and constituted. For there is no fixed, unified, or stable meaning to the democratic promise, only a history of meaning and usage to advance various projects. So our purpose should not be to recuperate some "pure," "original," or "authentic" model of democracy that can then be used to indict the current system for its failure to live up to its promise. Indeed, we must be more than a little suspicious of those who would seek to ground the democratic promise on firm foundations—be that foundation "the glory that was Greece," the European Enlightenment, or the founding fathers of the American Revolution. While we are committed to the project of recuperating and reappropriating the language of democratic public education and public life to give it new meaning, such a reappropriation, we believe, can occur only within the context of a recognition of the historical limitations and contradictions of democratic discourses of education and public life to this point.

Certainly, the "glory that was Greece" is still a foundational trope in Western, Eurocentric culture, so it should not be surprising to find that democracy is often considered a Greek production, as if the basic ideas and ideals represented by democratic forces in Greek culture at the time were somehow unique and new in the world, as if "humanity" had finally risen above the savage, animal world in a grand and glorious moment that was ancient Greece. This is a Eurocentric mythology that will need to be thoroughly deconstructed and critiqued before the idea of democracy can become truly global and multicultural; and this is a central challenge for progressive educators and cultural workers in the coming decades. The democracy of Classical Athenian culture was, after all, not only compatible with but seemingly dependent upon a large class of slaves—up to on-third of the population of Athens in the fifth century B.C.E. Indeed, all non-Greeks were classified as "barbarians" who presumably were not yet fully human, and thus not deserving of the full human rights granted democratic citizens. Similarly, Greek females, as Page DoBuis (1982) has observed, were relegated to a lower rung in the "great chain of being" that separated the fully human from the animal. The point here is that slavery was one extreme expression of a broader cultural discourse of inequality in Greek culture that constituted the democratic citizen only through the simultaneous process of constituting the non-citizen, the Other who was to be denied human rights as part of a project of domination. Thus, the "practices of freedom" in Greek culture that Michel Foucault (1986) looks to as a possible basis for re-thinking democracy, are practices he acknowledges were dependent upon an Other denied freedom. This is the central paradox of dominant discourses and practices of democracy in the West. Democratic discourses have been involved, in a contradictory way, in the construction of inequality along with equality, with oppression along with freedom. A democratic language will only be worth recuperating in the years ahead if we can begin detaching it from this dominant history of usage, this dependency upon an Other.

Then it is possible to talk about reappropriating and recuperating certain aspects of Greek democratic discourse and practice. In particular, we want to focus upon something that Pericles says in his famous defense of the Athenian democracy of his day, to the effect that Athens is the "school of Greece." At the heart of the Athenian conception of a democratic public, limited and exclusionary as that public was understood to be, was the idea that democracy is more than a process of decision making and self-governance. It is, more important perhaps, a way of living together in which people are always engaged in a form of self-education through public dialogue and debate, questioning their beliefs and stay open to new ways of thinking about what is good and just. As Nathan Tarcov observes, "The heart of Athenian democracy, the popular decision making of the assembly, was not a mere mechanism for satisfying popular preferences, but an arena of teaching and learning" (1996, p. 4). Interestingly, in a city so committed to the idea of continuous education and reeducation of the public through public dialogue and debate, there was no system of formal public education. Young people became educated "through democratic politics itself and the city's general way of life" (p. 4). This is an important point, we believe; and one that implications for public education that are compelling at this particular point in history. For one thing, the suggestion is that public education is something that occurs in the public, among all citizens, of all ages, at all times, as they engage in dialogue on public issues. Democratic societies are learning societies, and democratic communities are learning communities. This is central to what John Dewey (1916) meant when he said that democratic societies are "intentionally progressive." The belief is that through deliberate self-reflection and self-criticism, through questioning and debating in a public dialogue, it is possible to reconstruct self and society, to not be narrowly bound by what is or has been.

This kind of public education may occur partially in schools and colleges, but not exclusively or perhaps even primarily so. Outside of a broader context of public dialogue, what goes on in public schools and colleges is meaningless. The issue remains, then, as it did in Socrates's day, how to bring education into the streets and public gathering places, how to see public education as a broad project that goes on in many cultural sites, any where people gather to talk and reflect on the common and different concerns they face, their desires and dreams, their hopes and fears, and how to reach people in places where they engage in both reflexivity (reflecting back upon their taken for granted beliefs and practices) and the active production of culture and self. To think of the promise of democratic education and public life as related to the development of a public literacy, dialogue, and orientation toward critical literacy, and to reintegrate public education within the public—these are all ideas that have important relevance in thinking about how public education might be reimagined in the decades ahead.

Aside from the Greek tradition of democracy as primarily a way of life organized around habits of civility, practices of freedom, and public dialogue, the promise of democracy has been linked in American culture to a liberal Enlightenment discourse of contractual rights. This discourse of democracy constructs democratic citizens as contractual subjects, whose consent to be governed is made contingent upon the state, in effect, promising to protect their personal rights and freedoms through a system of laws and courts. In contemporary American cultural politics this liberal discourse of democracy most often is articulated with a conservative social and educational agenda. It is used, for example, to support a free market system of public education, in which autonomous consumer parents enter into contractual relations with private schools to educate their children. Conservative Christians also often invoke a language of parental rights—such as the right not to have one's children exposed to "immoral" literature, evolutionary theory, or sex education other than the "just say no" variety. But a democratic discourse of rights has historically been linked to progressivism as well; and in contemporary battles being waged over the course and direction of "progress" in American education, a language of rights continues to play a pivotal and guiding role. For example, current battles over equity in school funding, and adequate funding of public education more generally, are organized around a legalistic discourse of the rights of all children to a quality education. Similarly, progressives in education have advanced a legalistic rights discourse in support of affirmative action and Title IX (which prohibits school programs that discriminate by gender), both to ensure that they are enforced and to extend their meaning. In its most radical democratic forms in America, this legalistic rights discourse has been associated with movements and struggles to liberate, emancipate, enfranchise, and empower particular groups of marginalized Americans; and it must, be believe, play a central role in reconstituting public education along new lines in the years ahead.

Nevertheless, this discourse too needs to be critically interrogated and reconstructed if it is to take us much farther in a progressive direction. Once more, Foucault proves useful in this project. He argues that the liberal discourse of democracy has been deeply contradictory. On the one hand, it has legitimated the development of a vast network of courts, bureaucratic state agencies, and monitoring apparatuses as designed to protect the rights of citizens. On the other hand, once in place, this network of courts, agencies, record-keeping, and surveillance systems quickly establishes the basis for a new form of what Foucault (1986) calls "governmentality," a form that has the effect of restricting the rights of individual, autonomous citizens. Through the legalistic and juridical discourse of governmentality, the modern state actually produced the modern subject of power as a disciplined, subordinated, dependent subject—the opposite of the liberal, autonomous, free subject whose rights it claimed it was protecting. A rights discourse thus provided the conditions for new technologies of intervention, regulation, discipline, labelling, and policing of various sub-populations of students. Finally, a legalistic and juridical discourse provided the context for the emergence of a new class of professionals, armed with scientific knowledge, whose job it was to bring students (and teachers) under the gaze of a normalizing power. The battle over the rights of "special education" or "special needs" students is a good case in point. In order to protect the rights of special education students, they must first be constituted as special education students through the a rigorous process of identification and labelling. This process draws together professional educators, psychologists, and doctors in diagnosing the learning "disorders" of individual students and then prescribing a "treatment." The effect is that students are brought under a totalising and regulatory gaze, and teachers' role is reconstituted around testing, record-keeping, monitoring, and surveillance. While the inclusion movement in special education challenges the spatial marginalization of special education students, it does nothing to change this regulatory practice. Indeed, it involves more teachers in it. All of this means that battles in education to advance the rights of individuals or marginalized groups by expanding the state's regulatory power have limits, at least so long as they are framed within dominant discourses of governmentality *over* people.

Dominant discourses and practices of democratic education and public life, we have argued, are both contradictory and limited in forging a new progressivism, although we do not believe that it is wise to throw the baby out with the bathwater. Rather, we must find a way of using the language of democracy and practicing democracy that is neither *exclusionary* nor *disciplinary*, that neither excludes whole sub-populations of people from the full rights and freedoms of citizenship nor brings them under a governmentality of regulation, surveillance, and normalization. Is it possible for democracy to be re-invented so that it no longer is bound up in exclusionary and disciplinary practices but rather is constituted around practices of freedom and equality? Is it possible for the democratic subject of history to constitute itself without its its Other, the one who is denied rights, dominated, oppressed, and marginalized? These are the central questions of the age for progressives, and ones we approach with a sense of urgency. To the extent that we find reason to be hopeful, it is because democratic progressivism is a pragmatic tradition with the potential to continuously re-invent itself. Democracy, in a democratic pragmatic sense, is a moving target, an unfinished project, open to re-visioning, with no original, authentic, fixed, final, or unified meaning. Its meaning, rather, emerges within the context of its usage in concrete battles going on in various sites of cultural production, including public schools and colleges. At the same time, democratic pragmatism is not pragmatism without any coherent direction or aim. It is progressive in its commitment to a radical democratic vision of a "good society," one that is more equitable, caring, and humane.

In this sense, it is still possible we believe to speak about promises to keep. At this historical juncture, the promise of democracy implies working to open up more space within public schools and colleges for teachers and students to practice freedom, that is, to practice assuming control over their own teaching and learning, and to negotiate their relations with fellow teachers and students around equity and respect for difference. It means waging legal battles over the rights that young people have in public educational institutions, including the right not to be harassed or bullied. It means affirming academic freedom in the face of state efforts to make teachers accountable to "teaching to the test." But these efforts will not in themselves be enough to change the course and direction of public education. The democratic promise at this point in history must also be about forging a discourse and movement capable of re-directing the state toward new forms of governmentality and hence new forms of public education, linked to a reconceptualization of both curriculum and pedagogy. Finally, the democratic promise must be about the reappropriation of the very modernist and now thoroughly-deconstructed idea of "progress." If progress can never be guaranteed, and history does not lead, transformation through transformation, to the good society, it is important that progressives not abandon the language of progress, or the related notion of promises to keep. Promises help us set a course in a rapidly-changing culture. We always, in this sense, have promises to keep. Conservatives like to argue that the democratic project has brought us as far as it can take us, and that we are, for all practical purposes, at the "end of history" (Fukuyama, 1992). Democratic progressivism presumes that there is no end of history, that progress toward a better, more humane, equitable, and caring world is always being challenged, that we must continuously think anew as we move upon an historical stage that is open and unfinished.

Education and the New Progressive Cultural Politics

The new cultural terrain of the postmodern age is not overly hospitable to a radical vision of the promise of democratic education and public life. Inequalities are increasing between the haves and the have-nots within the United States, and between economically elite nations and the "developing" world. It is an age of hyperconsumerism in which one's sense of self and identity is defined by what one consumes in popular culture icons and styles marketed in the new shopping mall public. It is an age of backlash and resentment against the gains made by people of color, women, gays and lesbians, and other marginalized identity groups, and a time of the rise of religious fundamentalism in both in America and around the world. And it is an age in which conservatives use the democratic language of equity to oppose affirmative action and "special rights" for gay people. In public education, it is an age of a corporate state discourse of high-stakes testing, "accountability," "standards," and "efficiency," an age of preparing America's young people to be more competitive and productive in the new global labor market. Meanwhile, commercialized popular culture is busy blurring the lines between "reality" and "hyperreality," the material world and the virtual world. It is an age in which identity is constructed around performance, style, and image, and hybrid, border-crossing identities subvert the naturalness of race, gender, and sexual identity categories. All of this is part of postmodernism as a term that designates the cultural, economic, and political terrain emerging in a postindustrial information age.

Related to this, "postmodernism" is a term applied to a general shift in progressive cultural politics, and in critical educational studies. In this form, postmodernism tends to be a construct that takes on meaning only in relation to that which it negates, modernism. Postmodernism represents a critical moment of negation, a movement within modern culture to create a discursive space from which it becomes possible to cast a critical gaze back on modernism, to question that which modern culture has taken for granted (Butler, 1999). The aim of postmodernism is thus to push modernism to supercede itself and become something new. Postmodernism is not, in itself, a sufficient basis for forging a new progressivism in American education and public life. But it does play an important role in establishing the conditions for the emergence of a new progressivism, for allowing us to unthink modernism and rethink it in new ways.

Within the binary opposition that has been discursively established between modernism and postmodernism, the term "modernism" has been used to stand for a whole range of interrelated beliefs, values, epistemologies, and practices. For example, it has stood for unifying models of society, for explanatory models that make everything fit together nicely into a coherent whole. Modernism also has been associated with the idea that knowledge, or language, refers back to a "real" world, and that the objective of the educator and scholar is to reveal that world in a language of clarity, one that cuts through the distortions of ideology and common-sense knowledge to get to the truth beneath the distortion, to set the record straight. As Joan Scott observes, "a metaphor of visibility as literal transparency" has been crucial to the modernist project (1992, p. 23). Finally, in its critical and social reconstructionist forms, modernism has been associated with the idealistic Enlightenment language of democracy: liberty, social justice, equity, and community, and the more radical Hegelian and Marxian language of liberation and emancipation, of the oppressed and the oppressor.

Postmodernism begins with a critique of all discourses of unity, and of an authoritative, unified, "objective" truth, associating unity with antidemocratic, authoritarian projects that attempt to erase difference. In place of the trope of unity, postmodernism valorizes the trope of chaos and disorder, of differences that cannot be brought together under an "whole," of truth that is always partial, contested, and positional. Language is no longer understood as a transparent lens to reveal a world "out there," but rather a lens that actively shapes and constructs that world, a discourse in which words take on meaning only in the play of difference with other words, in which there is no firm foundation upon which to build authoritative truth claims, in which unintelligibility is a basis fact of life. In the postmodern world, truth is representational; it is something that is actively produced through the process of representing reality one way or another, with one discourse or another. This, obviously, is consistent with an interest in popular culture, not in terms of whether it represents the world "accurately" or "realistically," but in terms of *how* it represents the world and thus how it produces certain truths about "the way things are." Finally, postmodernism deconstructs all belief in a unifying logic or directionality to history, and deconstructs the category of the "oppressed" as too unifying, too idealistic, too indebted to a modernist belief that one either is or is not oppressed, one either is or is not an oppressor. The world is never that neat for postmodernists, and so the "oppressed" become the marginalized, the Other, those groups subjugated within the dominant discourse; and the aim is no longer emancipation so much as some limited freedom for self-production, some limited room for alternative discourses and practices. In place of the idealistic democratic language of the Enlightenment, postmodernism offers a more pragmatic democratic language, one that focuses on how democratic language takes on meaning within particular concrete battles over power and knowledge in specific sites.

Taken as an autonomous discourse and movement, postmodernism is fundamentally limited. For one thing, it fails to provide much of a base for bringing various movements together around even a contingent "united front" politics or discourse of the "public good." Also, and perhaps even more significant, the naive idealism and utopianism of the modernist democratic project is matched only by the cynical pragmatism and dystopianism of the postmodern moment. But we do not have to choose one over the other—modernism or postmodernism, naive hope or cynical pragmatism, unity or difference, scientific objectivity or the subjectivism of narrative, and so on. We can work the borders between these binary oppositions, opening up a hybrid space for intellectual work and critical pedagogy, a space within which the promises of democratic education can take on new meaning. We want to turn, now, to explore this hybrid progressive space between modernism and postmodernism in a bit more specificity, although the picture we intent to paint is still necessarily one of broad strokes.

For purposes of analysis, we want to limit our comments here to a discussion of four interrelated shifts in progressive discourse associated with postmodernism, each of which raises questions about the meaning of democracy and democratic education in new times. First, what is the continuing relevance of Marxism and Marxist categories in understanding the existing system of schooling and the basis for a critical pedagogy? In the 1970s and 1980s progressives were highly influenced by Marxist theory in its various forms. Now Marxism has gone out of fashion, along with class analysis generally. What can or should progressives salvage from the ashes of Marxism to both critique existing educational practice and reconstruct it a more democratic form? A second set of questions has to do with the challenge to un-think Eurocentrism in American education and culture, and in American progressivism. In this regard, what is the relevance of post-colonial narratives and discourses? A third set of questions focuses on how progressives can respond to far-reaching shifts occurring in youth identity formation, including class, race, gender, and sexual identity formation. What do these shifts mean for the way we view schools and other educational institutions as sites of identity formation? How can educational institutions be reorganized as sites where young people are involved in the construction of affirming, empowering identities? A final set of questions focuses on the meaning of community and the progressive idea that public schools and colleges should be "embryonic communities" that induct young people into democratic community life. How can progressives move away from unified and homogeneous constructions of community without abandoning the idea of community, like that of consensus, as inherently oppressive? In raising these questions, we do not propose to answer them, but rather suggest that questioning is a good way to proceed in constructing a new progressivism. For questions invite dialogue, and a new progressivism can emerge only out of dialogue among a broad coalition of actors in which answers are necessarily strategic and partial.

Marxism and Post-Marxism

Neo-Marxism was the reigning metanarrative in critical theories of culture and schooling in the 1970s and to a lesser extent in the 1980s (Whitty, 1985; Young, 1998). In its various guises, neo-Marxism provided a comprehensive and sophisticated metatheory of the role of state schooling and popular culture in the reproduction of the social, technical, and economic relations of advanced capitalism. Public education, according to structural Marxists such as Louis Althusser, is an "ideological state apparatus." It is one of those institutions that has assumed a heightened role in the modern age in "constituting concrete individuals as subjects" of power and domination (1971, p. 138). An economic system such as capitalism must gain dominance through more than a means of production. It must also "reproduce" the means of production, and more particularly labor power. Ideology thus operates to create an imaginary relationship between individuals and the world, one in which they learn to accept their own subjugation as natural. For Althusser and other neo-Marxists, ideological domination is increasingly important in late capitalism, although repressive forms of domination, such as police and military control, continue to be used when ideological control does not work. Public schooling, along with the mass media, thus are central ideological state apparatuses in late capitalism, and their specific form and functioning is fundamentally determined by this fact. At best, schools enjoy a "relative autonomy." The formal curriculum of schooling is an expression of bourgeois ideology. The organization of the learning process, along with the social relations of the school and classroom, are about socializing young people into the "social and technical relations of production," inculcating them with the attitudes, dispositions, and skills corporate elites want in workers destined for various rungs of the labor hierarchy.

One of the most fruitful lines of inquiry that "fleshed out" this neo-Marxist structural theory of schooling was associated with the theory of cultural capital and social capital, developed most elaborately in the work of Pierre Bourdieu and John Passeron (1977). According to the theory of cultural capital, one way that ideology works is by devaluing the culture and linguistic styles of some people and simultaneously privileging the culture, attitudes, and linguistic styles of others. As an ideological state apparatus, schooling privileges the cultural capital of the middle class, and it disadvantages the cultural capital of working-class and poor youth. Though Bourdieu and Passeron focused on a class analysis, this idea obviously has relevance for understanding how schools work to reproduce the cultural capital of those white youth who have learned a standard, or "normal" English in the home and in the community, since linguistic codes are linked to race as well as class in America. Cultural capital is more than linguistic "competence," however; it is those attitudes and set of beliefs that get rewarded in schools having to do with individualism, competition, motivation to "succeed" within the system, and a certain disciplined performance of self. Middle-class youth, presocialized into these attitudes, beliefs, and styles of self-presentation in the home, have a great advantage in schooling. Social capital, which refers to the network of "connections" middle-class youth have that other youth do not, pays off particularly once they graduate from college, but it also pays off to some extent in K–12 education. Middle-class parents, after all, are more likely to intervene with school administrators and teachers to demand that their children be treated "fairly," and this represents a form of cultural capital.

This neo-Marxist structural theory of schooling was complemented by ethnographic research on everyday life in schools and other public sites to explore how class identity was being constructed. This research continues to have important implications for the study of identity and resistance in schools and other sites, even if it has been the subject of an extensive critique. Paul Willis's classic study, *Learning to Labour: How Working Class Kids Get Working Class Jobs* (1977), showed how a group of working-class students in an England high school (the self-identified "lads") actively resisted the middle-class values and norms of the school and resisted its attempts to discipline and subordinate them, to make them submit to the school's authority and deadening routine. The irony, as Willis saw it, was that this resistance, this collective solidarity and refusal to submit to the authority of the schooling process over them, actually served to reproduce their "tracking" toward manual labor, shop-floor work. Thus, the affirmation of a working-class identity came at a cost, but then so did abandoning that identity.

Finally, Marxist discourse in education provided an anchor for "critical pedagogy" in the 1970s and 1980s. The Frankfurt School of Social

Research, and in particular the work of Horkheimer and Adorno, offered critical pedagogy a theory of the alienated worldview and consciousness of late capitalism, including the ascendancy of "instrumental rationality," a narrow means-ends thinking that also was associated with the objectification and commodification of both knowledge and human subjectivity. The Frankfurt School's critical theory, unfortunately, offered little beyond a cynical and gloomy critique of how the capitalist worldview had become hegemonic in the modern age, and how popular culture was turning people into docile consumer citizens. To complement critical theory, Henry Giroux, Peter McLaren, and others in the United States looked to the work of the Brazilian educator and political activist Paulo Freire, whose *Pedagogy of the Oppressed* (1970) continues to be a central text in defining the radical democratic project in education. In such a form, Marxist discourse pointed to ways in which educators can help oppressed and marginalized peoples demystify the ideological beliefs that keep them oppressed and silenced, and can move beyond "dependent consciousness"—characterized by the presumption that you cannot think for yourself, are undeserving, and are therefore dependent upon the "master." Marxism in this least-deterministic form emphasizes the active role the people assume, or potentially can assume, in "making" history and self. The irony is that the Marxist theory of schooling suggested that there was precious little room to do critical pedagogy in public schools and colleges, since they were presumed to be largely determined institutions.

Though Marxism served as a metanarrative for many progressives throughout much of the 1970s and into the 1980s, its future was on shaky ground by the mid-1980s. Its rather rapid decline as a metanarrative among progressives certainly cannot be separated from the decline of Marxist socialism as a political discourse and movement. In a general sense, the decline of Marxism was related to a growing movement against all metanarratives, all grand narratives that claimed to fit everything neatly together in a grand theory of a system, fixed in time. The decline of Marxist theory was, as well, related to shifts occurring in the academy. Marxism became the critical discourse of choice during a time when many white males of working-class background were entering the academy, working their way up through graduate departments and into junior faculty positions. Such a movement into higher education had been made possible in the 1960s by high state subsidies that kept tuition costs at an all-time low. White males of working-class background were the single largest group to benefit from such access to higher education. Marxism was a vehicle for the expression of their working-class rage, their alienation within a system of higher education that continued to be elitist and a bastion of "high culture." By the 1980s, however, new groups were entering the academy in significant numbers for the first time, at least partially because of affirmative action, including (most notably) women and African American and Hispanic students and faculty. For these "outsiders" in the academy, the universalistic language of Marxism did not resonate so well, and they resisted having their struggles reduced to class struggle. Meanwhile, tuition increases once more put higher education beyond the reach of many working-class youth, regardless of race or gender, so there was a decline in interest in class issues among students.

For whatever combination of reasons, the demise of Marxism, at least as a unifying metanarrative, came quite quickly. By the mid-1980s, the post-Marxism era had begun. For some progressives, this meant the whole-sale abandonment of Marxist theory and Marxist categories of analysis—an unfortunate situation in our view. For others, who have sought to reclaim Marxism in some limited form, the work of the early-twentieth-century Italian Marxist Antonio Gramsci has been very important. Perhaps no single book symbolized both the challenge to Marxism on the democratic left and the turn toward Gramsci than Ernesto Laclau and Chantal Mouffe's *Hegemony and Socialist Strategy* (1985); and in many ways the "radical democratic pluralism" they sketch in that book continues to guide the neo-Gramscian project in education and in cultural politics. The primary criticism leveled by Laclau and Mouffe against Marxism, includ-ing neo-Marxist resistance theory, was that "in the final analysis" resis-tances were always contained within a system of domination. "In the final analysis," everything was explainable in class terms. "In the final analysis" no institutions or sites in the public were treated as if they had any auton-omy from economic relations and worldviews. Marxism had taken for granted a structural theory of society in which every institution serves its assigned role in propping up the whole. But society is not, from a post-structural standpoint, a whole. There is always an "outside" to the domi-nant culture and ideology.

Culture is, from a Gramscian standpoint, produced through battle, which means that the dominant culture is only constituted through oppo-sition and negativity. There always is an "outside" space in modern culture for difference and for an oppositional language and practice. Democratic space outside of the dominant discourse and practice is thus always to be found, although it is a space that is never fully autonomous or free because it is always constituted relationally. Because culture is produced out of the battle between dominant and oppositional narratives and discourses, between what Gramsci called "hegemony" and "counterhegemony," public institutions such as schools are understood to be non-determined, even if they are by no means free or autonomous either. The trouble is, in order to mount an effective counterhegemonic movement, one that would set the stage for a fundamental reconstruction of public education and public life, progressives will need to come together around some unifying discourse and cultural politics. Gramsci, as a Marxist, understood class as the primary glue that held democratic left politics together. But postmodern Gramscians tend to see no struggle as having any necessary primacy or determinacy in forging a counterhegemonic discourse and movement. Laclau and Mouffe, for example, argue that postmodern democratic cultural politics must be based on "articulating" or interweaving various discourses associated with new social movements on the left. But the specific movements that come together at any given time will very much depend upon the situation at hand, as will the focus of political mobilization. Sometimes it might be best to focus on gender issues, and other times on environmental issues, and other times on the oppression of sexual minorities. Aside from strategic alliances, the only thing to hold a progressive counterhegemonic movement together, according to Laclau and Mouffe, is a common commitment to allowing identity and affinity groups the maximum possible freedom to define themselves, to represent themselves, to speak for themselves.

The "radical democratic pluralism" that Laclau and Mouffe saw emerging on the horizon in progressive cultural politics in the mid-1980s has fully arrived. Any talk of a "unified" progressive voice or agenda is, deservedly in our view, scorned by most progressives. At the same time, we share a concern voiced Peter McLaren and Ramin Farahmandpur that many of the new social movements associated with radical democratic pluralism "are primarily organized around the interests of the middle class," and that in such forms the new cultural politics may be just another variation on liberal pluralism (2000, p. 29). As such, it may be unable to bring together various movements on the democratic left (constituted around class, race, gender, sexuality, and ecological politics) on any fundamentally new vision of democratic education and public life. We suspect that if a powerful new counterhegemonic discourse is to emerge on the democratic left, class will assume a privileged status as an analytic category. Certainly the reproduction and resistance theories of schooling and the related theories of cultural and social capital have continuing importance in both critiquing existing practices and calling for something new. As Cornel West observes, the Marxist intellectual traditions remain "indispensable," particularly in accounting for economic oppression and the power of oligopolies and transnational corporations in shaping public life. "At the same time," he writes, "I am against general theories of oppression," which means placing a stress on "concrete circumstances and situations" (1999, p. 27).

This leads us to a final idea worth appropriating from the Gramscian tradition, that of the "organic intellectual." Gramsci argued that hegemony is increasingly established through battles in "civil society," outside the state. The organic intellectual emerges out of a particular class or identity group and helps that class or group engage in both critique and re-presentation, in both deconstructing the hegemonic "common sense" that keeps them oppressed and constructing a counterhegemonic voice as part of a project of empowerment. Organic intellectuals write new histories and provide new interpretations of social problems, and they recover the stories of those whose voices have been silenced. They contest dominant narratives of the oppressed and marginalized as passive and culturally deficient, along with narratives based on an attitude of paternalism and pity. This implies a new disposition for progressive educators and researchers today. It means speaking less in a universalistic voice, and more in a positioned voice, from a point within the battle. And it implies that all educators need to think of themselves not only as teachers, but also, and more fundamentally, as intellectuals engaged in public debate and dialogue, helping groups articulate their concerns, advocating for their interests. This should not mean abandoning all belief in critical reason, in seeing things as clearly as possible, in speaking the truth as much as we know the truth. But it does mean moving away from the modernist pretense that there is a space apart from the battle, an outside space from which the educator/scholar/scientist views the world with cold detachment and objectivity.

Postcolonialism and the Project of Un-thinking Eurocentrism

As we move into a post-Marxist era, the Gramscian notion of hegemony is being applied in new contexts. Most notable, perhaps, is its application within postcolonial discourse to refer to the hegemony of Eurocentrism, with Eurocentrism here understood as a commonsense worldview or, in Foucault's language, a discursive formation involved in the formation of subjectivity and culture. Marxism always spoke in a Eurocentric voice, a voice of universal human development, in which various non-European peoples played the role of the "primitive," the "prehistorical," and the "underdeveloped" (Mills, 1997). Postcolonial discourse is informed by Marxist analysis, and certainly includes a critique of the role of capital and capitalist culture in the "development" of "underdeveloped" nations and peoples. But it also turns a critical gaze on Marxism as the master narrative of critical theory in the West, revealing just how much it has failed to question its own taken-for-granted colonial worldview.

In helping un-think colonialism and Eurocentrism, Edward Said's *Orientalism* (1978) has been one of the most generative and seminal texts to appear in recent years. Said begins with the observation that the Orient exists only in the colonial imagination. "The Orient was almost a European invention," a space of romance, exoticism, of "haunting memories and landscape," a cultural landscape upon which the West painted its Other—an Other it both feared and desired. By projecting its alterity, its "contrasting image" upon the Orient, Europe came to know itself and define its mission. The Orient as an image of Otherness thus assumed a critical role in the construction of European material culture, and its institutions of colonial domination. Said coins the term "Orientalism" to refer to a complex set of discourses, narratives, mythologies, and apparatuses and technologies of power that are involved in producing both the colonizer and the colonized and that create the conditions for the rapid expansion of industrial capitalism and European military and economic hegemony. Orientalism is "a style of thought" that has changed and evolved over time and that has taken on somewhat different meaning in different European contexts. It is a hegemonic discourse that "unilaterally determines what can be said about the Orient" (p. 2). It is a discourse of identity that has made European culture very powerful by disempowering the Oriental

Other. While the era of direct colonial domination of Third World peoples is almost over, Said raises questions about the extent to which Orientalism, or something like it, might still be part of the dominant cultural hegemony in Europe and America.

One way Eurocentric mythology works is by making Europeans the narrators and subjects of history, who claim the right to speak for and represent colonial Others. Said finds this attitude everywhere in French and British literature and popular culture during the height of the colonial era, this sense that colonial people, like the Egyptian courtesan Flaubert describes who "never spoke of herself," who never represented her own feelings or self-presence. "He spoke for her and represented her" (p. 6). Of course, Said is also pointing to another aspect of Eurocentric mythology, its treatment of woman as Other along with Africans, Asians, and Arabs. The Eurocentric gaze is particularly patriarchal, associated with a form of domination that is ritualized in the home and workplace in the domination of women. To be European, wealthy, and male has put one in a position to not only possess and dominate people, as Flaubert possesses the Egyptian courtesan, but to speak for them as well, to tell their stories, to make them represent the exotic Other. But why is this othering process so central to the Eurocentric colonial mind-set? For Said, the answer is quite simple. The major thrust of European culture over the past several centuries has been to make that culture hegemonic on a world scale, to affirm the idea of European identity "as a superior one in comparison with all the non-European peoples and cultures." So, the "scholar, the missionary, the trader, or the soldier" knew where they were going before they arrived in the Orient (p. 7): they were going to an inferior land of inferior people. These peoples were the subject of study by anthropologists, who understood them as representatives of the "primitive" and who placed them and their "artifacts" in museums. And they were made the subject of study by developmental economic theorists who questioned how (or indeed whether it was possible) to "modernize" them, to bring them up to a development parity in some distant time with "civilized" Europeans.

Said is primarily interested in turning a critical gaze on Eurocentrism and on Orientalism as a particular expression of Eurocentrism. But he does not dismiss European culture outright. He looks for a time when Europeans and European-Americans can begin to un-think their own Eurocentrism. One way to do this is through a critical, deconstructive reading of histories, documentaries, and movies in which East meets West. How do these texts mythologize the meeting? This question is the focus of Ella Shohat and Robert Stam (1994) in their book, *Unthinking Eurocentrism*, a study of how colonial peoples are represented in hegemonic Hollywood narratives and of the counternarratives former colonial peoples are producing through film. They point to the persistence of colonial tropes in even the most liberal and supposedly "politically correct" representations of American history. For example, a 1991 PBS television series titled *Columbus and the Age of Discovery* seems, at least on the surface, to be balanced in its treatment of Columbus, asking at the outset, "Should we celebrate Columbus' achievement as a great discovery . . . or should we mourn a world forever lost?" But surely this is a highly dubious choice, one that Shohat and Stam observe leaves "no room for contemporary indigenous identities or for activism in the present." The series is also organized as a voyage of discovery into Columbus's mind, so that he is always the focus, always the center of knowing. Indigenous people are merely a backdrop to his story, to his journey out. Why are so many people obsessed with replicating Columbus's journey of "discovery"? It is, Shohat and Stam suggest, because his voyage speaks to them "in quasi-mythic terms" (p. 66). It is part of a Eurocentric mythology of origins around which European identity has been constructed. Can European-Americans begin to construct their identity around a non-Eurocentric mythology in the decades ahead, or will the mythology of Orientalism come back with a vengeance? These are open questions, posed to point to the critical role that public educational institutions might play in reconstructing the mythology of American public life and retelling the stories of American history.

Post-colonial discourse presumes that to un-think Eurocentrism one must do more than deconstruct its representational logic. One must also engage in the recovery of countermemories and counternarratives in the process of constructing a counterhegemonic discourse that offers more democratic and empowering ways of seeing the world. Post-colonialism is about reading colonial texts alongside texts written from the perspective and standpoint of former colonial and subjugated peoples. For these peoples to free themselves of the colonial mind-set, and to actively resist subjugation, they must engage in the process of representing themselves, in telling their own stories, in regaining control over their own representation in popular culture. This implies a narrative strategy designed to document subjugated accounts of reality, something that is also associated with critical race theory. Thus, Charles Lawrence observes of critical race theory that it aims to reclaim counternarratives of African American struggle and resistance, and to produce a countertext, "a text that constitutes another community in which those who are objectified by the dominant society become subjects" (1995, p. 349). These counternarratives and counterrepresentations do more than "correct" history. They also re-represent history in ways that open up democratic possibilities.

The Troubling of Identity

Education is not, from a progressive standpoint, about the transmission of knowledge so much as the formation of identity—a sense of self in relation to others. This is because most struggles over social justice are about the domination, silencing, oppression, and marginalization of specific identity groups. Identity thus has much to do with power (either empowerment or disempowerment) and with learning to position oneself within historic struggles over power. For those individuals who are members of identity groups that have been historically marginalized, education must be a process of learning to both affirm identity (through solidarity with others similarly disempowered and/or oppressed), and to reconstruct and represent identity in ways that challenge dominant negative representations and stereotypes. Consequently, shifts occurring in the ways identity is theorized, in the ways identity is represented in popular culture, and in how identity is actually lived and experienced have profound implications for the reconstruction of democratic education.

Within modernism/postmodernism dualism, modernism has been associated with two quite distinct views on identity, one of which has far more value in forging a new progressivism. According to one discourse, identity is something we are given or are born with. This discourse of identity is the one that has been most open to critique. Identity is treated as if it has an "essential" or "authentic" character and a "natural" basis. It also tended to be treated as unified, stable, and one-dimensional. Identity, from this standpoint, provides people with a solid grounding under their feet, a natural foundation upon which to construct a stable sense of self. Although this modernist view of identity tends to be most associated with conservatives, it has been influential among some progressives. Thus, some feminists, particularly those writing in the 1970s and 1980s, advanced the idea that there is a woman's way of knowing that is the basis for forging a feminist ethics, pedagogy, and so forth (Gilligan, 1982; Noddings, 1984). Some strands of Afrocentric discourses also may be associated with the essentializing of an African identity, seeking to unify blackness around a mythology of authentic origins and stability over time. If we believe in an essentialistic theory of identity, then the implications are quite clear for curriculum and pedagogy. For women to be empowered through the educational process, their ways of knowing have to be respected rather than treated as deficiencies. For African American youth to succeed in education they need a curriculum and pedagogy that incorporates Afrocentric principles. There is much good sense in all of this. At the same time, that good sense comes wrapped in a theory of identity that may not take us very far in a progressive direction.

A second discourse of identity, one that has influenced a more radical strand of progressivism in the modern era, is social constructivist and dialectical. For Hegel and for Marx, identity emerges out of the master/slave struggle and thus has no autonomous meaning. Identity is always constructed in relation to our Other in that struggle, so that identity is either privileged identity or subordinated and resistant identity, master or slave. Within this tradition, which has had a major influence over postmodern thinking about identity, we need to both affirm and question identity simultaneously. We need to affirm it because we are defined by our position and location within historical struggles between dominant and subordinate identity groups. We cannot walk away from these struggles and identities even if we might want to. For the forms of consciousness that prevail at any given moment in the history of a culture are themselves inseparable from the struggle over identity. They are forms of independent consciousness or dependent consciousness, forms of consciousness that either keep people disempowered or give people power over other people. So, for Hegel and Marx, we are pretty well trapped within the consciousness of the age, and unable to think very far beyond it. Our identities are social constructs, constructed in the mirror of the Other. But for those who are disempowered, their identities are also the basis for the organization of collective movements of liberation and freedom. Only by becoming "working class," or "woman," "black," or "gay," for example, can people fight to take back control over their lives and resist domination. The irony is that battles for freedom must be waged around identity even as these battles must also hold out the promise that one day identity itself will disappear, when there are no more masters and slaves. This, of course, is the utopian vision of a reunification of oppositions that is to come at the end of history. From this standpoint, education is about helping young people, particularly those from marginalized identity groups, to challenge their marginalization and resist their domination, and to do so in ways that are not self-defeating. It is about learning to understand oneself as situated in an historical drama, about developing a collective sense of solidarity and political struggle with others who are similarly marginalized and oppressed. For those privileged within identity binaries, education is about questioning one's privilege. This Hegelian and Marxian understanding of identity is, of course, central to the discourse of critical pedagogy.

Postmodernism certainly deconstructs all essentialistic understandings of identity. But what about the Hegelian and Marxian understanding of identity? It does, after all, recognize that identity is not given but rather actively constructed in relation with others, and that it is not static but rather emergent. Indeed, the Hegelian and Marxian understanding of identity is very postmodern in this sense. The trouble, from a postmodern perspective, is that identity is still represented in terms of the splitting of a whole self into two opposing selves, and about their ultimate reunification at the end of history. Unity is thus still a dominant trope, and disunity is associated with a split into two halves, the identity of the master and the identity of the slave, the oppressor and the oppressed. This means that differences among various groups are reduced to differences between two oppositionally defined identities, caught in a dialectic that ultimately leads toward reunification. In the meantime, however, it leads toward protracted struggle and the deferral of liberation or freedom until a later point in history. Postmodernists suggest that as this dialectic opposition is of our own making, so we need not wait until the end of history to walk away from it. We can construct an identity that is not based on negating another identity, an identity that is different from but not in opposition to other identities. We can walk away from identity as we have known it and construct new, hybrid identities. The aim of a progressive education from this standpoint is to help young people construct different but not oppositional identities and to encourage them to continuously engage in the creative reconstruction of identity that crosses borders and moves outside of binary oppositional logic. Hybrids, Creoles, mestizos—these are names for a new form of post-modern subject who no longer is caught in what Donna Haraway (1991) calls the "spiral dance," a subject who no longer needs an Other to define itself, a subject that is continuously engaged in "stitching" itself together and "assembling" itself out of various identity parts available in popular culture and everyday life, none of which fit together too neatly or hold together too long.

The characteristic postmodern attitude toward identity is parody or play, subverting the normal performance of identity, troubling what people think they know about identity (Butler, 1990). According to Stuart Hall, play suggests, on the one hand, "the instability, the permanent unsettlement, the lack of any final resolution." The meaning of "blackness," or "womanness," or "gayness" is always in play in this sense, always shifting and changing in response to a play of cultural forces. On the other hand, "play" suggests a subversion of the reigning binary oppositions that define identity, a play-ful movement across boundaries so that identity categories are no longer understood as mutually excluding categories. Since the meaning of cate-gories of identity is always found in the play of differences within a dis-course, their meaning is never completed or settled. Through such serious and subversive play, Hall argues, we may be able to move beyond the need for an authentic, foundational identity, and beyond the need to fight mis-representations and stereotypes with a supposed "truth." We may be able to constitute ourselves "as new kinds of subjects" engaged in our own self-production outside reigning identity binaries (1996, p. 120).

The radical freedom and openness that seems to characterize postmod-ern identity formation has its appeals. Hip-hop culture provides a good case in point. At its best, hip-hop culture has been deeply subversive of estab-lished racial representations and categories, as witnessed by the growing sense of collective identity among hip-hop youth of all racial and cultural backgrounds. It also has offered black youth a sense that they are control-ling their own representation, that they are in control of their own cultural identity and are creatively shaping and molding language, style, and self into something new (Dimitriadis, 2001a). Of course, in some dominant, highly commercialized and commodified forms, hip-hop culture also rein-forces dominant representations of blackness and depoliticizes resistance by black youth. Hip-hop culture, like postmodernism more generally, may offer youth an image of identity without much substance beneath the image. That substance comes from anchoring identity in historic and ongo-ing struggles over power and knowledge.

Community in a Postmodern Age

This leads us to a final theme we want to associate with the new progres-sivism. As people become hybrid subjects, crossing the boundaries that sep-arate various cultural traditions, they build new networks of affinity, identity, and lifestyle that replace modernist forms of community life. Modernist community life was, and to a large extent continues to be, organized around the idea of a common culture, and schools were supposed to socialize young people into this common culture. Of course, this common culture, this common conception of the public good that public education was to foster, was not in any way common to all or even most Americans. But the idea of a common culture of reason, and of a public language that all could participate in, continued to guide democratic progressives through much of the twentieth century. Now, as modernist narratives of community life organized around the idea of a "common culture" are rapidly breaking down, and as newer forms are not yet firmly established, we are entering a period in which everyday public life appears increasingly alienating, threatening, and chaotic, and this is reflected in popular culture. Established codes of public civility are often abandoned. A recent incident in Seattle provides a good case in point. A suicidal woman held up commuter traffic for several hours while police tried to talk her out of jumping off a bridge. Finally, disgruntled motorists began to yell at her, and a chant went up among the commuters who had stepped out of their cars to watch this "media event" unfold: "Jump, bitch, jump." In a culture dedicated to the autonomous individual, with the commuter SUV a primary symbol of individual autonomy and power, the kind of caring and respect necessary to establish democratic community life erodes.

Democratic communities must be more than a collection of individual commuters who huddle in their cars and occasionally take out their "road rage" on each other or on unfortunates like the suicidal woman on the bridge. In the midst of this erosion of community life, it is important to resist nostalgia for a romanticized *Brigadoon* or *Happy Days* mythology of community life—a mythological space of homogeneity and conformity in which nothing ever changes. For the "good old days" of community life in America were not so good for many people. The dominant model of community life throughout the modern era in America was what might be called (referring to Foucault) a "normalizing" community (Carlson, 1997). Normalization, as Foucault characterizes it, is the process of organizing everyday life around a primary binary opposition that divides the normal from the abnormal. Those defined as abnormal in one way or another may be excluded from community and relocated in a marginalized space (a ghetto, a space on the other side of the tracks, or segregated schools, for example). Alternatively, those defined as abnormal may be integrated within public life but expected to assume the role of a stereotypical Other, or to remain invisible and silent, or to stay in the closet while in public. In either case, normalizing communities are organized by inclusion/exclusion binaries. When we apply this to an analysis of community life in America in the twentieth century, it is clear that communities have been democratic only in a very limited, normalizing sense. Those defined by the dominant culture as normal are granted the full rights of participation in democratic public life, while those represented as abnormal are excluded from such rights. And who has been given the role of playing the abnormal Other in American community life? The list is long, but it certainly includes those marginalized by class, race, ethnicity, language, sexual orientation, gender, religion, lifestyle and other markers of difference. One might say that difference itself is marginalized within normalizing American communities.

Postmodern subjects thus inhabit the borderlands of contemporary communities, as insider/outsider subjects (Anzuldúa, 1987). They inhabit, again, a territory of those who "crossover, pass over, or go through the confines of the 'normal'" (p. 25). They prefer an "affinity politics" of personal communicative freedom and strategic political mobilization over a politics of building community in any unifying sense (Haraway, 1991). The postmodern social theorist Zygmund Bauman (2001) argues that community is at best something that exists only in concrete form, as particular groups of people with shared interests and concerns come together across their differences to participate in demonstrations, festivals, marches, and so on. Perhaps the November 1999 mobilization of a protest movement to confront the World Trade Organization (WTO) in Seattle might serve as an example of such an enacted community. As an event, it coalesced around the actions of individuals and small groups increasingly connected on a global Internet grid. In effect, an invitation went out worldwide for people to come to Seattle to participate in the protest. Who came? Privileged white middle-class kids committed to global ecopolitics came, as did Third World peoples and indigenous peoples, elements of organized labor, antiracist and civil rights groups, gay rights groups, ecofeminists, and animal rights activists. All found a common ground of affinity, an admittedly unstable and provisional space to come together amid their differences. Interestingly, C-Span broadcast portions of a premarch meeting led by Starhawk, a popular ecofeminist novelist and activist. Here was a perfect blend of science fiction and reality, with Starhawk admonishing the demonstrators to go into the protest with love rather than hate, to refuse appeals to violence and nihilism, to find their own space and decide for themselves what they were going to do. And so the protests and marches went off in their own chaotic way. People differed as to tactics and objectives, but little effort was made to paper over or erase these differences. Instead, they were made visible as signs of the strength of the movement. Meanwhile, everyone participated in the web of Internet and e-mail communication that was moving throughout the "community."

These changes in the meaning of community have important implications for a new progressive discourse in American education. If we think of education as occurring in learning communities, in which individuals are inducted into particular discourses of self-production and meaning making, then it is clear that these communities must now be understood as speaking in diverse voices, as organized around affinity at least as much as geography. Thus, progressives often support some version of choice in public education, such as charter and magnet schools, which at least potentially allow marginalized groups to constitute themselves around empowering narratives of self-production and community. Of course, this could also lead to an isolation of various affinity and identity groups and a failure to come together around any shared visions of democratic public life. Perhaps a better response among progressives would be to support heterogeneity within schools, with space allowed for the constitution of groups around difference and identity, and also for the crossing of borders and the construction of hybrid, non-essentialistic identities. What is needed, in this case, is a curriculum and pedagogy that is about reading different cultural traditions in relation to one another, so that, for example, the canon of European literature is read concurrently with contemporary novels by African American or Hispanic authors, or Eurocentric histories of America are read along with histories written by those subjugated, excluded, and silenced in dominant narratives of American community life, along with narratives that bring into view "the subaltern gaze on the eye of power, while simultaneously problematizing the very construct of center and periphery" (McCarthy, 1998, p. 155). Democratic communities of learning in the twenty-first century must be communities of difference without normalizing centers; and public education, we believe, must play a major role in building and sustaining such communities.

Cultural Studies and the New Progressivism

Cultural studies, traditionally associated with the work of scholars at the Birmingham Center for Cultural Studies in England, offers a useful starting point to explore these issues. Scholars and researchers in this tradition have looked closely at the everyday cultural practices of ordinary people, including popular culture, to see how they might inform a progressive political agenda (Grossberg, Nelson, and Treichler, 1992). Early scholars in cultural studies were drawn together by the belief that "culture is ordinary," to use Raymond Williams's phrase, that it did not reside solely in the realm of "high art." This work had a mooring in class and class-based politics, and looked at the working class not as a static entity which could be defined *a priori* but as an emergent phenomena, constructed and reconstructed through material practices. For example, E. P. Thompson's *The Making of the English Working Class* (1963) argued that "class is a relationship, and not a thing," one "embodied in real people in a real context" (pp. 1–2). Thompson's focus, in trying to understand the constitution of the English working class, was not "official history" but the lives of "ordinary" people—"the poor stockinger, the Luddite cropper, the 'obsolete' hand-loom weaver, the 'utopian' artist" among others. It is here that class culture is made and remade. Though Marxism was central to cultural studies, for these scholars and researchers it was (contra Orthodox Marxists) a "Marxism without guarantees" (Morley and Chen, 1996).

We see this, as well, in books like Richard Hoggart's *The Uses of Literacy* (1961) and Raymond Williams's *The Long Revolution* (1961). In the *The Uses of Literacy*, Hoggart looks at the ways traditional English working-class culture changed with the rise of mass forms of contemporary entertainment—how spicy magazines, commercial popular songs, and sex-and-violence novels (among other popular forms) usurped and supplanted local cultures, that had been created by and for the working classes themselves. For Hoggart, the cultural dimensions of working class life, not just the material ones, were intrinsic to revolutionary class consciousness. In *The Long Revolution*, Williams argues, quite similarly, that democratic and industrial processes were inextricably intertwined with cultural ones. All were implicated in global movements for democracy and self-determination that Williams saw burgeoning in the early 1960s. He writes, "Our whole way of life, from the shape of our communities to the organization and content of education, and from the structure of the family to the status of art and entertainment, is being profoundly affected by the progress of democracy and industry, and by the extension of communications." For Williams, however, these are not one-way or determining processes. He continues, "This deeper cultural revolution is a large part of our most significant living experience, and is being interpreted and indeed fought out, in very complex ways, in the world of art and ideas" (p. xii). Though culture is ordinary, it is also a site of struggle and contestation.

As cultural studies has traveled across the globe, it has taken on the concerns of different and distinct local contexts (Gaonkar and Nelson, 1999). As Nelson, Treichler, and Grossberg (1992) write, "cultural studies . . . has no distinct methodology, no unique statistical, ethnomethodological, or textual analysis to call its own. Its methodology, ambiguous from the beginning, could best be seen as a bricolage. Its choice of practice, that is, is pragmatic, strategic, and self-reflective" (p. 2). Most important, "the choice of research practices depends upon the questions that are asked, and the questions depend upon their context" (p. 2). These questions have always been linked to progressive political agendas, so that these agendas that have animated cultural studies from the beginning—from Marxism to feminism (e.g., the work of Angle McRobbie) to critical race theory (e.g., bell hooks and Cornel West) to "queer theory" (e.g., Isaac Julian) to disability studies (e.g., Paula Treichler) and beyond. "The commitment to imagine a more democratic society," as Norman Denzin (2001b) writes, "has been a guiding feature of cultural studies from the very beginning" (p. 3).

Cultural studies thus offers educators the opportunity to ground our social and cultural analyses in the everyday lives of youth and their material practices; it also encourages us to look beyond them. "Cultural studies," Nelson, Treichler, and Grossberg (1992) write, "offers a bridge between theory and material culture"—its politics are contextual, local, strategic, and always open to rethinking and re-visioning (p. 6). It should come as little surprise, then, that cultural studies has its origins not in the elite or "pure" disciplines, but in the everyday realities of adult education in England. Stuart Hall, Raymond Williams, and Richard Hoggart, for example, all taught adult education or "extramural education" courses for returning students at British universities. "Such pedagogical contexts," according to Lawrence Grossberg (1998), "existed outside the formal educational institutions of the state [and] served people (primarily women and the working class) who were deprived of any opportunities for, indeed actively 'blocked from' any higher education" (p. 375). In these contexts, according to Williams, students demanded to discuss what they learned "in a context to which they brought their own situation, their own experience." This meant looking beyond the formal strictures of disciplines, forcing teachers to acknowledge the fact that "specific disciplines might be inadequate to address the questions that students were raising" (p. 375).

We call here for a broad rapprochement with these impulses in cultural studies—the pedagogical effort to imagine more democratic futures rooted in the lived realities of multiple constituents. In its broadest sense, we envision the "cultural studies of education" as an interdisciplinary space to critique how education is represented and enacted within given particular cultural sites and also to imagine it otherwise (Greene, 1999). For too long, education issues have been separated from the study of culture and turned into either managerial or psychological issues. We call for a movement away from these confining and prescriptive discourses and toward the dynamic contextualization of education within culture, history, and politics, opening a space to think about what it means to be an educator in much more expansive and ecumenical ways. Just as E. P. Thompson looked beyond "official history" to the practices of "the poor stockinger, the Luddite cropper, the 'obsolete' hand-loom weaver, the 'utopian' artist" to understand class, we must look beyond the conscripted area of school research, with its delimited parameters, to a broader theater of action, both practically and theoretically. According to Grossberg, "if we are to imagine a different, a better future, we need to consider the different ways people participate in social, cultural, economic, and political life." He continues, "for it is here, as teachers, that we can examine how people make history and articulate what history we would—collectively—hope to make" (p. 390). In particular, we see cultural studies of education as actively engaged in forging an alternative discourse on the renewal of public education, one linked not so much to education policy as to new social movements in the public that potentially have the power to articulate a counterhegemonic discourse to the dominant corporate state discourse of "high stakes" testing, teacher "accountability," and higher "standards" and to re-vision the relationship between educators and their communities.

In this project, a number of critical discourses and traditions seem promising, and one of our aims in this regard is to integrate newer discourses and theories with some of those that have guided progressivism and critical education studies in the past. We see the space of cultural studies as one that can entertain multiple perspectives without the kind of linear, exclusive focus that demands that one school of thought supplant another. We do not see, for example, critical pedagogy supplanting the "new sociology of education," or cultural studies supplanting critical pedagogy, though we recognize each might better address particular kinds of concerns than might others. We offer this work very much in the spirit of the "bricoleur," as we make space for multiple methodological and theoretical traditions throughout (Denzin and Lincoln, 1994, p. 2). We see the cultural studies of education, ultimately, as having certain "uses."

Cultural studies has a particularly strong influence on three subfields or interpretive communities in education: the reconceptualist curriculum movement, critical pedagogy, and social foundations of education. We turn now to an exploration of how each of these discursive spaces is being reconstituted and reoriented around cultural studies.

The Reconceptualist Curriculum Movement

Cultural studies is rapidly reconceptualizing the curriculum field. An earlier reconceptualization brought new life into a traditional, "moribund" field in the 1970s (Schwab, 1969) by drawing upon a number of hermeneutic or interpretations traditions of scholarship such as existential phenomenology, autobiographical and subjectivist approaches to literary criticism, psychoanalytic theory from Freud to Lacan, and (to a lesser degree) neo-Marxism and the so-called new sociology of education informed by the sociology of knowledge. While each of these theoretical traditions has added something to our understanding of how education operates to keep people disempowered, the reconceptualist movement has traditionally lacked a critical discourse that is attuned to shifts occurring in the academy related to interdisciplinarity, postmodernism, and new approaches to thinking about what constitutes a "text" and what constitutes a critical reading of a text. This is changing, however.

Cultural studies, as a space opened up in the academy around these shifts, provides a way of reconceptualizing yet again. A number of studies recently published suggest a shift toward a strong cultural studies orientation in curriculum, but for purposes of illustration we want to point briefly to two. Both contextualize key identity constructs through historical analyses, giving educators new ways to think about the histories we occupy. Marla Morris, in her book *Curriculum and the Holocaust: Competing Sites of Memory and Representation* (2001), looks at the role of "historical memory" and how the Holocaust has been coded and recoded in and through multiple texts, both in and outside of school. Her effort is a personal, autobiographical recognition of the overwhelming power and pain of this event, one that opens it up to new political possibilities and forms of resistance—including the recognition that we must fight othering practices in our own culture that would turn some into scapegoats for our problems. William Pinar raises similar concerns in *The Gender of Racial Politics and Violence in America: Lynching, Prison Rape, and the Crisis of Masculinity* (2001). Pinar excavates in excruciating detail two key events in American race relations—lynching and prison rape. Pinar argues that disturbing psychosexual dynamics are at the core of these events, which have largely been written out of traditional curricular texts and their treatments of race relations. What gets written out, most notably, is an understanding of how racial domination in America has long been linked to particular construc- tions of masculinity and, more specifically, of masculine sexuality. The lynching of black men in the Jim Crow era in the South was a public spec- tacle and ritual of power in which black men were both symbolically and literally castrated, in which white masculinity was asserted around the demasculinization of the feared black Other. The ritual of prison rape, which often reverses and subverts the traditional roles of black men and white men, must be understood, Pinar argues, within this context of the ritual of lynching. All of this raises troubling questions about the con- struction of white and black masculinity in a racist culture.

Critical Pedagogy

Cultural studies perspectives entered educational discourse through critical pedagogy, and particularly through the work of Giroux. Though Freire had constructed critical pedagogy around a project of literacy education for economically and socially oppressed villagers in northeastern Brazil, people who had no exposure to the mass media, the situation is different in America. Giroux pushed critical pedagogy to acknowledge and account for the role of popular culture in maintaining relations of domination and marginalization in American society, and in youth identity formation in particular. He also reconstructed critical pedagogy around an emergent post-Marxist, postmodern politics of difference that emphasized struggles over race, gender, and sexuality as well as class. By the mid-1990s, critical pedagogy was closely interconnected with a broader cultural studies discursive community in the academy, which focused on questions of pop- ular culture. In fact, Peter Trifonas defines critical pedagogy as a "political economy of signification" (2001, p. 24), an approach to reading the world that requires interrogating the political economy and cultural politics of signs and locating signs within struggles over power and knowledge.

We see these concerns with signification perhaps most fully developed in the work of Giroux. For example, in several recent volumes, Giroux (1996, 1999, 2001a, 2001b) has explored how films like *Pocahontas*, *The Lion King*, *Beauty and the Beast*, and *Aladdin* promote racist and sexist stereotypes. Perhaps the most blatant example is *Aladdin*, which takes pains to construct Middle Easterners as savages or barbarians, as evidenced by soundtrack songs like "Arabian Knights" (1999, p. 104). Giroux's readings of this and other films are instructive for educators in that they raise questions about the degree to which Disney texts reinforce some very stereotypical and nor- malizing constructions of gender and race, to say nothing of class and sex- uality. For example, "In both *The Little Mermaid* and *The Lion King*," Giroux writes, "the female characters are constructed within narrowly defined gender roles." He continues, "The rigid gender roles in *The Little Mermaid* are not isolated instances in Disney's filmic universe; on the contrary, Disney's negative stereotypes about women and girls gain force through the way in

which similar messages are consistently circulated and reproduced, to varying degrees, in many of Disney's animated films" (p. 100). But Giroux also
frames his discussion of the hidden gender, racial, and class codes in Disney
films within the context of an analysis of their production, and the increasingly central role that major corporations like Disney and Viacom (which
owns the cable networks MTV, BET, and Comedy Central) play in producing the postmodern subject as a consumer of commodified images of self.
Corporations like Disney, he says, are able to effect "the concentration of
control over the means of producing, circulating, and exchanging information" in important and debilitating ways (2000b, p. 108). "This focus on
films must be supplemented with an analysis of the institutional practices
and social structures that work to shape such texts" (1999, p. 97).

Social Foundations of Education

Finally, cultural studies perspectives have begun to influence on what traditionally has been called the "foundations of education" or the "cultural
foundations of education," and more particularly the subfield identified as
the sociology of education. These perspectives are opening up space for
research that has progressive promise and that is attuned to social and
material shifts in the cultural terrain. Drawing on a hybrid form of qualitative sociological research informed by cultural studies perspectives, the
social foundations of education's focus is not on the study of curriculum as
a text or even pedagogy, at least not in any direct sense. Rather, its subject
is youth identity formation in the age of representation and hyperreality,
changing conceptions of "community" and the "public," global capital and
the restructuring of postindustrial labor, and other aspects of the new postmodern cultural terrain that are affecting education. This movement in the
cultural foundations of education thus links the study of everyday life
among young people, and the processes by which they construct and perform identity in relation to various Others, with a study of popular culture
and the representation of identity. And it embeds the study of both everyday life and popular culture within an analysis of real material changes that
are occurring in a rapidly globalizing society.

In a particularly fascinating study along these lines, Nadine Dolby (2000;
2001) explores how young people at a high school in South Africa ("Fernwood High") negotiated ideas about race in the aftermath of apartheid.
Here, music and fashion became ways to represent ideas about being
"white," "black," and "coloured," at a moment when a priori racial categories were called into question. These popular symbols circulated and
were ascribed different meanings at different times. "Rave music," for
example, "is understood specifically as 'white' music. A coloured student
who listens to rave would be ostracized by her or his classmates, and seen
as a threat to 'coloured' identity" (2000, p. 906). In sum, she argues, Race
at Fernwood "reinvents itself (as it does constantly) as a site of identification that takes its meaning, in large part, from affect and affective invest-

ments. Students are invested in the emotions of desire that surround consumptive practices, particularly the practices of global youth culture" (p. 903). In a similar vein, Yon's (2000) ethnographic research in a multiethnic high school in Toronto ("Maple Heights") focuses on the ways in which young people negotiate their day-to-day identities in relation to others. Yon offers portraits of different young people and their creation of complicated identities through their investments in popular culture. He writes, "Many of the signs and symbols of the popular cultures of these youth, like dress codes and musical tastes, are racialized. This means that the signifiers of race can also change with the changing signs of culture and identity, and what it means to be a certain race is different from one context to the next" (p. 71). He offers several examples of young people constructing complex identities through popular cultural texts. These include a Canadian-born black, a white youth who identifies with black culture, as well as a black immigrant from the Caribbean—all of whom use popular culture to negotiate and stake out particular notions of who they are.

Recent ethnographic work in the sociology of education has also looked to other sites where education is taking place today, including community-based organizations. Youth marginalized by race, class, gender, sexual orientation, and other markers of identity often view schools as oppressive sites, and they respond by dropping out of them both explicitly and implicitly in myriad ways (Fine, 1991; Weis, 1985, 1990). These young people are looking to various youth clubs, church groups, community centers, gay and lesbian drop-in centers and support groups, shelters for battered women, and so on as sites where they may engage in developing affirming identities in dialogue and interaction with others, and where they can engage in the active production of meaning. Lois Weis and Michelle Fine's notion of "free spaces" highlights much of the imaginative work young people invest in creating "spaces" out of the "places" made available to them in the everyday. "Young men and women," they write, "are 'homesteading'—finding unsuspecting places within their geographic locations, their public institutions, and their spiritual lives to sculpt real and imaginary corners for peace, solace, communion, personal and collective identity work. These are spaces of deep, sustained community-based educative work, outside the borders of formal schooling" (Fine, Weis, Centrie, et al., p. 132). This notion of free spaces, which operate inside and outside of schools, highlights the expansive work of the imagination that is becoming so much a part of the postmodern everyday. These are "spaces in which 'difference' signals interest, engagement, commitment, and opportunity," and which look beyond the "walls of school" (p. 149).

Cultural Studies and Education

These examples and others mark a new kind of disposition in education scholarship, one that agonizes over a broad and diverse range of sites, settings, and texts. At this new intersection of curriculum theory, critical pedagogy, and the cultural foundations of education is a hybrid and interdisciplinary or even postdisciplinary space, one that falls under the useful rubric of "the cultural studies of education." This is a space that gets us closer and closer to our constituencies where they live their lives—a particularly important gesture at this moment when we seem uncertain about what exactly "education" does and can mean. Such a space is necessary if we in education are going to rearticulate a relationship with young people and their ever more complex lives, and if we are to imagine, with them, a more democratic future.

Yet we do not want to construct a new metanarrative here that replaces or unifies diverse discourses in these and other fields of critical education inquiry. That is, we do not present the cultural studies of education as a new field or subfield in education that replaces other fields. Nor do we mean to view it as an interpretive community within curriculum theory, critical pedagogy, or the cultural foundations of education. It is best approached, we believe, as an intersection, a space where people working in all of these areas can find some shared language and overlapping interests. It is, at best, a borderlands space, constructed and maintained through dialogue among border crossers. Out of such dialogue and border-crossing, it is our hope, nevertheless, that new progressive counternarratives may be constructed that have the promise of significantly redirecting public discourse on democratic educational renewal. At the very least, we want to see what such a discourse can do, where it can take us. Cultural studies, as we use the term, implies a willingness to clear interpretive and methodological space to engage the vital project of democratic renewal in as expansive a fashion as possible.

Chapters

The following twelve chapters are presented as counternarratives in this project of reinventing and reimagining democratic education and public life. As such, they move back and forth between critique and possibility, between a micro- and macroanalysis, between theoretical and concrete analysis, between concerns with curriculum and pedagogy and broader concerns with the role that public education could serve in rebuilding democratic public life in these unsettling times. Essays in the first section, Education and the New Cultural Terrain, explore how shifts occurring broadly in postmodern America—related, among other things, to the new economic order, changes in youth culture and popular culture, globalization, the information superhighway, and shifting political coalitions—are influencing public K–12 education and/or higher education. The authors pay particular attention to the consequences of these shifts for the lived identities of contemporary youth. The authors also suggest some ways to move beyond the broken promises of democratic public education and public life, to recuperate or advance democratic progressive traditions in American public life.

McLaren and Farahmandpur powerfully set the stage in the first chapter, "The Globalization of Capitalism and the New Imperialism: Notes toward a Revolutionary Critical Pedagogy." According to McLaren and Farahmandpur, our moment is marked by a new articulation of old-fashioned imperialism, a lethal combination of "military and financial practices" that attempt to "impose the law of the market on the whole of humanity itself." Though often eclipsed in contemporary discussions around postmodernism and poststructuralism, questions of class struggle are fundamental to any rethinking of schools today. Indeed, these logics have permutated education at every level, offering critical pedagogues a new set of challenges. "A revolutionary critical pedagogy," they write, "must begin by reaffirming its commitment to the struggle for emancipating humanity from its own inhumanity." Kathleen Knight Abowitz follows with "Civil Society and Educational Publics: Possibilities and Problems," arguing for the importance of rethinking traditional notions of the "public" in "public education." Drawing on the work of Nancy Fraser, Abowitz critiques the idea that power can easily be bracketed in public discourse. The notion of a unified public sphere can itself, like other Enlightenment ideals, work to cloud and (thus) reproduce extant power relations. It is difficult, if not impossible, for people to simply debate as if they are equally powerful in other realms. More important is the nurturing of new "counterpublics" in education, sites and spaces where alternative discourses about the public can be created. "Educational publics," she writes, "forming in this sphere of civil society, can use the energy of cultural mobilization to form creative alternatives that may seriously challenge the universal public school ideal. At the very least, these alternatives offer an expanded public debate on the purposes and aims of education."

Building upon the concerns of Abowitz's article Weis and Fine's "Extraordinary Conversations in Public Schools" powerfully demonstrates how pockets of productive dialogue can happen in public schools today. The authors draw on ethnographic data from two sites: a sexual abstinence program, My Bottom Line, and a detracked and racially integrated world literature class. In the first example, the authors show how the program participants stretched beyond the official intent of the program to "traverse a variety of subjects regarding race, gender, sexuality, and men." In the second, the authors show how a world literature class can be a powerful space to debate and explore questions of identity and difference. Students learn, they write, to "engage in this space, for forty-five minutes a day, with power, 'difference,' and a capacity to re-vision. Some with delight and some still disturbed, but they know that everyone will get a chance to speak and be heard."

In "A Talk to Teachers: James Baldwin as Postcolonial Artist and Public Intellectual," Dimitriadis and McCarthy elaborate upon the importance of James Baldwin for contemporary dialogues on democratic renewal and pedagogy. Extending concerns with the public sphere opened up by Weis,

Fine, and Abowitz, the authors show how Baldwin's work offers us a new way to think about what an engaged pedagogy might mean. We see a pedagogy that is enmeshed in individual biography, exceeds the concerns of particular disciplines, engages with the popular, links the local with the global, and is intensely concerned with social change. We see a pedagogy that yearns for authentic, deliberative conversation that stretches beyond school walls and looks toward a broader theater of action. Baldwin collapses distinctions between art, criticism, and pedagogy, giving educators a broader range of resources for re-imagining and re-visioning their vocations.

In the final article in this section, "Promises to Keep, Finally? Academic Culture and the Dismissal of Popular Culture," Weaver and Daspit address these questions of popular culture, academics, and democracy, arguing that academics must renegotiate and rearticulate a relationship with the public by "resituating [themselves] within the realm of democratic tastes." This means rethinking a long intellectual tradition, from Plato through Adorno and Horkheimer, that has regarded the public and its tastes with great suspicion. They sum up, "Without these shifts there is no hope for an alternative approach to academic work, and even worse, there is no promise to keep because there will be no democracy to build from, only the illusion of a democracy."

In the next section, Reimagining Curriculum and Pedagogical Practice, the authors point to ways in which school curricula may be reconceptualized and reenacted in relation to cultural studies perspectives and shifts occurring in culture. In particular, the authors stress the ways in which proliferating media forms and representational texts have saturated the rituals of everyday life, becoming the new education curricula for many. The authors here provide concrete examples of the pedagogical uses, or possible uses, of these cultural texts within specific educational contexts. Particular attention is paid to new ways of thinking about these texts—how they can be critically demystified, deconstructed, and reconstructed, as well as how they can help us revision educational practice more broadly.

In his chapter "Stan Douglas and the Aesthetic Critique of Urban Decline," Crichlow opens up a fascinating discussion about the complex links between aesthetics and democracy through an exploration of Canadian artist Stan Douglas and his installation piece *Le Detroit*. The installation art of Douglas, Crichlow shows, is cognitive and perceptual, contingent and open in its "reading" of Detroit. In Crichlow's words, Douglas's installations allow us to envision "the unwritten future of the city," opening up imaginative possibilities for what might be otherwise. Douglas's insights, as read by Crichlow, are valuable for all of us wrestling with how to understand contemporary urban life and its implications for education.

Denzin, in his article on Hollywood's cinema of racial violence, "Screening Race," develops several critical, converging and diverging, historical and textual trajectories. In particular, Denzin explores the black arts movement of the 1960s and 1970s as a model for understanding how aesthetics can serve as a constitutive part of emancipatory political movements. Denzin reads this communal, deeply ethical, and participatory movement against recent urban cinema (for example, the Hughes brothers' *Menace II Society*) before returning us to a discussion of what he maintains are more progressive contemporary black films (for example, Carl Franklin's *Devil in a Blue Dress*). In the absence of realist claims to narrative closure, these films are deeply ethical and pedagogical, echoing the best impulses of the black arts movement.

Drawing on a Nietzschean vision of history, Carlson's chapter on Rosa Parks, "Troubling Heroes: Of Rosa Parks, Multicultural Education, and Critical Pedagogy," argues for a more multifaceted understanding of how this icon, so popular in the new multicultural canon, has been mobilized and contextualized through different political agendas. The effort of conservative William Bennett to take Parks out of her historical context and turn her into a timeless fable (alongside Chicken Little and Hansel and Gretel) is particularly telling. By exploring Rosa Parks as a complex icon, Carlson asks us to be responsible for how we navigate a historical terrain that leaves us no alibis for our effectivities—an important lesson for educators.

Susan Schramm-Pate and Dennis Carlson follow up on these concerns in "The Symbolic Curriculum: Reading the Confederate Flag as a Southern Heritage Text." They trace the struggles over the Southern Confederate flag, demonstrating how this highly charged symbol in the New South is open to a variety of interpretations, and they draw on qualitative study of how one social studies teacher in South Carolina dealt with the complexities of this symbol in the classroom. Echoing Dennis Carlson's article on Rosa Parks, the authors conclude by calling for educators to help students become more self-reflective and autonomous in their self-fashioning as historically informed citizens, to move beyond a reductive pedagogy that requires simple "yes" or "no" or "correct" answers. The "popular" offers no such easy referents.

Henke and Freedman continue to explore issues of schooling, but they expand the methodological scope of discussion. Indeed, both wrestle with the multiple tools of qualitative research—textual analysis and focus group interviews, among them—in their efforts to understand key representations of urban life and their effects. Henke's chapter, "Urban Education, Broadcast News and Multicultural Spectatorship," looks at the spectacular arrest of Pharon Crosby, a black teenager in downtown Cincinnati. She shows, through interviews with teens and newspeople, as well as critical analysis of news shows and newspapers, how this event was open to multiple meanings and interpretations. Ultimately, however, she shows how a particular, regressive meaning was mobilized, and how new links between law enforcement and public schools emerged. By describing the construction of these links, she shows us their durability as well as the possibility that things could have been otherwise.

In turn, Freedman's chapter, "'They Need Someone to Show Them Discipline': Preservice Teachers' Understandings and Expectations of Student (Re)presentations in *Dangerous Minds*," explores the complex intersections between teachers' education and popular culture. Specifically, Freedman looks at the TV show *Dangerous Minds*, which was based on a popular movie that was based in turn on a white urban teacher's memoir, and its messages about urban schooling. The program's images, she shows, do not do justice to the complexities of young people's identities, opting instead for simple one-dimensional representations that buttress the grand "hero" narrative of teacher LouAnne Johnson. These images of schooling were often picked up by the preservice teachers in her study in fairly monolithic and predictable ways. There seems to be little room for resistant readings, though they are clearly emergent, prompting Freedman to call for a more nuanced discussion about the pedagogies of popular culture. She reminds us as well that some of the more important—if problematic—education about education is taking place through popular culture today.

Finally, in "Schooling in Capitalist America: Theater of the Oppressor or the Oppressed?" Carlos Torres takes us onto new political and discursive terrain. Here, Torres decenters his authorial voice, writing a play that incorporates the voices of several distinct social actors—from a seventeen-year-old gang member, to a Los Angeles public school teacher, to a former college professor turned principal, to an elite university professor with an endowed chair. Torres evokes and orchestrates their voices inside and outside the classroom, their political struggles, their moments of hope, their feelings of despair. In abandoning traditional academic form and opening up a polyvocal space, Torres both questions his own complete control over an increasingly difficult set of issues and tensions and opens up new ground for intellectual participation around questions of democracy and education.

I.

Education and the New Cultural Terrain

1

The Globalization of Capitalism and the New Imperialism: Notes toward a Revolutionary Critical Pedagogy

Peter McLaren and Ramin Farahmandpur

> My father, the head of the family, was a rural teacher in the days of [Lazaro] Cardenas when, according to him, they cut off teachers' ears for being communists.
> —Subcomandante Marcos

> The Third World War has already started—it is a silent war, not for that reason any less sinister. This war is tearing down practically all the Third World. Instead of soldiers dying, there are children dying; instead of millions wounded, there are millions unemployed; instead of the destruction of bridges, there is a tearing down of factories, hospitals, schools and entire economies.
> —Luiz Inacio da Silva

The clock of history does not wind itself; its hands are moved by the sweat and blood of men and women who choose to be fully present on the stage of time. It is a stage often dressed for the bloodiest of wars. This present moment is no exception. Unwilling to forfeit the retrospective illusion of its own Manifest Destiny, a political regime at the helm of a mighty global empire is setting its course for a Pax Americana the likes of which has not been seen since the days of Imperial Rome. Determined to refight the old adversary of its Christian ancestors, Araby, with the unappeasable savagery of the legendary Crusaders, only this time augmenting its instruments of war with weapons of mass destruction, the United States marches forward to face its future. The movement of capital will delineate the horizon of this struggle. As educators wait in air-conditioned anticipation for a indication of what war might mean for the children of the Homeland, some waiving flags and some holding placards of protest, life grinds on in the classrooms of the nations' schools, unemployment lines grow longer, and citizens from countries already devastated by underdevelopment dream of finding a way into the streets of Los Angeles. Welcome to the age of neoliberalism where few moments of history belong so captivatingly and completely to the ruling elite.

The globalization of capital and its profane partnership with neoliberal politics pose unique and urgent challenges to today's progressive educators. The central questions that were raised by George Counts in the 1930s and by Henry Giroux in the 1980s need to be raised again: Dare schools build a new social order? What purpose do schools serve and in whose interest? Faced with the erosion of the welfare state, with the unpalatable certainty of continuing crises of overaccumulation and overcapacity within capitalism worldwide, with the persistence of structured unemployment, with attempts by the state to coerce disaffected workers back to nonexistent jobs and to convince temporary and contingent workers that they are fortunate to have any jobs at all, with the increasing privatization of schooling, and with the pacification of the victims of current relations of exploitation made so visible with the expanding U.S. prison industry, educators need to unthink their current relation to pedagogical practice as decoupled from the infrastructure of capitalism's deep value system and ruling moral syntax. Caught between economic meltdowns and the savaging of global ecosystems, between the ideological shock troops of the Christian Right and the steely-eyed hawks of Bush *hijo*'s war machine, between the McCarthy-like mechanism of the Total Information Awareness Agency and the vulgar nationalism of the U.S. PATRIOT Act, the time has come for a serious politicization of teachers' work, for exploring how the business of schooling is linked to the 'businessification' and environmental destruction of the wider society, how the idea of citizenship has been sutured to the mass appeal of fascism, and how education can be transformed in the interests of social justice.

This is especially urgent for schooling within the United States at a time when the invisible hand of the market has become a clenched fist and neoliberalism has given it brass knuckles. The United States was willing to put the whole world at risk of nuclear obliteration in order to carry out its Cold War anticommunist strategies; and now that communism has fallen onto global hard times that threatens its very existence, the United States places the world at a different—but no less serious—risk by attempting to push through its neoliberal imperialist agenda that includes preemptive military strikes against any country that is deemed a threat to U.S. interests and hence must be evil. Committed to the idea that a transformative change in education policy and practice cannot occur without challenging the current seismic shifts in the strategies of global capitalism to subject the lifeworld to what philosopher John McMurtry calls "transnational money sequencing" (2002, p. xvii) we will begin our discussion with a critique of economic globalization as a process of the "new imperialism." Further on, we will link global capitalism to the recent efforts of corporations to take over the business of education and to produce human capital for the international labor market. We will conclude our essay with a provisional sketch of what a Marxist-driven pedagogy of anticapitalist struggle might look like.

Globalization and Capitalism

The resignation produced by the seeming inevitability of capitalist society and its attendant relations of exploitation digs like a spur into the flesh of everyday consciousness, rendering us sick from exposure to too much reality. But as Marx argues, capital is an historically produced social relation that can be challenged (most forcefully by those exploited by it). A renewed engagement with and challenge to capital by means of Marxist theory fibrillates our social imagination which largely has been flatlined since the ascendary of Ronald Reagan and Margaret Thatcher and their evisceration of Keynesian welfare state capitalism. The advance of contemporary Marxist scholarship (Rikowski, 2001a, 2001b; Hill, 2001; Hill and Cole, 2001; M. Cole, 1998; McLaren and Farahmandpur, 2000), critical theory (Giroux, 1981, 1983b), and a rematerialized critical pedagogy (McLaren, 2000; McLaren and Farahmandpur, 2001) in the field of education—although still modest glimmerings—is, in our view, sufficient enough to pose a challenge not only to neoliberal free market imperatives but also to post-Marxist solutions that most often take the form of social movements grounded in identity politics.

Neoliberalism ("capitalism with the gloves off" or "socialism for the rich") refers to a corporate domination of society that supports state enforcement of the unregulated market, engages in the oppression of non-market forces and antimarket policies, guts free public services, eliminates social subsidies, offers limitless concessions to transnational corporations, enthrones a neomercantilist public policy agenda, establishes the market as the patron of educational reform, and permits private interests to control most of social life in the pursuit of profits for the few (i.e., through lowering taxes on the wealthy, scrapping environmental regulations, and dismantling public education and social welfare programs). It is undeniably one of the most dangerous politics that we face today. As described by Robert McChesney, neoliberalism is "the immediate and foremost enemy of genuine participatory democracy, not just in the United States but across the planet, and will be for the foreseeable future" (1999, p. 11). John McMurtry avers, noting that the restructuring of the United States economy constitutes the "revenge of the rich against those who advocate a more democratic and egalitarian social order" (2000, p. 10). So much has been made of the wonders of the U.S. economic model, yet it's so-called success can be measured in its complete rejection of social and environmental capital for the short-term gains of investors and consumers. As McMurtry remarks:

> Cheaper goods and costs come by the loss of tens of millions of secure domestic jobs. Real lower taxes for upper income brackets are achieved by stripping social assistance programs for the poor and unemployed. Equity values are increased by non-productive mergers, laundered drug billions, internet stocks

with no earnings, and leveraged debt and asset-flip money. Low unemployment figures are achieved by massive increases in part-time and starvation-wage jobs and a staggering 2,000,000 citizens in prison off the employment rolls (over 12 times the number of US citizens caged as in 1968, and about six times the Western European rate). The new regime rules the globe behind bars of money and iron. (2000, p. 10)

Neoliberal free market economics—the purpose of which is to avoid stasis and keep businesses in healthy flux—functions as a type of binding arbitration, legitimizing a host of questionable practices and outcomes: deregulation, unrestricted access to consumer markets, downsizing, outsourcing, flexible arrangements of labor, intensification of competition among transnational corporations, increasing centralization of economic and political power, and finally, widening class polarization. Neoliberalism is currently embarking on ways of "re-imagining" democracy through the importation of the market discourse of parasitic financial oligarchies into increasingly domesticated democratic practices and through the valorization of capital and the unrestrained economic power of private property (Teeple, 1995).

Under the tutelage of neoliberialism's celebrated economic engineers, Milton Friedman and Friedrich Von Hayek, the 1980s and 1990s became a showcase for an orchestrated right-wing backlash against the civil rights of working-class minority groups, immigrants, women, and children. At the turn of the new millennium, capitalism continues to run brakeless and at brakeneck speed across regional and national borders as global carpetbaggers looking to become the New World Order's latest centillionaires take advantage of increasing opportunities for business owners worldwide—privatization, budget cuts, and labor "flexibility"—because of the engineered absence of government constraint on the production, distribution, and consumption of goods and services brought about by global neoliberal economy policies. Stacking the shelves of Planet Mall with goods shaped for designer lifestyles has become the operative strategy. Following in the wake of a push-cart, no-frills, bootstrap capitalism are the cultural flotsam and jetsam produced by the Starbucking and Wal-Marting of the global landscape as the tyranny of the market ruthlessly subjects labor to its regulatory and homogenizing forces of social and cultural reproduction. The juggernaut of capitalist gobbelization seemingly has no outer limits to its frenzied overreach.

It should not be surprising that the increasing unavailability of health care for needy families drastic reduction of social services for the poor, and proposals for Social Security officials to connive with Wall Street brokers have coincided with the stagnation of wage growth and declining economic prosperity for most working-class men, women, and children. These recent trends have helped to hasten the shrinking of the middle class in the United States. Given such a daunting scenario, democracy seems perilously endangered. Indeed, the frontiers of human freedom are being pushed back as "free" market forces are being pushed forward.

In the wake of relentlessly expanding social and economic inequality, capitalism has never been so blindly infatuated with its own myth of success. Corporate leaders in the United States and dominant media have inured us into accepting the capitalist marketplace as the only possible social reality. Walter Mosley puts it thus: "The juggernaut of capitalism, having broken the bonds of its imprisonment—national borders—exacts its toll in an equal opportunity manner. It is the nature of capitalism to apply its value system to everything" (2000, p. 11). Echoing a similar sentiment, David McNally writes: "Having vanquished all challengers, having apparently tamed labor, anti-imperialist, and radical social movements, [capitalism] can now calmly go about the business of making us all rich" (1999, p. 134). McNally traces the current capitalist triumphalism to the antihistorical character of bourgeois ideology. He also notes that contemporary procapitalist ideology "betrays a remarkable amnesia about capitalism itself: it forgets its bloody past, its recurrent crises; it denies everything that hints at the historically specific limits of the capitalist mode of production" (p. 135). To wit, it naturalizes the exploitation of the world's poor and powerless and the normative disorder of its inner logic, reducing workers to the market price of their sweat and blood. If U.S. capitalists could have their own way, they would market for sale the tears of the poor. Are readers old enough to remember the sale of "pet rocks"?

Capitalism has become our ticket to the gaudy world of tinsel dreams and chloroformed hope, to a subterranean public sphere where *American Psycho* replaces Che Guevara as the icon of the postmodern revolution, where Americans feel at home in the illusory forms of commodity fetishism, where the studied immobility of Anna Nicole Smith's consciousness becomes the winning formula for self-production, and where memories of the revolutionaries of the Paris Commune are replaced in the structural unconscious of the nation's left by the "postmodern" bohemian revolutionaries of the *Moulin Rouge*. Under the beguiling eye of "high stakes" financial investors, a two-tiered laboring class has been created, with low-skill, low-paid service workers toiling alongside a small segment of highly skilled and well-paid workers. For the millions of people whose lives remain commodified and regulated in the charnel house of "fast-track" capital accumulation and its seductive companion, consumer ideology, the clearly visible contradictions within capitalist social and economic relations of production have become too obvious to be recognized. They have been naturalized as common sense. After all, the buying and selling of human lives as commodities—the creation of what Marx called "wage slaves"—must be guaranteed as a constitutive factor of our democracy, so this condition is carefully disguised as a "voluntary contractual agreement," even though the only alternatives the regulating presuppositions and life-destructive practices of capital accumulation are starvation, disease, and death. Liberals and conservatives alike love to heap fulsome praise on the United States as the world's bastion of freedom while ignoring the fact that its grandiloquent dream for saving the world has been a dismal failure and has unleashed a hyper-Leviathan among the aggrieved populations of humanity. For the most part, they have chosen to disregard abysmal disparities between effort and reward that accompanies real existing capitalism. Marxists know otherwise. Beneath the myth of meritocracy that undergirds the American Dream, and that locksteps with images of happy consumers in a breathless quest for an earthly paradise, lurks the enslaved consciousness of primitive patriotism and the increasing polarization between the rich and the destitute. The only "free" cheese is in the mousetrap. To be free from necessity is a constitutive impossibility within a "democratic" structure of private appropriation and corporate commodification. To be "free" in an advanced capitalist economy means being free to choose between being the exploiter or the exploited. The backwardness of the economies on the periphery *has become a necessary condition* for the flourishing of the economies of the center (Kagarlitsky, 2001, p. 58).

The challenge of turning the country into one giant theme park to entertain the ruling class has not been met in all corners of the globe, but the opposition is withering away by the minute. More and more countries are donning what William Greider has called globalization's "golden straightjacket" of "follow our orders, and we will make you rich (someday)"—forced austerity programs orchestrated by institutions such as the International Monetary Fund and World Bank that dictate what foreign governments may or may not do (2000, p. 14).

The closure of the second millennium represents at once the incalculably expanded scope of the culture of consumption and the implosion of social relations into a universal signifier—namely capital, which Marx metaphorically referred to as the "universal pimp." Marx likened money to a "visible god" that in the generalized commodity form "spreads this illusory perception throughout society, dissolving all previous identities and distinctions, and remolding human consciousness in its own image. In the fully developed form of capital, money achieves an active, self-regulating power through which it shapes the lives of concrete individuals" (Hawkes, 1996, pp. 101–102).

For those who believe that uninterrupted accumulation and increasing international concentration of capital is a good thing, that the shift from an international economy to a world economy is a sign of progress, that the feedback mechanisms of the unfettered "free" market are fair, that only democracy will spring forth from the market's spontaneous order, and that the common good will magically advance from its networked complexity, there is reason to be wildly optimistic about the future. Imagine the possibilities for privatizing remaining public spaces and spreading neoliberal domination over vast exotic populations hitherto unconquered! But for educators who reject the idea that the social system under capitalism is a self-organizing totality and who view the globalization of capital as an irredeemable assault on democracy, the future appears perilous indeed.[1] We refuse to elevate the victimization of the working class to a regulatory ideal of democracy and decline to treat the economy as an inert "thing" or endow it with self-evident democratic agency. After Marx, we view the economy as a social relation and not a self-sustaining natural entity. Capitalism is not powered by a transcendental metaphysic but is a social relation overburdened by exploitation, accumulation, endless growth, and class conflict. It remains predicated on the extraction of surplus value from workers (value produced by workers beyond that which the capitalist must pay out in wages so that the workers can reproduce their labor-power).

Despite all the fanfare surrounding the promises of free trade, it remains the case that advanced and developed countries have been hurt by globalization. Only a few metropolitan centers and select social strata have benefited, and it is no secret who these select occupants are. It's not the case that the poor are next in line to become millionaires. That's not part of the overall scheme. The overnight success of the television game show, *Who Wants to Be a Millionaire*, has brought with it its repressed double, the unemployed victim of corporate downsizing who returns to visit the scene of his firing to do some 'firing' of his own, only this time through the barrel of an automatic rifle as he guns down his former boss and coworkers. Such an act serves as an index of capitalist society's hubristic rejection of a social world in which corporate profit take precedence over human needs. No, the poor are not next in line to enter free market heaven, but the belief in overnight wealth and security success continues to be creatively engineered in the dream factories of corporate advertising.

In fact, the poor are completely written out of the script of the American Dream; they serve as permanent extras for the background shots for larger millionaire *novelas* of fame for the lucky few, and misery and poverty for the unlucky many. The functional integration among production, trade, global financial markets, and transport and speed technologies that make financial transactions instantaneous has facilitated the redeployment of capital to "least-cost" locations that enable exploitation on the basis of advantages it will bring to those wishing to become part of the "Millionaires-R-US Club."

As global assembly lines increase and as speculative and financial capital strikes across national borders in commando-like assaults ("move in, take the goods, and move out"), the state continues to experience difficulty in managing economic transactions but has not yet detached itself from the infrastructure of corporate imperialism. Transnational corporations and private financial institutions—Gold Card members of the leading worldwide bourgeoisie—have formed what Robinson and Harris (2000) call a "transnational capitalist clan." And while the emergent global capitalist historic bloc is marked by contradictions in terms of how to achieve regulatory order in the current global economy, national capitals and nation-states continue to reproduce themselves. Home markets have not disappeared from the scene since they continue to provide ballast for the imperialist state through ensuring the general conditions for international production and exchange.[2]

Liberal democracies like to pretend that the state is a separate and autonomous sphere of activity because that way they can set up convenient smokescreens against the internal workings of the capitalist production process. They can also prevent the staggering exposure of capitalism's zero-sum game and hinder our understanding of the invidious ways in which the state functions to sustain and promote the capitalist system. Not to mention the ways in which the state *nomenklatura* ideotypically locates blame within individuals (they are too lazy, ignorant, unskilled) rather than within their conditions of existence (i.e., the value form of wealth that is historically specific to capitalism). Within liberal democracies, individuals are conveniently held responsible for their own poverty as blame is shifted away from the capitalist "race to the bottom" to see who can prosper with the minimum or lowest standards of social and economic justice as well as environmental protection and sustainability. The blame is always shifted away from the means by which surplus-value is created through the internal and dialectical relation that exists between labor and capital—that is, away from the way workers are locked into an internal and antagonistic relation to capital in the most alienating and dehumanizing of ways—and away from the fact that exploitation is a constitutive feature of the capitalist production process (Allman, 2001).[3] The globalization of capital has dramatically occasioned what Mészáros (1999) describes as the "downward equalization of the differential rate of exploitation," in which workers all over the world—including those in advanced capitalist countries such as the United States—are facing a steady deterioration of working conditions because of structural crisis of the capitalist system, a crisis of monetarist capitalism and the aggressive marketization of social relations.

Unlike its well-known predecessors—the plutocracy that relied upon slave labor slavery and feudalism—capitalism is predicated on the overaccumulation of capital and the superexploitation of rank-and-file wage laborers. The irreversible contradictions inherent within capitalist social and economic relations—those between capital and labor—are taking us further away from democratic accountability and steering us closer to what Rosa Luxemburg (1919) referred to as an age of "barbarism." Peery (1997) makes the point that in comparison to the political economy that sustained slavery or feudalism, the social and economic contradictions in the present-day capitalist mode of production are much more virulent and unremitting. This is because the production, distribution, and consumption of commodities are in constant contradiction with labor power and prevents the logic of capital from validating any logic other than its own. McMurtry argues that the "sixty-five-hour-a-week job of the Nike running-shoe producer in a sweatshop of the new 'free labor zones' of the East or South, with a wage of less than $40 a week, is arguably less free than the work of a nineteenth-century field slave" (1999, p. 176).

Capital's cheerleaders have hidden its diabolical nature and its refusal to be accountable to democratic interests behind the non-sequitur claim that the free market promotes democracy. In fact, self-determining governments only get in the way of the goal of transnational corporations, which is "to open all domestic markets, natural resources, built infrastructures, and labor pools of all societies of the world to foreign transnational control without the barrier of self-determining government and people in the way" (J. McMurtry, 1999, p. 58). The real agenda of transnational corporations is, in other words, to create an anti-welfare capitalism with a human face while drawing attention away from the paradoxical congeniality of capitalism and its repressed underside.

The McLaw of Value

Today we can't simply talk about the capitalist law of value, but we rather need to address the "McLaw of value," in which a corporation that sells hamburgers has more clout under NAFTA than many governments of the so-called Third World. Why is it that the World Trade Organization can determine that a corporation like Time Warner AOL can sue the government of India if it permits an underground market in compact disks by Michael Jackson, but remains silent about enforcing human rights and conditions for workers (C. Leys and F. Yeskel, 2000)? Imperialism has arrived unannounced, this time in a Vegas-style stretch limousine where financial oligarchs and their banker servants and parvenus plot ways to accelerate the concentration of capital and the formation of monopolies, oblivious to the economic refugees languishing on skid row, their shopping carts in tow. But this kind of information will never make the evening news precisely because it draws attention to what McMurtry calls "the money death-sequence of value"—the global market's value imperialism (J. McMurtry, 1998, 1999).[4]

McMurtry asserts that free market democracy is a self-certifying term premised on the most odious of lies. Corporations steward us in the direction of market doctrine, a doctrine of legitimized by its baptism in the fire of commodity production. He asks: Who are the producers? They are, after all, owners of private capital who purchase the labor of those that produce, including, notes McMurtry, "that of white-collar managerial and technical workers" (1998, p. 174). While some investing owners may also be producers—paying themselves as managers in addition to the renumeration they receive as owners—most corporate "producers" do not actually produce goods. These owners have no roles in the production process and are constituted as fictitious legal entities or "corporate persons." The real producers—the workers—are reduced to faceless "factors of production" employed by the owners of production. There is no freedom for the actual producers within the "free-market economy." This is because the real producers belong to the employer, and they serve as the instruments of the employer's will. What little freedom exists is located at the top levels of management, but even here freedom exists "only so far as it conforms to the ruling command of maximizing profitability for stockholders and owners" (1998, p. 175). McMurtry maintains that obedience to the market god has been perceived as the only path to freedom and fulfillment. He writes:

Freedom is not simply a slogan, but requires an option to do other than what is prescribed. Few agents of the market system are in truth free, even those at the top. In the end, then, only the "free market" itself is free or self-regulating. As in other fundamentalist creeds, however, obedience to this god is conceived as the acme of personal freedom and self-realization. (1999, p. 178)

The present generation has been sacrificed in advance to the globalization of capital. This poses a major dilemma for teachers and cultural workers. Why try to help young people adapt to a system that is designed to exclude them? As Viviane Forrester has noted, education under capitalism has caught today's youth in the fabrications and deceits of history, teaching them "about the rudiments of a life already denied to them, an already confiscated life, a life of which they are deprived in advance [and a life no longer viable anyway]." (1999, p. 70). The system does provide roles for our young people, but these are mostly roles as castaways or as pariahs. How is it possible to teach today's youth to become part of the very society that rejects them (Giroux, 2000a, 2000b)?

The current mind-set of global capitalism can, in fact, be traced to the Trilateral Commission of 1973 (composed of the world's leading corporate CEOs, academics, government officials, etc.) who argued that there existed "an excess of democracy" in the Western world and who advocated the legitimacy of hierarchy, coercion, discipline, secrecy, and deception, as well as the non-involvement of a governable democracy (McMurtry, 1999). Mutagenic capitalist values have transmogrified into a social ethos, making it easier for flimflam financial ventures to proliferate, breaking the tenuous accord that has long existed between labor and capital. Adam Smith's notion of the market as a servant of the public good through the shared "wealth of nations" has achieved the status of a good joke in bad taste. Arching over the blandishments of the value program of the global market is the aerosol figure of George "Dubya" Bush, who is not content to have stolen the election through voter cleansing in his brother Jeb's state of Florida, but is determined to realize his potential for manifest delusion and to exercise a stubborn willingness to give away billions of dollars of tax cuts to the wealthiest 1 percent of the population. Armed with the world's mightiest-ever army, the United States looks more like a military industrial complex disguised as a country than a country supporting a military-industrial complex.

The Failure of the Free Market

In more specific terms, how has the globalization of capital fared? The economic performance of industrial countries under globalization in the 1980s and 1990s is much poorer than during the 1950s and 1960s when they operated under a more regulated social-market economy (Singh, 2000). Economic growth and GDP growth have dropped, and productivity has been cut in half; in addition, unemployment has risen dramatically in the OECD countries.[5]

Latin American countries that have liberalized their trading and external capital regimes have suffered from severe financial crises, including the "peso crisis" of 1994–95 in Mexico and the "Samba effect" of 1999 in Brazil. Latin American countries following the Washington consensus have, since the late 1980s, experienced a long-term growth rate reduction from 6 percent per annum to 3 percent per annum (Singh, 2000).[6]

The battle over free trade is not only about profits. It's also about manufacturing ideology. Globalization has been a dismal failure for the vast majority of the world's capitalist nations. And yet the corporate elite refuse to concede defeat. In fact, they are boldly claiming victory, and they insist that history is on their side. In a sense they are correct. But we have to understand that they are claiming history for themselves. They have been victorious. In fact, they've made millions. The question remains: At whose expense?

Global capitalism has won the battle over ideology hands down. Global capitalist monocracy has declared itself victorious over socialist and communist ideologies. The latter are being auctioned off at Sotheby's as relics of class struggle from bygone eras, to be archived in museums dedicated to democracy's glorious victory over the evil empires spawned by Mr. Marx. For now, capitalism has succeeded in steering the wheels of history to the far right, to a head-on collision with the reigning neoliberal bloc, where postmodernized signposts on the streets declare the triumph of privatization over socialization, econometrics over ethics, individualism over collectivism, lifestyle identity politics over class politics, cynicism over hope, and barbarism over civilization.

The decaying carcass of communism lies in its red iron casket, only to have grave robbers from the International Monetary Fund stir its bones by removing anything left of monetary value. It wouldn't surprise us if statues of Lenin have been melted down to produce slot machine tokens for Las Vegas gamblers. Fading socialist dreams in the former USSR memorabilia can be purchased by credit card on the Internet by graying radicals from 1968 (the *acht und sechziger*).

The fall of the Berlin Wall and the cataclysmic social and political implosions in Russia and eastern European countries coincide with the premature "end-of-ideology" proclamations and correlative self-canceling pronouncements about the end of history hailed by conservative social theorists such as Francis Fukuyama. In classic red-baiting style, Fukuyama has announced the end of revolutionary movements and the demise of socialism altogether. However, in their mad dash toward capitalist utopia, the growing lumpen-proletariats in Russia and in ex-socialist European countries, drunk on the prospect of get-rich-quick schemes and of reaping enormous windfalls, are stumbling over the balmy corpse of Lenin and learning the lessons of privatization and the empty promises of market socialism the hard way. According to Arrighi, Hopkins, and Wallerstein (2001), "the hold of Milton Friedman on the hearts and minds of his Eastern European and Soviet disciples" is so considerable, and their embrace of the monetarist ideology of the West is so maddeningly strong, that they "have to yet realize that this road is leading them—or at least most of them—not to the promised land of North America but to the harsher realities of South America or worse" (p. 43).

Of course, workers in Russia and the former eastern bloc countries are not the only ones being deceived by capitalism's promises of prosperity. Thousands of workers in Latin American countries whose dictators borrowed from the World Trade Organization—and who stealthily pocketed most of the profits—are suffering through imposed austerity programs in which they have been made to assume repayment of international loans. If the postmodernists want to brag about the disappearance of the U.S. working class and celebrate the new culture of lifestyle consumption, then they need to acknowledge that the so-called disappearing working class is reappearing again in the assembly lines of China, Brazil, Indonesia, and elsewhere, where there exist fewer impediments to U.S. profit making (Žižek, 2000).

The engines of globalization are powered by two interlocking phenomena (Went 2000). The first can be described as the "long-term development of capitalism" dating back to the 1870s, marked by the accumulation, concentration, and centralization of capital. The second phenomenon is associated with the neoliberal social and economic policies put into motion in the 1970s, which ignited the shift toward the liberalization, deregulation, privatization, and flexiblization of the labor markets. The social and political antagonisms haunting capitalism today are manifold and can be discerned and challenged by utilizing the optic of historical materialist critique. On the one hand, we witness the vast profusion of material resources able to sustain the livelihood of the six billion inhabitants of the earth, and provide basic necessities including full employment, housing, and health care. On the other hand, the growing bipolarization and the overaccumulation of capital by the new breed of opulent gangster capitalists from reigning global mafiacracies has reduced the odds of surviving hunger, poverty, malnutrition, famine, and disease for a growing segment of working-class men, women, and children who are now joining urban ghettos and global slum dwellers in their *casas de carton* all over the world. We are not talking only about Calcutta and Rio de Janeiro, but our own urban communities from New York to Los Angeles that have been placed epochally at risk.

Instead of celebrating the advance of democracy worldwide, we are facing growing inequality the proportions of which stagger the imagination. As Willie Thompson notes: "The trend is precisely in the opposite direction, toward intensified polarization, the concentration of misery, suffering, deprivation and hopelessness at the lower end of the scale, mirrored by exorbitant and unceasing accumulation [of capital] at the other pole" (1997, pp. 224–25). Whether by increasing the extortion of absolute surplus value through the proliferation of *maquiladoras* along the U.S.-Mexican *frontera*, or increasing relative surplus value extortion through increasing the productivity of labor and reducing the value of labor power, capitalism continues to hold living human labor hostage, fetishizing its own commodity logic and valorization process, and recasting the world into its own image. Value—the medium and the outcome of abstract labor—binds individuals to its law of motion. Like Ahab, lifelessly thrashing about on the body of Moby Dick as the White Beast submerges itself into the icy fathoms of eternity, we are carried into the future on the backs of our worst nightmare, in a ghoulish parody of life. Spawned in the social universe of capital, our nightmares chart the course of civilization, illuminated by the dark lamp of history. According to James Petras: "The boom in the U.S. is fueled in part by an exaggerated speculative bubble that is unsustainable. Stocks are vastly overvalued; savings are negative and the performance of the productive economy has no relation to the paper economy" (2000, p. 16). He further notes that it is clear "that one quarter of the capitalist world cannot prosper when three quarters are in deep crisis—the laws of capitalist accumulation cannot operate in such restricted circumstances" (p. 16).

Teresa Ebert captures the understanding of globalization that we wish to underscore in this essay when she describes globalization as the unfolding of capitalism's central contradiction: the separation of the worker from the product of her labor. Ebert is worth quoting at length:

> Globalization . . . is . . . above all, about the structured inequality in the contemporary world, and contesting theories of globalization are really contestations over how to understand and engage this material inequality. . . . Globalization, as Marx and Engels describe it, is a dialectical process. Contrary to its official propaganda, globalization is in no way a remedy for inequality. It reinforces inequality: the fact that it provides jobs for the jobless in no way means that it changes the social relations of production. In fact, globalization is the internationalization of these social relations of production—the internationalization of class structures. (1999, pp. 390, 399)

Teresa Ebert has provided a lucid and incisive "materialist" critique of two approaches to globalization—what she calls the globalization-as-transnationalism argument and the political theory of globalization. The former representation of globalization refers to the putative emergence of a new world community based on a shared cosmopolitanism and culture of consumption. This perspective shares a culture and a state orientation. The cultural orientation emphasizes global symbolic exchanges relating to values, preferences, and tastes rather than material inequality and class relations. It is essentially a form of cultural logic. The focus on the state explores the relationship between the local and the global and whether globalization means the reorganization or disappearance of the nation-state. The political theories of globalization generally argue about the sovereign status of nation-state. They maintain that local legal codes, local currencies, and local habits and customs that enables the rise of capitalism now serve as constraints on capital so that now the new transnational institutions more suitable to the new phase of capitalism are developing.

Ebert's materialist conception of globalization asserts that both cultural and political theories of globalization bury issues of production and labor under questions of consumption of the market. Here, consumption is effectively naturalized as questions of taste, value preference and sensibilities erase the more fundamental issue of labor and production. Ebert rightly stresses the importance of production and highlights what the politics of globalization is really about: the continuous privatization of the means of production; the creation of expanding markets for capital and the creation of a limitless market of highly skilled and very cheap labor so capitalists can maintain their competitive rate of profit. In short, this process is all about the internationalization of capitalist relations of exploitation.

Global Capitalism as the New Imperialism

Numerous social and political theorists have studied the phenomenon of globalization extensively and have pronounced it a discomfiting inevitability for some but a powerful, life-enhancing economic tonic for many. In our opinion globalization represents an ideological facade that camouflages the manifold operations of imperialism. In fact, the concept of globalization has effectively replaced the term "imperialism" in the lexicon of the privileged class for the purpose of exaggerating the global character of capitalism—as an all-encompassing and indefatigable power that apparently no nation-state has the means to resist or oppose. Furthermore, it deceitfully suggests that capitalism no longer needs the protection of the nation-state. This position occludes the fact that a large portion of production in western European countries takes place within national boundaries. Moreover, the globalization thesis maintains that whereas state power can be used in the interests of the large multinational corporations, it cannot be employed in the interest of the working class.[7]

We are using the term "imperialism" here after Lenin (1951) to refer to the merging of industrial capital via cartels, syndicates, and trusts, with banking capital, the result of which is *finance capital*. To call globalization a form of imperialism might seem a rhetorical exaggeration. But we believe that this identification is necessary because the term "globalization" is calculated by bourgeois critics to render any radical politicization of it extreme. The ideology of this move is invisibly to frame the concept of globalization within a culturalist logic that reduces it to mean a standardization of commodities (i.e., the same designer clothes appearing in shopping plazas throughout the world). By contrast, we see the process as inextricably tied to the politics of neoliberalism, in which violence asserts itself as stability through a recomposition of the capital-labor relationship. Such a recomposition entails the subordination of social reproduction to the reproduction of capital (Dinerstein, 1999), the deregulation of the labor market, the globalization of liquid capital, the outsourcing of production to cheap labor markets, and the transfer of local capital intended for social services into finance capital for global investment.

The "new" imperialism to which we refer is really a new combination of old-style military and financial practices as well as recent attempts by developed nations to impose the law of the market on the whole of humanity itself. Having obscured the distinction between the sacred and profane, the global aristocracy's new world order has set out to expand the free market in the interest of quick profits, to increase global production, to raise the level of exports in the manufacturing sector, and to intensify competition among transnational corporations. It has also benefited from part-time and contingent work, reduced the pool of full-time employment, and accelerated immigration from Third World and developing countries to industrial nations (Bonacich and Appelbaum, 2000). In addition to our description of globalization as imperialism we might add the following: imperialist military intervention primarily disguised as humanitarian aid, the submission of international institutions such as the United Nations to the social and economic demands of imperialist conquest [witness the recent subservience of the U.N. to the demands of the U.S. in the context of weapons inspections in Iraq] and the instigation of ethnic and nationalistic conflicts to weaken nations refusing to submit to the rule of the market (Azad, 2000).

While we agree that capitalism has, since its inception, functioned as a world economy, we also want to stress what we see as a powerful new movement in contemporary capitalist production and global relations of power. This movement provides the groundwork for a more centralized and unitary regulation of both the world market and global power relations that tend toward " a single supranational figure of political power" and that introduce "a new inscription of authority and a new design of the production of norms and legal instruments of coercion that guarantee contracts and resolve conflicts" (Hardt and Negri, 2000, p. 9). But we stress here that these movements are today only tendencies—not a paradigm shift. Interimperialist rivalry is still strong, and the global landscape is still replete with a multiplicity of contesting capitals. In the face of such an intensification of global capitalist relations (rather than a shift in the nature of capital itself), we need to develop a critical pedagogy capable of engaging everyday life as lived in the midst of global capital's tendency toward empire, a pedagogy that we have called revolutionary critical pedagogy.

According to Samir Amin (2001), historically there have been three stages of imperialism: the European conquest of the Americas; the colonial subjection of Asia and Africa during the industrial revolution; and the intervention of the Triad (United States, western Europe, and Japan) in situations in which "rogue nations" interfere with democracy and the free market. The first stage of imperialism saw the rise of the mercantilist system of Atlantic Europe coincide with the genocidal destruction of Native

American civilizations as well as their Hispanicization–Christianization. According to Amin, The second stage resulted from the creation of a second Europe by the United States by means of the advances brought about by the industrial revolution. It marked the opening up of global capitalist markets and a seizure of the natural resources of the globe. In this stage inequality grew from a maximum ratio 2:1 (around 1800) to around 60:1 today. The third stage in Amin's model is underwritten by a justification of any military aggression useful to the United States and the quest for international markets and the unimpeded opportunity to loot the earth's natural resources. It also involves the super-exploitation of the labor reserves of the peripheral nations. The third stage of imperialism is also marked by the perceived "convergence" of democracy (modern management of political life) and the market (capitalist management of economic activity). Amin argues that, in reality, democracy and the market are divergent but that this divergence is progressively concealed as democracy continues to be emptied of all its content that is dangerous for the smooth functioning of the market.

A symptom of a new stage of imperialism can be seen in the arena of recent international military conflicts involving NATO and its allies. For instance, Hardt and Negri (2000) trace the Gulf War (and we would also include the bombing of Kosovo in this category) to the concept of *bellum justum*, or "just war" whose genealogy can be traced all the way back to the biblical tradition. Today the concept of *jus ad bellum* (right to make war) has been both reduced and banalized to the status of police action or routine police repression and sacralized as an ethical instrument used against an "absolute" enemy. And though the concept repeats ancient or medieval notions, it also represents a shift in practice: since it is no longer an activity of defense or resistance but an activity *that is justified in itself* (Hardt and Negri, 2000).

Contrary to popular opinion, wealth depletion among developing nations is not rescued by capital from the imperialist activities of advanced capitalist countries. This is because transnational corporations drain the local capital from poor countries rather than bring in new capital. Because their savings are often low, banks in developing countries would rather lend to their own subsidiary corporations (who send their profits back to advanced nations) than to struggling local businesses in developing nations. Faced with low prices for exports, high tariffs on processed goods, and a lack of capital and rising prices, local businesses are locked into entrenched impoverishment because of structural adjustment measures to balance the budget. Such measures are financed through cuts in spending for human development (Imam, 1997). The World Trade Organization does not permit poor countries to prioritize fighting poverty over increasing exports or to choose a development path that will advance the interests of the countries' own populations. By 1996, the resulting concentration of wealth had "the income of the world's richest individuals . . . equal to the income of 52 percent of humanity" (Imam, 1997, p. 13). Big business is in control of the government and is making its move to cash in on the recent theft of the White House by George Bush *hijo*.*

Bush's "appointment" as president of the United States has made a mockery of the idea that you can reform capitalism through the existing electoral process. And his White House *caudillismo* has made it clear that helping the poor and powerless is not on the agenda at all. When we arrive at a juncture in our political history at which General Motors is bigger than Denmark in wealth; Daimler Chrysler is bigger than Poland; Royal Dutch/Shell is bigger than Venezuela—and when the United States basically is dedicated to serve profits rather than its citizens—we need to stand back and take a deep breath, asking ourselves who, as citizens of the world's poster-child democracy, we really serve and for whose benefit. In 1990, the sales of each of the top five corporations (General Motors, Wal-Mart, Exxon, Mobil, and Daimler Chrysler) were bigger than the GDPs of 182 countries.

The Corporatization of Public Education

As the logic of capital accumulation shifts toward knowledge-based economies and as new forms of computer technology and biotechnology are integrated into today's high-tech economy, information itself is fast becoming a high-priced new commodity. Transnational corporations are laboring vigorously to privatize the socially produced knowledge associated with the educational system. Decreased government funding of public education has encouraged alliances with private corporations, which seek to create "high-tech knowledge industries" (Witheford, 1997). Transnational corporations are sponsoring research centers in universities across the United States by donating millions of dollars for the research, development, and production of for-profit technologies. This has resulted in the "high-tech colonization of education," transforming public universities into corporate-operated "techopolises" that have little interest in coexistence with the poor (Witheford, 1997). This has brought the spread of quantitatively measurable accountability schemes interpreted from a managerial point of view (Ollman, 2001).

Under the command of the market economy, not even universities, colleges, and vocational schools are immune from the economic policies favoring capital accumulation. Niemark (1999) reports that social policies that support for-profit universities have made higher education an extension of the market economy. She writes that social policies that support privatization have moved in the direction of

> establishing for-profit degree-granting institutions (such as the University of Phoenix); outsourcing curriculum, instruction, counseling, operations, and administration (in such areas as bookstores, food services, libraries, computer

---

*hijo is spanish for "son."

operations, plant maintenance, security, printing, and payroll); signing campus-corporate research and development partnership and licensing agreements; and selling exclusive on-campus marketing rights to companies that sell products as varied as soft drinks, fast food, computers, and credit and telephone calling cards. The campus is becoming virtually indistinguishable from the marketplace, and both universities and their faculties are becoming entrepreneurs. (p. 24)

The restructuring of higher education can be seen as reinforcing class inequality and exposing public higher education to social and economic policies governed by the laws of the market economy (i.e., commodification, proletarianization, and capital accumulation). It also visibly functions as an impediment to the education and active participation of citizens in a democratic decision-making process dedicated to coexistence (Niemark, 1999). The far right, supported by organizations such as the Heritage Foundation, continues to be represented by powerful conservative political figures such as Jesse Helms, Edwin Meese, William Bennett, and Newt Gingrich, who blame the government for the declining social and economic status of the United States in the global economy. The goal of these pundits and their corporate allies is to decentralize education and privatize public schools. The religious right has attacked the government for promoting homosexuality, secular humanism, and scientific creationism; banning school prayer; and downplaying the importance of family values. Neoconservatives supported by organizations such as the American Enterprise Institute have largely positioned themselves as political centrists who in their frenetic drive for academic excellence advocate a strong role for the federal government and support for private schools. Many of these conservative groups reflect a plangent yearning for the heterosexist patriarchy and still-born democracy of *Leave It to Beaver* and *Lassie*, pop culture's Elysian Fields as dreamt by Norman Rockwell on melatonin. We are living *Nickelodeon* reruns of the American Dream, only in reverse.

The shift toward the privatization and corporatization of public education is best exemplified by the corporate raider Michael Milken, the Wall Street wizard and junk bond king of the mid-1980s who lured investors into high-risk investment schemes. Milken has returned to the business world, this time by focusing on the lucrative $800 billion education market and has decided to create for-profit education enterprises with the help of his powerful—yet comparatively obscure—$500 million company known as Knowledge Universe. Milken has invested heavily in several companies producing educational materials. Knowledge Universe owns companies such as Children's Discovery Centers, Bookman Testing Services, Pyramid Imaging Inc., Nobel Education Dynamics, and Leapfrog, which produces educational tools used at learning centers of the Riordan Foundation (Vrana, 1998). In a recent interview with the Los Angeles Times, Milken calculated that if the net worth of the United States is placed at $120 trillion, roughly $75 trillion consists of human capital. This means that every American is worth $400,000 to $500,000 (Vrana, 1998). In short, Milken has discovered that the knowledge business is profitable.

Corporate Philanthropy and the Neoliberal Agenda

A significant part of the neoliberal agenda has been directed at the business of education—literally. We are referring not only to the growing commercialization and corporatization of public schools, which are now at the center of much-heated public debate and controversy, but rather to the businessification of schooling: for-profit education with the extraction of surplus value as the bottom line (see Kincheloe, 1993, 1998). Coca-Cola, McDonald's, and Exxon are among a long list of corporations that are providing financial help to some of the nation's eighty thousand public schools. Indeed, many urban school districts have accepted corporate funding because of a shortage of qualified teachers, school textbooks, resources, and materials.

The Center for a New American Dream (2000) reports that since 1980, advertising expenditures in the United States doubled from 1980 to 1998, rising from nearly $106 billion to $200 billion. More than $2 billion alone is spent annually on advertising that specifically targets children, twenty times more than a decade ago. Channel One, the brainchild of Chris Whittle, has a captive audience that is nearly fifty times larger than the number of teenagers who watch MTV. The average child of today is exposed to twenty thousand to forty thousand commercials each year. From the ages six to eighteen, children view nearly sixteen thousand hours of television programming and are exposed to four thousand hours of radio and music programming. Children also spend more time viewing television and commercial programs than they spend in school. Nearly one of four children under the age of six has a television set in his or her bedroom. Jean Kilbourne (1999) writes: "The average American is exposed to at least three thousand ads every day and will spend three years of his or her life watching television commercials. Advertising makes up about 70 percent of our newspapers and 40 percent of our mail" (pp. 58–59).

In 1996, corporate philanthropy funneled nearly $1.3 billion into the education marketplace, constituting 20 percent of the $6.3 billion in total corporate handouts. According to Corporate Watch (2000), the education industry consists of: (a) public schools sponsored by corporations such as American Express, Celebration School, American Bankers Insurance Group; (b) corporate charter schools or educational maintenance organizations such as the Edison Project, Advantage Schools Inc., Educational Alternatives Inc.; (c) marketing and investment companies in the school business, such as Lehman Brothers, EduVentures, and Kid Connection; (d) corporations offering sponsored educational materials, such as Lifetime Learning Systems, Enterprise for Education, the Mazer Corporation, Media

Options, Inc., Youth Marketing International; (e) in-schooling advertising firms such as Scholastic Inc., Adopt-a-School, Cover Concepts Marketing Service, Inc.; (f) lunch programs funded by Pizza Hut, Subway, Arby's, and the American School Food Service Association; and (g) conservative and right-wing think tanks that influence education policies, such as the Heritage Foundation, the Educational Excellence Network (which is part of the Hudson Institute, overseen by Chester Finn and Diane Ravitch), and the Landmark Legal Foundation.

Supported by a complex infrastructure, McDonald's global empire (which consists of twenty-five thousand restaurants in over one hundred countries) is aggressively pursuing its ultimate goal of the "McDomination" of the fast-food industry (see Kincheloe, 2002). McDonald's has a state-of-the-art university, Hamburger University, located in Oak Brook, Illinois (there are also branches in England, Germany, Japan, and Australia), where it trains its future managers. In a concerted effort to increase consumer loyalty, McDonald's provides public schools with free educational materials. At Pembroke Lakes Elementary School in Broward County, Florida, students are introduced to the world of work by learning how a McDonald's restaurant is operated and managed, how to complete an employment application, and how to interview for a job at McDonald's. Students are also required to learn about the nutritional values of the high-fat, high-cholesterol foods served at McDonald's. By providing free educational material and resources to schools, McDonald's is able to achieve two important goals. First, it expands its market share and influences public school curricula. Second, McDonald's secures the foundation for recruiting future employees from a vast pool of working-class and minority students of color in urban schools, thus making the transition from school to work more efficient.

Although there has been vociferous public protest against the corporate takeover of education, corporations have aggressively fought back with boardroom-style aggression against student, teacher, and parent activism. In public schools, colleges, and universities across the country, students have been penalized for resisting corporate colonization. In 1998, Mike Cameron, a senior at Greenbrier High School in Evans, Georgia, was suspended for wearing a Pepsi T-shirt on the day the school was participating in Coca-Cola's "school-sponsored Coke day," a national competition with other schools to win $10,000 (Klein, 1999). Jennifer Beatty, a college student who attended Morain Valley Community College in Palos Hills, Illinois, protested against the growing corporatization and commercialization of colleges and universities by chaining herself to the metal mesh curtains of McDonald's Student Center. Beatty was arrested and expelled from the college (Lasn, 2000).

In recent years, the profit-driven corporate coup d'état has shifted toward a "corporate sponsored curriculum" supported in part by AT&T, McDonald's, Nike, Coca-Cola, PepsiCo, the Campbell Soup Company, and other corporations that are eagerly seeking new consumer markets. Corporate propaganda has been successful partly because of its ability to associate corporate interests with environmental and health issues. For example, Nike provides teachers with "sneaker-making kits" that teach students how Nike shoes are assembled; the lesson also focuses on how Nike is protecting the environment.

Today, the impress of capital is found in the subjectivities of young and old alike. Children spend $35 billion of their own money annually, while influencing their parents to spend an additional $300 billion. In consumer culture, brand awareness and consumer loyalty are the key ingredients for the successful cradle-to-grave marketing strategies of corporations. To lure potential consumers, corporations devise slick advertisement campaigns that frequently involve giving away merchandise and prizes. In short, the commercialization of public schools through campaigns such as Pepsi Stuff, Marlboro Gear, Camel Cash, McDonald's Happy Meals, and the Budweiser Frogs attests to the disturbing, growing trend of the privatization of the public sphere and the increasing transfer of capital from the public to the private sphere.

It is not unusual these days to see school buses in certain states covered with advertisements for Burger King and Wendy's fast-food chain restaurants. It has become fashionable for elementary school children to carry books wrapped in free book covers plastered with ads for Kellogg's Pop Tarts and Fox TV personalities. School districts have gleefully granted Coca-Cola and Pepsi exclusive contracts to sell their products in schools. In health education classes, students are taught nutrition by the Hershey Corporation in a scheme that includes a discussion of the important place of chocolate in a balanced diet. A classroom business course teaches students to value work by exploring how McDonald's restaurants are operated and what skills are needed to become a successful McDonald's manager and provides instructions on how to apply for a job at McDonald's. Ecological and environmental education now involves students learning ecology from a Life of an Ant poster sponsored by Skittles candy and an environmental curriculum video produced by Shell Oil that concentrates on the virtues of the external combustion engine. Finally, a new company called Zap Me! offers schools thousands of dollars' worth of computer equipment, including a satellite dish, fifteen top-flight personal computers, a furnished computer lab, and high-speed Internet access in return for a constant display of onscreen advertisements in the lower left-hand corner of the screen (see Fischman and McLaren, 2000). Lasn (1999) writes,

> Your kids watch Pepsi and Snickers ads in the class-room (The school has made the devil's bargain of accepting free audiovisual equipment in exchange for airing these ads on "Channel One"). . . . Administrators in a Texas school district announce plans to boost revenues by selling ad space on the roofs of the district's seventeen schools—arresting the attention of the fifty-eight million commercial jet passengers who fly into Dallas each year. Kids tattoo their calves with swooshes. Other kids, at raves, begin wearing actual bar codes

that other kids can scan, revealing messages such as "I'd like to sleep with you." . . . A few years ago, marketers began installing ad boards in men's washrooms on college campuses, at eye level above the urinals. From their perspective, it was a brilliant coup: Where else is a guy going to look? But when I first heard this was being done, I was incensed. One of the last private acts was being co-opted. (pp. 19–21)

A math book published by McGraw-Hill is spiked with eye-catching references to Nike, Gatorade, Disney, McDonald's, Nabisco, Mattel Barbie dolls, Sony PlayStations, Cocoa Frosted Flakes, Spalding basketballs, and Topps baseball cards (Collins and Yeskel, 2000, p. 78). John Borowski, a public school teacher, recently noted in *New York Times*,

At least 234 corporations are now flooding the public schools with films, textbooks and computer soft-ware under the guise of "instructional material." A lesson in self-esteem sponsored by Revlon includes an investigation of "good and bad hair days." In a history lesson, Tootsie Rolls are touted as a part of soldiers' diets during World War II. Exxon provides a video on the Valdez spill playing down its ecological impact. And Chevron, in a lesson for use in civics science classes, reminds students that they will soon be able to vote and make "important decisions" about global warming, which the company then rebuts as incomplete science. (1999, p. A23)

Channel One, a commercially produced news station, has forged contractual agreements that require teachers to broadcast Channel One programs in class for ten minutes a day in return for a satellite dish, videocassette recorders, and as many television sets as they want. A study of its effects revealed that the students were no better informed than their contemporaries but that the advertisements broadcast on the channel had a significant effect on their consumer tastes (Aitkenhead, cited in M. Cole, 1998, p. 327).

Henry Giroux (2001) warns that with the advent of neoliberalism, public schools are no longer seen as a public asset but rather as a private good. Advocates of neoliberalism, he says are "aggressively waging a war against the very possibility of creating non-commodified public spheres and forums that provide the conditions for critical education." (p. 30). Here neoliberalism is conceptualized "as both a set of economic policies and an impoverished notion of citizenship . . . [that not only includes] a series of market-driven programs but also a coherent set of cultural, political, and educational practices" (p. 30). Giroux is worth quoting further:

Neoliberalism works not only to produce a depoliticized consumer culture, it also limits the possibilities for *any* noncommodified social domains where young and old alike can experience dissent and difference as part of a multicultural democracy, locate metaphors of hope, respond to those who carry on the legacies of moral witnessing, and imagine relationships outside of the dictates of the market and the authoritarian rule of penal control. Educators and others need to rethink what it means to not only challenge a system that turns its children into a generation of suspects, but also how it might be possible to radically transform a social order marked by zero tolerance policies that reinforce modes of authoritarian control and social amnesia in a vast and related number of powerful institutional spheres. This suggests the need for both a collective struggle for public space and a public dialogue about how to imagine reappropriating a notion of politics that contributes to the development of authentic democracy while simultaneously articulating a new discourse, set of theoretical tools, and social possibilities for reviving civic education as a basis for political agency and social transformation. (p. 58)

Democracy in Crisis: Decoupling Democracy from Capitalist Development

Samir Amin's discussion of the relationship between democracy and development is both lucid and challenging and offers critical educators an important vantage point from which to consider present-day capitalist social relations. Amin argues that "there can be no socialism (if we use that term to designate a better, post-capitalist alternative) without democracy, but also there can be no progress in democratization without socialist transformation" (2001, p. 18). Amin rhetorically poses the question of why, for instance, Soviet Marxism did not bring about democratization. One answer he provides is that private property was never fully replaced by social ownership, a process that would have taken many generations, "gradually transforming themselves by their own action," to achieve. Another answer is that totalitarianism is common to both socialism and democracy, although the Western version was "softer" because it had already become cushioned by greater development. The ideology of the modern capitalist world privileges the rights of the individual even over those of society and at best is only a precondition for liberation. More likely it will lead to horror and destruction. Amin writes that the unilateral ideology of the rights of the individual—whether in the popularized versions of Sade and Nietzsche or in the American version—can only produce horror and, if pushed to its limits, autocracy, hard (fascist) or soft. Amin criticizes Marx for underestimating the danger of the ideology of the individual over collective rights, especially the powerful reactionary potential of the former.

In arguing that there is no "natural" convergence between democracy and the market, Amin makes the case that development through the market is incompatible with the exercise of an advanced degree of democracy. He argues that globalization is by nature polarizing and that development must take place within an alternative, postcapitalist society. We must abandon the "thesis of convergence" between development and democracy and accept the fact that "the conflict between the logic of different domains is the prerequisite for interpreting history in a way that potentially reconciles theory and reality" (2001, p. 19). Abandoning the thesis of convergence also is "the prerequisite for devising strategies that will make it possible to take really effective action—that is, to make progress in every aspect of society" (p. 19). The real relation we should be pursuing is not between already existing democracy and development, but rather *democratization* and real social development (because the term democratization stresses the idea that democracy is still an unfinished process).

Following Amin, we believe that it is important to resist attempts to devalue the term "democracy" by vulgarizing it and domesticating it as synonymous with community development that "negates the unity of the human race in favor of 'races,' 'communities,' 'cultural groups'" and the like (2001, p. 20). Democracy is "necessarily a universalist concept." Amin argues that dividing democracy into isolated communities based on race, class, gender, and sexual orientation is an example of "apartheid that is not acknowledged as such." Of course, we must be attentive to concrete struggles and acknowledge particular cultures of oppression and resistance. But the idea that particular identities can protect people from the overall crisis of capitalist democracy is an illusion to which Amin gives the name "culturalism." To critique culturalism is not the same thing as saying that subjectivity and agency are not important. Amin asserts that the only way to affirm diversity is by practicing genuine democracy, possible only in a socialist economy. As we ourselves have asserted on numerous occasions (McLaren and Farahmandpur, 2000, 2001), social movements based on the priority of ethnic, racial, gender or sexual diversity over class differences *a fortiori* can serve the ends of dominant capital and, in fact, can be openly reactionary. According to Amin, "[d]ominant capital knows this . . . and supports their demands" (p. 23). In fact, dominant capital invokes democracy and the rights of people as a "political means of neoliberal management of the contemporary world crisis, complementing the economic means" (p. 23). In the final instance, identity politics embodied in many of the new social movements "is entirely subservient to the priorities that the strategy of the United States Triad tries to impose" (p. 23). Amin proposes to this a corollary that we strongly agree with: "Those social movements whose demands are connected with the fight against social exploitation and for greater democracy in every domain are progressive" (p. 23).

Toward a Revolutionary Critical Pedagogy

In the space that follows, we attempt to sketch out in broad strokes the key characteristics of a revolutionary critical pedagogy (we borrow this term from Paula Allman, 2001) that attempts to move beyond current liberal and left-liberal efforts at making capitalist schooling less barbaric and more democratic. The revolutionary critical pedagogy that we envision here agitates on behalf of pedagogical practice connected to a larger socialist political project. This struggle targets not only the globalization of capital but capital itself (Mészáros 1995).

Glenn Rikowski has pointed out that educational theorists who analyze social class focus too narrowly on issues of stratification and social inequality and in the process literally abandon the notion of working-class struggle. We use the term "class struggle," after Rikowski (2001a), to denote a social relation between labor and capital that is integral to the existence of capitalist society: "an element of the constitution of a world struggle" (2001a, p. 1) that exists everywhere in capitalist society. Education is a key process in "the generation of the capital relation." Education "links the chains that bind our souls to capital. It is one of the ropes comprising the ring for combat between labour and capital, a clash that powers contemporary history: 'the class struggle'" (2001b, p. 2). Schools therefore act as vital supports for, and developers of, the class relation, "the violent capital-labor relation that is at the core of capitalist society and development" (2001a, p. 19). As Massimo de Angelis remarks:

> Education is crucial for capital if it wants to rely on a strategy of continuous displacement of the class composition. An educated worker in today's paradigm is a worker who is able to adapt—who is able to take over one job one day and another job the next day—who is engaged in life-long learning as a continuous process, which means updating their skills to suit the market. That is essential to maintain social cohesion in a context in which there is continuous displacement of the class composition of what kind of work is done. (2000, p. 10)

We share Glenn Rikowski's perspective that the class relation *is* the capital-labor relation that forms the "violent dialectic" that generates all value. Class struggle is born out of the antagonistic relation between capital and labor. Rikowski argues that class struggle occurs *intersubjectively* as well as collectively as a clash of contradictory forces and drives within the social totality. Rikowski notes that

> the class relation *runs through our personhood.* It is internal to us; we *are* labor, and we *are* capital. We are social beings incorporating antithetical social drives and forces. This fact sets off contradictions within our lives, and their solution can only come from the disintegration of ourselves as both capital and labor and our emergence as a new, non-capitalised life-form. (2001a, p. 20)

This split within capital-labor itself is founded on the issue of whether labor produces value directly or through labor power.

In sum, class struggle has to be linked to the relation internal to all labor, the split or rift within labor as a form of social existence within capitalist society. Class struggle is implicated in the truism that labor creates its own opposite (capital) which comes to dominate it. The issue of class struggle needs to be approached from the perspective *of a critique of capital and its value form of labor.* As Ebert argues: *"Globalization begins with the com-*

modification of labor-power itself—when human labor becomes a commodity like all other commodities and is exchanged for wages. The commodification of labor is the condition of possibility for 'profit'" (2001, 397, italics in original).

We believe that Rikowski's adaptation of Marx's value theory of labor compellingly reveals how education is implicated in the social production of labor power in capitalism. Rikowski's premise, which is provocative and compelling (and perhaps deceptively simple), can be summarized as follows: Education is necessary to the direct production of the one commodity that generates the entire social universe of capital in all of its dynamic and multiform existence—labor power. Within the social universe of capital, individuals sell their capacity to labor—their labor power—for a wage. Because we are included in this social universe on a differential and unequal basis, people can get paid above or below the value of their labor power. Because labor power is implicated in human will or agency, and because it is impossible for capital to exist without it, education can be redesigned within a social justice agenda that will reclaim labor-power for socialist alternatives to human capital formation.

Rikowski notes the important point that as capital becomes a living force within the human, it works to make us extrahuman or "transhuman." We are transhuman as life-form within the social universe of capital precisely because we are capitalized. Over the last several centuries, humans have become capitalized, as the form that labor power takes in capitalist societies—human capital—constitutes as an extrahuman social existence that education is actively engaged in promoting (Rikowski, 2001b). Rikowski argues that the key Marxist insight here is to recognize that education is implicated in the social production of the one commodity (which Marx referred to as a "special" commodity) underpinning the maintenance of capitalist society: labor power. As a consequence of this, we need to devise forms of labor power expenditure and development *not tied to the value form of labor*. Rikowski asserts that while teachers are surely helpful in reproducing the ideological fabric of capitalism, they are also potentially "dangerous to capital and its social domination." Educators constitute the "guardians of the development of the one commodity that keeps capitalism going [labor power], whilst also being in a structural position to *subvert the smooth flow of labor power production* by inserting *principles antagonistic* to the social domination of capital. Such principles include social justice, equality and solidarity for progressive social change" (2001b, p. 38, italics in original).[8]

Recognizing the "class character" of education in capitalist schooling and advocating a "socialist reorganization of capitalist society" (Krupskaya, 1985) are two fundamental principles of a revolutionary critical pedagogy. Following Marx (1973), we argue that it is imperative that teachers recognize the contradictions of "free" and "universal" education in bourgeois society and question how education can be "equal" for all social classes. Education can never be free or equal as long as social classes exist. We believe that the education and instruction of working-class students must be linked to productive labor and also to social production. Thus, we envision a revolutionary critical pedagogy that pivots around a number of key linkages: the production of critical knowledge and productive work; the organization and management of critical knowledge and the organization and management of production; and the utilization of critical knowledge for productive consumption (Krupskaya, 1985).[9]

Furthermore, the severing of workers from the products of their labor under the capitalist mode of production *mirrors in a number of basic instances the separation of the production and consumption of knowledge among students.* For instance, in public schools today, theoretical knowledge is seldom linked to labor practices. Our vision of a revolutionary critical pedagogy, in contrast, consists of teaching students how knowledge is related historically, culturally, and institutionally to the process of production and consumption. The more these relations are disavowed, the more cynical students become, largely because they already have some understandings of these connections but need a language to explore them further. The more cynical students become, the more they are likely to cathect their anxieties to fundamentalist celebrations of vulgar patriotism and ethnic triumphalism.

Revolutionary critical pedagogy, in our view, should focus on problematizing the production of value through the work experience. This should include, but not be limited to, *four relations* that lie at the center of the work experience in U.S. society. Marx described these four relations as constituting what he termed "alienation." These are summarized by Ollman as follows:

> (1) the relation between the individual and his/her productive activity, in which others determine how it is done, under what conditions, at what speed, and for what wage or salary, and even if and when it is to begin and end; (2) the relation between the individual and the product of that activity, in which others control and use the product for their own purposes (making something does not confer any right to use what one has made); (3) the relation between the individual and other people, particularly, with those who control both one's productive activity and its products, where each side pursues their own interests without considering the effects of their own actions on the other (mutual indifference and competition become the characteristic forms of human interaction); and (4) the relation between the individual and the species, or with what it means to be a human being. (2001, p. 111)

Capitalist production and consumption constitute a totality of interconnected social relations that can be divided into productive and unproductive consumption. While productive consumption satisfies the physical, spiritual, and social needs of individuals, unproductive consumption (its antithesis) appropriates and transforms the surplus-value of labor into capital. Thus it is imperative that teachers and students question how knowledge is produced and ask the following: Who produces it? How it is appropriated? Who consumes it? How is it consumed? Revolutionary critical pedagogy gives analytical priority to the struggle between labor and capital, to the relationship between the forces of production and the means of production, and to the relationship between nature and society (Hill, McLaren, Cole, and Rikowski, 2002).

In a provocative discussion, David Harvey (2000) suggests that Marx did not openly endorse the concept of social justice because Marx believed that the struggle for social justice was limited to the redistributive characteristics of the capitalist mode of production. For Marx, a redistribution of wealth and income merely addresses one of the several "moments" or dimensions of the mode of production that includes production, exchange, distribution, and consumption, all of which constitute the elements of an "organic totality." Emphasizing one "moment" while ignoring other moments does little to advance the elimination of exploitation. However, in our view, this does not mean that Marxists should abandon the *idea* of social justice or the struggle to bring it about. Far from it. Critical educators must work toward liberating the concept of social justice from those ideological boundaries drawn by capitalist social relations of production.

Of course, to offer an alternative to capitalist social relations is a daunting struggle, and one that has untiringly exercised socialists for generations. Once such struggles occupied the efforts of labor unions, but especially since the demise of the Soviet Union and the eastern bloc countries, unions have been all too happy to coexist with the value form of labor under capitalism. In our view, education will play an increasingly important role in years to come in the production of critical agency. There is a growing need for the development of a revolutionary critical pedagogy that is not only *capable* of challenging but also *willing* to challenge the rule of capital in everyday life.

Teachers as Intellectual Workers

A revolutionary or "remilitarized" critical pedagogy requires moving anticapitalist struggles in the direction of a new transnationalism that extends beyond the nation-state. Organizing teachers as part of a larger compendium of social movements struggling toward a set of common objective goals (such as the abolition of economic exploitation, sexism, and racism) is necessary for the development of an effective revolutionary politics—one that can effectively and demonstrably create the necessary conditions for disenfranchised social groups to empower themselves (McLaren, 1998b; McLaren and Farahmandpur, 1999a, 1999b, 2000). This is not a romantic call to don a *bleu de travail* and rush the corporate barricades erected by procapitalist ideologues but to understand how the forces of globalization and neoliberalism are not forces in their own right but are connected to a wider system of exploitation that is as old as capitalism itself. We do not seek to answer the question of whether or not a new capitalist class has been created by the globalization of capital, but rather emphasize the competitive struggles among various capitalists in the context of the tension between labor and capital and the link between horizontal intercapitalist relations and vertical class relations and class conflict (Allman, 2001). The connective tissue that holds the various social movements in place should not be a commitment to a diffuse counterhegemonic struggle but a dedication to the achievement of proletarian hegemony.

We use the term "proletarian," which may seem antiquated, to identify all those whose labor is exploited for its surplus value in the interests of profit. While admittedly there has been a global restructuring of the class composition of wage labor, we are using the term in its broadest sense. There is a danger here that the drive toward socialism advocated by some Marxists will be restricted mainly to an ethical socialism, socialist republicanism, or market socialism. Though an ethics that supports the global abolition of power, the struggle for world citizenship and international social solidarity, and participatory, nonbureaucratic democracy is surely worth defending, it often supports a citizenship of the proletarians rather than a proletarianization of the citizenry. While certainly the historic bloc that we envision includes the bourgeoisie as well as the working class, we believe it is important not to abandon the idea of the working class as the central agent in the struggle for a socialist society.

While we need to focus on multiple forms of oppression such as racism, sexism, and homophobia, we believe that these are best understood within the overarching system of class domination and the variable discriminating mechanisms central to capitalism as a system. This position is emphasized by Foster when he insists that

> It is a serious mistake to view the working class, except as an artificial abstraction, as cut off from issues of race, gender, culture and community. In the United States the vast majority of the working class consists of women and people of color. The power to upend and reshape society in decisive ways will come not primarily through single-issue movements for reform, but rather through forms of organization and popular alliance that will establish feminists, opponents of racism, advocates of gay rights, defenders of the environment, etc. as the more advanced sectors of a unified, class-based, revolutionary political and economic movement. (2002, p. 45)

Revolutionary critical pedagogy seeks to create a context in which freedom from the enslaving subordination of the individual to the crisis-prone nature of capital accumulation replaces the arid realm of necessity, where the satisfaction of social need replaces imprisonment within the division of labor, where the development of the creative capacities of the individual replaces the laws of capital and landed property, where worker self-rule and the free development of individuals replaces the current entrapment in the Byzantine maze of capitalist bureaucracy and the bureaucratization and atomization and alienation of social life. As Marx and Engels wrote in the

Manifesto, the goal of socialist society is expressed as "an association, in which the free development of each is the condition for the free development of all."

Teacher educators as part of a broader revolutionary anticapitalist movement based on the development of a new transnationalist class politics (in the form of an historical bloc rather than a political party) must be attentive to the diverse social and political interests as well as the needs of different constituencies in the struggle. Furthermore, Marxist revolutionary theory must be flexible enough to reinvent itself in the context of current social, economic, and political restructuring under the economic policies of neoliberalism. As Marx noted, theory becomes a material force when it grips the masses. Good theory not only attempts to understand the complex events that mark the current historical juncture and develops in step with new conflicts and challenges but also attempts to transform existing social relations. Revolutionary educators do not have to endure the Golgotha of revolutionary praxis, as in the historical example of Che Guevara, in order to effect mindful social transformation. Marxist theory is set forth here not as a universal truth but as a weapon of interpretation. No theory can fully anticipate or account for the consequences of its application but remains a living aperture through which specific histories are made visible and intelligible. In this sense, Marxist theory provides the oppressed with the theoretical knowledge for analyzing and challenging capitalist production. It is here that Marxist theory can be used to advance proletarian hegemony through the work of organic and transformative intellectuals (see Giroux, 1988) engaged in revolutionary socialist praxis aimed at the transformation of the bourgeois state. We don't believe that we are destined to live our lives forever in the whiskey-soaked and blood drenched Hobbesian universe of "The Gangs of New York."

The battle in Seattle (as well as other anti–World Trade Organization demonstrations in Quebec City and throughout Europe) can teach educators important lessons (Rikowski, 2001b). There are times when anticapitalist struggles require an organized revolutionary class that has, in the course of its protracted political activities, gained a significant measure of class consciousness and recognizes itself not only as a class in itself but as a class for itself. At other moments, anticapitalist struggles take the form of what Jim Hightower (cited in Marshall, 2000) refers to as "spontaneous and unauthorized outbreaks of democracy," as in the case of the anti–World Trade Organization protests in Seattle. There are moments, too, when class struggle consists of individual and collective acts of resistance against corporate colonization and commodification of the life world. A case in point is the French farmer José Bova, who protested against genetically modified food by driving his tractor into a McDonald's restaurant under construction in the south of France. All of these efforts have their importance. The main point we wish to emphasize here is that it is crucial to struggle against all attempts to decenter political struggle so that the social basis of exploitation is dissolved beyond class politics. In this regard, the concept of globalization needs to be reformulated so that historical subjects or actors are given the basis to challenge the hegemony of international capital in the defense of justice, solidarity, and the working class. Those who are prevented from creating history—or worse, who choose to remain passive in its wake—are forced to recycle the past, combing the shoreline for dreams washed up in bottles of Pepsi and Coca-Cola, as the river of time, which waits for no one, rushes by in a vast swirl of regret. We must not allow our individual acts of resistance to lead to reformism or economism or to derail the proletarian and popular movements from their focus on anticapitalist struggle.

Class: The Outmoded or Forgotten Antagonism

We do not believe that class struggle is outmoded, but rather that it constitutes one of the crucial missing dimensions of contemporary educational criticism (McLaren, 1998b). We are rejecting the neo-Weberian concept of class based on consumption-based patterns, status, and occupational hierarchies that tell us little about the relationship between social classes. Along with British Marxist educators, Dave Hill and Mike Cole, we reject technicist reductions of class into "fractions" or segments that hide or disguise common interests (i.e., common consciousness among these groups comprising the working class in opposition to the exploiting capitalist class) (Hill and Cole, 2001).

We feel it is important for the education researcher to recognize both the political and the pedagogical import of the predicament put forward by Ellen Meiksins Wood (1994): "Once you replace the concept of capitalism with an undifferentiated plurality of social identities and special oppressions, socialism as the antithesis to capitalism loses all meaning" (p. 29). Here the critical education researcher challenges the relativism of the gender-race-class grid of reflexive positionality by recognizing that class antagonism or struggle is not simply one in a series of social antagonisms but rather constitutes the part of this series that sustains the horizon of the series itself. In other words, class struggle is the specific antagonism that assigns rank to and modifies the particularities of the other antagonisms in the series (Žižek, 1999).

Despite recent attacks on critical pedagogy as universalist and totalizing (see Lather, 2001), the critical educational researcher refuses to evacuate reference to historical structures of totality and universality by recognizing that class struggle itself enables the proliferation of new political subjectivities. Both conservative and liberal bourgeois anti-Marxists refuse to see how class struggle structures in advance the very terrain of political antagonisms. Such a failure of recognition has led them to annex the enterprise of progressive educational criticism to the discourse of liberal democracy (albeit cloaked in fashionable transgressive attire). Postmodern theorists recognize these contradictions hidden in the arid soil of advanced capitalist democracies but are largely unable to develop an anticapitalist political agenda except by restricting their observations to cultural formations and thereby obfuscating the political economy of real existing capitalism. Neil Larsen warns:

> At best, the culturalist account of globalization results in mere descriptivism. . . . At worst . . . it results in the kind of pseudo-theory that simply reads off certain of the lateral effects of globalization (e.g., the hybridization of national cultures or the manipulation of global opinion through the mass dissemination of CNN-type 'news' simulacra) as the fantasmagorical sites for its subversion or its eternal replication. This is reified thinking taken to the extreme of mistaking the empty shell of a globalized commodity form for the social, human content that it progressively fails to contain. (2000, p. 4)

On the other hand, we are confronted by the protestations and denunciations of some Derridean poststructuralists who reject Marxism, *tout court*, as hopelessly outdated. Patti Lather's (2001) denunciatory cry of "Ten Years Later: Yet Again" (which is intended to raise the issue of why Marxists pedagogues still work within supposedly received and exhausted masculinist categories after poststructuralists had—ten years earlier—shown them how to be less self-assured and to adopt a less transparent analysis under the advance guard of "teletechnic dislocation, rhizomatic spreading and acceleration, and new experiences of frontier and identity") is the latest example. We maintain that such condemnations amount to little more than intellectual scrap metal and should be read against another cry in the face of the barbarianized academy: "One Hundred and Fifty Years after the Communist Manifesto: Ruling Class Pedagogues Cloaked as Avant-Gardists Defending the Capitalist Class, Yet Again." Bourgeois educational theorists from today's battered and beleaguered left who write under the sign of anti-Marxist chic have largely abandoned the struggles of the world's poor, uncoupling history from the fight for liberation. Michael Parenti writes:

> Most Left intellectuals in the United States are busy fighting the ghost of Stalin, dwelling on the tabloid reports of the "horrors" of communism, doing fearless battle against imaginary hordes of "doctrinaire" Marxists at home and abroad, or in some other way flashing their anti-communist credentials and shoring up their credibility. So busy in these pursuits are they that they seem relatively unconcerned about the real dangers we face, about how the rights and life chances of millions of people throughout the world have been seriously damaged. (2001, p. 158)

Patti Lather (2001), in particular, not only demonstrates an understanding of human agency as untethered to social relations of production but also unwittingly advocates a move toward a centrist politics that etherealizes class struggle into questions of anti-essentializing epistemology and evacuates historicity under the guise of a fashionable anti-Marxism. Her position, popular in the postmodern academy, represents what E. San Juan (1999) calls "the new conformism." E. San Juan's comment is apposite here:

Anyone caught "totalizing" or rehearsing "grand metanarratives" of the Eurocentric variety can be flunked, denied tenure, ostracized. But the new conformism that claims to be more radical than anything proves, on closer examination, to be just an application of the old paradigm of close New Critical reading—a more sophisticated encoding/decoding exercise—to shopping malls, television and film, museums, rituals high and low, and the practices of everyday life. The hermeneutics of Lyotard, Baudrillard, de Certeau, Clifford, etc. is now in vogue. The "linguistic turn" in the seventies, together with the uncritical appropriation of Althusser and other poststructuralist doxa, may be responsible for the return of formalism and metaphysics in new guises. Could this have been anticipated if the Williams road of the "long revolution" were followed? (1999, p. 119)

According to Slavoj Žižek, class struggle "is not the last horizon of meaning, the last signified of all social phenomena, but the formal generative matrix of the different ideological horizons of understanding" (2001b, pp. 16–17). In Žižek's terms, class struggle sets the ground for the empty place of universality, enabling it to be filled variously with contents of different sorts (ecology, feminism, antiracism). He notes, important for our purposes, that "the economy is at one and the same time the genus and one of its own species" (2001a, p. 193).

Conclusion

What might constitute the main pillars of a revamped, retooled, and reinvigorated Marxist pedagogy? What can Marxist educational theory offer educators in the wake of the dictatorship of the financial markets, in which, in the words of Robert Went (2000), the "invisible hand" of the market is mercilessly and ruthlessly obliterating the lives of millions of working-class men, women, and children? How do we liberate creative human powers and capacities from their inhumane form, namely capital?

We believe that a revolutionary critical pedagogy must begin by reaffirming its commitment to the struggle for emancipating humanity from its own inhumanity. For Marxist education theorists the challenge of critical pedagogy is intimately linked to the following questions (following the conviction that a good question is half of the answer): What does it mean to be human? How can we live humanely? What actions or steps must be taken to be able to live humanely? We believe that these questions can be answered in the course of revolutionizing educational practices in the context of class struggle (Hill and Cole, 2001).

Our vision of a revolutionary critical pedagogy is informed by Marx's historical materialist method of social inquiry. To engage in Marxist analysis and praxis does not mean plumping for the standard bearers of the Second International. We do not agree with post-Marxists who continue to criticize—often adventitious and carelessly—Marx's historical materialist method of inquiry as dogmatic and mechanically reductive (which is not to say that all examples of historical materialism claiming to be derived from Marx's writings escape dogmatism and/or economic reductionism). However, we believe that Marx's approach to historical materialism is, in the main, a human science that can restore humanity to human society (C. Smith, 1996). For Marx, the question of what it means to be human was not bound to or constrained by an eternal or fixed concept of human nature. Rather, Marx maintained that the question of what it means to be human was conditioned by the specificity of the sociohistorical conditions and circumstances of human society, particularly the social relations of production. Marxism is not used here as a codicil of revolutionary amendments to the radical literature on education, as a collection of unchallengeable postulates enjoined upon the faithful, or as an ideology used to target constituencies of the masses; rather, Marxism as a practice hews closely to its notional starting point in dialectical analysis. We are using Marxism not as a radical critique of society but more importantly as a negative theory against capitalist society. As John Holloway (1993, 1994) puts it, Marxists are not bent on understanding social oppression as much as they are determined to unmask the fragility and vulnerability—i.e., the contradictions—of capitalism. The contradictions of capitalism do not exist independently of class struggle. This is because capitalism relies on human labor while human labor does not rely on capitalism. Using negative categories to understand capitalism from the standpoint of non-capitalism, Marxists such as Holloway view the objective conditions of class struggle as alienated expressions of the power of labor. As long as capital is dependent upon the power of labor, the powerless can realize their power through class struggle. In this view, Holloway notes that there is no room for the concept of historical necessity. This is because, when we view the world as continuous struggle, we must evacuate the notion of certainty and historical determination. Following Marx, we believe that the purpose of education is to enable people to realize their powers and capacities. Whereas liberal approaches to education and self-development attempt to liberate individuals *from* the social, revolutionary critical pedagogy attempts to help individuals liberate themselves *through* the social, through challenging, resisting, and transforming commonly held discourses and practices. Thus the objective of revolutionary critical pedagogy is the liberation of both consciousness and labor from the shackles of capital and the creation of a society in which each person participates according to his or her abilities for the benefit of his or her needs.

How can teachers recognize the important role they play in the battle between labor and capital? How can they develop a revolutionary ideology? Part of the answer to these questions will depend upon the ability of teachers to cultivate the potential of schools as sites for capacity building and democratization, and for fostering a spirit of popular activism and socialist militancy. And while it is true that teachers take part in reproducing class relations (pedagogically), they can at the same time utilize their pedagogical skills and expertise to resist and to challenge capitalist schooling. And even if it is true that "a single, homogeneous working-class of the type described in the works of traditional Marxists does not exist . . . anywhere" (Kagarlitsky, 2001, p. 64), a class movement is nevertheless possible in the form of a popular front.

A revolutionary critical pedagogy is grounded in an analysis of capitalist society that is untethered from the compromised language of identity politics associated with many education postmodernists such as Patti Lather, a language whose nomenclature and systems of intelligibility remains tributary to anti-capitalist struggle. It is a pedagogy that is underwritten by a unified struggle over collective needs in contrast to the individual's right to compete in the marketplace and become rich beyond the imagination. A revolutionary critical pedagogy is premised upon a socialist commitment to an egalitarian distribution of economic power and exchange and a mutually beneficial division of labor coupled with a realization that you "simply cannot have private property in the means of production, finance, exchange and communication and at the same time have an unalienated, socially just, and democratic social order" (Panitch and Gindin, 2001, p. 199). It is a Marxist-driven pedagogy that revives the fecundity of human agency in the service of the oppressed. It is not the hidebound and doctrinaire pedagogical Marxism of the Second International, so the anti-Marxist gaggle need not expect a tongue-wagging Josef Stalin to spring out behind every mention of class struggle.

Panitch and Gindin argue for bringing a new conceptual layer to Marxism by developing the concepts of capacities and potentials. Here they refer to capacities and potentials as new productive forces such as "the collective capacities to govern democratically everyday life, the economy, civil society, and the state" (2001, p. 196). Panitch and Gindin wish to utilize the study of capacities as a way to help us "to inhabit capitalism while building bridges to those individuals/institutional capacities to get socialism on the agenda" (2001, pp. 196–197). Socialism, as we conceive it, means the creation of a vibrant life economy. According to John McMurtry, "a functioning life economy consciously selects for life goods, rather than against them. At the most basic, it selects for life capital—means of life that produce more means of life . . . all life is a process, and this process always follows the pattern of the life sequence of value" (2002, p. 139). Life capital is wealth that produces more wealth, with wealth in this instance referring to *"life capabilities and their enjoyments* in the individual, the bio-regional, or the planetary form" (2002, p. 139). Life capital is the *"life-ground in its economic form"* (2002, p. 142) and in capitalist society it is subjugated to money-sequence capital.

In an insightful passage in *Capital*, Marx declares: "A spider conducts operations which resemble those of a weaver, and a bee would put many a human architect to shame by the construction of its honeycomb cells.

But what distinguishes the worst architect from the best of bees is that the architect builds the cell in his mind before he constructs it in wax" (1977, p. 284). In other words, the fundamental distinction between humans and other species is that humans are endowed with a social imagination, one that operates as a tool for transforming their social conditions. Marx believed that although consciousness is conditioned by social and economic structures, it remains a powerful mediating force in transforming the existing social and economic structures that constrain it. This is especially true of a critical consciousness minted in the service of revolutionary praxis, a praxis that is not limited to, in the words of Marx and Engels (1850), "the smoothing over of class antagonisms but the abolition of classes, not the improvement of existing society, but the foundation of a new one." In this regard, revolutionary critical pedagogy is designed to dispel the necessary misrecognition of the inner structure of antagonisms informing capital, to peel away its occult quality and to reveal to the light of day capital's subterranean connection to alienation and exploitation.

Panitch and Gindin remind us that the current pessimism that surrounds us can be broken by "drawing inspiration from the continuity between the utopian dream that predates socialism and the concrete popular struggles in evidence around the world as people strive, in a multitude of diverse ways, to assert their humanity. . . . [A]bove all, it means apprehending what the very power of capital is inadvertently proclaiming as it overruns, subordinates, and narrows every aspect of our lives: that capitalism is 'the wrong dream' and that only an alternative that is just as universal and ambitious, but rooted in our collective liberating potentials, can replace it" (2001, p. 199).[10] Here what we call revolutionary critical pedagogy can take flight on the wings of a new political imaginary and ascend toward an imaginative socialist empyrean. Samir Amin makes an important point when he argues that neither modernity nor democracy has reached the end of its potential development. This is why he prefers the term 'democratization," "which stresses the dynamic aspect of a still unfinished process, to that of democracy, which reinforces the illusion that we can give a definitive formula to it" (2001, p. 12). In our view, socialist democracy can be deepened by its engagement with revolutionary critical pedagogy and vice versa. By challenging the rule of capital, we simultaneously engage in a revolutionary process of democratization.

Critical revolutionary educators speak truth to power not by attempts to expand the parameters of liberal democracy but by challenging the very core of liberal democracy. Slavoj Žižek expands on this idea in his discussion of Lenin's role in Soviet and world history. According to Žižek, Lenin understood that liberal democracy is a vehicle that gives ballast to capitalism rather than challenges it. In fact, Lenin was all too aware that liberal democracy was an otiose development as far as economic equality was concerned and had become the political arrangement which best facilitated capital's ongoing survival. Žižek argues that challenging liberal democracy today represents Lenin's "ultimate lesson" since "it is only by throwing off our attachment to liberal democracy, which cannot survive without private property, that we can become effectively anti-capitalist" (2002, p. 23). Žižek notes that "actual freedom of thought means the freedom to question the predominant, liberal-democratic, "postideological" consensus—or it means nothing" (2001, p. 194). For instance, to believe that land distribution in Russia in 1917 could have been accomplished through parliamentary means is, notes Žižek, the same as believing today that "the ecological threat can be avoided by applying market logic (making polluters pay for the damage they cause)" (2002, p. 10).

Žižek argues that from Lenin we can learn to escape the "lure" that "one can undermine capitalism without effectively problematizing the liberal democratic legacy which (as some leftists claim), although engendered by capitalism, acquired autonomy and can serve to criticize capitalism" (2001, p. 196). Žižek describes this lure as "a rhizomatic monster/vampire that deterritorializes and swallows all—indomitable, dynamic, ever rising from the dead, each crisis making it stronger, Dionysis-Phoenix reborn" (2001, p. 196). Lenin's historical lesson avoids what Jacques Lacan refers to as the "narcissism of the lost cause" whereby pseudo-leftists can participate in struggles against the state that are perceived by the public as too extreme and thus are always already doomed to fail so that these individuals never have to put their politics on the line or encounter "the extreme violence of the real." This sounds a lot like the plight of today's postmodernists who have toe-tagged the project of social transformation before engaging it. The narcissism of the lost cause prevents an authentic "explosion of emancipatory potential" brought about by true spontaneity (see Žižek, 2002, p. 16) that Žižek believes rests at the center of any true liberatory politics, and what he feels Lenin's politics best exemplifies. Žižek emphasizes that Lenin "was fully aware that true spontaneity is very rare: in order to achieve it, one must get rid of false, imposed ideological spontaneity" (2002, p. 23). Lenin's challenge, Žižek proclaims, is how to "invent the organized structure that will confer on this unrest the *form* of the universal political demand" (2001, p. 197). Lenin's lesson can be summed up thusly: "politics without the organizational form of the party is politics without politics" (2001, p. 198). According to Žižek, then, Lenin's reproach to liberals could be pitched as follows:

> They only *exploit* the working classes' discontent to strengthen their position vis-à-vis the conservatives, instead of identifying with it to the end. Is this also not the case with today's left liberals? They like to evoke racism, ecology, workers' grievances, and so forth, to score points over conservatives *without endangering the system.* (2001, p. 198)

We therefore need to retrieve what Žižek calls the "Lenin-in-becoming." We do not want to recapture the old Lenin in a gesture of nostalgia; rather, we wish, in Žižek's terms, to "repeat Lenin." To repeat Lenin is to admit that the old Lenin is dead and to advance the notion that we must act within the field of possibilities that he opened up but could not succeed within. Žižek writes that to repeat Lenin

> Is thus to accept that "Lenin is dead"—that his particular solution failed, even failed monstrously, but that there was a utopian spark in it worth saving. To repeat Lenin means that one has to distinguish between what Lenin effectively did and the field of possibilities that he opened up, the tension in Lenin between what he effectively did and another dimension, what was "in Lenin more than Lenin himself." To repeat Lenin is to repeat not what Lenin *did* but what he *failed to do*, his missed opportunities. (2001, p. 198)

Repeating Lenin means that we must not only take an anti-capitalist position, but also problematize capitalism's political form, which, as Žižek reminds us, is the liberal, parliamentary, democratic consensus. There is a split between pure politicians who have abandoned the economy as the site of struggle, and the economists who preclude the possibility of a political intervention into the global economy. This split must be overcome.

Lenin chooses to go a different path than those who want to wait until the moment is ripe for revolution, according to the necessity of historical evolution, or those who wish to seize the moment that emerges since there is no historically proper time to revolt. Lenin's achievement was a prolonged explosion of utopian energy which, Žižek notes, should be christened "The Event of Lenin." Of course, we believe that there is more to appreciate in Lenin than "Lenin as an Event" or "utopian spark" since his writings constitute some of the most important analyses of the state and the politics of imperialism ever produced. But Žižek's point on the importance of Lenin's praxiological moment is well taken.

We seek a politics where we can both be disciplined and compassionate, where we can be moved by the sound of Beethoven's Appassionata or carried away by Nathalie Cordone singing 'Hasta Siempre' without forfeiting our daily commitment to and rigorous engagement with revolutionary praxis and where we can remain steadfast to anti-capitalist struggle without being dogmatic or inflexible, and without sliding inexorably toward the political swindle of pragmatic compromise that follows from today's post-modern/post-political premise that universal forms of emancipatory praxis can only lead to problems greater than the ones that they are attempting to transform.

2

Civil Society and Educational Publics: Possibilities and Problems

Kathleen Knight Abowitz

We are indisputably in an era of "school choice." Even if we discount those children whose parents choose their residence based on their desired school district, nearly one-quarter of U.S. schoolchildren attend a school—private, public, or in the home, through charter, voucher, or magnet programs—that was chosen for them (Henig and Sugarman, 1999, p. 29). Many progressive educators bemoan the era of choice as an end to the ideals embedded in universal public schooling, viewing "choice" as the beginning of the end of the common school ideal. But is the choice to leave a traditional public school a choice to leave *public* education?

"Civil society" is a term for the relatively autonomous public sphere that exists in the spaces between state, markets, and the intimacies of domestic life. Civil society offers a public alternative to both the state and market spheres. Though civil society is vulnerable to the corrosive effects of both aggressive markets and instrumental individualism, it remains a vital arena for public life and activity. Indeed, civil society is now becoming a sphere in which new *forms* of public schooling are being tested and tried. In this essay, I explore the idea that the notion of a universal public as inherent in traditional public schooling is giving way to a more pluralistic notion of multiple publics vying for recognition and resources to pursue their educational visions. As choice plans proliferate and educational alternatives are now being generated by diverse publics seeking to reconstruct or exit the public schools, we see the existence of what I label educational publics. I develop the meaning of the term "educational publics" by using the critical theory of Nancy Fraser (1997). I argue that civil society offers hopeful ground on which educational publics might be cultivated and used to rejuvenate the current system, expand beyond its current parameters, and even rebuild it in creative ways. Civil society does not offer a democratic utopia, however. I conclude this essay by noting some of the important limitations from a perspective of justice that this pluralistic model presents.

What Is Civil Society?

Political theorists commonly divide social life into several parts: the state or government sector, the market, and the voluntary sphere of associations that we call civil society. These are public spheres, and until relatively recently, were clearly and purposefully distinguished from private spheres of domestic, sexual, and other intimate relations. Thanks to the work of feminist scholars and activists, it is possible here to discuss public spheres without automatically invoking the public/private dualism.

Civil society, in fact, is generally considered to be the sphere and spaces where so-called private individuals become public participants. Habermas states it this way: "Civil society is composed of those more or less sponta-neous coalitions, organizations and movements which respond to the res-onance that societal problems have found in the private sphere, and which condense them and amplify them in the direction of a public sphere" (quoted in Carleheden and Gabriels, p. 7). These coalitions, organizations, and movements are incredibly diverse: from the local PTA to the Black Panthers, from Internet-based home schooling coalitions to labor unions, from religious groups to professional organizations. Individual, family, or domestic concerns, not yet recognized as shared or public, become directed toward the larger society: a parent who becomes involved in the PTA is motivated, at least in part, by a devotion and commitment based on domestic relations of love and care, often thought of as "private" or unreg-ulated by government. This parent may also be motivated by a more amor-phous commitment to the general good of the school and those who attend it—this parent's neighbors, friends, and even strangers, all of whom deserve a good education. Civil society marks, therefore, a political sphere that is not directly part of government, but which is a neutral ground medi-ating between the shared interests of persons as "private" citizens and between persons as citizens of the state.

As Keane (1988) notes, however, civil society as a sphere separate from government is a relatively recent concept—it did not originate until the eighteenth century. Up until this time, Western political philosophy held that "to be a member of a civil society was to be a citizen—a member of the state—and, thus, obligated to act in accordance with its laws and with-out engaging in acts harmful to other citizens" (p. 36). This classical con-ception of state and civil society became separated by social upheavals in Europe and America during the period of 1750–1850. During this time, the idea of a civil society arose in part to "posit a synthesis between a number of developing oppositions that were increasingly being felt in social life . . . between the individual and the social, the private and the public, egoism and altruism, as well as between a life governed by reason and one gov-erned by the passions" (Seligman, 1992, p. 25). Civil society slowly began to be seen as a sphere that is independent from the state; civil society was increasingly used as a term to describe autonomous social groups that were to help guard against the authoritarian potential of the state, and to bridge the gap between domestic and broader concerns.

A special function of civil societies is to maintain a relatively autonomous sphere for public dialogue and debate, apart from the government or the state. According to Tocqueville, civil society must maintain autonomy from the state and especially from "the control of the public administration," whose influence could be seen in the state's monopoly of public instruction, health care, and provision of support for the unemployed (see Keane, 1988, pp. 57–58). In this sentiment, Tocqueville articulates a republican and conservative understanding of civil society that remains influential today. Keane summarizes Tocqueville's vision:

> Tocqueville never tired of repeating the point that the "independent eye of society" . . . an eye comprising a plurality of interacting, self-organized and constantly vigilant civil associations—is necessary for consolidating the democratic revolution. In contrast to political forms of involvement (such as participation in elections or jury service) which are concerned with the wider, more general community interests, civil associations consist of combinations of citizens preoccupied with "small affairs." (p. 61)

Civil associations enable citizens to negotiate political actions of all kinds, from voting blocs to neighborhood watch programs to school funding initiatives. More contemporary republican notions of political life follow this ideal, promoting a strong, active sphere of civil society operating in a decentralized state. "According to the republican view, the citizens' political opinion- and will-formation forms the medium through which society constitutes itself as a political whole. . . . [T]his leads to a *polemic understanding of politics directed against the state apparatus* (Habermas, 1996, p. 26, italics in original). The state would be a weakened force in such a society, because the voluntary civil society would attend to its own needs. Classic republicanism, in its current forms, seeks to diminish the state's role to the point of nonexistence; state-run schools would be replaced by a variety of schools meeting the public's wide interests. Libertarians would also seek to diminish the state's role in education but for different reasons. Libertarians see society not as an arena for coalitions and associations but for individuals and consumers; a republican defense, in the classical sense, is not an argument based in individual consumer choice but in democratic involvement and local participation.

Classic republicanism stands in subtle contrast to a civic republican tradition that, in educational thought, traces its roots back to Horace Mann and remains influential in its contemporary communitarian manifestations. The civic republican vision, which seeks a weak state to meet the administrative needs of a strong public, is achieved by "exploring common ground, doing public work, and pursuing common relations" (Barber, 1998, p. 37). Civic republicans believe, to various degrees, in government as a provider of basic services, including schooling. The role of schooling is to help promote civic virtues and knowledge with the aim of socializing an active citizenry. Public schools get their strength not from a strong state but from a strong, active, multivoiced public that, as Barber (1996) argues, aims at common ground and "consensual (that is, integrative and collaborative) modes of action" (p. 271). Public education is the education system created, maintained, and reflecting the interests of civil society and the public (widely shared) interests of citizens, as opposed to the interests of the state, of the market, or the instrumental interests of individuals. Republicans, to various degrees, see the state's role in education as minimal (as in the case of civic republicanism) or nonexistent (as in the case of classic republicanism). Republican views coalesce around a vision of public life that is vital, collaborative, relatively independent of the state and market, and oriented toward a multivoiced consensus.

Critical theorists, of course, start from a very different picture of social life than the republican view; critical views on civil society emphasize the conflicts and struggles among unequal classes and social groups. Gramsci's assessment captures important elements of the critical view of civil society. In a sphere between the economic structure and the state (armed by coercion and aided by legislation), civil society is a realm constantly under pressure to conform to the economic structure. In this realm, dominant groups organize consent by hegemony, and dominated groups organize to work against that hegemony (Forgacs, 2000; see also Brosio, 1993). The critical theory tradition views the public sphere not as a totality but as a fractious playing field of stronger and weaker players. In our current economy, with the gap between rich and poor increasing and the globalized economy exerting enormous influence over our lives and culture, this critical view of civil society is extremely persuasive.

If we accept the critical perspective on civil society—as I do here—then a problem of justice becomes central. How can the playing fields of the public spheres be made more democratic? That is, how can different players participate as equals in political discussions and decisions?

There are (at least) two very different responses to this question from critical theorists: one view suggests that the public sphere needs to be made more universal, more open, and accessible to all, while another view suggests that the trouble lies precisely within the notion of a universal, Enlightenment-based conception of a public sphere. Jürgen Habermas's communicative ethics represents a powerful body of work articulating a vision and defense of a universal public sphere. Nancy Fraser, critically reconstructing Habermas's concept of the public, argues against Habermas's idealized public sphere and instead suggests a pluralized sphere composed of multiple publics and counterpublics.

In his communicative ethic theory, Habermas lays out the method by which discursive public spheres can be made accommodating to all voices and all perspectives, no matter how subordinated or historically silenced. His ideal is lodged in the Enlightenment development of a bourgeois public sphere. Calhoun "The bourgeois public sphere institutionalized, according to Habermas, not just a set of interests and an opposition between state and society but a practice of rational-critical discourse on political matters" (1992a, p. 9). An educated elite emerged in the expansion of market capitalism in Western liberal democracies in the eighteenth century, and this bourgeois public sphere presented an "idea of the public . . . based on the notion of a general interest sufficiently basic that discourse about it need not be distorted by particular interest (at least in principle) and could be a matter of rational approach to an objective order, that is to say, of truth" (Calhoun, 1992a, p. 9). In other words, the Enlightenment model of a public sphere is that of the bourgeois public sphere of rational debate. Instead of the speaker's status determining the import or weight of his or her comments, the crucial feature of debate was instead the rational argument or view presented by the speaker. Habermas sees this ideal of public sphere debate as practically difficult but the only alternative to resolving our shared problems through violent means: "Once you invent these universalistic Enlightenment concepts, forms of communication, like court cases, that are meant to settle practical conflicts in terms of mutual understanding and intended agreement manifestly rely on the force of more or less good reasons as the only alternative to overt or covert violence" (quoted in Calhoun 1992b, p. 467). As Benhabib (1992a) notes, a universalistic public sphere should give all participants "an equal chance to make assertions, recommendations, and explanations; all must have an equal chance to express their wishes, desires, and feelings" (p. 89). The only alternative to this public sphere, Habermas suggests, is conflict leading to violence.

Fraser rejects the universalistic public sphere put forward by Habermas as inherently and practically problematic.[1] Habermas idealizes the model of the bourgeois public sphere, a sphere Fraser (1997) argues has always been exclusionary. "We can no longer assume that the liberal model of the bourgeois public sphere was simply an unrealized utopian ideal; it was also an ideological notion that functioned to legitimate an emergent form of class (and race) rule" (p. 76). Fraser contends that the aims of democratic equality are "better achieved by a multiplicity of publics than by a single public." In a society stratified along class, race, and other lines, "subaltern counterpublics" are alternative publics in which "members of subordinated social groups invent and circulate counter-discourses, which in turn permit them to formulate oppositional interpretations of their identities, interests, and needs" (p. 81). As an example, Fraser points to the late-twentieth-century U.S. feminist subaltern counterpublic, which has produced a formidable array of journals, bookstores, publishing companies, films, conferences, festivals, reading groups, and local meeting places. This counterpublic has, among other achievements, produced and introduced a new lexicon into larger society, emblematic of the larger ideological and legal changes it has brought about in the last century. Terms like "date rape," "sexism," and "sexual harassment" are now part of a common American vocabulary. These terms symbolize the feminist counterpublic's engagement with wider publics, with the effect of influencing the prevailing understandings and notions about gender and power in American life.

As the example of feminism makes clear, these counterpublics are both interpublic and intrapublic. Counterpublics are formed in the important debates and interactions among members, and these serve to help members articulate needs, problems, and even to form and enact their social identities. Counterpublics also have important interpublic functions, or interactions, relations and conflicts with other publics in the larger social sphere. This is what separates counterpublics from the narrow aims of special interest groups or enclaves that exclusively promote their own privatized goods in public discourse and policy. As Fraser points out, counterpublics in stratified societies have a dual character: On the one hand, they function as spaces of withdrawal and regroupment; on the other hand, they also function as bases and training grounds for agitational activities directed toward wider publics. It is precisely in the dialectic between these two functions that their emancipatory potential resides (p. 82)." Fraser argues that the republican conception of public spheres assumes that public deliberation is talk about the common good, ruling claims of self-interest or group interests out of order. But deliberation, states Fraser, is a process aiming to help "participants clarify their interests, even when those interests turn out to conflict" (p. 87). Additionally, if participants have experienced subordination, the discovery of a common good in the republican conception will not offer a way to articulate and understand conflicts of interest. In stratified societies, Fraser states, we cannot assume that there are no conflicts of interest, and thus there "is no warrant for putting any strictures on what sorts of topics, interests, and views are admissible in deliberation" (p. 87). Therefore, Fraser's counterpublic allows us to see the public sphere of Habermas in a more fragmented way, one that puts less of a premium on consensus. Broad consensus does matter, for in wider arenas, multiple publics will agree on some basic democratic ideals: Rights to freely associate and express ideas, or the right to be heard in state governments and courts. But in the smaller, narrower publics that Fraser calls counterpublics, members will have concerns and needs that will likely not be heard in larger public arenas. The multiple publics are themselves layered and fluid: An African American woman will participate in an African American public but may also participate in publics largely concerned with women, or with African American women, or with women of color. Publics are fluid and our membership shifts, but their existence helps to expand recognition and representation of the needs of all citizens, especially those who are marginalized in our society.

As critical theorists, Habermas and Fraser agree that civil society is a sphere of unequal power relations. Their respective solutions for the problem of making public spheres more egalitarian and more responsive to the concerns of the marginalized and oppressed are somewhat distinct, though both argue that the advancement of capitalism has a directly negative influence on the expansion of democracy and public spheres. Beyond curtailing the influence of free-market capitalism, Habermas hopes to advance the Enlightenment utopia of public reason, and to continue to work toward the ideals of a universal public debate. Fraser has a layered, fractious view of public spheres, and her counterpublics are spaces where marginalized groups can both retreat into discourse between and among members, and can disseminate that discourse into wider arenas.

The tensions between a universalistic public sphere and multiple publics that are presented in the comparison of Habermas's and Fraser's work are more than the abstract musings of scholars. Theorists who study social movements in democratic civil societies argue that a number of alarming shifts are occurring in public spheres and civil society in Western democracies. These shifts concern many citizens and scholars who embrace a universal notion of the democratic public sphere. Seligman (1992) notes that the rise of liberal individualism has eroded the sense of trust and solidarity implicit in the traditional notions of civil society in the West. Putnam (1995) is among the social scientists who study fragmentation and decreased participation in traditional associations such as labor unions, bowling leagues, and mainstream houses of worship. He argues that his findings present "striking evidence . . . that the vibrancy of American civil society has notably declined over the past several decades" (p. 3). In "A Call to Civil Society," Jean Bethke Elshtain (1999), the chair of the Council on Civil Society, goes beyond a thesis about organizational forms of civic life, staking a claim about a national moral crisis. "What ails our democracy is not simply the loss of certain organizational forms [houses of worship, civic organizations, arts institutions, local government, local schools] but also the loss of certain organizing ideals—moral ideals that authorize our civic creed, but do not derive from it" (p. 17). The notion that all persons possess equal dignity represents a moral truth, Elshtain suggests, that no longer is widely embraced in our society. The "homeless public," as labeled by Barber,[2] lacks the organizational forms, political activity, and moral idealism that a vital civil society uses to construct visions and articulations of the common good or goods necessary to guide policy and law. Seligman (1992), tracing the idea of civil society through modern Western intellectual history, poses the problem this way:

> The problem of civil society (whether in the eighteenth century or today) remains that of positing a model of the social whole that would overcome (while not negating) the inherent universal/particularity of its members. The problem of civil society is thus, in its essence, the problem of modern natural law—of constituting a *universitas* that would include (or rather, represent the ties binding) a *societas* of individuals whose very compacts or contracts tend to highlight the autonomy and independence of each rather than their fundamental communality. (p. 99)

Fraser is among those theorists who would argue that our civil society has never lived up to its communitarian, egalitarian ideals; to decry a decline in civil society, or a dissolution of shared moral ideals such as human equality, is to nostalgically recall a past that never existed for entire classes and groups of citizens. Fraser's model of counterpublics attempts to show that in a stratified, capitalist society with very loose or nonexistent ties among diverse citizens, the public problems of fragmentation and moral decline are not solved by attempting to mend the social whole but by working to strengthen the multiple parts constituting that whole. The communality of individuals can be highlighted within smaller publics that satisfy both particular and universal ends—the need for particularity in intrapublic relations, and the need for universal relations and debates in interpublic communication with other publics in the larger, wider public sphere. In this way, the model of multiple publics and counterpublics represents an alternative view to those provided by the scholars who find cause for alarm in the so-called decline of civil society. Fraser's model represents a critical perspective on civil society as an idealized public sphere that both conceptually arises from a divided, stratified society and that continues to stratify and marginalize in practice. Using Fraser's framework, a fragmented civil society may be presenting open spaces or opportunities for a variety of counterpublics and social movements that have been underrepresented in public debates and policy. In the next section, we test this notion through an exploration of a phenomenon I call educational publics.

Civil Society and Educational Publics

Competing republican and liberal ideologies have helped to construct the notion of a universal, common public school. The free public school, open to all, has symbolized a sacred public ideal for some, a highly contested public ideal for others. Activists of many types fought throughout the late nineteenth and twentieth centuries to have the public schools live up to their public, universal ideals. Though quite imperfectly, public schooling has integrated our public lives by bringing together different races and classes in ways that few other public institutions have been able to do. Yet there are signs that the symbol of the universal public school is tarnishing in the eyes of many Americans, as the notion of a universal public for a universal public school system is increasingly challenged in contemporary school debates and political battles. Of course, for some Americans who have been economically and socially marginalized, American schools have never lived up to this universal ideal. For a variety of reasons, Americans of different classes, ideologies, and races are questioning the validity of universal public schooling. To put such a claim in perspective, let us look briefly at the development of this universal ideal.

Public schools are a mix of tradition and competing ideologies, but among the powerful influences shaping the development of public schools have been republican and liberal ideologies. Public schools, in many ways, were conceptualized in the nineteenth century by those embracing a republican ideology. Schools were to be a site where individuals became citizens and acquired the knowledge needed to debate issues and participate in public life. Schools were also influenced, however, by liberal notions of freedom and the welfare state. Liberal notions of freedom shaped the idea that public schools are to "guarantee an essentially non-political common good by the satisfaction of private preferences" (Habermas, 1996, 27). Liberal notions of a welfare state, in contrast, lead to a vision of the political state as a protector of liberties and welfare, with special concern for the poor and the marginalized.[3] While common school reformers like Horace Mann made use of capitalist (training workers) and republican arguments (assimilating immigrants, creating citizens) to persuade states to create public school systems, he and his cohorts also argued that "the state should assume educational responsibilities previously reserved to parents" since a privatized system resulted in educating wealthy and poor students differently and unequally (Kaestle, 1983, pp. 116–117). Thus, a mix of ideologies lent themselves as rationale for a universal public school system: a republican notion of democratic citizenship for all, accompanied by liberal conceptions of autonomy and of the welfare state as inclusive of the poor. Public schools were free for the poor and rich, and the system evolved as universal in the sense that it was designed, by and large, to serve the children of all families regardless of status or wealth.

The universal public school—as the school that enrolls a major part of the children of the society—is still the place where most American children go to school, but its predominance in our national consciousness, personal allegiances, and political prioritization has clearly declined. David Matthews, president of the Kettering Foundation, which researches public participation in democracy, issues bleak warnings about public schools' future. "The public school system, as we have known it, may not survive the next century," said Matthews, who conducted in the late 1990s a national study of the public role in education issues. "There are evidently a great many people who don't believe that the public schools are their agents" (quoted in Willard and Oplinger, 1999, p. 1).

Bradley (1996) lists reasons why our ideals of publicly funded and publicly governed schools are currently under special scrutiny. First is the demographic fact that only about 25 percent of households have school-age children, an historic low. Increasingly, therefore, taxpayers are looking at education as a financial investment that benefits other people's children.[4] Second, Bradley suggests that the public's faith in and support of its institutions have "withered" (although this seems to be a misleading generalization).[5] Third, the public has reacted with confusion and conflict to efforts to improve schools. Moreover, there are signs of growing support for alternatives to public schools, such as magnet schools, vouchers, charter schools, and home schooling. "Support for giving parents greater discretion over where to send their children to school has recently been growing," Gold-haber writes (1999, p. 16). According to the National Association for Independent Schools, enrollment in private schools is up nearly 17 percent in the past decade across the country; and the number of charter schools nationwide grew by 40 percent during the 1998–99 school year (DiFilippo, 2000; McQueen, 2000). The privatization of public schools, moreover, is also a problem, as voucher programs now have Supreme Court approval and as for-profit corporations run more and more schools. Mathews (1996) pointedly asks, "Is there a public for our public schools?"[6]

There are certainly reasons to believe that the public is abandoning a meaningful notion of public schools in favor of various forms of privatization. The public sphere as fragmented, homeless, and colonized by market values of greed and competition are popular and indeed plausible explanations for the public disenfranchisement with its state-supported schools. The number of for-profit educational companies is expanding, and despite their general lack of profitability thus far, "entrepreneurs are still optimistic about the possibilities of for-profit public education" (Engel, 2000, p. 3). Managing entire school districts and a growing number of charter schools, educational management organizations see the education of children as a "vast consumer base" with an "enormous potential for growth" (pp. 5, 4). A market ideology is not only feeding the corporate approach to educational management, it also is feeding the growing belief among parents that education is primarily for individual advancement, rather than for democratic equality or social efficiency. As Labaree notes: "public education has increasingly come to be perceived as a private good that is harnessed to the pursuit of personal advantage" (1997, p. 43).

Additionally, the state's past record and future success in realizing the ideals of the common school and success for all children is exposed to increasing skepticism. Take, for example, Orfield and Eaton's (1996) findings that racial segregation in some American schools is at levels equal to or surpassing the levels in existence when the *Brown v. Board of Education* decision was handed down.[7] Or consider, in another example, the lawsuits filed against the states on behalf of poor school districts protesting the huge differentials in per-pupil spending in rich and poor districts across the nation. The state, subservient to economic forces and absent the voices of a strong, active public citizenry, may no longer hold the legitimacy or authority necessary to run public school systems that uphold public virtues such as universal access and equality of opportunity in learning-centered, high-quality schools.

American publics may be abandoning the traditional public school because of the dominance of market ideology, an increasing focus on individual advancement over common aims, or due to a growing distrust in the legitimacy of the state to run schools that help all students achieve appropriate academic, social, and moral outcomes. Yet, I wish to argue that a move away from state-run schools is not necessarily an abandonment of the notion of a school as a public institution. In the future, it may no longer be accurate to continue to automatically equate *state-run schooling* with the notion of *public schooling*. In education, the public is increasingly taking the form of multiple educational publics, thereby shifting the conception of public schools from more universalist traditions to more particularist forms. Educational publics are sites where parents and educators can resist or reconstruct the state's goals for education and schooling, debate and agree upon various shared educational needs and visions, and hold the state accountable for helping them to implement these visions. The state, in turn, must assume a more regulatory role in assuming fair and appropriate educational settings and outcomes for all children.

Educational publics are groups of citizens mobilized by their common concerns and critiques of schooling. These educational publics fit the description of social movements as defined by Melucci (1989):

> First, a social movement is a form of collective action which involves *solidarity*, that is, actors' mutual recognition that they are part of a single social unit. A second characteristic of a social movement is its engagement in *conflict*, and thus in opposition to an adversary who lays claim to the same goods or values. . . . Third, a social movement *breaks the limits of compatibility of a system.* Its actions violate the boundaries or tolerance limits of a system, thereby pushing the system beyond the range of variations that it can tolerate without altering its structure. (p. 29; italics in original)

Energized and mobilized by similar complaints of the public school system, educational publics represent counterpublics as put forward by Fraser. Educational counterpublics are spheres of solidarity for members; through dialogue and interactions, members identify and name their educational interests and visions, which are—not coincidentally—aligned with their social identities (understood in a postmodern, nonessentialized sense). Educational counterpublics are also interpublic spheres in which members engage with larger publics, often on terms of conflict regarding interests and resources. Educational publics are frequently in conflict with the public school system (this, of course, feeds the solidarity among members); their emergence in contemporary life is driven by what some consider to be an overly intrusive, hegemonic, or hopelessly inept state-run public school system. Educational counterpublics have, through their mobilization and interpublic work, placed great strain on the existing model of the universal public school. As a result, we see school choice plans proliferating, private school enrollment increasing and educational alternatives such as home schooling experiencing new popularity. Educational publics alter the public educational landscape for society as a whole. As the system becomes less centralized and more open to alternatives, more educational publics proliferate around new schooling concepts and visions enabled by a more decentralized structure of state-sponsored schooling initiatives.

Let us discuss two very different examples of educational publics as a way to further explore this concept. When charter school reforms became popular in the 1990s, critics feared that these schools would become elite organizations made up of middle-class white kids whose families were flee-ing integrated public schools. In fact, researchers have shown that a healthy number of charters are attempting to serve families and commu-nities that have traditionally been ignored or underserved by public schools. In a study of California charters, Wells et al. (1999) wrote:

> Groups of parents, students, educators, and community activists in low-income communities of color are using charter school reform to gain free-dom from state-mandated curricula in order to embrace their own cultural heritage. After forty years of unsatisfactory progress with reforms designed to improve unequal distribution of resources across schools or help margin-alized groups gain access to mainstream institutions, members of these com-munities now seek to create schools of their own. (p. 175)

According to the *State of Charter Schools 2000*, about one in four charter schools "established their charter to serve a special population of students, often students considered 'at risk.'" (p. 42). It seems that, at least in a few cases, educational publics consisting primarily of low-income communities of color have formed to bring about and take advantage of charter school-ing laws.[8] These publics can base their charter schools on more localized problems and values. Such grass-roots charter schools, as studied by Wells and her colleagues, "have the potential to be politically empowering for formerly disconnected and disempowered parents" (1999, p. 194).

In the California study, Wells also noted another educational public that was taking advantage of charter school alternatives: homeschooling fami-lies. Though this public is not nearly as historically or materially marginal-ized as, say, low-income communities of color, homeschooling families, for a variety of reasons, do not feel well served by traditional public schools. Home-schooling families are networks of parent/educators who want to pursue localized, individualized educational options for their children. Homeschoolers represent a counterpublic inasmuch as many of these fam-ilies are seeking to escape and challenge what they consider to be the hege-monic public schooling system run by the government. The label of homeschooler can be a pejorative one for many educators, conjuring up images of "David Koresh" types who "keep their children home because they don't want them to mix with children of other races or faiths" (Schnailberg, 1996, p. 2). The author of one study of homeschoolers states that stereotypes that many hold about this group are rarely borne out: "The popular myth out there was that this was kind of a monolithic group moti-vated by religious attitudes" (in Archer, 1999, p. 5). While religion often figures prominently in a family's decision to educate their children at home, this growing group cannot be simply cast as religious fanatics. "Any way you slice the American pie, you're going to find homeschoolers," states the founder of one home schooling publication (Archer, 1999, p. 5). Van Galen and Pitman (1991), in their study of homeschoolers, categorized families as ideologues or pedagogues in their study, based on the parents' motivations to teach their kids at home. The group labeled ideologues are typically Christian fundamentalists who object to what is taught in public and private schools and seek to strengthen family relationships. The group labeled pedagogues, on the other hand, are highly independent families with a broader interest in learning and a critique of the bureaucratization and inefficiency of modern institutions, including schools. Van Galen and Pitman's study is a now a decade old, but even at that point in the home-schooling movement, these researchers found a diversity of ideologies and views. A *Time* cover story in August 2001 represented this movement in a similarly diverse fashion:

> Homeschooling is still growing at 11% a year, and it's no longer confined to a conservative fringe that never believed in the idea of public schooling anyway. . . . According to [a recently released] Federal Government [report], up to three-quarters of the families that homeschool today say they do so pri-marily because, like so many of us, they are worried about the quality of their children's education. (Cloud and Morse, 2001, p. 49)

Estimates of school-age children being homeschooled in 1999 were placed at 1 million ("Homeschooling," 1999).

All educational publics must be judged on both their intrapublic and interpublic relations. Though some homeschooling groups break off from traditional schools to isolate their families from outside influences, confin-ing their social networks to only communal members, homeschooling publics that are truly *public* in orientation have arisen as the movement has grown in number and diversity. Educational publics like homeschoolers are forming informal networks for specialized study and activities—like writing groups or math clubs—and forming associations, support groups, legal aid societies, publishing networks, and Internet sites to support homeschooling families and connect them with one another. Far from a closed private world based on the domestic expression of religion, many homeschooling families are connected pedagogically and politically with other families who share in the discourses of homeschooling. Inasmuch as these families engage in interpublic and intrapublic dialogue and activity, homeschoolers form educational publics. In addition, the type of education provided by educational publics is critical. A charter school serving low-income Latino families will both nurture Hispanic identities and traditions as well as immerse children in the language, discourses, and traditions of broader cul-tural and political contexts. Families and schools (or other institutions) should not only be helping them to become members of their particular communities or publics; these educational publics should also be prepar-ing children for, and immersing them in, broader public settings, dis-courses, and activities, so as to foster and strengthen their identities as participants in multiple political spheres. When and where this is not happening, I would argue, educational publics are not publics at all, but domesticated and enclosed spheres of dangerously limited learning and growth.

The public may be abandoning the notion of a state-run school system as the exclusive educational system for all citizens. In so doing, however, Americans are not necessarily may not be abandoning all notions of publicness. There is no doubt that some or even most American families who are choosing alternatives to universal public schools are doing so for privatized reasons: to flee the racial or class diversity in public schools, or to make sure their kids get access to the best colleges and jobs in order to enter the upper classes of society. But some of the exodus from traditional public schools may also signal the existence of multiple educational publics in which groups of citizens are forming spheres of debate and action around common identities and shared educational concerns. As more alternatives for these educational publics exist to form and shape their own visions of education through choice schemes of various types, we may see a dramatic shift in the notion of a universal public and the traditional public school.

The current formation of civil society as a fragmented sphere of associations is viewed as a flawed version of the original conception. That is, our present civil society is often seen as broken, experiencing a malaise characterized by instrumental individualism, a lack of trust and solidarity, and the lack of public spaces and institutions that genuinely cross class and other categories of human difference. Yet if civil society is seen as layers of publics, multiple publics that *both* withdraw from larger public spheres *and* enrich these larger, more universal spheres with their participation and perspectives, then perhaps civil society is not as diseased as many believe it to be. At the same time, however, civil society as a sphere for educational publics is a terrain that is not without serious limitations and problems.

Limitations and Dangers

Thus far, I have pointed out the ways in which multiple publics and counterpublics might enrich public life by promoting coalitions and associations that broaden formal education for diverse persons and perspectives. I have purposefully made extensive use of the hopeful possibilities to be found in the shift from a universal model of the public sphere, in part because I believe that these possibilities have been overlooked by those on the left who decry these shifts with relatively blunt accusations that Americans have an increasingly privatized or otherwise diminished conception of public education. In discussing civil society as a sphere for multiple educational publics, however, I would be remiss if I did not point out the serious limitations and even dangers that the shift away from a notion of universal public school represents. I highlight three major limitations here: the economic context of aggressive global capitalism, the problem of inequality among publics, and the problem of illiberal educational publics. I also, in conclusion, briefly address the cultural and civic problem of segregation related to the shift away from a universal public school ideal.

Critical theorists like Habermas and Fraser agree that democratic public spheres of any kind are undermined and destroyed by the expansion of capitalism, and we are currently in an era in which our economic structure is permeating all aspects of our cultural life. Capitalism, because it is a system that values the pursuit of profit and the accumulation of private capital over and above public goods, works against full democratic participation and the equalization of the public spheres through the redistribution of wealth. In education, the expanding influence of capitalism on school structures, policies, and curriculum has been documented (Boyles, 1998; House, 1998). In this context, the universal school system may provide a stronghold, albeit a possibly weakening one, in which various groups can sustain a public space, committed to equality and inclusiveness, against the expansion of market logic and ideals. Giving up a universal ideal may pave the way for schools to become entirely run on a market model, either run by for-profit companies or by organizations set up to compete with one another for dollars, students, and resources. Already we see a growing number of charter schools run by for-profit companies, and these companies may not have the long-term best interests of all children in their mission.[9] Civil society may be less autonomous from the influences of capitalism than I argue here, and may have few defenses against the erosion of schooling for public aims into schooling for private gains. One solution to this problem is to severely curtail the ability of for-profit corporations to run schools, though the trend in most states is moving in the opposite direction, throwing open more avenues for for-profit education rather than fewer.

Civil society has no mechanism to deal with the problem of inequality among educational publics, but this second major limitation of my argument can be addressed through state interventions. We cannot pretend that all educational publics are equal in terms of membership, recognition, or resources. Studies of charter schooling demonstrate the import of this point clearly, as Wells and her colleagues (1998) argue: "Without additional resources targeted toward the poorest communities, charter school operators have little power to overcome existing inequalities within the large and uneven public education system" (p. 306). Even with all the federal money now flowing to charter schools, charters find it difficult to raise money for facilities (Bowman, 2000). Marginalized groups may find fundraising even more difficult than other groups who have more connections with private venture capitalists. As Walzer (1999) suggests, state programs should target such publics. The state should provide a myriad of ways to fund the educational visions of the diverse publics related to education, but provide more opportunities for publics formed largely of poor and disadvantaged families. Educational publics are both diverse and conflicting; the state should administer help (e.g., financial resources, consulting, institutional models) to those groups who lack the necessary cultural capital to bring their education visions to life. Political connections, knowledge of funding sources, or private sources of funds are all aspects of the requisite cultural capital that has advantaged middle-class charter schooling initiatives and served to further the inequalities between rich and poor publics. The state at least attempts to formulate remedies to level the playing field of schooling, and the courts can be used by citizens to seek remedies to funding inequalities. Civil society has no such mechanisms and as such provides a field in which, absent state intervention or assistance, these existing inequalities can be exacerbated.

Civil society is also a unequal sphere in terms of recognition and rights, both within publics and between publics. As Phillips (1999) wryly notes, as a feminist she sees "the same patterns repeating themselves in every sphere of existence. Same old pattern of dominance, same old pattern of exclusion, same old problems whether in family, market, civil society, or state" (p. 56).[10] Fraser (1997) admits that some counterpublics are "explicitly antidemocratic and antiegalitarian" (p. 82). Fraser states that these antidemocratic counterpublics can be forgiven for these exclusions "insofar as these counterpublics emerge in response to exclusions within dominant publics" since they help expand discursive space (p. 82). This problem that Fraser forgives presents a serious dilemma for education, since schools that perpetuate these qualities of dominance or exclusion will be affecting the future lives of schoolchildren, possibly disabling them from living full lives as equal citizens. If a school based in Afrocentric values, set up by an educational public emerging in response to exclusion from dominant educational publics, were to perpetuate and exacerbate gender inequality in its curriculum, this presents serious harm to the girls in that school.

I conclude with a final, and more personal, comment on a detrimental effect of civil society as a sphere for the proliferation of educational publics. Attending public schools in my rural, southern hometown, I was the first in my family to have a K–12 schooling experience that brought white and black children together in the same classrooms. I am convinced that, despite the imperfections that existed and still exist in desegregation plans, my educational experience was dramatically enhanced by attending integrated schools. Whether it enhanced the educational experience of the African American students in my classes, I cannot say; I can say that the experience qualitatively changed my views of other races and classes from the beliefs that I had learned in my family. Part of the common school dream is to help children understand the diversity of cultures and lives that constitute this nation, and the universal public school ideal is still embraced by many with this dream in mind. Educational publics may exacerbate the levels of racial- and class-based segregation already seen in public schools today. Perhaps this dream is a necessary casualty for marginalized publics to find a fair shake in publicly funded schools, as advocates of segregation argue. But as a middle-class white person, I can say that this casualty would represent a serious loss if charter schools were to exacerbate the already growing segregation of different races and classes in American public schools.

Civil society as a terrain for growing educational publics is fraught with problems, and I raise only a few of the more serious ones here. Yet in a society more and more run by markets and market values, civil society represents some hopeful possibilities for democratic public life. As Habermas (1996) notes: "Civil society provides the social basis of autonomous public spheres that remain as distinct from the economic system as from the administration. This understanding of democracy suggests a new balance between the three resources of money, administrative power, and solidarity, from which modern societies meet their needs for integration" (p. 28). Autonomous public spheres are decentered rather than emanating from a social whole of state, as in liberal theory, or from a totality of political community, as in republican theory. They are decentered from the authority of the economic sphere and from the sphere of the state that exists to administer the policies and law that emanate from public sphere will formation. This does not mean public spheres are impervious to the influence of the capitalist economy, but that civil society is, in some sense, a domain autonomous from both the economy and the state. It is a "porous" sphere, as Habermas describes it, with fluid movement throughout; market influence moves through it but does not define nor contain it. Without wishing to draw the boundaries between domains too strictly, the decentered public spheres are the culturally mobilized domains in which people gather "critical potential" through critiquing existing structures or policies, discussing issues, and seeking agreement on their needs and desires. Educational publics, forming in this sphere of civil society, can use the energy of cultural mobilization to form creative alternatives that may seriously challenge the universal public school ideal. At the very least, these alternatives offer an expanded public debate on the purposes and aims of education. At worst, however, these alternatives may make schooling less public and less just for families and groups historically oppressed or marginalized in traditional public schools.

3

Extraordinary Conversations in Public Schools

Lois Weis and Michelle Fine

Over the past twenty years, scholars have amassed an impressive array of work aimed at uncovering the ways in which schools reproduce social inequalities. Forming a corpus of structuralist interpretation, such studies wind through the ways in which curriculum (Apple, 1982; Anyon, 1983; Gaskell, 1992), standardized testing (Haney, 1993), political economy and bureaucratic organization (Anyon, 1998), teacher practices (Kelly and Nihlen, 1982), and university preparation (Ginsburg, 1988) sustain broader social inequalities. Although it is well understood that schooling plays a crucial role in offering opportunities for individual social mobility, it does, at the same time, serve to perpetuate and indeed legitimate widespread structural inequalities.

Much work over the past twenty years focuses on the ways in which social inequalities along racial, social class and gendered lines are sustained through schools. And, indeed, we have contributed writing in this area (Fine, 1993; Weis, 1990; Weis and Fine, 1993). Recently work has also been done on the ways in which schools inscribe heterosexuality and able-bodiedness through curriculum and social practices as well, and excellent work has been done in this regard (Barry, 2000; Sapon-Shevin, 1993; Fine, 1988; Friend, 1993; Whatley, 1991). Additionally work has focused on the ways in which students themselves, through resistant cultures, further inscribe their own subordinate positions (Willis, 1977; Solomon, 1992; Giroux, Valli, 1986) along social class, race, gendered, and sexual lines. In the case of gender, for example, Angela McRobbie (1978) has argued persuasively that it is the girls' own culture, even more than what the school expects of girls, that ensures their (our) position in an ongoing set of patriarchal structures.

This vibrant research agenda has taken us a long way toward understanding how it is that schools sustain that which they purport to eliminate. Nevertheless, in examining the reproduction of social inequalities we may camouflage those truly outstanding moments in today's schools—instances of teachers and kids working against the grain to create more critical and egalitarian structures, to imagine more open opportunities for all, to truly challenge all that is inscribed in the American mosaic. These spaces (Katz, 1996; Keith and Pile, 1993) reflect and blend many of the commitments of critical race theorists (e.g., Ladsen-Billings, 2000; Delpit, 1988; M. Foster, 1997; Matsuda, 1997), feminist pedagogy (Ellsworth, 1989; Lather, 1991), and resistance theorists (Giroux, 1983a; Cochran-Smith and Lytle, 1992), but with a profound sense of place and space borrowed from radical geographers like Katz (1996) and Keith and Pile (1993). Organized to create and sustain a sense of intellectual and political community among differences, with a critical eye on power asymmetries within and outside the room, these educators have crafted rich and fragile spaces within public schools—currently sites of enormous surveillance and pressure toward reproduction. Here we wish to honor two such sites—instances of forceful pedagogy that deliberately and directly challenge inequity; sites which are sustained over time by critical educators working toward a larger political and intellectual project. We suggest, then, that these disruptions deserve critical understanding as politically and pedagogically strategic moments, within traditional schools, for identity and movement work.

Social Spaces for Challenge

Data reported here were collected as part of a larger study on "urban spaces" (Fine, Weis, Centrie, et al., 2000). As we have argued elsewhere, education does not just take place in schools, as anthropologists have long contended. It occurs at dinnertime, in front of the television set, on street corners, in religious institutions, in family planning clinics, and in lesbian and gay community groups. In the deindustrializing Northeast, those cities ravaged by the collapse of the private sector and the often wholesale abandonment of the public sphere wrought by late-twentieth-century capitalism, some poor and working-class youth find the strength and fortitude to continue educating themselves and each other in spaces they craft and tenaciously hold onto, often against great odds. Young men and women are finding unsuspected places within their communities, their educational institutions, and their spiritual lives to sculpt real and imaginary corners for peace, solace, communion, social critique, personal and collective work. These are spaces of deep, sustained community-based educative work—in many cases, outside the bounds of formal schooling.

Serious (re)educative work can flourish in these spaces. Not necessarily rigidly bounded by walls/fences, these spaces often are corralled by a series of fictional borders within which trite social stereotypes are precariously contested. Young men and women, in the constant confrontation with harsh humiliating public representations of their race, ethnicity, gender, class, and sexuality, use these spaces to reeducate, to break down public representations for scrutiny and invent new ones. It is within this broader theoretical context that the two projects discussed here were conceived.

Unlike many of the other sites connected to our larger theoretical project, though, these two are set specifically in public schools and focus on youth, as well as the adults who are connected to these youth, and begin with the question: How do adults establish and secure an environment within which critical reeducative work with and for youth can flourish across social class, race and gender lines? And, how do students participate in environments that stretch toward this end?

Political scientist Nancy Fraser (1993) argues that it is advantageous for "marginals" to create what she calls "counterpublics," in which they may oppose stereotypes and assert novel interpretations of their own shifting identities, interests and work. She theorizes that these are formed, ironically, out of the very exclusionary practices of the public sphere. We, too, have found that in the midst of disengagement by the public sector and relocation of private sector jobs "down south," or, more likely overseas, it is into these newly constructed "free spaces" as Sara Evans and Harry Boyte (1992) would call them, that poor and working-class men and women, boys and girls have fled from sites of historical pain and struggle and reconstituted new identities. It is to these "free spaces" that we have been led. Together and separately, young people are shaping identities that do and do not resist the structures around them; that will and will not transform their material conditions; that at base promise to inspire reeducative possibilities; new ways to produce "common sense" and reimagine social possibilities.

What we offer here is a theoretical extension of our previous work in this regard. In two public schools we observe and participate with committed adults who push the boundaries of what "would be." These are educators who intentionally and self-consciously challenge the reproductive instincts of public education and create spaces in which youth can challenge "common sense" about themselves and others, and engage intellectual and political projects that are, indeed, counterhegemonic. Further, these are not simply "liberatory" spaces for historically oppressed or marginalized youth, but perhaps more pedagogically treacherous, they are integrated sites in which youth with biographies of some privilege sit side by side with youth of poverty, working for a public common understanding across lines of race, ethnicity, and geography. And finally, these educators are not simply engaged in practices of resistance but have designed and crafted spaces of public responsibility and intellect, carved by a racially and ethnically diverse group of educators for youths in ways that can easily (and accurately) anticipate opposition from community members, administrators, colleagues, some parents, and many youth.

We argue that counterpublics, such as those described by Fraser and others, can and do exist in public arenas such as schools. As public monies are increasingly withdrawn from institutions that serve poor and working-class youth, it is absolutely essential for the community to reclaim these spaces. Those of us who work with public schools cannot sit by and accept that schools do no more than reproduce social inequalities, though this may certainly be the case much of the time. We must engage in the creation and protection of counterpublics, spaces where adults and youth can challenge the very exclusionary practices currently existing in public institutions, practices that inscribe inequalities by social class, race, gender, and sexuality.

We have no illusions about the ease, political or pedagogical, of creating or sustaining these spaces; indeed, we are sure (and have lots of evidence) of the likely resistance. We write, instead, with respect for the efforts that are going on and hope to join a public conversation of support for such educational practices within (not despite) the public sphere of public education. As we suggest here, it is not enough to let this form of challenge go on in alternative sites, as important as these alternative sites might be (Bertram et al., 1999; Fine, Weis, Centrie, et al., 2000, forthcoming; Morton-Christmas, 1999; Reichert, 2000). Here we focus on two projects which push against the grain. The first, a voluntary girls group that meets in an urban magnet school in Buffalo; and the second, a detracked ninth-grade social studies class in Montclair, New Jersey.

Pushing the Borders of Gender and Race

Data for the first project considered here were gathered during spring semester 1997 at "Arts Academy," a 5–12 magnet school geared toward the arts in Buffalo, New York. Students must be accepted into the school on the basis of an audition, either in dance, theater, music, visual arts, or radio and TV. The school draws broadly from the city of Buffalo, although many of the students reside in poor and/or working class neighborhoods within a ten-minute ride of the school. The school is located just south of downtown Buffalo and, like all magnet schools in the city, as part of the desegregation plan ostensibly acts as a magnet for white students to attend school in neighborhoods populated by people of color. The school is highly mixed racially and ethnically, having 45 percent white, 45 percent African American, 8 percent Latino/Latina, 1 percent Native American, 1 percent Asian students. The ethnic/racial montage is everywhere visible, as students from varying backgrounds participate in academic pursuits and arts endeavors ranging from jazz combo to ballet.

Data were drawn from within a school program called "My Bottom Line," the officially stated goal of which is "to prevent or delay the onset of sexual activity, build self esteem and increase self sufficiency in young women through an abstinence based, gender specific prevention education program." Students voluntarily attend the program during study halls, participating one or two times a week, depending on the schedule. The guidance counselor actively recruited Womanfocus, a nonprofit agency, to deliver the program to local area schools. It has the strong backing of the guidance counseling staff, and group meetings are held in the large, centrally located conference room of the guidance office.

As Shirley, a guidance counselor, states,

I really want these girls to take good risks with their lives and escape negative situations. I want them to be empowered to make good choices, to be able to leave town for college, to take internships, to take advantage of opportunities, to be able to leave their neighborhoods. Too many are trapped. I want them to delay sexual activity without being a prude so that they will be able to live fuller lives. Too many of these girls don't realistically see what a baby does to one's life. They have babies to make up for their own lost childhood and want to give to the baby what they themselves did not have. But they do not have the resources or maturity to give to their baby what they didn't have.

Shirley invited Womanfocus into the school, and used all school resources possible to support the program. She talked with teachers on a regular basis, urging them to send students during their study halls, and worked with teachers to make attendance possible.

My Bottom Line is run by Doris Carbonell-Medina, a Latina Womanfocus staff member. Lois participated in all meetings for a full semester and acted, at times, as co-facilitator of the group. The program runs fifteen weeks. Although the program targets young women in seventh, eighth, and ninth grades, young women from grades 7–12 participated, at the explicit request of Doris. Seventh- and eighth-graders meet together, and high school students meet in a different session.

Proposals for the program targeted girls in the seventh, eighth, and ninth grades, and this is, in fact, where funding for abstinence-related initiatives is found (Mecklenburg and Thompson, 1983; Wilcox, 1998).[2] However, Doris insists on working with the older girls as well, specifically tying her decision to the rhetoric of abstinence:

Many people interpret abstinence-based programs as, you know, very conservative, sort of right-wing, concepts. Like that abstinence means they have to be "clamped shut," and you're saying, "that's it." And that's why we target those seventh, eighth-, and ninth-grade girls, because those are the years that they're going to be facing those crucial decisions in their life, as to whether or not they want to be having sex. And those are the years that girls choose this for their lives. But, on the other hand, those high school girls that have already made that choice [to have sex], or some that haven't, they also need some sort of intervention, and that knowledge that simply because you've been sexually active in one relationship doesn't mean that you have to be sexually active in another relationship. And, you know, young girls need to be given that information, or at least to be given the confidence to say, "Hey, you don't have to sleep around with every single guy." There are some standards that you should have. There are some criteria that you should have in establishing your relationships. And I think those lines get blurred once you become sexually involved, and once you get into that whole world of adolescence and sex.

This space was, then, in addition to dealing with issues of sexual abstinence, intentionally established to empower young women, particularly in their relationships with young men. For Doris and Shirley, women's bodies must be under the control of women themselves, and should not be a site for male control, abuse, or exploitation. Both state strongly that women need to evidence choices over their bodies and minds, and that the lack of such choices means that these teen women will never venture outside their neighborhoods or their lived economic marginality. Empowering them to stay away from situations of abuse lies at the center of the unofficial programming. This is not, then, simply a program about abstinence, although the abstinence strain is there. Here, mainstream sexuality education curricula are used as the basis for important discussions about gender, sexuality, and, indirectly, race.

In this space, which adults establish and facilitate, teens actively interact. Although the official intent of My Bottom Line is sexual abstinence, there is much other work going on in this site, both by adults and youth, which offer it as a powerful space for re-visioning gendered and race subjectivities as students gain a set of lenses and allies for doing social critique. As we have argued elsewhere, most youth have the potential for social critique, but this critique fizzles as they grow older (Fine and Weis, 1998; Weis and Fine, 1996; Fine, 1993). Here we focus on the preliminary consolidation of critique and enter the site, as Lois lived in it and worked with it, for six months. It is the gender and race work we visit here, work done under the explicit tutelage of Doris Carbonell-Medina, Esq.[3]

Baring Secrets

A cornerstone of the group is confidentiality, which enables the girls to bare secrets without fear of recrimination or gossip. As Doris states,

> I tell them at the very beginning that this issue I take very seriously. And when we say that in order to build trusting relationships, in order to build relationships [in the group] where we can open up and tell our stories, that we have to be mature. And mature means that you don't go around and you gossip and stuff. Then I say that I get so crazy about this stuff that if it comes back to me that you've opened your mouth and blabbed—and that's how it's seen—you know, we'd ask you to leave. And that would be the way that we separate you from us, because we don't want you to be in our group if you can't keep our secrets. They're very careful about it I tell you. And they don't reveal anything [in group] that they don't want people to know. And then, if they've really got to get it out—and many of them have done this to me—they have said, "Can I talk to you after the group?"

Embedded in the weaving of a new collective of young women across race lines is the baring of secrets. The group is a space within which young women tell a great deal about their personal lives—the illnesses within their homes, the violence in their relationships, their fears spoken aloud when their "stepfather's moving back in with mom." Girls share secrets as they share strength and hope, jumping in to help each other with problems, sometimes life threatening and other times mundane. As they share secrets, they examine self and weave new identities, individual and collective. What is particularly striking in these data is the extent to which young white women reveal pieces of their lives normally not told. Although they are relatively quiet in group, as compared with African American girls, for example, those who do open up contest the suffocating silence which envelops them. White women, whether adolescents or adults, are the most silent/silenced group with which we have worked (Weis and Fine, 1998; Weis, Marusza, and Fine, 1998), speaking, always softly, about the horrors in their lives only in one to one interviews, never in a group context. But not so here. White girls are cracking that silence so typical of the group, sharing secrets in protected environments, working beyond the one to one encounters. They are hearing each other out as they unburden their problems. Girls from a variety of backgrounds unravel their stories within the group context. Listen to Tiffany, who speaks with Lois and Tia in group:

TIFFANY: I love my mother dearly. But, OK, she's manic-depressive, but I love her dearly.

LOIS: Is she really manic-depressive?

TIFFANY: Yeah, like she's got medication and everything. She's a manic-depressive and my dad is schizophrenic—which is great for me [sarcastically]. . . . She doesn't make friends easily. I have to watch what I say, because I don't want to get her in a bad mood. She's on medication now. She's very caring, but she's smothering. Like, it's my birthday Monday, right. I'm like, since I was like nine, I have like, each birthday, I have a half an hour later that I can stay up. I mean, right now it's 9:30, and all my friends are sitting there going to bed at 11. And on Monday, I get to go to bed at 10 o'clock and that makes me so happy because I can go to bed at ten [laughs].

Tiffany speaks candidly about her clinically ill parents, weaving through her discussions throughout the term her own feelings as she attempts to live in her mother's house. She is not the only one who speaks so openly about home-based problems, and the uniqueness of this, particularly among white girls, should not be underestimated. My Bottom Line offers a space within which such secrets can be shared. Tiffany, of course, does not receive professional help in a group of this sort. What she does receive is support and understanding from her peers, monitored by an adult who is sensitive to these issues. In addition, and perhaps most importantly, Tiffany feels less alone with her problems since she has shared them and learned, oftentimes, that she is not the only one who has such problems. While teenagers, to be sure, often complain about their parents, this should not be seen simply as a "gripe session." Tiffany's parents are ill, and the sharing of this information, like the sharing of incidents of domestic violence, of violence in a personal relationship, represents one step toward acknowledging the problem and obtaining long-term help. When Doris meets with girls outside the group, in a more confidential context, she frequently wages them to seek additional help.

Distancing

Able to bare secrets, young women use the space of the program to fashion and re-fashion individual and collective identities. Under Doris's expert guidance, it is a space within which selves are tried on, experimented with, accepted or rejected. A key piece of this identity work among participants involves distancing self from those perceived as "not like us." In this space, in this time, they pull away from others. Unlike previous work, however, which suggests that this form of identity work in urban schools takes place largely along we/they racial lines (Fine, Weis, and Powell, 1997; Weis, 1990; Fine and Weis, 1998; Bertram et al., 2000), particularly among working class whites, and most particularly boys and men, the particular form this distancing work takes here is that of distancing from other neighborhood youth, and, more broadly, from other girls/women thought to be heading down the wrong path. Virtually all of the girls, irrespective of race/ethnicity, who attend the sessions use the space to distance themselves explicitly from those they perceive to be "other" than themselves; those who will not make it, those who will end up pregnant at an early age, those who will be beaten at the hands of men. This is not an idyllic presentation of cross-race interactions and friendships, but rather reflects the observation that when "difference" is constructed in group, it is not constructed along racial lines. Girls from all communities articulate carefully that they wish to be different from those in their neighborhoods, those whom they leave behind in their pursuit of schooling and success. Though this may not translate into intimate friendships across racial/ethnic lines, it does mean that the racial Other is not constructed as the "fall guy" for any of the groups under consideration, contrasting sharply with Julia Marusza's data on girls in a white lower-class community center (2000). For none of the groups under consideration are the racial borders specifically erected against which one's own identity is then elaborated. Rather, identity is elaborated across racial and ethnic groups as girls distance self from the Other whether male or female, who will not make it. Certainly there is much racial identity work going on in other sites that reaffirms whiteness, for example, in opposition to blackness, much as previous work suggests (Bertram et al., 1998; Weis, Proweller and Centrie, 1997). However, in this site alternative positionalities are developed.

Witness Connie and Ayisha, Connie, a white girl of modest means who lives in one of the racial borderlands of Buffalo, a place which is formerly Italian but now largely Puerto Rican and African American. Although Connie draws an Other, this Other is racially like self:

We live in a really small house. I don't have the things my friends have, like all of them at this school are having big graduation parties; I asked my mom to get some small invitations from Party City so that we could at least have the family over; she hasn't even done that. I guess I won't have any celebration. All my friends are having these really big parties. They all have much more money than we do. We live in a really small house; I have a really small bedroom. My one sister lives with us with [her] two kids; another sister lives in a house owned by my father on Fourteenth Street. All my sisters are on welfare. We have been on welfare when my father wasn't driving truck. When he lost his job, we didn't even have food in the house. I would go over to my boyfriend's house to eat. His parents are real nice to me. I have no friends in the neighborhood. All I know is that I don't want to be like my sisters and my mother. Their lives have gone nowhere. I don't want to be like them. I want to have lots of money—and food. I want to go to college [she is currently attending the community college]. . . . My dad is an alcoholic. He drinks all the time. One time he grabbed my mom's face and held it really hard. He really gets out of control when he drinks. I don't let him put me down, though—I just tell him off.

Connie spends much time in the group discussing her own emotional/physical distancing from her alcoholic father, her immediate family, and neighborhood. The group offers a "safe space" in which she can air these problems and receive support for remaining emotionally separate from her family, for not being dragged down. At the moment, her boyfriend also offers this "safe space." He is twenty-three; they have known each other three years and are engaged. Because of Connie's father's alcoholism group members are concerned that Connie may fall into a pattern of drinking. Doris and the other group members also check to make certain that Arturo (Connie's boyfriend) is not abusing her physically; they generally are supportive of the relationship, however. Unlike other white girls and women whom we have interviewed extensively, Connie and other group members talk relatively freely about family histories of alcoholism and physical and/or sexual abuse, thus engaging in a language through which one's own and others' circumstances can be understood. In putting this language on the table, they bury such histories far less often than previous research suggests (Weis, Fine, et al., 1998). Additionally, in breaking the silence about alcoholism, welfare, and/or violence in the white family, they shatter the myth that the white family has no problems, thereby encouraging young women across race/ethnicity to understand that such problems are indeed shared, as well as helping young women to face their own situations.

Ayisha, an African American woman of sixteen who has a one-year-old daughter, also sees her task as one of distancing herself from the neighborhood in which she grew up. This distancing is nuanced, however, since she is entirely dependent on her family, boyfriend, and her boyfriend's family in order to raise her daughter. She walks a fine line—distancing from those who will hold her back, but simultaneously recognizing and respecting those who help her move forward. All live in the same neighborhood.

> Actually there is a small percent who are going to do something with their lives. I hate to see 'em like that, but it's like they're all going to go off, smoke weed and drink, go to parties, and hang around the fellows. You know, my mother always told me, "it's not ladylike to sit there and drink on the corner." It's just . . . I mean, they just don't care about their body. It's terrible to see. And I'll be trying to say, you know, I have some friends and they go do that. And I'll be like "You all shouldn't do that." "Well, just because you don't do it. . . ." "OK. Whatever. Whatever you decide to do, I'm behind you. If that's what you're doing, OK, that's what you're going to do." But they're always calling me a preacher or something, you know, every time I try to talk to them.

Many of these young women, particularly the African Americans, are very much connected to their families and neighborhoods, passionately caring about what happens in their communities, while at the same time drawing discursive boundaries around themselves which enable them to go to school and stay on the right track. They engage the Other constantly, telling them that they are going down the wrong path, while at the same time setting them up as radically different from themselves.

This work of othering is done similarly across race and ethnic lines in the group, thus rewriting dominant race scripts of difference in poor areas (Fine and Weis, 1998) at one and the same time as they sculpt alternative forms of femininity/womanhood. All are concerned with elaborating a positive present and future for themselves and see themselves in relation to community Others; those who do drugs, drink to excess, wear tight clothes, sleep with a lot of guys, walk the streets, don't take school seriously, see older men. The group provides an arena for dialogue, a space within which these constructions get worked through, between, and among participants. Witness, for example, the eighth-grade group below.

An Eighth Grade Group

> Lois: OK, talk to me about the women in your community.
> Krista: About 10:20 they come out. [laughter]
> Danielle: Just about every girl, like, on my street, had babies when they were about fourteen, fifteen . . .
> Krista: And I know this one girl, she doesn't live on my street anymore, but she had a baby when she was like fourteen or fifteen, and she went back to the same guy and got pregnant again, so now she's got two kids. And I don't know a lot like that. But I know her, because I think she used to baby-sit me when I was little, but I don't know if he's there and will come back to her, you know, better and everything. But she got pregnant again.

LOIS: What about some of the other women?

SHANTELLE: Well, some of them is fast. They talk to the boys on the corner. All boys on the corner is not bad. They wear a lot of showy clothes.

TONIKA: I was watching Jenny Jones, this twelve-year-old girl, she wore so much make up, she acts like she's about twenty-three. And the makeup and stuff. All these girls had these shirts like this [indicates very short], their chest sticking out. I mean, all these short shorts, look like underwear.

TISH: My underwear is not going to be that short.

TONKA: I mean, they're wondering why they'd be getting raped and stuff, even though it's [rape] wrong, but if you walk out of there with your chest sticking out in some short shorts, which is what they do, it's kind of like, what kind of attention you're going to get? You think you're going to get positive attention, you know?

SHANTELLE: OK. A lot of girls like have babies around my neighborhood. They don't have an education, so like they are kind of, they're low educated, ain't got no money, broken-down house and everything, and they're talking to the people in the weed house and everything.

GLORIA: The girls around my neighborhood, they all 'Hos'. And they wear nasty outfits, and they go out with older guys.

DELORES: They [older guys] just be using, they use you, and they have like three other girlfriends, and they try to play it off. When they get caught, they'd be trying to like, well, you shouldn't have been doing all this, and all that stuff. And they [the girls] can't do nothing about it.

The eighth-grade group, most of whom are African American at this particular session, use the space to talk about other girls and women in the neighborhood, carefully distancing themselves from them, and asserting that they are different. By publicly solidifying the boundaries of good behavior, they hope to hang together and remain without problems.

This actual (and potential) discursive work takes place across racial and ethnic groups. The fall guy is not a constructed racial other, as is so common in urban (and suburban; see Kress, 1997) schools, but rather those neighborhood youth who are perceived to be headed down the wrong path. In the case of young women, it is those other girls and women, those who are fast, wild, wear tight clothes, who enact femininity and sexuality differently from the ways they feel are appropriate and safe, who provide the primary Other against which their own individual and emerging collective self is created. Though this may seem to mirror the good girl/bad girl distinction so deeply etched in male culture, and indeed it does in some ways, the fact is that these young women are working cross-racially to live productive lives, lives that enable choices to be made and that are free from abuse. The eighth-graders know that the "older guys just be using them [these other girls]"; they have "three other girlfriends, and they try to play it off." When the guys are caught, they blame the young women for doing something wrong—"You shouldn't have been doing this and that." These thirteen-year-old girls understand this full well and use the group to talk about it. It is exactly this situation which they are trying to avoid, and they know that things only get worse as women grow older. They want to stay in school in order to assert some control over their lives, enabling them to make choices regarding sexuality, men, marriage, and a future devoid of physical and sexual abuse and harassment. Though the officially stated goal of My Bottom Line is to encourage abstinence, clearly much more is happening in this context; it can be argued that young women are weaving a form of collective strength that goes beyond individual abstinence—they are gaining a set of lenses through which to do social critique and opening up the possibility of cross-race political work in the future.

It is most interesting in this regard that although "race work" is not in the official curriculum of this project, it is done all the time. The distancing discussed above, which is a by-product of "baring secrets," encourages a form of gender collectivity that works across traditionally antagonistic race lines. Abstinence work, on the other hand, which is the official curriculum, is done some of the time, raising interesting questions as to what constitutes the lived curriculum as opposed to the intended curriculum of this or any other project. Curriculum theorists (Cornbleth, 1990; McNeil, 1986; Apple, 1982) have, of course, alerted us to the fact that what is distributed as curriculum in actual classrooms bears, at times, little resemblance to what is seen as the legitimate curriculum (that which is written). The same dynamic is at play here. Doris intentionally stretches what is presented to these teen women as she moves well beyond notions of abstinence in her own understanding of what these young women need. The girls, too, stretch the project in that they interact with what is presented and create something new, in this case, a girls collectivity that works across race lines. By baring their secrets, they create a community, at least in this space at this time, which transcends individual racial and even social-class identities. It is the dialectic of lived curriculum creation which is so noteworthy in this particular context—the context of teaching about abstinence. We will see this even more clearly in the next section.

In a contradictory way, of course, these young women, while struggling for their own future health and safety, are positioning themselves as different from "like Others" in their communities of origin, thus cutting themselves off potentially from what Robinson and Ward (1991) refer to as group-based "resistance for liberation." At the moment, though, any potential future psychic pain involved in this move and possible inability to do future political work around categories of community of origin cannot be acknowledged. Indeed, it can be argued that these young women must engage in such a move, even if only temporary, in order to save themselves from what they fear is their fate. The moment of disruption chronicled here is not, though, without its own contradictions.

Contesting Social Stereotypes

Spaces such as this can offer places where trite social stereotypes are contested; where individuals and collectivities challenge definitions and constructions perpetuated through media, popular culture, and so forth. This is highly evident in this group, in that the girls use the space, under the guidance of Doris, to challenge hegemonic constructions of femininity and race. Doris's role here is important. She urges these young women not to accept prevailing constructions of femininity and masculinity, and to challenge race and gender scripts directly.

February 10, 1997 (Field Notes)

> Doris and I [Lois] were waiting for the girls to come in for group. Just then Tia walked in for the fifth-period meeting. Tia talked about her former boyfriend, who got a thirteen-year-old girl pregnant and "now it is too late to do anything about it since it is her fourth month." The girl lives two doors down from her. Her mother's best friend is the mother of the young man involved, and that is how she found out. They had broken up already because she [Tia] had no time to see him, with school and working at Wegmans, but she still cares for him. The boy, as it turns out, is nineteen. Tia can't even look at the girl. She considers her a "slut." She forgives the boy, because "she made him do it," but not the girl.
>
> DORIS: "What do you mean you forgive the boy but not the girl?"
> TIA: "But she made him do it!"
> Doris: "She made him put his penis into her vagina? He had nothing to do with it at all?"

Tia admitted that he had something to do with it, finally, but she still hates the girl because she is a "slut." Since the baby will live only two doors from her, she will see the baby a lot, and she is angry about that. "How is she going to take care of a baby at only thirteen? She is a slut."

Working off of prevailing understandings that boys are not responsible for their sexual activity because they are hormonally programmed to want sex, unlike girls, whose job it is, therefore, to make sure that boys do not get aroused, Tia's response mirrors notions of sexuality and gender circulating in the broader society and available, as Fine (1988) and Whatley (1991) note, in sexuality curriculum. These understandings have it that if girls get in trouble, it is their fault, since they have the responsibility of ensuring that boys are not enticed by sex. This positions women as sexual victims of hormonally programmed males. Under this formulation, the only subject position for females is when they keep men from being aroused. Doris intentionally interrupts this set of understandings by posing the question, "She made him put his penis into her vagina? He had nothing to do with it at all?" Though it is not clear that Tia accepts the validity of Doris's disruptive practice, Doris's continual challenges are not without consequence in the group.

Below, Doris guides the girls into specifically gendered understandings, offering them space to challenge deeply rooted notions.

April 22, 1997; Eighth-Grade Group

DORIS: Is it good to be friends before having a boyfriend/girlfriend relationship?

DELORES: I think you should be friends first, then if it don't work out, you can still be friends.

AYISHA: That don't work.

PATRICE: I hate it when you make friends with a boy and then he doesn't want to take you out because he think you like a little sister.

TONIKA: I hate it, most of the guys are taken, conceited, or gay. [All laugh.]

DORIS: [TO THE GROUP] How old are you? [She already knows how old they are.]

RESPONSE: Thirteen, thirteen, thirteen.

DORIS: Don't you have a long way to go?

TONIKA: No.

AYISHA: This one guy likes me. Everywhere I go he right there. When I go to my friend Phalla's, he right there.

DORIS: Why is that a problem?

AYISHA: Cuz I don't like him. I don't want him to be around me.

DORIS: Is this a form of sexual harassment? We walk down the street and someone calls after us. Don't we want real romance? You meet and fall in love?

TISH: But then you find out he's married.

PATRICE: He's married and he's got a girlfriend.

DELORES: He's married, got a girlfriend and got kids by both of them.

DORIS: What do we do when someone is in an unhealthy relationship?

TISH: Try to help them out.

PATRICE: Get a restraining order.

TONIKA: Talk about violence! When my mom was pregnant, her boyfriend hit her.

PATRICE: My mom got beat up, then she left.

DORIS: Well, we all know that relationships are bad if there is physical abuse.

Doris offers, in the above, the language of sexual harassment and makes certain that the girls understand that violence in relationships should not be tolerated. While these are obviously complicated issues and suggest no easy solutions, it is key that these discussions are taking place in a public school, under the guidance of a trained adult, who is suggesting that women need to develop their own power in relationships and not passively accept notions that whatever happens to them is their fault. She is, through the group, encouraging the girls to reconstruct what it means to be a woman/girl, working against the grain, offering an alternative voice to the deafening victim mentality. Helping the girls establish their bottom line— a bottom line that recognizes that women ought not be victims—comes through loud and clear in the group interactions.

Situated in the middle of a public school, young women traverse a variety of subjects regarding race, gender, sexuality, and men. Moving through these issues, under the watchful and caring eye of Doris Carbonell-Medina, young women begin to form a new collective—a collective that surges, at least for the moment, across race and is based on a woman/girl who is different from those left behind emotionally in the neighborhood. We now move to our second instance of "disruptive practice"—this one in a ninth-grade detracked social studies class in Montclair, New Jersey.

Creating an Intellectual and Ethical Community
across Borders

With texts, students, anxieties, memories, colleagues, budget crises, faculty cuts, and wild anticipation, the year opens. It's September in a public school, ninth grade. Students bend the spines of new books, launch new lives, try novel identities, and sneak toward new relationships. Their fourteen- and fifteen-year-old bodies are filled with delight, dread, hormones, excitement, premature boredom. For some, the room is filled with friends. For all, the room is also filled with strangers. The room doesn't look like my other classes. Not everybody looks like me. Everyone's in the room, and the teacher thinks that's a good thing. What am I in for? These data are drawn from a two-year ethnography of a world literature class, detracked and racially integrated, studied by Michelle Fine (see Fine, Weis, and Powell, 1997), in a racially integrated high school of approximately fifteen hundred youth, just over 50 percent African American and over 40 percent white, ranging in social class from well under the poverty line to extremely wealthy.

The teachers open the year with Name Pieces, an invitation to revisit the origins, the histories, and the herstories of student names. And so we hear, from a young man I [Michelle] had written off as disengaged.

> My real name is Carlos, but my mother calls me John. She says John means "son of kings." But I know it means a man who hangs out with prostitutes or a toilet. And even though God loves men who pay for prostitutes, and prostitutes, I wish she would call me Carlos.

Next we discuss *Of Mice and Men*, in particular George and Lennie's relationship at the end of the book. Carlton Jordan, teacher, asks his students to form what he calls a value line: "Stand on my right if you think it was right for George to kill Lennie. Stand on my left if you don't. Stand in the middle if you are of both minds."

Much to my surprise (and dismay?), the room tips to the right. The crowd moves in those loud clumsy teenage feet over toward the "it's okay to kill" side. I look for patterns by gender, race. Nothing. To the left wander three boys, a bit surprised and embarrassed, two white and one black, feeling like they are going to lose. "But it's never okay to kill a friend," insists Joshua.

Carlton, momentarily stunned but never stumped by his "pedagogical failure" to get equally distributed groups, undermining his "plan" to set up pairs to discuss their positions, invites them to sit in common position groups and discuss whether or not George should appeal.

The "it's okay to kill a friend" group gets loud, committed, animated, vile. "Lennie's stupid." "He's the biggest retard in the world. He likes to pet dead rabbits. He don't need to live," shouts Kizzy—Muslim, brass, wonderful, noisy, always the voice that provokes Darren, an African American boy, to respond with emotion. Sofia continues, "He should have killed Lennie long ago; he's a burden." Kizzy continues: "He's stupid. He murdered cold-blooded. We got to make him bad if we're gonna get George off." Eli joins, "By killing him, it was like saving a life."

Carlton and I exchange glances. I'm thrown by the raw but vicious analyses of these young adolescents and their endless creativity. The screams of "stupid, useless, dumb" are rusting my soul.

Carlton is as visibly shaken as I am. A strong, bold African American educator, he begins to teach, to preach, to speak with his heart, his eyes, his arms, and his mouth. "Let me say something about Lennie, because, as I walk around, I am disturbed. What are the characteristics of Lennie?"

The class volunteers: "Stupid, slow, dumb!"

Carlton continues. "Dumb. Retarded. When you use language like that, I have to speak. You may say it was right for George to kill Lennie because Lennie killed someone else or Lennie would have been killed. There are many reasons. But because [he] is stupid, slow, no. Some of you have learning disabilities. Some of you have persons with autism or retardation in your family. And none of us knows what's coming next. It is important to see Lennie as a man, as a human being, not as something that should be destroyed."

Kizzy: "But he stupid. You are coming down on our group."

My mind wanders. Remembering the calls [from some white parents] to the superintendent about "them," remembering talk at the school board about how "those students" will hold back "the motivated ones," I am brought back to the room by Carlton's voice. "Some of you have been called stupid by others. You have to think about what it's like to be in a world where everyone seems to be getting it right, and you don't even know what you don't know. Some of you sit in lunch room and won't eat tuna sandwiches because you're going to save the baby whale, but you'd laugh at Lennie in our school. Some of you will send money to Rwanda and Bosnia to save children over there. But you would make fun of Lennie, throw stones or shun Lennie over here." The students have reproduced the discourse being narrated about them. "George should not be burdened by Lennie." That is just what some at the school board meeting were implying.

Carlton: "Let me say, I take this personally. If you can't walk with Lennie, if you can't see Lennie as a human, as a brother, what future is there for our community? What possibilities are there for us as a whole?"

Class is over. I'm feeling exhausted and depleted, and amazed at the strength of a teacher willing to speak, interrupt, listen, and educate. After a weekend of worries and exchanged phone messages with Carlton, I returned to class on Monday to refind "community," orchestrated by Carlton, already at play.

The lecture opens with a discussion of first-person and third-person narratives. Carlton asks students to "turn to a page of *Of Mice and Men* where George and Lennie are interacting. I want you to rewrite the passage as Lennie. In first-person narrative. To see how Lennie's wheels turn."

"What wheels?" snipes Paul.

The students clip through the text, muttering, but writing eagerly. Carlton waits patiently for volunteers. Hands shoot up. "I am just a happy man, likin' my rabbits." "Why George callin' me a stupid so and so." Hands of all hues fill the air. The room is alive with Lennies.

"How do you feel?" asks Carlton. "Stupid?" The point was made. Carlton was crafting a community not yet owned by students, but the students were growing extensions with which to connect in the room and beyond.

A parallel exchange occurs in Dana's classroom, early in October. Note how powerfully the character of George is relentlessly protected by the students, while Lennie is ruthlessly discarded as if disposable.

CHARLES: George is trying and Lennie is holding him back.

ERIKA: Lennie died happily. George did what he had to do. He gave a final request about rabbits. It's not right to kill, though.

ANGELA: Whether it was right or wrong, George was the one who had to sacrifice. It was a judgment call. He'd be lonely without Lennie.

DANA: Anyone want to respond?

DENNIS: It was a sacrifice. He was sad. Steinbeck tried to make it like he was sad.

MIKEL: Maybe he had a bit of remorse because he hesitated, remember? But he thought it was the only decision he could make. They did try to escape.

[Dana comments on their desire to protect George, render him a victim. Lennie is somehow deservedly dispensed with; George is seen as the victim.]

BEN: It's not George's fault.

DANA: Why not?

BEN: If he had known what Lennie was thinking, maybe. But George is off the hook.

DANA: Who is solely responsible for ending the life of Lennie?

ANGELA: I still feel exactly the way I did before what you said. Lennie couldn't live. . . .

SHANA: It was a hidden message. When George shot Lennie, it was his way of setting him free.

DANA: Was it fair for Lennie?

SHANA: George wanted Lennie to die. It's not fair for Lennie. Maybe George, in the back of his mind, Lennie was such a burden.

SHANA: Proof he was a burden because George said, "I could do all this stuff, without Lennie."

MIKEL: I'm not sure, Curley was going to do something. George protected himself.

LIZA: Lennie is a nothing. He's a *sausage*!

DANA: Is it hard to hang out from Lennie's point of view?

STUDENT: Lennie isn't given a point of view in the book.

[Dana and Carlton insist, but don't yet prevail. The students in September and October refuse to view social relations from the bottom.]

Across the five classes echoes a ringing, shared, often painfully victim-blaming consensus, in September and October, in which most *who speak* agree that Lennie is a "loser," a "leech," a "sausage," and that social relations are inherently and fundamentally hierarchical, competitive, and back-biting. These are the Reagan-Bush and now Clinton babies of the '90s. These are the children who have been raised on policies that are anti-immigrant, antiwelfare, anti–public sector, pro–death penalty, anti–affirmative action, "national/maternal" ideological milk. And they swallowed. If I were only to report on what I heard from September through November, the right could relax. These adolescent youths have been well trained by a nation armed with victim-blaming rhetoric. . . . In the beginning of the year, though there are pockets of silence and some raised eyebrows, moments of, "Wait a minute . . ." we hear mostly that "murder and crime can keep the population down," that George was "entitled" and Lennie "dispensable." And so, too, we witness fatigued teachers, still standing in the front of the room, trying to create a space in which could enter a view from the bottom, a moment of empathy, a peek from another angle, a reanalysis of youth's assumptions.

Having finished *Of Mice and Men*, Dana's class has moved on to *Two Old Women* by Velma Wallis, a Native American woman from Alaska who retells a story told to her by her mother. The story tells the tale of two old women left to die, abandoned by their community.

DANA: In the book *Two Old Women*, where two Alaskan women are left to die by their tribes, should the two old women have forgiven the tribe?

BEN: Maybe they should. It was their time to go. It was their survival.

DANA: I heard that for George [protection of the powerful].

MICHAEL: I don't think they should forgive because they weren't helpless or lame. Just old. It wasn't right. They shouldn't forgive.

ANGELA: I was raised to believe old are wiser and keep heritage alive. From old you get new experiences, but young have little to offer. Even though they were old they were strongest in the book. Like Lennie.

BEN: If they didn't forgive, they couldn't last long. If we saved all old, we'd be overpopulated. Murder and crime may keep this earth's population in balance.

DANA: Do we bear *no responsibility* in the taking care of?

In the beginning of the school year, there are typically few who will publicly annotate a perspective from the bottom. And yet, by November students like Michael [black boy] and Angela [white girl] are beginning to chance another point of view, beginning to notice that something is different. Their teacher is not simply a carrier of dominant views, reinforcing only the view from above. Dana and Carlton are offering many lines of vision and insisting that when challenging whispers are voiced, usually late in a class, quietly, in an embarrassed "Please don't read this out loud" paper in an after-school private meeting—that they get a hearing.

It is toward the end of this season of victim-blaming chill, when parental calls to the superintendent start to come in, demanding to know why Candace didn't get an A on the first draft, why Dana is "bending over backward for *some* students," why Carlton is having "political" and not "literary" discussions. These are the days when "everyone has a choice" is declared as truth by some students, when victims are blamed and those who challenge social arrangements grow suspect. Students and teachers alike. But work is yet to be done. And at this point in the class, all students suspect that something is up. The dominant conversation prevails, but on its last legs for the year. A new moon is rising.

December through February: The Melting, and Then Partial Restoration, of Privilege

Creating a safe space for all means breaking down the invisible walls that segregate those historically privileged from those historically silenced; that separate traditionally "smart" from traditionally "slow"; that challenge the categories and "right" answers that fit so well in the past. Forcing students to "come out" from behind their performances of nerd, athlete, scholar, quiet, clown, or dummy, these educators invite them to reveal their deeper, more complex selves. They venture well beyond the borders of intellectual and political work, modeling, chancing, and pushing the very categories usually taken for granted, categories that have elevated some (smart?) while stunting others ("at risk").

By December, it is clear that the teachers invest in what might be called standpoint theory, an understanding that people think, feel, see, express, resist, comply, and are silent in accordance with their social power and that a view from the "bottom" may diverge dramatically, critically, and brilliantly from a view from the "top." But a view from the bottom may be as "smart."

Discussion in small groups: What are the experiences you have that told you/taught you "your place"?

CRIS: [Black boy] Mr. G. [former principal] told me I am a shitball and would never develop into nothing.

DEL: [Black girl] I got kicked out of graduation dinner dance. I was mad and depressed. I just got out of the hospital.

CARY: [White boy] Me and my friends couldn't see an R movie. We were kicked out cause of age.

ELI: [White boy] I can't think of one.

NASHAMA: [Black girl] You don't expect racist comments, like from white friends, so you don't know what to say.

Even if a view from the "top" has been the standard, accepted as "best," assured an A+ to date, those standards, oddly, no longer operate. Equally rigorous new standards emerge. We turn now to a discussion of the book *Nectar in a Sieve*, an analysis of dharma, fate, and hope, to notice the early awkward stages of trying to get *all* voices heard.

SERI: [Mixed-race boy] People *live* based on hope.

ALISON: [White girl] I think that's *sad*. If it's just based on hope, you need to study.

PAM: [White Girl] You need not just *hope* but *goals*.

CECIL: [Black boy] My *hopes* are to do the best that I can, be a musician and NBA player.

DANIELLE: I think it's true. Everybody has *one dream* and they have to accomplish the dream.

CARLTON: What keeps you in school?

CHRIS: [White boy] I think about school, it's the future. College and further, career, family, and support.

JAMES: [White boy] *Work hard*.

SARA: [White girl] My *goals* are based on education, not McDonald's.

CECIL: I would rather have McDonald's.

SARA: I don't want to *depend* on a husband or taxpayers or my parents.

ALISON: Most people only have *hope*. That's sad.

KAREEM: [Black boy] Animals don't have hope, only people. Animals have instinct.

MICHELLE FINE: (Field notes) It's polarizing: Blacks defend hope and Whites defend ambition/goals as if hope were silly, as if this dichotomy made sense!

CARLTON: Are people different from animals?

URI: Some animal types that have leaders hope to be the leader in the pack.

HANNAH: [White girl] Lennie doesn't know what hope means but he hopes to be as smart as George.

QWUINETTE: [Black girl] He does have hope.

ALISON: Maybe ignorant people have more hope and smarter people are more cynical.

CECIL: You've got to be kidding!

Cecil carries the momentum here. The room spirals, the conversation stops and then begins again, changed. These critical turns, upon which our pedagogy relies, are as necessary as they are unpredictable. We yearn to understand how we can nurture, cultivate, fertilize our rooms so that critical turns get a voice and eventually get a hearing.

At this point, "smarts" are popping out of unsuspected mouths, bodies buried in oversized jackets. At the same time, perhaps in response, there is a parallel move, a polarizing performance. So, for instance, blacks defend hope and whites defend ambitions, goals as though these were separable. As previously unheard voices sing, there is a subtle polarizing, a freezing of positions. Now that the voices are up, there is nothing automatic about creating a community of differences in this space.

It's becoming clear that student identities ranging from "smart" to "disengaged" to "at-risk" are unraveling—not so predictable. In integrated schools, as Du Bois worried, sorting (Bowles and Gintis, 1976; Ryan, 1981) takes a particularly perverse form. Some students, usually white and/or middle-class students in an integrated school, rise like cream to the top. They blossom as institutional signifiers of merit, smarts, advanced achievement. It is their loss most profoundly dreaded by public education. Today urban and suburban school boards live in terror of losing whites and middle-class students across races and do all they can to keep them, even if that means holding other students hostage (Kohn; Sapon-Shevin). And yet this categorical elevation is, as Eve Sedgwick (1992) would argue, not absolute. It is fundamentally relativistic, parasitic. It *requires* that others (blacks, working class/poor, disabled students) are seen as Not, Lacking. Funneled through a lens of hierarchy and limited goods, standards, achievements, and excellence demand exclusivity. But, in this class, the metric for status enables excellence from otherwise marked bodies.

As new voices emerge, mostly heretofore unheard black voices, a kind of polarizing occurs. Again a small group of white students may decide to sit together, to reinforce each other's points, synchronize eye rolls when a student of color speaks. In ironic similarity to the oft-repeated, "Why do all the black students sit together?" at this point in the semester, there is a consolidation of a white-resistant position—not all, just a few—but enough to chill the room. The days of listening to "them" are over. It's important to note that most white and most black students don't glacialize. But most are at a loss for how to engage this conversation outside the polarities. In February, Chante [black girl] talks to me about this problem.

CHANTE: Our teacher don't care 'bout the groups, just look at the class. They're all sittin', I'm not gonna say, but just look. At least, when Ms. Little made the groups mixed, we talked to each other, one black boy, one white boy, one black girl, one white girl, and we say how we feel. Now, they all sittin' together and scared to talk to us, scared we're gonna yell at them, so they just talk to themselves.

ERICA: When Devon [black boy] was talkin', and Eli [white boy] jumped on him, we all talked but the bell rang and then the conversation went back to the book. But we can't talk about the books until we finish that conversation.

I have a frightening thought: Is it possible that whites work "optimally," that is, uninterrupted, when we *don't* have to discuss race and ethnicity and that students of color can be engaged and most unburdened only when race and ethnicity are squarely on the table?

Returning to the dynamics of Linda Powell's Achievement Knot (1997), it seems likely that students of color are "stuck" until "race" is discussed, while white students are "stuck" once race is discussed. Then the teacher (or black students) get blamed for dwelling on race—again! And a few outspoken white parents "save" the white students (through phone calls) from the conversation. This is not simply about "race," it's about what constitutes good and responsible education in a pluralistic society.

By January, midterm grades are in and the old stratification system is not layered like it used to be, no longer a two-tiered white-and-black cake. Carlton and Dana have been reading aloud to the class some of the writings of students who sound like poets, like journalists, like creative writers. Sometimes a white kid raises an embarrassed hand when Carlton asks, "Whose paper is this?" As often an African American boy from the back of the room will lift a reluctant finger, or an African American girl will hide her giggle as she sachays up to the front of the room to reclaim her text. This moment is one of both racialized melting and desperate consolidation of racial privilege—a tight moment of entrenched contrast sails through a room. The stakes are growing clear, and the educators are riding broncos of resistance. This is a crucial moment in an integrated space, one in which many give up. But not these educators.

At this point, a small number of relatively well-off white students (not all, but a few in particular and in full voice) search to reclaim status by displaying their family treasures, what Pierre Bourdieu would call cultural capital. "My mother is a literary agent, and she said *Two Old Women* never would have been published if the author wasn't a Native woman." "Have you read any of Sigmund Freud? My father is a psychoanalyst, and he would contest your interpretation." "My mother is the chair of the board of_____, and she said that Newark is lucky that outsiders have invested money because there was *nothing* there before." Some, at this point, less decorated with biographic merit badges, simply assert, "Today, in this coun-

try, we *all* have choices." Oppression and history are deemed largely irrelevant. A few gracefully sneer or turn away when students of color talk
about race (not again!). I [Michelle] time the conversations that address
race: The average conversation lasts thirty seconds. The record conversation lasted forty-five seconds before someone shifted to "But I don't think
it's race, it's class." "It's age." "What about Whites in basketball?" "What
about sexism?" "How about when you say faggot?" "But the Holocaust
was. . . . ." And we're off. . . .

Old lines are being redrawn, gentrification in academic blood. A sharp-
ened white line of demarcation is being drawn. Interestingly, most white
students refuse to employ these displays or barricade themselves but don't
know what else to do. They can't yet invent another discourse of whiteness. And so they retreat to a kind of silence, sometimes wonder, sometimes embarrassment. A few seem delighted that those who have always
"won"—from prekindergarten to eighth grade—are not the automatic vic-
tors in this class. Like a fight in a hockey game, it is part of the work—not
an interruption and not a failure. Re-vision. There is more to learn on the
other end of this struggle.

March through April:
Playing with Power, Shifting, and Reversals

It's been a long stretch but some of those students who never expected to
be seen as smart, never expected to get a hearing from teachers or peers,
are now opening their mouths, challenging myths and stereotypes and
lines of vision from the top represented as if "natural" or, even worse,
inherently correct. And getting a hearing. There is a long conversation
about the story *La Llorana*, by Rudolpho Anaya, a literary giant of a text in
which the story of Cortes and Malintzin, the conquest of Mexico, unfolds
with the final scene, in which Cortes is invited to return to his homeland,
Spain. Cortes insists upon taking his sons to Spain, lest they become "savages" and "uncivilized." Malintzin, their mother, a native unwilling (and
uninvited) to go to Spain kills the boys in a belief that after their deaths,
their spirits will liberate the people of Mexico. Dana has invited the students to prepare a mock trial of Malintzin.

"Is she guilty for having killed her children?" The pros and cons polar-
ize almost immediately. White students form a chorus, "You should never
kill your children." "She must have been crazy." Most African American
students circle around another question: "What do you do to survive
oppression?" Four black boys refuse to take sides, "You never kill, *and* it
was a time of incredible oppression." And then Aziz, an African American
boy, breaks the stalemate, reversing the power and insisting that the trial of
Malintzin is itself contained within colonialism. He queries, "Why is Malintzin on trial? Why isn't the Captain [Cortes] on trial?" At once the air
thins, the fog lifts, the fists of power are sitting in the center of the room.

The debate is not about Malintzin's innocence or guilt, the debate surrounds the question of who decides what is the crime, colonialism of a race or murder of two.

Now, three-quarters through the term, questions of power are engaged (and enraged), often by an African American male like Aziz, even more often by an African American female who may press so hard that the white students back off *and* the African American boys move to censure her. Back to another class on *Two Old Women*.

DANA: What's wrong with giving up pride?

PAT: [white girl] It makes me feel lower. Not better.

MANDY: [white girl] It's shocking to realize maybe they're better than me.

DANA: It's really based on a hierarchy? Do we define ourselves hierarchically in relation to others? What if it's [social relations] not a triangle [draws on the board] but a flat line [draws]?

MANDY: Then it still goes zero to ten.

DANA: [Looking horrified] What if it's a circle [draws circle]?

COLETTE: [white girl] I'm on top of the circle.

LAMAR: [black boy] In the center!

SERGE: [black boy] It's like heliocentric versus geocentric. Older ways saw the sun rotating around the earth, but really we're not the center. You're not the center.

NIA: [black girl] If you're not the center, you're right next to it.

DANA: It has to do with who we value and why. What if I said there is no such thing as better, less-than or equal? We made that up. We made up that conversation. It's a lie.

JOANNA: [white girl] We were taught *all* our life to be the best.

NEFRETITI: [black girl] Not everyone.

MF: *Here's the challenge.*

JOANNA: *Everyone* wants an A in school.

SERGE: It's how *a lot of people* see things. Superiority complex.

SHARON: [black girl] I have to disagree with Joanna. Not everyone is taught to be all you can be. Some are raised to grow up and try as hard as you can. Most parents don't talk to kids about getting an A. Half the time parents don't care.

NINA: [white girl] *Everyone* is taught being the best even though no one taught us. It's there. Everybody gets it. And then there are those who acknowledge they are not going to be the best, but they know everybody thinks they should be.

DANA: Is a triangle really the structure of the school? How is it arranged?

CARL: [white boy] In groups, in classes, outside of school, popular and not so popular and those who couldn't care.

RAVONA: [black girl] I'm not better than anyone else. No one is better than me. Zero to ten, triangle doesn't make sense. The only one who is superior is God. Not everyone is taught to be better. Some parents put their children down. Not everyone is raised in that way; it's good for parents to say to try. Not "you better be on the honor roll or I'm going to beat your behind."

JESS: [black boy] For all the people. You get good grades. My mother expects me to do what I have to do. She wants me, my life, to be better than her life. She doesn't expect me to be better than anyone else. She knows everyone's a pawn in life.

PATRICE: [white girl] My dad says if I get a C, don't come home. *Society and parents say do good* and be better than others.

JOANNA: My parents never pressure me, but I am expected to because my sister did. As a society *everyone wants to be rich, famous,* and we believe we have to be better than everyone else.

MANDY: What Joanna said is true. There is an expectation, you are going to college. You have to be better than everyone else. It's a drill. My parents don't want me on unemployment lines. You have to be better.

SHARON: I have a question for you [two white girls]: How can you be better than someone else?

PAT: They might have tried harder.

SHARON: There's racism out there. Most people have to work hard all the time.

PAT: Like levels of self-esteem. Ones who can go farther than those who say "I can't."

MARY: [White girl] And that's who people want to hear. That makes you better. Everyone is equal but not quite.

DANA: Nobody buys that we are equal? [Fainting] Here are my questions, tonight's homework. What does it mean to be successful? What does it mean to be better than? What does it mean to be a good student? What if these distinctions didn't matter? What if there was no such thing as better, less than, or equal?

The theater is alive. Girls, for the most part, are carrying on the debate about social injustice. Some black girls assert their position in a discourse of power and inequality. In response, some white girls displace a discourse of power with a discourse of psychology, motivation, and equal opportunity. These white girls, trying to be sympathetic and inclusive, offer up universals "everyone . . ." while black girls, equally insistent, draw attention to power, difference, and inequality. Typically an African American girl presses a question of race, class, and gender at once, with the white boys flushed, the white girls scared, and the black boys actively engaged in muzzling her! And yet she stands sturdy, bold, and alone, courageous even without a support in the room. The room coalesces around its desire for her to just stop.

The end of the year is riddled with a series of power eruptions. Sharice has cracked the dominance in the room, and Rose takes up her analysis. The dominant hold is cracking and freeing everyone. Splinters fly.

April through June:
Coalitions, Standpoints, Speaking Truth to Power . . .
Preparing for the "Real World"

This course is messy. Little can be said that is linear, developmental, moving forward in a predictable line. And yet, on our well-toiled intellectual and emotional grounds, with the reading of great literatures, these educators invite young minds to travel. With a pedagogy that encourages multiple readings, they are asked to tackle the perspective of others, to review their perspectives of self. In this context, there are sometimes fleeting and sometimes sustained moments of coming together.

Students agree to stretch, as a collective, to cross borders of race, class, gender, and "difference" and meet each other in a June Jordan poem, mourning for Rukmani, angry at Cortes, reciting what Lennie, in *Of Mice and Men*, might have really been thinking. These moments of coming together are, for us, the hope, the point, the real metaphor for America as it could be. For in these moments of coming together, students and faculty embody their differences in a chorus of voices, in a tapestry of cloth. Very smart and bold, not compromising, not "whiting out" differences, not "not noticing," but standing together, even if for a moment, challenging the separations that we adults—the "other" America—try to impose on them. Coming together to build knowledge, community, and serious intellectual work through and across race, ethnicity, class, and gender.

From April through the end of the term, students engage in this space, for forty-five minutes a day, with power, "difference," and a capacity to re-vision. Some with delight and some still disturbed, but they know that everyone will get a chance to speak and be heard. They will be surprised, still, to learn that "*she* said something so smart" or "*he* plays golf?" By now (finally), it is no longer rare to hear white students refer to, grow a conversation off of, interrupt with praise or even disagree with students of color. Or African American students challenge, extend, or ask a question of a white student. These may sound like minor accomplishments, but in a sea of parallel lives stratified by geography, class, color, friends, language, dress, music, and structures of tracking around them, the moments of working together, not always friendly or easy but engaged across, are worth comment. For these are moments which, once strung together, weave a frayed tapestry of cross-racial/class practice inside and outside of schooling. Students may risk a statement anticipated to get support from peers; they may dare to not support a lifelong ally/neighbor/friend; they may wander into a more treacherous alliance with someone very different, but nine months' worth of interrupting across the room; they may challenge a comment that sounds, on its face, racist or homophobic even if a black person, or a white person, uttered it. They may opt for a coauthored poem, a joint extension project. It is in this moment when, after a protracted conversation about race and power, John, a young man I had "coded" as middle class and black, offered: "These conversations are very hard for me.

I understand both points of view. You all think I'm black, but actually my mom is white, and I could take either position in the room. But I don't talk much because I don't think anyone will catch my back." His eyes fill with tears, as do those of many others in the room. There is a stunning silence. "I just felt confused." At which point from across the room, on the diagonal, arise the sounds of applause, strong, hard, deliberate. Eddie has begun the pulse of clapping that waves across the twenty-four young men and women. This course is transformative, and yet it is a moment. Given the ruthless commitment to tracking students, they are, largely, resegregated in tenth through twelfth years—but there was that moment.

Conclusion

We offer these two scenes, not to argue against reproduction theory, for we are deeply implicated and persuaded by such analyses. But we seek to agitate, at the same time, for analyses that reveal where, under what conditions, and with what effect schools are promoting extraordinary conversations for and by youth. Though critical scholars have spent the past thirty years engaging in important analyses of reproduction (and later resistance in schools), we now extend the room under the umbrella of critical scholarship for a feminist and antiracist responsibility to produce extraordinary educational projects (see Cochran-Smith and Lytle, 1992).

Social reproduction theorists, and we include ourselves here, have been perhaps too glib in overlooking moments of interruption, material and discursive, within deeply reproductive educational settings. In this essay we have taken seriously these buried moments, what Chantal Mouffe (1988) might describe as ripples in an otherwise toxic sea, to try to theorize what it is that youth gain, learn, and teach in these spaces. We offer scholarly respect for educators who dare to carve out such spaces.

These educators, across sites, work with feminist and critical race texts, and strategies, to accomplish a set of common aims. We elaborate these aims and their associated pedagogies in an effort to make explicit the micropolitics of these deeply "disruptive" and responsible pedagogical sites. When we say disruptive, of course, we mean disruptive to reproduction, not necessarily to schools or students. Although it needs to be said that any act designed to disrupt the asymmetric relations embedded in a capitalistic economy and racism will indeed provoke ripples of resistance inside schools, communities, faculties, and indeed the student body. No one should be surprised at such fallout. We challenge institutions and communities to generate more such dissonance within educational sites for youth.

First, across these two sites, these educators work to create spaces of difference, not merely to engage in practices of resistance. They struggle to create what Mary Louise Pratt calls "contact zones . . . social spaces where cultures meet, clash and grapple with each other, often in the context of highly asymmetric relations of power" (1991, 496). They dare to search for the common among differences.

Second, these educators situate, at the center of their intellectual work, crucial questions of power and privilege, standpoint and knowledge, and difference. At once they decenter privilege in the room and in the canon and seek to hear voices of youth whose biographies range broadly (see Hall, 1991).

Third, these educators reframe "private problems" as public issues. In the spirit of C. W. Mills (1959), they make explicit the issues that many youth are grappling with, as though they were normative, including domestic violence, racism, pleasure, surveillance. These issues are posed as intellectual and social concerns, and as potentially shared, not as sources of individual humiliation. By so doing, youth see themselves in a social world, and can review themselves as agents with choices rather than victims swept into a corner of shame with no recourse.

Fourth, these educators work through intersections normally not acknowledged, such as those of race, class, disability (in the New Jersey case), and gender. Thus, all students potentially come to recognize that while they bring situated knowledge from one set of race, class, and gender intersections, other knowledges flood the room. "Organic intellectuals," as Gramsci (1971) has argued, emerge; but so do critical allies from unsuspecting corners.

Fifth, these educators have a complex relation to youth voice. Though they embody Freirian commitments to voice, critique, and liberatory knowledge, these educators also embody a firm standpoint toward community, and social justice that requires listening and reflecting. Indeed, like historian Joan Scott (1992), they understand that "experience" marks the beginning of a conversation, not the end; that "evidence of experience . . . reproduces rather than contests given ideological systems. . . . Experience is, at once always already an interpretation and in need of interpretation" (p. 37). All youth deserve spaces in which they can engage with critical and supportive analysis, involving prodding and facilitating by other youth and adults.

Sixth, these educators work, at one and the same time, on individual development and community building. That is, they presume and educate toward individual growth but also toward a sense of community, interdependence, and collective responsibility. They refuse to engage what Pierre Bourdieu (1998) would call "the return of individualism, a kind of self fulfilling prophecy which tends to destroy the . . . notion of collective responsibility" (p. 7).

These two instances raise questions about the power of disruption. While most educational settings still fail to educate most poor and working-class youth, and while most schools reinforce structurally and discursively class, race, ethnic, gender, and sexuality stratification, we are taken by the power of spaces designed explicitly to interrupt such dynamics. We are impressed, further, by the consequences of such spaces with respect to young people's ability to review critically social arrangements, challenge stereotypes foisted upon them and others, and realign socially and politically with differently situated young adults. We are not so naive as to imagine that a pregnancy prevention of whether length of power conversation is sufficient to disrupt the weight of structural stratification. Nor do we believe that the introduction of a single detracked course, even if mandatory, can derail the sleek and efficient machine of tracking. But we do ask readers to indulge in the possibilities of interruption. We invite theorizing and strategizing about the potential of stringing together sets of disruptive practices and sites, rather than posing simply unilateral assault on what we still know to be deeply reproductive settings.

That is, we maintain our challenge to educational settings as reproductive sites. Further, we recognize the power of some faculty, community members, and young people to resist. We add now that we encourage spaces that radically alter the power relations around and within school. We add to the progressive political agenda, the generation of multiple disruptive sites in which social critique, new alliances, and alternative readings of common sense are available, nurtured, and supported by and among youth, particularly poor, working class youth of varying racial and ethnic backrounds.

As strategies for change move away from democratic public education and onto neo-liberal private support for vouchers and tax benefits for the wealthy, we find it imperative to return our gaze to spaces inside public schools such as those focused upon here and to demand more. Thus, we offer these scenes as we promote a collective analysis of the ways in which schools must dare to interrupt reproduction, must engage young people in conversations of intellect and courage, and dare to educate for critical inquiry and civic participation across lines of "difference."

4

A Talk to Teachers: James Baldwin as Postcolonial Artist and Public Intellectual

Greg Dimitriadis and Cameron McCarthy

As critics and scholars we face a tough road. The pressures are on for us to atomize our roles—work within delineated theories, choose clear methods and disciplines, remain professionals. Political interests and commitments are circumscribed within particular—albeit contentious—discourses like multiculturalism, postcolonialism, feminist theory, and critical race theory. We are encouraged to work within single genres of writing and to communicate our work to a body of our peers—narrowly defined—preferably as a single author. For those of us in education—a field seemingly rooted in praxis—these pressures can be particularly debilitating and are linked to a whole host of corporate imperatives and *ressentiment* logics operating at all levels of the educational enterprise (McCarthy and Dimitriadis, 2000). For example, for those of us in elementary, middle, and secondary education, high-stakes testing and accountability measures have become all-important, largely circumscribing the role of the teacher as a transformative intellectual. In turn, for those of us in higher education, an increasing reliance on adjunct teachers, enrollment-driven resource allocations, assaults on tenure, and corporate "distance learning" initiatives, have all conspired against the intellectual freedom once associated with graduate education and the professorate.

In facing this stultifying *realpolitik*, we (Greg and Cameron) have struggled in search of new models, new theories, new intellectual ancestors, new ways of thinking, acting, and being as transformative intellectuals and pedagogues. Our journey has taken us away from the increasingly circumscribed field of "expert" research and theory to the overlapping spaces of postcolonial art, music, novels, poetry, and criticism—to the work of authors such as Wilson Harris and Toni Morrison, painters like Jean-Michel Basquiat, Gordon Bennett, and Arnaldo Roche-Rabell, and public intellectuals such as C.L.R. James and James Baldwin (Dimitriadis and McCarthy, 2001). In this chapter, we extend this and related work on James Baldwin, paying particular attention to the implications of his life and work for our project of revisioning public education and reimagining what public democratic pedagogy might look like in our moment of "difference" (Dimitriadis and McCarthy, 2000).[1]

In particular, we explore James Baldwin as a postcolonial artist and public intellectual, with much to offer contemporary dialogues on democratic renewal and pedagogy. As we will make clear, Baldwin wandered the globe in the middle part of the last century in a sincere effort to break down the constraints of racial origin, geographical locations, and disciplinary boundaries and vocabularies and to offer new, emancipatory social and political visions. We find in Baldwin a postcolonial artist whose global migrations allowed him to link local concerns to broader global struggles in what was a profoundly pedagogical project. Baldwin was broad in scope in terms of what he studied and the genres he wrote in. He was an essayist, novelist, poet, playwright, and script writer. He was a public, political figure, involved in many high-profile (and dangerous) political struggles, including the civil rights movement in the United States, which he linked to colonial struggles around the globe. Finally, he was very much interested in the complexity of popular representation. He wrote a book on film (*The Devil Finds Work*) and never stopped interrogating the "hieroglyphics" of the popular in an effort to understand the complexities of race relations both nationally and internationally. Baldwin, we argue, serves as a shining light in an educative field that typically stresses genre confinement in writing, elides personal narrative, addresses narrowly defined and circumscribed audiences, and atomizes the role of an intellectual. In his critical reflection on his own life and the world, Baldwin serves as an exemplar to an intellectual field sadly bereft of examples like him.

Baldwin in the Village

Baldwin's life was complex, and its details are the stuff of legend, as he worked and reworked the contours of his personal biography so often in both his fiction and nonfiction. Baldwin struggled early on with the Baptist church of his parents. He was a widely known preacher from a very young age in Harlem, New York, though the church came to symbolize for him a constrained and painful life, embodied by his bitter, rage-filled, and later insane father, with whom he had a contentious relationship. In addition, the church precluded, for Baldwin, his growing sense of gay sexuality, a dynamic touched upon in his short story "The Outing."

The church refused Baldwin full human actualization, denying him the ability to answer what he saw as his most basic of callings—to write. The "street" beckoned him, symbolizing, as it did, all aspects of a forbidden vernacular culture—including blues and jazz—as well as the freedom to explore multiple intimate relationships. This struggle between life inside the church and life outside the church was drawn on in his play *The Amen Corner*, novels such as *Go Tell It on the Mountain*, and several essays, including *The Fire Next Time*.

Soon after he left the church, Baldwin traveled abroad to Paris and then

Switzerland, where he wrote his first novel, *Go Tell It on the Mountain*, and continued to explore racial dynamics, both in the United States and internationally. Many of his most significant works were written abroad, including his important critiques of Richard Wright, "Many Thousands Gone" and "Everybody's Protest Novel," as well as "Stranger in the Village," about his stay in Loche-les-Bains. Like many, Baldwin developed an international perspective that helped him to gain a clearer focus on his own situation "back home." In fact, Baldwin commented in an important lecture that his trips abroad gave him the courage and critical apparatus to visit another seemingly foreign country—the American South.

After returning to the United States, Baldwin mobilized his growing fame to address issues of racial inequality in novels and essays, including his best-selling and most popular account of race relations in the United States, *The Fire Next Time*. He was frequently interviewed, appeared on the cover of *Time*, went on a speaking tour for the Congress of Racial Equality (CORE), worked with Medgar Evers to investigate lynching in the South, worked with SNCC on voting drives for poor blacks, and was called upon by politicians including Robert Kennedy to discuss racial issues and tensions in the United States.

The Fire Next Time is particularly illustrative of Baldwin's unique angle of vision on the civil rights movement. Baldwin begins the book with an open letter to his nephew and namesake—"My Dungeon Shook: Letter to My Nephew on the One Hundredth Anniversary of the Emancipation." Here, Baldwin talks to his nephew about the complexities and paradoxes of self-determination in a profoundly debilitating, racist U.S. culture. "This innocent country set you down in a ghetto in which, in fact, it intended that you should perish," he tells him (1963, p. 7). The only hope, it seems, is a kind of near-religious faith in experience, in passionate involvement and ecumenical investment in the world. "Take no one's word for anything, including mine," he says. "The details and symbols of your life have been deliberately constructed to make you believe what white people say about you. Please try to remember that what they believe, as well as what they do and cause you to endure, does not testify to your inferiority but to their inhumanity and fear" (p. 8). For Baldwin, whites have fled from the reality of an inextricably intertwined world—dehumanizing themselves in the process. The only hope here, he says, is to "cease fleeing from reality and begin to change it," or, as he tells his nephew, to make "America what America must become" (p. 10). This volume thus begins on a very personal note—indeed, a pedagogical note, with Baldwin in intense dialogue with his nephew.

Much of *The Fire Next Time* deals with Baldwin's reflections on the civil rights movement in general and Elijah Muhammad and the Nation of Islam in particular. Baldwin begins by discussing, as he so often does, his youth and the various "nets" or "traps" that surrounded him, which vied for his allegiances early in his life. Among these were the church and the streets, each of which tried to "claim" him and those around him. "Some went on wine or whiskey or the needle and are still on it," he writes. "And others, like me, fled into the church" (p. 20). All were ways to avoid the "horrors of the American Negro's life"—horrors for which, he writes, "there has been almost no language" (p. 69).

Baldwin thus understands the power and pull of religious transcendence—in his own life and in the life of others. Clearly, Baldwin appreciated the force with which the Nation of Islam resonated, the way it turned an insidious and all-pervasive black-white binary on its head:

> God is black. All black men belong to Islam; they have been chosen. And Islam shall rule the world. The dream, the sentiment is old; only the color is new. And it is this dream, this sweet possibility, that thousands of oppressed black men and women in this country now carry with them after the Muslim minister has spoken, through the dark noisome ghetto streets, into the hovels where so many have perished. The white God has not delivered them; perhaps the Black God will. (p. 57)

For Baldwin, the Nation of Islam spoke to the dispossessed with brutal clarity, their claims sealed with the secure knot of ideological closure.

Baldwin pushes the reader here, however, pushes us to see the ways in which "color"-based doctrines, whether black or white, lock us into what he calls an "impossible water wheel." Race, for Baldwin, is a fiction that white people mobilize to oppress in all manner and form—it is embedded everywhere, from the violence of the police to the nuances of culture and language. He writes, "as long as we in the West place on color the value that we do, we make it impossible for the great unwashed to consolidate themselves according to any other principle. Color is not a human or a personal reality; it is a political reality" (pp. 103–104). This is the terrain upon which Baldwin pushes us, the political uses to which "race" is put. It is a global terrain, one in which no one is innocent, everyone is implicated.

Indeed, Baldwin saw civil rights struggles in the United States as inseparable from more global struggles for independence. Baldwin's trips to France, where he was able to see how similar kinds of colonial oppression affected the lives of Algerian immigrants, were extremely instructive in forming his globalized social and political vision. In some sense, he stressed, all colonizers share something vital, as do all colonized people. He writes, in *No Name in the Street* (1972),

> Any real commitment to black freedom in this country would have the effect of reordering our priorities, and altering our commitments, so that, for horrendous example, we would be supporting black freedom fighters in South Africa and Angola, and would not be allied with Portugal, would be closer to Cuba than we are to Spain, would be supporting Arab nations instead of Israel, and would never have felt compelled to follow the French into Southeast Asia. (p. 178)

These struggles were inextricably intertwined for Baldwin, who continually problematized the "here" in light of the "there."

Throughout it all, it is critical to note, Baldwin documented his most personal relationships, as if they held some key to unlocking the ever-inscrutable problem of race in the United States. He soon fell out of favor with a new generation of black radicals, who demanded clearer and more unilateral statements on "the black problem" and wanted no part of the emergent ecumenical order for which Baldwin called. His critique of "the impossible water wheel" of race was tantamount to treason for many, especially to those building political empires by "consolidating" color in different of ways. We recall Eldridge Cleaver's famous attack, in *Soul on Fire*: "There is in James Baldwin's work the most grueling, agonizing, total hatred of blacks, particularly of himself, and the most shameful, fanatical, fawning, sycophantic love of the whites that one can find in the writings of any black American writer of note in our time. This is an appalling contradiction and the implications of it are vast" (1968, p. 99). The attack would not be an isolated one. Baldwin soon fell out of favor as a "spokesperson" for issues of race in the United States. Later in life, he left the United States again, this time for Istanbul. He died in 1987 in St. Paul-de-Vence, France, leaving behind a body of work that included plays, essays, novels, poems, and even a screenplay (for a proposed film on Malcolm X).

Considering the above, it is indeed deeply problematic that Baldwin's work is not read as widely as it once was (though it is currently being reevaluated, most especially vis-à-vis "whiteness studies" [see Lipsitz, 1999; Roediger, 1998]). Baldwin, in essay collections like *Notes of a Native Son* and *Nobody Knows My Name*, spoke to the complexities of the colonial encounter and the multiple and often contradictory ways it registered on the psyches of both oppressed and oppressors. These questions were inextricably intertwined for Baldwin, who famously commented "by means of what the white man imagines the black man to be, the black man is enabled to know who the white man is" (1955, p. 167). Baldwin did not write "protest literature," nor did he interrogate the "black problem." His project of documenting the deeply wrought psychic and material dimensions of black-white relations was more complex.

Key here is the brilliant essay "Stranger in the Village," in which Baldwin foregrounds several tensions worth exploring. These include the constant push and pull between assimilation and separation that marks the United States's particularly configured "melting pot" as well as the global circulation of identities and histories that radically situate subjects around the world. We recall here the fascination of the children in the distant village toward Baldwin: "If I sat in the sun for more than five minutes some daring creature was certain to come along and gingerly put his fingers on my hair, as though he were afraid of an electric shock, or put his hand on my hand, astonished that the color did not rub off" (p. 162). We recall, as well, how quickly this innocence—a theme throughout Baldwin's work—

turned to fear and loathing: "But some of the men have accused *le sale negre*—behind my back—of stealing wood and there is already in the eyes of some of them that peculiar, intent, paranoiac malevolence which one sometimes surprises in the eyes of American white men when, out walking with their Sunday girl, they see a Negro male approach" (p. 168).

Ultimately, Baldwin's work foregrounds the radical dynamism of race, its variability and changeability, the multiple nature of its representational character, and the multiple purposes to which such representations might be used or deployed. He particularly highlights, as the above quotes suggest, the constant play and push and pull of the social and psychological dynamics of attraction and repulsion, desire and fear, in black-white relations. And, Baldwin opened up discussion of the way in which race relations constitute a field of vigorous contestation over tendentious cultural signs, symbols, and representations to which social combatants attach powerful racial meanings and associations. These are registered most clearly in his autobiographical work, which addressed the most profound of political questions through the complexity of the everyday.

Baldwin used his life as a resource—one he could draw on in the always uncertain task of speaking to broad, multiple constituencies, building empathy while never settling for, in Patti Lather's language, "comfort texts" (1997, p. 286). His life was filled with complexities and paradoxes: he was black, gay, heavily influenced by the church, a (willing or not) spokesperson for African Americans, an artist struggling with existential demands. He continually used these complexities and paradoxes to challenge himself and his readers, processes that, for Baldwin, were inextricably intertwined.

Not surprisingly, given his own engagement with the media, Baldwin had a particular interest in popular culture. In a passage from "Many Thousands Gone," he notes: "As is the inevitable result of things unsaid, we find ourselves until today oppressed with a dangerous and reverberating silence; and the story is told, compulsively, in symbols and signs, in hieroglyphics" (1955, p. 24). For Baldwin, music and film were both "hieroglyphics," cultural signs that were inscrutable yet filled with meaning, telling painful and highly conflictual tales that did not find easy resonance in language itself. He continued, "The ways in which the Negro has affected the American psychology are betrayed in our popular culture and in our morality" (p. 24). These hieroglyphics register key cultural dynamics in important ways, and he made many attempts to decode them through interrogations of his own life, most especially in his book on film, *The Devil Finds Work* (1976). When discussing *In the Heat of the Night* (1967), he comments on "the anguish of people trapped in legend. They cannot live within this legend; neither can they step out of it" (pp. 55–56). These legends are bigger than any one person, but they do not let anyone get beyond them. We are doomed to live in and through them, speaking as they do to the deepest tensions that inhere in the particular colonial encounter in the United States.

Baldwin's complex use of personal narrative is worth pursuing further. Baldwin looked beyond all ready-made explanatory frameworks, noting that "all theories are suspect" and that "the finest principles may have to be modified, or may even be pulverized by the demands of life" (1955, p. 9). In his treatment of popular culture as elsewhere, Baldwin did not merely open up his life in a confessional manner, as in much autobiography, nor did he merely proselytize, reconstructing his own life as a kind of ad hoc justification for a particular political platform. Rather, he mobilized the complex details of his life as a kind of resource, one that moved personal narrative from the traditional terrain of self-disclosure to that of ethics, using his experiences to address contemporary concerns in compelling ways.

But ethics are, for Baldwin, anything but simple and prescriptive. Baldwin precedes his discussion of the horror film *The Exorcist* (1973) with a brief meditation on the nature of evil for whites in the West and for African Americans in Harlem. Drawing both on his experience of church rituals as well as black vernacular forms such as the blues, he writes:

> In our own church, the Devil had many faces, all of them one's own. He was not always evil, rarely was he frightening—he was, more often, subtle, charming, cunning, and warm. So, one learned, for example, never to take the easy way out: whatever looked easy was almost certainly a trap. In short, the Devil was the mirror which could never be smashed. One had to look into the mirror every day—*good morning, blues / Blues, how do you do? / Well, I'm doing all right / Good morning / How are you?*—check it all out, and take it all in, and travel. The pleading of the blood [a church ritual in which participants threw themselves at the alter] was not, for us, a way of exorcising a Satan whom we knew could never sleep: it was to engage Satan in a battle we knew could never end. (1976, p. 116)

The kind of evil in *The Exorcist*, in which possessed bodies spat up venom and contorted in inhuman ways, served only to purify a white audience, to make them pure and real in relation to what they were not. "The mindless and hysterical banality of the evil presented," Baldwin wrote, "is the most terrifying thing about the film," justifying, as it did, all manner of atrocity—from the state of schools and prisons to the "ruined earth of Vietnam" (pp. 121–122). Ethics, for Baldwin, is a terrain of struggle, one that draws together the intimately personal and the profoundly political.

Indeed, in *The Devil Finds Work*, Baldwin speaks to his profound ambivalence about popular representation and the ways he himself charted his life, so filled with similar ambivalence, through film itself. As noted, Baldwin faced a very stark split early on between life inside and outside the church—a split that film played a central role in. Film was a part of a kind of self-definition that could not take place inside the strictures of the church. In fact, film was very directly responsible for his leaving the church. He writes of a challenge from his early childhood friend Emile Capouya:

On the coming Sunday, he would buy two tickets to a Broadway matinee and meet me on the steps of the 42nd Street Library, at two o'clock in the afternoon. He knew that I spent all day Sunday in church—the point, precisely, of the challenge. If I were not on the steps of the library . . . then he would be ashamed of me and never speak to me again, and I would be ashamed of myself. (p. 32)

Quite clearly, for Baldwin, the "devil found work" in film and he himself did indeed sneak out of church that following Sunday. Baldwin's use of the term "devil," however, has a kind of dual meaning, as Baldwin was also quick to point out how constricting the images in film could be. In his famous "talk to teachers," he commented that one of the things that teachers should impart to students is the fact that "popular culture—as represented, for example, on television and in comic books and in movies—is based on fantasies created by very ill people, and he must be aware that these are fantasies that have nothing to do with reality" (1988, p. 11). However, it is also quite clear from his work that he sees these "fantasies" as pervading our lives in ways that cannot be so easily sidestepped (recall the earlier discussion of *The Exorcist* and evil). These fantasies are imparted with a kind of psychic historical weight that has accumulated from years of circulation in the Americas.

These representations have provided us all with deeply problematic "legends"—that, as noted, are not of our own making but must be worked through. Commenting on the film *In the Heat of the Night*, Baldwin writes:

The history which produces such a film cannot, after all, be swiftly understood, nor can the effects of this history be easily resolved. Nor can this history be blamed on any single individual; but, at the same time, no one can be let off the hook. It is a terrible thing, simply, to be trapped in one's history, and attempt, in the same motion (and in this, our life!) to accept, deny, reject, and redeem it—and, also, on whatever level, to profit from it. (1976, p. 56)

This can be terribly painful, to chart one's life through these inescapable narratives and their histories. But one has, really, no other option. These histories cannot be ignored, but, as Baldwin says they can be profited from.

Baldwin interrogates several such histories or legends in *The Devil Finds Work*, reading them through select stars, icons, and archetypes. Key here is the classic and ever-inscrutable figure of the American gangster. Indeed, the gangster has been a constant source of fascination for both black and white audiences in the United States—from *Angels with Dirty Faces* (1938) and *The Godfather* (1972) to *Superfly* (1972) and *Menace II Society* (1993). In fact, Baldwin says that *"le gangster"* and the *"nigger"* have a similar place in the popular American imagination, an insight that helps explain the phenomenal commercial success of contemporary "gangster rap" (p. 23).

Baldwin, however, pushes us further. While discussing the film *Dead End*

(1937), he notes that he had known many figures similar to the gangster that Bogart plays, "with his one-hundred dollar suits, and his silk shirts, and his hat." Yet, he criticizes the film for its lack of broader human context. The heroine, he notes, seemed all too innocent:

> The severity of the social situation which *Dead End* so romanticizes . . . utterly precludes the innocence of its heroine. Much closer to the truth are the gangster, his broken mother, and his broken girl—yes: I had seen *that*. The script is unable to face the fact that it is merely another version of that brutal fantasy known as the American success story: this helpless dishonesty is revealed by the script's resolution. (pp. 26–27)

This narrative, this "legend," fails to account for this sadder and more complex picture. The plot itself, with its neat resolution, speaks to the harsher reality it works to silence. He writes of his response to the main character's decision to turn in the gangster, Baby-Face:

> I was by no means certain that I approved of the hero's decision to inform on Baby-Face, to turn him over to the police, and bring about his death. In my streets, we never called the cops, and whoever turned anyone into the cops was a pariah. I did not believe, though the film insists on it, that the hero (Joel McCrea) turned in the gangster in order to save the children. I had never seen any children saved that way. . . . I could believe—though the film pretends that this consideration never entered the hero's mind—that the hero turned in the gangster in order to collect the reward money: that reward money which will allow the hero and the heroine to escape from the stink of the children: for I had certainly seen attempts at *that*. (p. 27)

He goes on to argue that "even with some money, black people could move only into black neighborhoods: which is not to be interpreted as meaning that we wished to move into white neighborhoods. We wished, merely, to be free to move" (p. 28).

There are no "good guys" and "bad guys" in Baldwin's world (again, recall his discussion of *The Exorcist*). There is no recourse to a "happy ending." We have only his own complex biography engaging with these key "hieroglyphics," attempting to decode them somehow. The result is a narrative that is political as well as personal—his experience seeing the film, *Dead End*, intertwined with a discussion of key issues, including cultural autonomy and integration, and the problems and paradoxes of white authority. Throughout, he relied most clearly on his own experiences to narrate these concerns, experiences that constantly worked with and against these popular representations, experiences that spoke to the ways history situates us all in profound ways. Throughout, he critiqued "that brutal fantasy known as the American success story" with a unique, embodied social vision.

Final Thoughts

As noted at the outset of this chapter, the role of the teacher as transformative intellectual has been increasingly narrowed and circumscribed over the past few decades, as education has become less and less tied up with individual student and teacher biographies, interests, dispositions, and so forth (Apple, 1993). In his work and in his life, James Baldwin provides us with another (desperately needed) model for pedagogy—a pedagogy that deploys the particularities of autobiography in engaging with a broad range of texts—a pedagogy that wrestles with ethics as it aims to engage as wide and as disparate an audience as possible. Baldwin, in short, provides a shining exemplar for those of us working in the field of education today—a resource for "thinking beyond" the constraining logics so prevalent and pervasive at all levels of the educational enterprise.

Baldwin understood these logics well. "The purpose of education," he wrote in his famous "talk to teachers," "is to create in a person the ability to look at the world for himself, to make his own decisions. . . . To ask questions of the universe, and then to learn to live with those questions, is the way he achieves his own identity" (1988, p. 4). Societies can function only when engaged citizens continually question their circumstances, continually make and re-make themselves and their worlds. Yet, there is a paradox here, as "no society is really anxious to have that kind of person around. What societies really, ideally, want is a citizenry which will simply obey the rules of society. If a society succeeds in this, that society is about to perish" (p. 4).

Democracies, thus, cannot survive without a deliberative ethic, without the ability to invent and reinvent themselves. This is precisely the ethic Baldwin discussed in essays such as *The Fire Next Time*, where he struggled with the persistent and deluded racial project in the United States: "What it comes to is that if we, who can scarcely be considered a white nation, persist in thinking of ourselves as one, we condemn ourselves, with the truly white nations, to sterility and decay, whereas if we could accept ourselves as we are, we might bring new life to the Western achievements, and transform them" (p. 94).

Such transformations can only happen if we, as a nation and as a world, embody the ideals of democracy and democratic deliberation. These are the ideals, as has been maintained throughout this volume, that should be guiding the educational enterprise today. Yet, as noted, they are ideals which have been supplanted by more technical and technocratic ones. This is the great tragedy of our times. If current trends in education continue—trends, for example, toward strict accountability measures, high-stakes testing, and the de-skilling of teachers; trends toward a reliance on adjunct teaching, enrollment-driven resource allocations, and corporate "distance learning" initiatives—we are in danger of producing a disciplined citizenry that cannot sustain rich, democratic life. We are in danger of robbing teachers and students of the radical particularity of the pedagogical encounter, of teaching young people only to obey rote rules—not to fashion different kinds of futures—or to explore the complexities of their lives and the lives of others.

The work of Baldwin offers us a new way to think about what an engaged pedagogy might mean. We see a pedagogy that is enmeshed in individual biography, exceeds the concerns of particular disciplines, engages with the popular, links the local with the global, and is intensely concerned with social change. We see a pedagogy that yearns for authentic, deliberative conversation that stretches beyond school walls and looks toward a broader theater of action. Baldwin collapses distinctions between art, criticism, and pedagogy, giving educators a broader range of resources for reimagining and revisioning their vocations.

5

Promises to Keep, Finally? Academic Culture and the Dismissal of Popular Culture

John A. Weaver and Toby Daspit

For this chapter our contention is this: In the academy there have been no promises kept in regard to promoting a democratic society, because many academics have treated popular culture, or that which people value, with suspicion at best and abrupt dismissal at worst. To make our claim we want to draw on the work of three central figures in the Western academic tradition: Plato, Theodor Adorno, and Max Horkheimer. Much of Western criticism of popular culture is indebted to these three figures. In fact, it is easy to make the assertion that it is from Plato that the liberal arts curriculum, or the foundational basis of a traditional Western education, is developed, and it is from Adorno and Horkheimer (along with Marcuse and Benjamin) that leftists garner much of their moral authority to comment on popular culture. This is true, but both traditions are suspicious of popular culture and view it as the antithesis to a healthy society. For Plato, popular culture, especially that which is mimetic, represents the rule of the masses rather than the naturally ordained guardians. For Adorno and Horkheimer (1998), their suspicion is based on two sources. First, they saw how easily Nazis were able to manipulate popular images in order to garner mass support for their anti-Semitic and eugenic policies. Second, Adorno and Horkheimer constructed the "masses" as manipulable and gullible victims of the "culture industry." While we find the first source of suspicion a vital and understandable point to address, the second source prevents academics from exploring the massive and complex impact of popular culture in/on people's lives.

With these thoughts in mind, we want to highlight aspects of Plato's and Adorno and Horkheimer's thought that inform contemporary culture. From Plato, Western cultural criticism has adopted a kind of correspondence theory of reality or the belief that if people see or hear something they will do it. In the aftermath of the shootings at Columbine, this was a popular mantra repeated by media pundits and concerned parents, teachers, and administrators. Many who raised this issue insisted that there is a one-to-one correlation between what young people do and what they see and hear. Such a thesis demonstrates a deep distrust of popular culture and an even deeper distrust of young people. From Adorno and Horkheimer, critics have adopted a paranoid style, in which popular culture is constructed as a wasteland in which executives of the culture industry intentionally create programs that will control and manipulate "the masses" into doing things that will not be beneficial to their lives. We can see this influence in the proliferation of commentaries that focus on debasing programs such as WWF, Jerry Springer, and "reality" TV. We are not necessarily advocates for such programs, but our contention is that many critics are using these examples to simultaneously demonstrate that Western society is in decline and to dismiss all of popular culture as debased and unworthy of scholarly attention. After we discuss the work of these thinkers in detail we want to conclude with an alternative approach to popular culture that is more accepting, which does not mean less critical, of popular creations and, by extension, more democratic in its ethos and assumptions.

Before we do, it is appropriate to discuss our views of democracy. Above we essentially have associated popular culture and popular aesthetics with democracy, but by no means do we wish to reduce democracy to popular culture. There are other important dimensions of a healthy democracy, including the ability to freely express dissenting and assenting opinions and the right to influence the political process as much as any other individual and more than any corporation or entity in which profits dominate over the well-being and interests of individuals. Our point is this: A democracy flourishes best when the will of the people are honored, no matter how much they may clash with corporations, political barons, or academics. For a democracy to exist, the wills of people must be respected rather than dismissed, ignored, or condemned out of hand. We see no problem with raising doubts, as Plato, Adorno, and Horkheimer do, about the tastes of people or warning against the possible consequences of popular decisions. This academics have done well, and we hope they will continue to do so. Where we think academics have failed democratic ideals is in not giving popular cultures and tastes serious and sustained attention. For a democracy to develop, intellectuals have to treat popular culture with the utmost respect and seriousness. Without this respect, the wills of people will be ignored and erased, thereby assuring that academics will fail, again, to keep their promise of nurturing a democratic nation. As we wish to suggest below, there is not much of a tradition that, as academics, we can be proud of when it comes to supporting democratic ideals.

A Correspondence Theory of Reality
or the Academy's Numb Thesis

In Plato's *Republic* we see the origins of a correspondence theory of reality. There is a long-held belief in academia that if the untamed masses are exposed to something they will imitate it. If they see it in the movies, listen to it in music, or watch it on television, they will act it out in real life. This is a common argument heard today as adults grope to understand violence in the mimetic generation. When Klebold and Harris went on their rampage, it was spread through the Internet and television news programs that Klebold and Harris got their idea for a rampage from a scene in the movie *The Matrix* and *Natural Born Killers*. We also see the correspondence theory of reality in research that suggests members of the mimetic generation view hundreds of thousands of acts of violence, are now numb to these acts, and thus are more likely to perform acts of violence in real life. This thesis of weak causality, we want to demonstrate, begins with Plato's "Socrates."

Socrates spends most of his effort developing the correspondence theory of reality in book ten of the *Republic*. From this book we want to discuss three aspects of this theory of reality that outlines common beliefs academics hold in regard to popular culture. These aspects are, in the order we want to cover them: the masses gravitate to forms of popular culture because even if they were exposed to true art, they could not comprehend it; creators of popular culture are not intellectuals and only pander to the poor taste of the masses; the masses do not have the intellectual capacities to discern between reality and the created worlds of popular culture.

In book ten, Socrates questions Glaucon as to whether they should permit poets into their city. The issue of the intellectual capabilities of the masses to comprehend the underlying truths and meanings of art appears as Socrates takes up the characteristics of poetry and "whether it is ordinary or serious" (Bloom, 1991, p. 286). Within this context, Socrates asks Glaucon to judge the rational (public) and irrational (private) acts of a man who is suffering from the loss of a son or "something else for which he cares particularly" (p. 287). Socrates draws the conclusion that the deliberative man would not express his grief in public but would wisely choose his moments of grief and conclude that "one must not behave like children who have stumbled and who hold on to the hurt place and spend their time crying out; rather one must always habituate the soul to turn as quickly as possible to curing and setting aright what has fallen and is sick" (p. 288). To this analogy, Glaucon "plainly" accepts what Socrates has offered.

With this analogy of the deliberative man who grieves properly, Socrates draws the conclusion that such a principled approach to life's predicaments cannot be expected of the poet and most certainly not from those people the poets easily sway. He says:

> Now then, the irritable disposition affords much and varied imitation, while the prudent and quiet character, which is always nearly equal to itself, is neither easily imitated nor, when imitated easily understood, especially by a festive assembly where all sorts of humans beings are gathered in a theater. For imitation is of a condition that is surely alien to them.

Glaucon concurs that this is "entirely certain." Socrates adds, "Then plainly the imitative poet isn't naturally directed toward any such part of the soul, and his wisdom isn't framed for satisfying it—if he's going to get a good reputation among the many—but rather toward the irritable and various disposition, because it is easily imitated" (Bloom, 1991, p. 288).

In these passages, Socrates reveals his views of the masses. Socrates, in part, is inclined to prevent mimetic poets from coming into his city because the people are too easily influenced; they are like the child who "stumbles" and is unable to overcome his or her grief. The poets will pander to these childlike tendencies of the masses. Mimetic poets should also be banned from the city because even if they were among the rare poets who capture the truths of life in their works, the masses would not understand anyway. The childlike masses are festive theater goers who hear the poets and their words but are unable to comprehend the subtle meanings of those words. Contemplation is alien to them. The intellectual elite can, out of the goodness of their natures, open the doors of art to the masses, but it will not have any lasting impact on the capabilities of the masses. As a result, the masses flock to the imitative poets because these poets pander to their childlike nature and their proclivity to seek out those moments of entertainment that does not tax their minds.

Within this logic, we can see the beginnings of an academic tradition that treats anything the masses enjoy with intellectual suspicion and dismisses popular culture as a serious or deliberative form of study. If the masses are interested in the imitative poets, the logic is posited, then clearly the poets are not saying anything worthwhile, and, given this state of affairs, intellectuals need not investigate either what the poets are saying or why the masses find these poets so appealing. They are saying and thinking nothing. As the saying goes, fifty-four channels and nothing is on. This adage should be reformulated to state: fifty-four channels and as an academic I still do not see anything on.

This same passage in the *Republic* can be used as a transition to understand Socrates's dismissal of popular artists as lacking in intellectual potential and substance. As Socrates confides in Glaucon, the imitative poets want to pander to the "irritable disposition." It the source of their popularity. The imitative poets know it, and they probably know that it is not the most lasting and intellectually endearing course to take, but it is the course that gains them popularity. Socrates clearly understands this source of popularity, and this is why he is threatened by it.

This, however, is not the most revealing passage in book ten of Socrates's views on imitative poets. Earlier in book ten, Socrates enters into another lecture with Glaucon on the three arts found within things and painting. Socrates suggests to Glaucon that "for each thing there are these three arts—one that will use, one that will make, one that will imitate." Glaucon, like the faithful fan that he is of Socrates's art, concurs with a "yes" (p. 284). Of these three arts, Socrates, not surprisingly, is least impressed with the "one that will imitate." In dealing with the imitator Socrates suggests to Glaucon that "with respect to beauty and badness, the imitator will neither know nor opine rightly about what he imitates." Glaucon agrees (did you expect anything else?): "It doesn't seem so." With Glaucon's token approval, Socrates continues on with his diatribe against the imitator who "in his making, would be a charming chap, so far as wisdom about what he makes goes. . . . But all the same, he will imitate, although he doesn't know in what way each thing is bad or good. But as it seems, whatever looks to be fair to the many who don't know anything— that he will imitate. . . . The imitator knows nothing worth mentioning about what he imitates; imitation is a kind of play and not serious; and those who take up tragic poetry in iambics and in epics are all imitators in the highest possible degree" (pp. 284–285).

The imitator (poet or painter) or popular artist is a creator, but a creator who knows nothing of the inner workers of which he copies. The poet is just a charlatan imitating nothing of note and the painter is a poor imitator of the artisan who knows of the inner essence of his craft. The poet and painter do work, but it is not serious work that uncovers anything worthy for people to understand. Imitators will create their work simply to gain popularity from the masses, who will not understand anything of importance even if the imitator happens to uncover it. Applying this perspective to contemporary popular culture, we can see Socrates's understanding of imitators in academic commentaries. For most academics, popular culture is an imitative art form that panders to the lowest human desires. It is seen as a worthless endeavor that symbolizes the hedonism of our postmodern world. Critics do not interpret the work of popular artists as serious but fun; nor do they view these artists as having the capabilities to grasp the important intellectual ideas of our age.

The final aspect we want to cover is the idea Socrates develops concerning what we call the undiscerning masses. In the previous passages cited in this section, we get a glimpse into Socrates's lack of confidence in the ability of the masses to think. It is in an earlier section concerning the imitative tendencies of painters that Socrates reveals best his views towards the ability of the masses to discern the difference between reality and the creations of popular culture. Socrates asks Glaucon: "Now consider this very point. Toward which is painting directed in each case—toward imitation of the being as it is or toward its looking as it looks? Is it imitation of looks or truth?" (p. 281). Glaucon, habitually imitative, replies "of looks." Socrates continues:

> Therefore, imitation is surely far from the truth; and, as it seems, it is due to this that it produces everything—because it lays hold of a certain small part of each thing, and that part is itself only a phantom. For example, the painter, we say, will paint for us a shoemaker, a carpenter, and the other craftsmen, although he doesn't understand the arts of any one of them. But, nevertheless, if he is a good painter by painting a carpenter and displaying him from far off, he would deceive children and foolish human beings into thinking that it is truly a carpenter. (p. 281)

For Socrates, the imitator dupes children and foolish adults into believing that what they see is not a painting or a replica, but the real thing in all its inner truth. The masses are unable to discern what is real and what is an imitation. For Socrates this meant that most people were unable to discern between reality and the illusions presented by poetry and painting. Poets knew this, but they also knew their popularity was in their ability to please the masses, who wanted to be duped. For academics today, this translates into the belief that most people cannot make the distinction between violence in real life and violence they see on television or films.

Later in book ten, Socrates takes this argument one step further. The imitative form places us into an intellectual trance as we are lured by the mimetic and unable to discern between truth and the imitative. Socrates tells Glaucon, "Listen and consider. When even the best of us hear Homer or any other of the tragic poets imitating one of the heroes in mourning . . . you know that we enjoy it and that we give ourselves over to following the imitation; suffering along with the hero in all seriousness, we praise as a good poet the man who most puts us in this state" (p. 289). Glaucon, in a trancelike state responds, "I know it, of course."

With this last passage we can see what concerns Socrates and many academics today. They fear the mesmerizing powers of popular culture that even the greatest of minds cannot risk. This power is too much for anyone to resist. Once the masses and great thinkers of an age peer into the eyes of the poet and listen to their words, they cannot help but to be thrown into a state of pleasure and vulnerability. For Socrates and many academics today, the fear is giving oneself "over to following" the powers of imitation at the expense of all that the intellectual values, including the ability to discern and to think rationally. Poets need to be outlawed from Socrates's ideal city because they risk the perseverance of truth and natural law.

What has changed in these tales of poetry in relation to contemporary popular culture is that Socrates had no problem exiling poets, unless they could prove their intellectual value (without meter of course), but academics and cultural critics only call for the boycotting of some forms of popular culture. Nevertheless, underlining both of these reactions is distrustfulness of people to make their own decisions regarding matters of taste. Moreover, there is a continuity here in which popular culture is viewed suspiciously as inherently impoverished. We can see this suspicion in the work of some academics in recent years, including Henry Giroux and Douglas Kellner, who have found popular culture a fruitful field to canvass. These contemporary cultural commentators still concentrate their efforts on presumed dimensions of popular culture that are exploitative and the work of those who want to manipulate the masses into behavior they normally might not do. Such critics also assume that their interpretations are manifestations of the true nature of popular culture, thereby implying that the masses are unaware of those dimensions these cultural commentators expose.

There is one final dimension we want to cover in this chapter that we think is pertinent to mention. Throughout this piece we have included Glaucon's responses to Socrates to highlight an important dimension of academic work. Academics, for all their criticism and suspicion of popular culture, do not recognize the ways in which they act in a mimetic fashion and respond to the "classics" and great thinkers like the duped masses Socrates condemns in book ten. Academics, like the masses who flocked to hear the Athenian poets, make decisions as to who they are going to mimic. From Socrates to the present day, most academics have chosen to follow the modest witness. That is, the one who, for Socrates, did not speak in meter but plainly and clearly and, for contemporary scholars, the one who is a conduit through which truth speaks. Whether it is the Athenian poets or the modest witness, both traditions disguise their own voices and their own human role in the process of searching for truth. What has changed today is that the modern poets, popular artists, are no longer disguising their voices. They are telling you what they think and see, and they are doing it with a real attitude. Academics, however, still assert that they themselves really represent the truth rather than skillfully re-present a truth. The price has been a growing irrelevance of academic work in the lives of people at the same time that popular artists are coming into the mainstream, changing the mainstream, and sharing their insights with more people every day. Academics need to make a decision soon. Do they want to be like the popular artists, that is creative, real copies of a copy, or do they want to be like Glaucon, a copy of a copy disguised as an original?

The Culture Industry Reconsidered (Again):
Adorno, Horkheimer, and Their Legacy
in the Cultural Studies of Education

In the introduction of our edited book *Popular Culture and Critical Pedagogy* (Daspit and Weaver, 2000), we attempted to put forth two major points about critical pedagogy and cultural studies within education: critical pedagogues need to invite multiple perspectives into their writings, and critical pedagogy has to recognize the ways in which popular culture is a form of critical pedagogy. We did not want to deny that there are some long-standing tendencies within popular culture that objectify and cripple the ability of people to think and act in the world, but we wanted to draw attention to the fact that the legacy of the Frankfurt School of critical thinking still has a strong grip on the minds of those doing cultural studies within education. This grip does not take the form of a critical reductionism that interprets viewers and consumers as Nielson ratings or manipulated creations of the culture industry. Critical pedagogues have exposed and abandoned the theoretical dead end of a reductionist approach to popular culture. Yet the Frankfurt tradition still holds a prominent position in critical pedagogy and influences how popular culture is conceptualized and interpreted. With few exceptions, a deep suspicion of popular culture pervades critical pedagogy. This suspicion marks popular culture as the hegemonic playground for entertainment capitalists willing to exploit at every turn the unconscious and clueless viewers who want only to enjoy the football game. As a result, critical pedagogues focus on the exploitative possibilities within popular culture, and, unfortunately, thereby ignore what people actually do with, and how people actually work within, popular culture to construct meaning and act in the world.

In the second half of this chapter we want to revisit Adorno and Horkheimer's original attempt to tackle the culture industry. In our rereading of these essays (originally published in 1944, reprinted in 1998), we want to focus on the problems with assuming that popular culture is a wasteland loaded with pitfalls for the original and true intellectual who wishes to elevate his/her own mind and tastes. At the same time, we do not want to suggest that Adorno and Horkheimer were incorrect in their analysis. In the second part of this section, we will focus on their thoughts on viewers/audiences as objects and how their assumptions prevent cultural critics from entertaining the ways in which viewers/audiences play with the images of popular culture

Written as part of their more general treatment of the destructive tendencies of Western Enlightenment, Adorno and Horkheimer interpret the culture industry as another manifestation of modern control and destruction of the individual and his/her potential to create a culture that is liberating and uplifting. The culture industry is the homogenization of Western life in which distinctions of tastes are erased and "culture now impresses the same stamp on everything" (1998, 120). In this process of destroying distinctions, the culture industry embodies the Enlightenment ideals of efficiency, but like everything in the 1940s, it is taken to an extreme that threatens the very thing that made efficiency possible and desirable. With brutal efficiency, the culture industry turns films into a formula, radio into a pre-set script, television into a hypnotic experience, and viewers/audiences into helpless consumers unable to resist the enticing power of the movie studios, television companies, and radio stations. Whereas the telephone opened the possibilities for liberation, films, television, and radio are run by and through the principle of brutal efficiency. As Adorno and Horkheimer posited, "the latter [are] democratic: [it turns] all participants into listeners and authoritatively subjects them to broadcast programs which are exactly the same. No machinery of rejoinder has been devised and private broadcasters are denied any freedom" (p. 122). Creativity and spontaneity, unless they lead to higher ratings and public approval, have to be controlled. The process has to win out over any original thought if the industry is to guarantee its sources of profit and if it is to elicit the desired effect from the viewers/audiences, who are now turned into objects. Even when the so-called avant-garde attempt to try something new within the culture industry, they are permitted to do so only as long as it does not disrupt the generic formula that guarantees the success of the system. "Whenever Orson Welles," Adorno and Horheimer cite as an example, "offends against the tricks of the trade, he is forgiven because his departures from the norm are regarded as calculated mutations which serve all the more strongly to confirm the validity of the system" (p. 129). That is, when Welles tricked the world into believing that the broadcast they were hearing on the radio of H. G. Wells' *War of the Worlds* was real, it was acceptable to the culture industry because it figuratively glued people to their radio sets, guaranteeing sponsors that their advertisements would be heard. Such an approach within the culture industry prevented the clash of dialectical poles that was essential, in Adorno and Horkheimer's view, if the Enlightenment system of thought was not to turn on itself. By stifling these "essential tensions," to co-opt Thomas Kuhn's term from the history of science, the culture industry was turning the Enlightenment onto itself, thereby creating the same conditions that produced Fascism in Europe. Brutal efficiency was killing the individual psyche, stifling original thought, and promoting hyperenlightened thinking in the form of Fascism.

Brutal efficiency was not the only dimension of the culture industry; the dialectical poles within art of high culture and low culture were undermined to such an extent there no longer was a visible distinction. The culture industry turns the act of art into a "surrogate identity" of style in which art ceases "to be anything but style" (Adorno and Horkheimer, 1998, p. 131). Style in the culture industry is formulaic. It destroys the negative truth that art is suppose to extend our ability to understand life through painting, music, or words. Instead, style in the culture industry only confirms "obedience to the social hierachy" (p. 131). Style in the culture industry affirms what is and convinces the viewers/audiences that this is all that can be. The leveling of style within art opens the door for the dominance of kitsch art, as Velvet Elvis and Dogs Playing Cards overtake the market of taste for Rembrandt and Picasso, Jim Carrey replaces the Barrymores on the Shakespearean stage, and *Survivor* erases any illusions of television's golden age. As a result of this leveling of style, the masses become a part of the art scene only to be captivated by "the very ideology which enslaves them" rather than by an "autonomous art" that can reveal and liberate the masses from their oppression (p. 134).

The culture industry's reduction of art, in all its possible forms, to the lowest common denominator, has severe consequences on the individual psyche of the masses. Where autonomous, avant-garde art could create a path toward liberation, but the culture industry acts as a catalyst to reorient the masses to the dramatic changes of an automated, assembly-line world. "Amusement under late capitalism," Adorno and Horkheimer (1998) insist, is "the prolongation of work" (p. 137). It is sought as an escape from the mechanized work process "to recruit strength in order to be able to cope with it [work] again. But at the same time mechanization has such power over a man's leisure and happiness, and so profoundly determines the manufacture of amusement goods, that his experiences are inevitably afterimages of the work process itself" (p. 137). Amusement as a source of fun becomes another mechanism to remind the masses that what is, is all that can be. In the culture industry, amusement is an attack on the individual's psyche, a constant reminder that he or she must accept that the pace of the world is changing and that films, television, and the factories represent these changes. Cartoons, for example, "do [nothing] more than accustom the senses to the new tempo, they hammer into every brain the old lesson that continuous friction, the breaking down of all individual resistance, is the condition of life in this society" (p. 138).

These creations of the culture industry remind the masses of the shallowness of life. "There is laughter," Adorno and Horkheimer (1998) suggest, "because there is nothing to laugh at" (p. 140). Laughter replaces "real" happiness, and fun becomes "a medicinal bath" (p. 40). Laughter is a veil that masks the despair of life: "In a false society laughter is a disease which has attacked happiness and is drawing it into a worthless totality" (p. 141). In modern society, the culture industry reorients the world to the new rules of capitalist life, and the masses amuse and laugh themselves to death. For Adorno and Horkheimer, sitting in front of a television and laughing at the raw humor of the Bundy family is not a result of creative writers and talented actors who saw through the shallow rhetoric of late 1980s and early 1990s of the so-called family values movement, but a continued expression of the sickness the culture industry wishes to peddle as happiness.

A dimension of the culture that moves beyond the leveling of high and low culture is the role of advertisements in the culture industry. Advertising in the culture industry is "an open lie" (1998, p. 144). It is the culture industry's most effective medium to speak the illusion of opportunity and abundance. Adorno and Horkheimer claim that "the less the culture industry has to promise, the less it can offer a meaningful explanation of life, and the emptier is the ideology it disseminates" (p. 147). Advertising is the most effective means for the culture industry to transmit and disseminate its empty message. In advertising, the more illusions you create around a product or celebrity, the less meaning or substance there is to it. People don't buy products, they purchase the illusion, the open lie. Smoke this brand of cigarettes, and you instantaneously become the modern woman; drive this car and peace in a turbulent world will come upon you; and wear these sneakers and you will defy all laws of Newtonian physics.

Yet, advertising is more than an open lie for Adorno and Horkheimer. It is an obsession. "Advertising is [the] elixir" that cures the culture industry of ills that might surface (1998, p. 162). In part, foretelling the coming of Baudrillard and his free floating signifiers, Adorno and Horkheimer suggest that "innumerable people use words and expressions which they have either ceased to understand or employ only because they trigger off conditioned reflexes" (p. 166). Advertising creates a consumer culture. It gives the masses a sense of belonging to an elite culture of movie stars and robber barons. As an elixir for the culture industry advertising attacks individual psyches and further denies indivduals the opportunity to transcend their current repressive conditions. Advertising becomes the means through which the culture industry and late capitalism promises everything to the masses but delivers nothing. The lure of advertising is so seductive "that consumers feel compelled to buy and use its products even though they see through them" (p. 167).

Advertising blurs the line between reality and illusion and is the ultimate symbol of the reduction of modern society to a sameness that threatens the imagination. For Adorno and Horkheimer (1998), "the whole world is made to pass through the filter of the culture industry . . . [and as a result] no scope is left for the imagination" (pp. 126–127). As Adorno (1991) later states in his essay "The Schema of Mass Culture," "Imagination is replaced by a mechanically relentless control mechanism which determines whether the latest image to be distributed really represents an exact, accurate and reliable reflection of the relevant item of reality" (p. 55). Just as the reduction of high culture to the lowest common denominator threatens the ability of individuals to think, advertising attacks the imagination, rendering the individual helpless in the culture industry's world.

With these attacks on the distinctive, discerning, imaginative individual, the culture industry creates a new kind of person. It creates the masses as the rating point, the focus group, the object. "Now any person," Adorno and Horkheimer (1998) proclaim, "signifies only those attributes by which he can replace everybody else: he is interchangable, a copy. As an individual he is completely expendable and utterly insignificant, and this is just what he finds out when time deprives him of this similarity" (pp. 145–146). The individual is a copy with no meaningful original since s/he is utterly insignificant in the eyes of the culture industry that can replace one individual for another.

Adorno restates this perspective on the masses in his essay "Culture Industry Reconsidered." The masses "are an object of calculation; an appendage of the machinery. The customer is not king, as the culture industry would have us believe, not its subject but its object" (1991, p. 85). The masses, consumers, individuals are graph points to be studied, prodded, adjusted, persuaded, seduced, and probed. The master illusion of all of this is that while the masses are being treated like laboratory rats in a maze of cultural productions, they are made to feel like pampered kings and queens. It is an illusion that Adorno thinks the people want to live. Adorno concludes "The phrase, the world wants to be deceived, has become truer than had ever been intended. People are not only, as the saying goes, falling for the swindle; if it guarantees them even the most fleeting gratification they desire a deception which is nonetheless transparent to them" (p. 89). In his reconsideration of the culture industry, he asks his fellow elite thinkers not to blame the gullible masses. He urges his colleagues to reconsider their revulsion of the masses—after all they cannot help but be duped. Adorno writes: "If the masses have been unjustly reviled from above, as masses, the culture industry is not among the least responsible for making them into masses and then despising them, while obstructing the emancipation for which human beings are as ripe as the productive forces of the epoch permit" (p. 92).

For all of their dire warnings against the decline of culture, the blurring of reality, and the objectification of masses, Adorno and Horkheimer, and later Adorno alone, cannot see the ways in which they objectify "the masses." Whereas the masses are Nielson rating points or focus group studies to the culture industry, the masses are willingly duped buffoons to Adorno and Horkheimer. That is, Adorno and Horkheimer are guilty of the very act of objectification of "the masses" they have revealed within the culture industry, only in a different form.

In Adorno and Horkheimer's essays there is no interaction with "the masses," no interviewing nor observing. They analyze one symptom of "the masses" at the very same time they are reinforcing the assumption that the unintelligent masses are unwilling and unable to reflect upon their own condition. Adorno and Horkheimer, like many academics today, construct "the masses" as individuals unable to lead themselves. If they were given an opportunity to freely choose their destiny, Adorno and Horkheimer deterministically conclude, they would make the same decisions that enslave them today. Adorno and Horkheimer assume that "the masses" are incapable of making any nuanced judgments about popular culture and the culture industry. Because they do not possess the mental faculties to make nuanced decisions, "the masses" are putty in the manipulative hands of the culture industry, and they do exactly as the culture industry says and plans. There are no navigational and interpretive skills in the empty minds of "the masses" as far as Adorno and Horkheimer know or care to know. Without interacting with the diseased masses, Adorno and Horkheimer already know what they are thinking, if they were thinking, and how external stimuli influence their actions. Adorno and Horkheimer's objectification of "the masses" can be seen today as media pundits and cultural critics proclaim that the violent images generated and marketed by the culture industry encourage "the masses" to commit violent crimes. Like Adorno and Horkheimer before them, some critics today conclude that "the masses" sit in front of the television, listen to the CD player, or watch the movie screen and respond instintively: "Yes, Ice T says 'Fuck the Police' therefore I must go kill the police." Such a conclusion reveals nothing about the ways in which people negotiate media images but reveals everything about how cultural critics envision the intellectual abilities of people.

Perhaps more telling is the fact that, ironically, Adorno and Horkheimer do not reflect upon their own methods, nor do they reflect on the conclusions they draw. In other words, methodologically and interpretively they become what they argue against. Adorno and Horkheimer lose the imaginative powers and critical thinking skills needed to liberate themselves from the objectifying stereotypes they construct about "the masses." Because they fail to utilize their self-reflective skills when it comes to thinking about popular culture and the interpretive skills of "the public," they miss an opportunity to construct possible alternative explanations of the impact and power of popular culture and the culture industry on the mind-sets of people. One can assume too that they were so convinced that "the masses" were an inert group of manipulable Nielson ratings that even if they entertained alternative explanations they would still favor the conclusions they came to in their culture industry essays. As a result, Adorno and Horkheimer become the mirror image of "the masses" they construct in their essays. They become the very thing they fear.

Toward an Alternative Approach to Academic Work and Popular Culture

We have tried to present evidence from Plato and Adorno and Horkheimer that academics, in direct conflict with democratic ideals, have dismissed the overall potential of the majority of people to act as thinking individuals who are able to make informed decisions about their tastes, lifestyles, political situations, and economic standing. We believe an alternative vision would be for academics to assume that people are conscious of the decisions they make, that they are discerning individuals whose taste is not vulgar but as nuanced and diverse as Plato's and Adorno and Horkheimer's. To understand these discerning tastes, it will require academics to transform their methodological styles and assumptions about popular culture. If we work from an assumption, as Plato does, that the majority of people do not have the faculties to make wise decisions, then our research on popular culture can be done with ease. We merely have to assume the worst about "the masses" and take an opposite perspective. At the same time, if we believe that popular culture is merely a tool that corporations use to manipulate the masses, as Adorno and Horkheimer contend, then we merely have to follow the advertising executives and studio moguls around to see what they are thinking. From these perspectives our research can be done easily because we can ignore the very people we are trying to understand. However, if we accept that people are discerning individuals with complex views of taste, then our research shifts, and we are required to raise different questions. As academics we have to ask ourselves how individuals interact with popular culture texts, what they do with popular culture, why certain aspects of culture are popular, and why certain aspects of popular tastes are cultural.

To ask these types of questions, however, we not only have to change our research approaches, but we have to resituate ourselves within the realm of democratic tastes. This means that we have to become a part of people's lives and, at least, understand why they value what they do. Without these shifts there is no hope for an alternative approach to academic work, and even worse, there is no promise to keep, because there will be no democracy to build from, only the illusion of a democracy.

Resituating means we should recognize the dialogic nature of popular culture. For Plato, the mimetic poets fooled their listeners; for Adorno and Horkheimer, the "culture industry" manipulated its audiences. However, neither Plato nor Adorno and Horkheimer permitted these listeners and audiences to speak. To accept the dialogical nature of popular culture is to accept that "[l]anguage is not a neutral medium that passes freely and easily into the private property of the speaker's intention, it is populated—overpopulated—with the intentions of others. Expropriating it, forcing it to submit to one's own intentions and accents, is a difficult and complicated process" (Bakhtin, 1994, p. 294). No matter what dimension of popular culture we are studying, whether advertising agencies, media moguls, or mimetic poets, we have to permit the multiple voices into our thoughts and words. It is in these voices, not solely or primarily in the intentions of the manipulators and deceivers, that we will find an "overpopulated" world of intriguing, complex, and multiple but conflicting meanings impregnating the words and images of popular cultures.

Permitting the voices of the "public" into our work does not mean we have to somehow subordinate or ignore our own voices in our ventures into popular cultures. To the contrary, even if we are able to let the voices speak in our studies, it is still our work. They are our words, our framings, our conclusions. In this sense, by entering the "overpopulated" world of popular cultures, we are at best altering popular culture in a minimal way. That is, whether we let the voices of popular culture into our work or not, these voices will still weave themselves in and out of society, circulating as meaning. When we let the voices speak in our work, we are letting them speak through our work and in our words. The voices transform our work and words, and it is because of this transformation that academics will be better prepared to make promises about creating a democracy in America that is not based on opinion polls, consumer choices, or spending capabilities, but rather one that is based in words, deeds, and equal opportunities.

Another way of resituating ourselves in the realm of popular culture, and hopefully in a democratic society, is to find ways to unleash the "ungovernable." We co-opt this term from J. Hillis Miller, who writes that the ungovernable should be a foundation of all universities and embedded in all of our acts of reading, writing, and thinking as academics. Miller (1999) writes:

> Such [ungovernable] ideas [and readings] inaugurate something new, something unheard of before. Another way to put this is to say that the university is the place where what really counts is the ungoverned, ungovernable. The ungovernable does not occur all that often. Most of what goes on in the university is all too easily governed, In fact, it is self-governing, as when we say a machine has a "governor" that keeps it from running too fast. It just turns around at a moderate speed and keeps repeating the same. Nevertheless, the university ought to have as its primary goal working to establish conditions propitious to the creation of the ungovernable. (p. 181)

What better source to create and foster the ungovernable in the university than popular culture? In a democracy the will of the people is so ungovernable that the only people capable of governing are the people themselves. To recognize this trait about popular culture, we believe, is to finally keep our promise of creating a democratic society. We are not naïve in our proclamations about the potential of popular culture and academic work. We recognize that inviting the ungovernable into the university will inaugurate "new readings and new ideas," but it will also spur the "governors" of the university to view the entrance of the ungovernable into the university as a true sign of decay and decline. We also understand that to unleash the ungovernable in the university is to risk the current stability of the well-"governed" university, but we contend that it is worth the risk to incur the wrath of the governors in order to create new readings and new ideas that offer penetrating insights into the lives of people and the cultures they inhabit, rather than reducing them to objects who enter the university to take tests, meet influential people, and find a career.

II.

Reimagining Curriculum and Pedagogical Practice

6

Stan Douglas and the Aesthetic Critique of Urban Decline[1]

Warren Crichlow

But this is what I came so far to find, she told herself; I can't go back.
——Shirley Jackson, *The Haunting of Hill House*

Do you not feel the breath of an empty place?
——Nietzsche, quoted in Michael Taussig

There is a necessity for remembering the horror, but of course there is a necessity for remembering it in a manner in which it can be digested, in a manner *in which* the memory is not destructive.
——*Conversations with Toni Morrison*

I

Le Detroit (1999/2000), an installation project by the Canadian artist Stan Douglas, comprises a six-minute-long, 35mm black-and-white continuous film loop and a collection of thirty-two large-scale color photographs. The photographs depict manicured lawns, brush-entangled fences, and dusty vacant lots, as well as decrepit buildings, some partially demolished yet, all clinging to some mystical remnant of lost grandeur. With these classically composed shots, their strangely beautiful blue skies and ethereal white clouds as imposing background, Douglas proposes a doubly haunting and surreal evocation of the social conditions that give rise to urban decay in modern cities like Detroit.

Douglas typically conducts intense periods of research and photographic inquiry, often "scouting" a landscape site that might inspire ideas for a video or film project. Such architectural and landscape photography provides the foundational impulse for the specter of urban detritus displayed in *Le Detroit*'s film loop. In what follows, I will analyze this work as a means to characterize Douglas's aesthetic critique of urban decline, hoping to tease out its quasi utopian implications toward fostering a richer democratic public life. Here and throughout his ouvre Douglas offers the viewer an intensely deliberative space that imaginatively approximates and anticipates new and different kinds of futures—what might be otherwise.

Row Houses at Herman Gardens, 1997–1998. Courtesy of Stan Douglas and David Zwirner, New York.

II

The purring engine of a parked white Chevrolet Caprice,[2] announces Detroit's long-standing identification with the automobile industry and with its machine–modernity interface in general. The soundtrack is otherwise silent—or almost silent. As one might hear the wind blow through a desolate place, an abandoned housing project that was once the scene of a vibrant, productive and hopeful modernity, ghostly sounds of emptiness, of wind, slamming doors and fleeing footsteps now stand in for the ruins. Whether the events represented in this film installation are "real" or supernatural remain answerable only to the individual viewer. But the pervasive chill this loop effects suggests "an emptiness so empty anything could happen in [its] continuous blur" (Taussig, 1999, p. 1).

Le Detroit utilizes the ghost story genre.[3] In particular, the film projection draws its narrative structure from two literary sources. One is *Legends of lé Detroit*, Marie Caroline Watson Hamlin's 1884 chronicle of French-Canadian and American folklore and weird tales—what Hamlin called the "historical and romantic souvenirs [that] hang like tattered drapery around the fair city of the Straits" (p. 3). The other literary referent is Shirley Jackson's 1959 novel, *The Haunting of Hill House*, a Gothic thriller whose central protagonist travels by car to the secluded and dreary Hill House to participate in a study of psychic or poltergeist activity of some kind. The young black woman protagonist of Douglas's film bears the name Eleanore, a close resemblance to the young woman named Eleanor in Jackson's novel.

The scene of *Le Detroit* is set late at night in front of a remaining townhouse in Detroit's Herman Gardens, a 1930s-style, once all-white housing development that evolved over time into an all-black "project." Now the development is entirely abandoned and in ruin, crumbling from flight, displacement and neglect.

Eleanore stares at the building from the driver's seat of the white Caprice. The look on her face betrays both calm and dread. She may be returning to the scene of a crime or a traumatic event, but the viewer can sense that the protagonist has come to this place in search of something unknown, perhaps for some clue left behind.

She exits the car, placing a spotlight on the hood to illuminate the building shrouded by overgrown trees. She walks deliberately toward the building, a flashlight in hand. Once inside, Eleanore examines a single footprint left in the sediments of dust and dirt that cover the floor. Passing through the desolate rooms, her impassive look betrays a melancholic recognition of piles of cluttered remains scattered over the floor, social artifacts like computer monitors but also furniture and old photographs that appear antique, perhaps dating from the nineteenth century. Eleanore stops to pick up one of the remains, examines it momentarily and then uncannily seems to put it back in its rightful place.

Climbing the stairs to the second floor of the house, she blindly reaches inside a punctured wall searching for some hidden object until, startled by a slamming door, she hastily abandons the quest. Following the same path of her entry, Eleanore flees the building. All of the items she touches or opens as she enters the building either return or close to the positions in which she found them—things fall back into their original place as if the film were running in reverse, but it is not. Eleanore reaches the car, collects the now dimmed spotlight from the hood, and starts the engine. Through a seamless edit, however, the film imperceptibly begins again, leaving the moment of flight or return uncertain. Clutching the steering wheel, Eleanore stares pensively at the building, preparing to *again* confront a lone footprint that is perhaps her own. This harrowing scene of return is all the more bewildering in its dreamlike tedium endless repetition.

III

Many of Douglas's installation projects are concerned as much with the ghastliness of failed utopias as they are with what possibilities the past might bequeath to the present. *Le Detroit* is one such work. It considers a historical moment in the life of Detroit and its debris. In this case, the city is a site of calamity marked by fire, race war, urban rebellion, reaction and urban redevelopment. This vision is curious about, or perhaps it is a curiosity of, that compulsion to repeat both the horror and the horrible in modern urban life. Hence, the indeterminacy of the loop in which Eleanore seems trapped and that the viewer as well is is compelled to watch, voyeuristically, over and over again. If the viewer inadavertently walks into the projected light, her or his shadow participates in the murky events on screen. One's ghostly afterimage joins many others complicit in the remnant of shady events that continue even after one has passed out of the light. Repetition of horror always leaves traces, even if ignored or denied, on cultural memory. *Le Detroit* aesthetically frames these unsettling traces within the borders of vision and, in doing so, triggers questions about processes of urban renewal that seem so compulsively dependent upon reducing a place to abject obsolescence.

Le Detroit's combination of film montage projected on a hanging screen and accompanying still photographic works is an installation practice Douglas has employed with increasing acuity in both art gallery and public space since the early 1980s. In *Le Detroit*, these dual "ways of seeing" picture Detroit affected by the trauma of historical and material social change. But "far from the cliché of Detroit as a sad necropolis" (Art Gallery of Windsor, 1999, p. 3), both Douglas's still and moving images extract a sense of the "not yet" from an extreme example of a more general blighting of history. Disquiet is provoked by photographic and cinematic strategies that (re)turn, however obliquely, to the traumatic thrall of urban defacement. And it is the "fact" of such an experience that prevents the observing eye from easily turning away.

IV

I evoke the term *defacement* in the spirit Michael Taussig's recent analysis of the mystical, *Defacement: Public Secrecy and the Labor of the Negative* (1999). When something is defaced, like a human body, a nation, a flag, money, a public statue or a city, Taussig maintains that the very repulsiveness of the act arouses a strange surplus negative energy from within the defaced thing itself. To see the defaced thing or the wound inflected is to witness a certain form of desecration, that is, the thing made sacred. To deface is to render a thing or a space empty, but that emptiness contains its own negative energy. If I follow Taussig correctly, I suggest that walking through the secular streets of a defaced city is "the closest many of us are going to get to the sacred in the modern world" (p. 1). More importantly, however, defacement can also concern the effort to recoup a negative energy trace and to purposefully redeploy it as a form of unmasking or critique that offers to tell *a* "truth." Here truth is not a matter of mere exposure of, say, a "secret." Defacement does not necessarily destroy the secret: defacement can also produce a revelation. If one lets it, a revelation can, as Taussig emphasizes, "do justice to the secret" (Walter Benjamin, quoted in Taussig, 1999, p. 2).

Stan Douglas's *Le Detroit* project engages in such an attempt of revelation, revealing through the foreboding labor of the negative. Here the negative suggests two meanings. First, the way a photographic negative is produced through the exposure of film to light. A negative produces its own "truths" or revelations when it is reversed through the photographic process and is reproduced on paper or in the case of film montage, projected onto a screen. This reversal process also informs and undergirds *Le Detroit*'s formal operations. Negative and positive versions of the film are projected onto either side of a hanging translucent screen. An image of Eleanore's frightful travail is seen on one side of the screen while its negative counterpart, slightly out of synch by a few seconds, is shown on the other side. The result is that each projection seems to bleed through the porous screen so that the interaction of the two images produces frequent afterimages, shadowy forms that seem to blend into one another, producing a third ghostly, flaky effect on the action. These images appear to flicker and shatter on the screen, sometimes crystallizing into near sharp black-and-white focus before receding in a shimmering gray-white murkiness. In constituting a rather arbitrary interaction of positive image and its negative, Douglas aims to heighten the sense of the film's indeterminacy and to foreground the lurking threat that pervades the film's subject matter (Enwezor, 2000).

Taussig's second point regarding the labor of the negative, as he metaphorically imports (following Walter Benjamin), relates to "the burning up the husk of the beautiful outer appearance of the secret as it enters into the realm of ideas" (p. 2). Laboring in the negative in this sense does not reinforce the negative by dwelling on its material facts or its social conventions. Rather, to reveal is to scrutinize the economy of signs in a given historical field, perhaps mystically but always metaphorically, in order to unleash other energies or other possibilities for reading those signs differently in the social present.

Defacement, however, suggests a double-edged sword: powers of negation lie entirely in the mode of revelation it is made to seek or seeks to make (Taussig, 1999, p. 3). On the one hand, defacement as exposure can work positively to destroy or conceal a secret, particularly a "public secret," like the nature of urban development, one that has become socially routinized and naturalized in face of the hushed absence of a demolished neighborhood. (Africville, a once thriving black autonomous community located in Halifax, Nova Scotia, Canada offers but one immediate parallel.)[4] Such histories may not be spoken about precisely because they are such public secrets: visible and *"generally known but* [things that] *cannot be articulated"* (Taussig, p. 5). "Live and forget," or "We must go on!" are usually the justifying phrases for such insidious denial and silence.

On the other hand, defacement can also denote unmasking, or re-presenting a public secret in a manner that might produce a different revelation, one that does justice to the secret rather than render it silent. Taussig names this unmasking "the just revelation."

Like Taussig, however, Douglas is guardedly skeptical about the revelatory task, indeed his own task. In aiming for the "just" there is a distinct possibility of falling into error, and by extension, doubt that any outside or any "just revelation" of the secret can emerge where power lurks. Douglas, like any insightful artist, may see his work not as explanation but as characterization. Can explanation exist? For Taussig, such a task is "doomed to [failure] from the outset, a surrender to the way of the world, wanting to be one with and even devoured by the subject matter of the negative" (p. 2). This self-reflexive skepticism, one that recognizes the fundamental irony of both his—and any artistic work—is the most persuasive element of Douglas's critical practice. His capacity (though some might argue luxury) to make a work of art "talk" about contemporary dilemmas, while side-stepping the "closed text" allure of pure facts and certainties, yields an "open work" that provokes multiple interpretations and possibilities for making meaning.[5] *Le Detroit* approximates the bellowing question of Nietzsche's madman, "Do you feel the breath of an empty space?" (Nietzsche, quoted in Taussig, 1999, p. 1). Douglas's open response characterizes this space by creating a jointly figurative and illusive emptiness where innumerable happenings and meanings await.

V

Stan Douglas is a visual artist, not a sociologist of the urban. Born in Vancouver, Canada in 1960, he is among a number of Canadian artists who have, in the last decade or so, achieved critical international art world attention. But like those great observers of the city, W. E. B. Du Bois, Friedrich Engels, Charles Baudelaire, Georg Simmel, Sigmund Freud, Walter Benjamin, and Samuel R. Delany, Douglas engages in extended periods of photographic scouting and archival research to seek out "truths" hidden and repressed by/in the city's imposing public façade. These secrets, and the strange surplus energy they arouse, are subjects visually realized.

Douglas's work reflects a particular hybrid of film/video/photography installation that focuses on a number of issues in contemporary visual culture and theory. These include: the nature of aesthetics; the political structuring of the image and the cultural context in which the image circulates; the way sound envelops and alters space; and the use of both obsolete and new media technologies to render transparent—and thus open to reconsideration—the constructed nature of representation in the shadowy side of capitalism.

Though Douglas's projects are typically exhibited in spaces of art museums, his intense critical engagement in/with such spaces "challenges the notion of the museum as a space of containment, contemplation and reification" (Crichlow, 1999; Enwezor, 2000). In doing so his work, like any significant artwork, introduces difference into our present-day narratives and, if only momentarily provokes reflection over immediate comprehension.

From his earliest work, a 1981 panoramic photographic installation titled *Jericho Warf* for example, Douglas has assiduously inquired into the ways European and Euro–North American urban culture have attempted to deface both history and natural landscape with rationalized forms of modernity. His photographic research uncovers and examines artifacts of utopic "development" discourses visible in the sediments of decay. If there is a political intent here it is embedded in experimental images that, however obliquely, highlight how modernist discourses have yet to come to terms with indigenous cultures and how they consistently continue to occlude marginalized peoples and lifestyles.[6]

With *Le Detroit*, Douglas continues to push forms of cinematic meditation to further the iconography of the urban fabric. His eye is particularly drawn to the pastoral, as well as the uninhabited ruins of cities, to the palpable strangeness of nonhuman aspects of defaced human constructions. The resultant images depict, without didactic assessment or sentimentalism, the failure of modern utopias, which he theorizes as a pile of debris (Watson, 1983, pp. 226–255).

These concerns with the urban landscape, with urban renewal and the failure of urban modernisms are variously reflected in a series of film and video installation projects Douglas produced throughout the 1990s. From his perspective, forgotten or naturalized incidents of modern utopia hold within them counterfactual narratives of the past and reveal elements of the future as chance (as much as power) that do not guarantee the received wisdom of our present.

I offer but a few examples. Set in Paris, France, *Hors-champs* (1992) juxtaposes expatriate African-American free-jazz performance with a history of troubled and only partially realized human freedoms to raise questions about promises of liberty that modern utopias held out. Depicting Nootka Sound on the west coast of Vancouver Island, British Columbia, *Nu tka* (1996) conjoins the Gothic nature of conflict and paranoia of eighteenth-century imperialism and the haunting absent presence of aboriginal peoples in our postcolonial present. *Win, Place, or Show* (1998) is perceptually harrowing and offers an endless scrutiny of the claustrophobic social relations created by modern urban planning and architecture.

Given the Gothic themes of imperialist dispossession prevalent in his prodigious *oeuvre*, such as imperialist crime, malignant modernity, slippage of identity, and urban displacement, Douglas's sojourn north to Detroit was likely. Indeed, the Gothic is familiar territory for Douglas. As he writes in regard to *Nu tka*: "The Gothic romance was typically characterized by a return of the repressed: some past transgression haunts, then destroys, the culpable family, person or social order. It is no surprise that these narratives flourished during the era of high imperialism" (quoted in Augaitis, 1999, p. 43).

With *Le Detroit* Douglas once again visits the failed utopias of modernism, only configured now as urban legend meets capitalist hope through ruin. But here utopia is reversed. Many of the photographs picture modernist architecture abandoned and in collapse, but others reveal how the pastoral past both endures and returns. Yet in all of the images, it is a return haunted by the knowledge of past transgressions and by a discontented repetition of epic ruin. *Le Detroit* thus synthesizes the modernist urban schemes of *Win, Place, or Show* and the Gothic underpinnings of *Nu tka*. If *Nu tka* approximates Canadian Gothic, then *Le Detroit* offers an American Gothic.[7]

VI

I attended the opening reception of *Le Detroit* held at the Art Gallery of Windsor in November of 1999. I recall the four-hour drive west from Toronto, Canada—down the infamously traitorous Highway 401—and how relieved I was to finally exit to head north to Windsor. Visiting Windsor for the first time, I finally gained a material sense of that peculiar Canadian pride in the geographic fact that Windsor is the sole point from which the United States is *north* of the Canadian border.

I also remember driving down Howard Avenue toward downtown Windsor. It was dusk and I could see ahead a looming city skyline of towering buildings. Ah! I said to myself, "Windsor is a real city!" When I reached downtown I discovered that the skyscrapers that had piqued my interest from the outskirts of the city were actually across the Detroit River, in the United States, in the famous motor city of Detroit. I parked my car and walked quickly to a riverside tourist park to peer at the massive infrastructure lining the other side of the watery border. I looked with awe and a flaneur's delight at the facade of urban Detroit, but I was actually thinking, there is America!

I am "American," actually, but I had not visited Detroit since 1978 when I attended an academic meeting held in the August of that year. Twenty years later, I can still recall how struck I was by the emptiness of the central business district. I remember how eerily boarded up abandoned buildings and storefronts looked as I walked, perhaps a mile, from a dingy YMCA to the Renaissance Centre, that futuristic hotel, office, and retail complex where the conference was housed. I recall colleagues' telling me that the recently constructed complex was the multimillion-dollar focal piece of Detroit's urban redevelopment plan. It was emblematic of the city's touted comeback scheme orchestrated by the ruling elite in the early 1970s. The intention of this plan was to rebuild economic confidence in the city after the riots of July 1967. As these memories flooded back during that dusk view of Detroit from a spot on Windsor's riverside, my anticipation heightened as I tried to imagine what Stan Douglas envisioned in his *Le Detroit* project.

VII

What did Stan Douglas see? As I have suggested, the presupposition of *Le Detroit* is that Detroit is a city haunted by both the past and by uncertainties about the future. In many ways, the social and economic transformation that exemplifies urbanism's ambivalent future in North America over the past fifty years happened first in Detroit, and here most dramatically.[8]

The history and extremity of urban crisis in Detroit leaves the city situated in a particular liminal space, one that may be characterized as between the present and the future. The word *detroit* literally means "strait"—a place in between. French seventeenth-century explorers who first paddled along the rims of the Great Lakes and through the Detroit River named the region "the strait," deriving the term from their translations of the aboriginal names for the region. The strait was also the scene of colonial conquest of the region, marking a site that stood inbetween the new world and old but irrevocably set in motion the transition from one world to quite another. The early explorers who subsequently founded Detroit as a French outpost against English territorial encroachment were not only interested in the search for imperial glory and treasures. They were simultaneously determined to carry their flag and knowledge of their "true God" throughout the colonized "New World."[9]

Le Detroit thus signals the ghosts of an unspoken and occluded past that continue to haunt the present, Detroit's own and most other North American cities as well: aboriginal displacement from the land, as well as the displacement of the poor and the marginalized from the inner city. A past and present of shifting forms of overt and covert race and class conflict have afflicted Detroit since the mid-nineteenth century, as well as the alienation of hundreds of thousands of deindustrialized workers in the urban renewed present.

A strait is a channel that connects two bodies of water, but it may also refer to the passage from one psychic "state" to another, from the uncanny back to what has been always known and long familiar. It can also mark the frightening space between these states, between the real and the unreal. It is in such an in-between state that Douglas's vision of Detroit evolved. The project was researched and photographed mainly during the years of 1997 and 1998, as the city lurched forward in the frenzy of urban renewal. The project may also have residual origins in Douglas's childhood memories. At age seven, Douglas reports that his family drove through riot-stricken Detroit on their way back to Milwaukee after visiting the 1967 Montreal Expo (Laycock, 1999). In *Le Detroit*, one may witness the artist laboring to externalize the strait between what can remembered of a childhood trauma and what sense might be made of that trauma years later, in the present.

More concretely, I suggest that in *Le Detroit*, Douglas has accomplished a dispassionate form of visual inquiry that plays in urban time and space, simultaneously on the edges of what happened, what is happening and what might happen in the urban renewed landscape of Detroit. The film projection on the double-sided screen serves as a further strait between what can and cannot be fully taken in by vision—the viewer simply cannot see the flickering play of positive and negative interaction on both sides of the screen. On one side or the other, all we can see are the ghostly results of an interaction that continuously and inconclusively shifts from surfaces of violence to beauty, hardness to fragility, but always with a conceptual rigor that keeps the question of meaning open. Finally, the inconclusiveness of the film loop and the blending of positive and negative images of the same event slightly out of synch with one another both serve as a metonym for trauma but also hope. Douglas again suggests that things are not yet spent and there is no guarantee for the future.

VIII

The future often resides in the popular imaginary as a parody of the past. The 1950s, 1960s, 1970s, or even 1980s—anytime but now—constitute possible sites for return to the future. Once America's motor of industry and fourth-largest city, Detroit provides a frightening narrative of transformation. *Le Detroit* visualizes this tale's present offering a metaphorical window through which to consider a not-quite-yet-urban future. A June 11, 1805, stable fire razed virtually all of the budding Detroit river town, and the 1943 race riot of proved a violent culmination to wartime tensions in the booming city. Detroit's most recent ill-fated story line, however, moves with abrupt steadiness from civil rebellion in 1967 to the domination of corporate will over civic space and civil society. Its eerie plot shifts from "white flight" depopulating, deindustrializing, deservicing, and devaluing large neighborhood areas of the city to the massive leeching of its tax base, the de-skilling of jobs, and the displacement of everyday consumption from the central business district to the sprawl of new suburbs. This spatial and material reorganization offers a possible future that rests on a city defaced.

Like the return of the repressed, *Le Detroit* presents a dreamlike witnessing of urban decline. Within and beyond its visual frames, however, this work inquires into a future imagined on a slate cleared of the residues of a cataclysmic past. Most iconic public facades of downtown Detroit, along with its politicized public sphere, were demolished, neighborhoods razed,

Michigan Theater, 1998. Courtesy of Stan Douglas and David Zwirner, New York.

making it possible for developers, the new harbingers of the future, to work
a sleight-of-hand magic and get super-rich quick. By picturing stagnant
residues of a complex history of abandonment, Douglas anticipates the
unsettled future. That is, a future absent of such landmark civic and cultural
icons as the J. L. Hudson's Department Store building which has been crumbling in decay since closing in 1983; the grand proscenium and stage area
of the old Michigan Theater now a retrofitted parking lot; or the Herman
Gardens Housing Project, a last inkling of Franklin and Eleanor Roosevelt's
New Deal social-engineered (utopic) modernism returning to nature.

But what kind of future, *Le Detroit* asks, does redevelopment, new "good
time" entertainment zones, and gentrification announce? With the neoliberal accomplishment of a "new jack city," what is to prevent urban
dwellers from capitulating to the aggressively euphoric narrative of the
"end of history"? If such a belief in capitalist triumphalism prevails, Douglas argues, then what is being "made real" in urban-renewed Detroit and
in other urban centres around the globe, "is a [social] condition that
remains [as] false as it is predicated upon the triumph of rhetoric and
defeat of imagination" (1999, p. 68).

Such defeat, however, is only one possibility. The verdict is not out on
such a future, yet. We are, after all, talking about Detroit, Motor City, the
Dodge Revolutionary Union Movement (DRUM), the Motown Sound, and
a history of dancing in the streets by people who are very much alive. The
legacy of these collective narratives also comprise public secrets whose quo-
tidian traces lie just beyond the edges of Douglas's images. The unwritten
future of the city that Eleanore searches so furtively for, lies beneath the
sediment and debris of a politically and racially charged environment.
Longtime activist Grace Boggs (1998), moving between past and present, in
her twilight looking compassionately toward the future offers a cautiously
optimistic but apposite prophesy:

> I rejoice in the changing of the guard and at the fact that the new genera-
> tion, which is beginning to discover its mission, is more open than the gen-
> eration that led the movement in the 1960s. . . . I am glad that I am still
> around not only as a participant but as a griot to pass on the story of how we
> got to this place—because to paraphrase Kierkegaard, if the future is to be
> lived, the past must be understood. (p. 272)

Le Detroit additionally suggests a future possibility that negatively foregrounds the logic of defacement. The critique of urban decline is rendered
not as an end point, as yet another finality to be bemoaned. Rather, the
spellbinding eeriness unleashed by the emptying out of place gives these
images their critical revelatory power. It is not a matter of uncovering
truths that animate this visual imaginary, but of lending credence to the
unwritten future of this city, one that beckons social justice to be collectively imagined—and struggled for the knowledge that things past might
have been otherwise.

7

Screening Race

Norman K. Denzin

Presently in America a war is being fought. Forget about guns, planes, and bombs, the weapons from now on will be the newspapers, magazines, TV shows, radio, and FILM. The right has gotten BOLD . . . any piece of art that doesn't hold the party line is subject to attack. It's war in the battleground of culture.

—Spike Lee, *By Any Means Necessary* (1992)

A marginalized group needs to be wary of the seductive power of realism, of accepting all that a realistic representation implies.

—Lubiano, *But Compared to What* (1997)

Aesthetics then is more than a philosophy or theory of art and beauty; it is a way of inhabiting space . . . a way of looking and becoming. . . . I find compelling a racial aesthetic that seeks to uncover and restore links between art and revolutionary politics.

—hooks, *Yearning: Race, Gender, and Cultural Politics* (1990)

A single problem, moving in several directions at the same time, guides this essay.[1] I seek to understand Hollywood's cinema of racial violence, a cinema represented in more than twenty films released between 1987 and 1998. Produced by mainstream Anglo, African American, and Latino/a filmmakers, this cinema located racial violence in the black and brown public sphere, the hyperghetto, America's postindustrial wasteland.[2] Spike Lee is right. At one level, America's war on race occurred in the spaces and the battlegrounds created by these films. It was and remains a war fought on the battlefields of cultural representation.

The crack cocaine wars, the War on Drugs, and the "Just Say No to Drugs" campaign of the Reagans coincided with the appearance of a new war zone in the national popular imagination—the black and brown hood. In the spaces of this war zone, dark-skinned youth in gangs engaged in drive-by shootings as a new form of entertainment. Rap music and hip-hop culture became signifiers of a new and violent racial order. In the minds of many, rap music meant racial violence. And this violence was spreading everywhere, threatening white America. Joel Schumacher's 1995 film *Falling Down*, starring Michael Douglas, spoke for many male white Americans. They were not going to take this violence falling down. They were going to fight back.

The hood movies represented another version of this battle, another way of fighting back. These films framed a particular version of the violent, gendered, cinematic racial order. This cinema of racial violence was shaped by a politics of representation that valued whiteness and a new conservative cultural racism (see Pinar, 2001, p.18).

In this essay I offer preliminary observations on the possibilities of a critical, ethnic cinema, a cinema that honors racial and cultural difference. I begin with a brief aside on the hood movies, then turn to the aesthetic arguments of the Black Arts movement of the 1960s and 1970s. I next examine the didactic, realistic cinema of the new black aesthetic. I compare and contrast these two aesthetics, in the hopes of fashioning a counterhegemonic cinematic aesthetic for the twenty-first century. I write against the backdrop of the Black Arts movement of the 1960s and 1970s. I want their dream to live again.[3] I end with observations on critical race theory, a new aesthetic of color, and a radical cinema of racial difference.

Race in the Hood

The hood race films of the last decade came in two forms: action-comedy interracial cop-buddy series (*Lethal Weapon, Die Hard*); and films that emphasized didactic, social realist, social problems messages. These were utopian tales, shaped by a dialectic of fear and hope. There were some women's stories, but primarily these films were coming-of-age all-male narratives, dealing with violence on the streets and in prison. A uniform conservative moral message was conveyed. Young men must have strong role models. They must respect their elders, go to school, get a good education, and become responsible members of the black or brown middle class. These films do not take up critical race, Marxist, feminist, or postcolonial theories of racism, empowerment, and liberation. They articulate a neonationalistic, essentializing, homophobic, masculinist gender and identity politics. (Spike Lee's films epitomize these tendencies.)

The New Right blamed persons of color for the problems that were located in the ghetto. The repressive efforts of the right were anchored in the crack cocaine wars that extended from the mid-1980s to the mid-1990s (Reeves and Campbell, 1994; Reinarman and Levine, 1997). The hood films narrate the cocaine wars. These wars were accompanied by increased police surveillance in the ghetto. This new police state contributed to a sense that the ghetto had once again become a violent nation, or a crumbling internal colony within the great American cities of Los Angeles and New York. Black, brown, and Italian Mafias took control of an underground drug economy. Racial gangs on the street and in prison recruited youth of color for this project. Soon young men were shooting one another in drive-bys and gang wars. The police kept white America safe from the crazed violence that was operating in the ghetto.

These race stories are not progressive or subversive films. Indeed, they created deep generational, gender, and class divisions within the black and brown middle classes. Women called the films misogynist. The black and brown middle classes objected to the guns, drugs, and gang warfare. Black activists from the '60s said they were reactionary (Baraka, 1993, p. 153).

Sadly, as films about race and racism, they do not attack the essential, underlying ideologies and material conditions that perpetuate racial oppression in American today. This is the case even for the films made by black and brown filmmakers. These filmmakers seem unwilling and unable to attack the ideology they and their films are so firmly embedded in. They do not rupture the veneer of this larger racial apparatus. It is as if they are trapped by the very violence they want to criticize. Hence these are not politically subversive texts (see Comolli and Narboni, 1971/1976, p. 27; Denzin, 1995, p. 192). They do not advance the project of the earlier Chicana/o and Black Arts cultural movements.

The Black Arts Movement

Participants in the Black Arts movement of the 1970s waged a cultural war against centuries of segregation in the United States (W. Harris, 1998, p. 1344). This battle was ignited by the civil rights movement, the women's movement, the Chicano movement, and the antiwar movement. It drew upon texts and political figures central to the national liberation struggles in Africa, Asia, and Latin America, including Maoism in Asia, Castro in Cuba, Che Guevarism in Latin America, and Fanonists in Africa and Algeria (Harris, 1998, p. 1344; Masilela, 1993, pp. 107–108; Noriega, 1992a, p. 141; Diawara, 1993, pp. 3–11). Artists, poets, scholars, playrights, filmmakers, and performers of color, including Angela Davis, Jayne Cortez, Sonia Sanchez, Etheridge Knight, Lucille Clifton, Don L. Lee, Ishmael Reed, Amiri Baraka, Henry Dumas, Daniel and Luis Valdez, Gregory Naven, and Edward James Olmos called for a radical reordering of the Western cultural aesthetic.

They rejected the white, Eurocentric, Enlightenment model that called politicized art propaganda. They sought an art that was unique to their cultural experiences. Gayle argued, "few . . . would disagree with the idea that unique experiences produce unique cultural artifacts, and that art is a product of such cultural experiences" (1997, p. 1876). There was a conscious attempt to "forge an unbreakable link between artistic production and revolutionary politics" (hooks, 1990, p. 106).

Similarly, artists within the Black Arts movement crafted their version of an artistic and political aesthetic that advanced the cause of a radical, separatist black politics (Neal, 1988; Fuller, 1997; Gayle, 1997/1971). These artists sought empowerment through art. They rewrote history to include spaces for the black power (and Chicano) movement, the black church, links to folklore and the oral tradition, and the African and Latin diaspora. They used various regimes of realism to present stories and images about black and brown communities under siege. Soundtracks echoed themes from the civil rights movement.

The original Black Arts movement eschewed protest art because such art based its arguments on an appeal to white morality and a white Eurocentric artistic aesthetic. Etheridge Knight, quoted by Neal (1998), defines protest art thusly, contending that any black person

> who masters the techniques of his [or her] particular art form, who adheres to a white aesthetic, and who directs his [or her] work toward a white audience is, in one sense protesting. And implicit in the act of protest is the belief that a change will be forthcoming once the masters are aware of the protester's "grievance" (the very word connotes begging, supplications to the gods). Only when that belief has faded and protestings end, will Black art begin. . . . Unless the Black artist establishes a "Black aesthetic he [she] will have no future at all." (p. 1450)

Thus the black artist gives up on the project of speaking to a white audience (Gayle, 1997, p. 1875). The need to create a uniquely black aesthetic, to create new artistic forms and new values is very clear.

Gayle (1997, p. 1875) frames this demand in terms of W. E. B. Du Bois's concept of the veil. In an often-quoted passage, Du Bois (1903/ 1989) argued:

> The Negro is . . . born with a veil, and gifted with a second sight in this American world—a world which yields him no true self-consciousness, but only lets him see himself through the revelation of the other world. It is a particular sensation, this double-consciousness, this sense of always looking at one's self through the eyes of others, or measuring one's soul by the tape of a world that looks on in amused contempt and pity. One ever feels his twoness—an American, a Negro, two souls, two thoughts . . . two warring ideals in one dark body. (p. 3)

A black aesthetic would cut through this veil, and give black people a new mirror to look into, a mirror that did not hang behind a white veil. This mirror speaks to and from the souls of black folk.

This mirror, this aesthetic, is an ethics of representation that expresses the truth of racial injustice as lived by the oppressed. In this world ethics, epistemology and aesthetics will "interact positively and be consistent with the demands of a more spiritual world" (Neal, 1998, p. 1451). On this point Neal was clear: "The Black Arts Movement is an ethical movement" (p. 1451). This aesthetic creates new standards of beauty. Black is beautiful.

Blacks have style and flair, and their speech exhibits distinctive rhythms. This aesthetic rejects white standards of beauty, including those connected to white, or light, skin and straight hair (Fuller, 1997, p. 1813).

Gayle (1997) elaborates:

> The question for the black critic today is not how beautiful is a melody, a play, a poem, or a novel, but how much more beautiful has the poem, melody, play, or novel made the life of a single black [person]? How far has the work gone in transforming an American Negro into an African-American or black man? This Black Aesthetic, then, as conceived by this writer, is a corrective—a means of helping black people out of the polluted mainstream of Americanism. (p. 1876)

Gayle contended that black art required new standards and new tools of evaluation. According to Karenga (1997/1972) there were three criteria for black art: it must be functional, collective, and committed. Functionally, this art would support and "respond positively to the reality of a revolution" (1997, p. 1973). It would not be art for art's sake, rather it would be art for our sake, art for "Sammy the shoeshine boy, T. C. the truck driver and K. P. the unwilling soldier" (p. 1974). Karenga is clear: "We do not need pictures of oranges in a bowl, or trees standing innocently in the midst of a wasteland . . . or fat white women smiling lewdly. . . . If we must paint oranges or trees, let our guerrillas be eating those oranges for strength and using those trees for cover" (p. 1974; see also Gayle, 1971, p. xxiii).

Collectively, black art comes from people and must be returned to the people "in a form more beautiful and colorful than it was in real life. . . . [A]rt is everyday life given more form and color" (Karenga, 1997, p. 1974). Such art is democratic: it celebrates diversity, personal and collective freedom, and speaks to the everyday people and their concerns in the world. It is not elitist.

After Fanon, these filmmakers and artists conceptualized the ghetto as an internal racial colony (Diawara, 1993, p. 9; Fuller, 1997, p. 1813). This colony, like a cancer, was buried deep in the belly of the larger white racist society. The short-lived blaxploitation film movement of the 1970s embodied many of these values (Diawara, 1993, p. 9). As Diawara observes (1993, p. 9), Van Peebles's Sweetback can be read as a hero of decolonization. Sweetback represents all of the black outlaws who came before him: Stagolee, Bigger Thomas, Chester Himes's criminals, Ellison's invisible man, Malcolm X, the archetype of the black man running from the law.

The Black's Arts movement resurfaces in the 1990s with a new generation of filmmakers and is called the "new black realism," "the new black aesthetic" (Massood, 1996, p. 88; Diawara, 1993, p. 23; Boyd, 1997, p. 25). (The films discussed in this essay embody this aesthetic regime. They must bear witness to its own cinema of racial violence.)

A Cinema of Racial Violence

The New Right under the Reagan, Bush, and Gingrich administrations reversed the economic, educational, and political entitlements of the civil rights movement of the 1960s. These efforts had disastrous effects on life in America's inner cities. The politicians of the New Right made race visible in new ways. They succeeded in coding violence with race, with black youth, with gangs, drive-bys, rap music, and hip-hop culture.

The hood movies offered one set of responses to this so-called national moral crisis. This was a historical project. This group of filmmakers was responding to a particular set of economic, cultural, and political conditions. Thus was produced a complex politics of representation. The filmmakers were criticized for making violent films about the violence they said was in the hood. Directors from Edward James Olmos to Spike Lee, John Singleton, and the Hughes brothers argued that they were only telling it like it was, that the violence they represented was there because of what the right had done. It was a stand-off.

Using the apparatuses of cinematic realism, these films erased the notion of a unified or essential racial subject. Still, they created their own notion of the racial subject, the young black or brown man in the hood with a gun. These social problems–based films brought the violence of the hood directly in front of the viewer. These didactic texts called for an end to the genocide in the hood. "No More Packing" screams Spike Lee's billboards at the end of *Clockers*, and the Hughes brothers and Olmos have close-ups of little children holding guns.

The conservative political consequences of this new cinematic realism were made clear in California after the race riots in Los Angeles in 1992. On national television Pete Wilson, the governor of the state, suggested, "Everyone in America should see the movie *Boyz N the Hood*. In that movie, a strong father makes the difference for his teenaged son . . . [who is] about to rush . . . out and try to avenge his best friend who has just been gunned down in a mindless, senseless gang war. . . . Now . . . that movie says we need a strong father and welfare is no suitable replacement for that" (Reeves and Campbell, 1994, pp. 246–247).

A Mimetic Realism

Filmmakers using the new black aesthetic brought the "real" world of the hood in front of the viewer. Lubiano (1997, pp. 104–104), drawing on Mercer (1988), argues that their realist methods relied on the operation of four cinematic techniques: transparency, immediacy, authority, and authenticity. The hood filmmakers acted as if their cameras were neutral recording devices, presenting the hood as it really was, telling the truth through their slices-of life-imagery. Thus the films claimed a truth that was transparent—visible— in reality. This was not a personal cinema; it was objective and authoritative. The filmmakers used documentary-like footage (the opening scenes in *Menace II Society*) and shots of political posters (*Boyz N the Hood*) to lend historical authenticity to their texts.

Their invisible cameras offered detailed, close-up images that filled the screen. This was an authentic realism that was everywhere, but nowhere more visible then in the blood-soaked stains that spilled across sidewalks after drive-bys. The use of vernacular speech, rap music, and hip-hop fashion further authenticated the visual text and the spoken narrative, giving them an even greater aura of realism (Dimitriadis, 2001b). This social problems–based cinematic realism demanded that viewers react in horror to senseless, youthful genocidal violence.

The black filmmakers of the 1990s were committed to a mimetic conception of representation (Mercer, 1988, p. 53). They assumed that an objective reality was out there, that it existed, and that it could be captured cinematically. Thus they sought to present the referential realities of race using a grammar of visual or mimetic realism. Paradoxically, they sought to do this even as they resisted mainstream Hollywood and its racist cinematic apparatuses. But they were using the same codes, methods, techniques, and conservative, racist story lines as mainstream Hollywood.

Lubiano contends that a realism used thusly, and uncritically "as a mode for African American art implies that our lives can be captured by the representation of enough documentary evidence, or by insistence on another truth" (1997, p. 105). When the graffiti in *Do the Right Thing* reads "Tawana told the Truth" there is an assertion that her story was true and real, actual and concrete, that it was a story of a real rape (p. 105).

There are several problems with such assertions. First, whose truth is operating? Must Tawana be telling the truth before we can accept the "larger truth about sexual abuse of African American women by Euro-American men? Is this 'truth' compared to the 'truth' of their abuse by African Amercian men? Compared to what other African American women say? Compared to what Alice Walker . . . says about African American men?" (Lubiano, 1997, p. 105).

In staking out its claims to truth, this version of cinematic realism also creates the conditions for its own deconstruction, and this is so on multiple grounds. First, telling it like it is assumes that you can in fact tell it like it is, that there is but one telling. But this is not the case, for conservatives tell it differently than radical black feminists, for example.

Second, adherence to the regimes of white racial realism belies an acceptance of one version of what the real is, and one version of how the real is made visible. The apparatuses of mainstream realism lead to the production of films that have the authenticity of modernist, naturalistic ethnographies. These texts purport to present lived reality. In so doing they perform particular gendered versions of race, they reinscribe familiar cultural stereotypes. They reproduce white stereotypes of dark-skinned persons. These constructions and representations of "blackness" or "brownness" enter public discourse and are accepted as real (Lubiano, 1997, p. 107).

Third, this realist apparatus creates an implicit demand for members of racial minorities to set the record straight, to make public stereotypes and misunderstandings conform to the truth of the real facts. There is a risk in setting the record straight; namely, whose record is being corrected, with what methods and with what representations? By agreeing that the record should be set straight, one gives an authority to the existing representations. By using the selfsame methods that created the racist representations, one enters a battle over which record is truthful, accurate, or correct. Lubiano notes that the post–Harlem Renaissance "black aesthetic critics . . . built a political and intellectual movement around an assertion of a countertruth against the distortions of cultural racism" (1997, p. 106). This has not been the case for users of the new black aesthetic.

Fourth, the reproductions of the sounds and sights of African American (and Hispanic) vernacular culture is problematic. There is a danger in "repeating the masculinism and heterosexism of vernacular culture" (Lubiano, 1997, p. 196). Further, there is no guarantee that a text will be counterhegemonic just because it represents, romanticizes, or criticizes the vernacular (see Lubiano, 1997, p. 119, n. 19).

Indeed, fifth, the use of the vernacular as a method for establishing authenticity can reproduce a problematic version of essentialism; the belief that certain characteristics are "inherently part of the core being of a group" (Lubiano, 1997, p. 109). These kinds of representations may contribute to a naive and stereotypical notion of the unified racial subject. Thus hip, cool, jiving black males have a "predilection for playing craps, drinking, using or selling drugs, or raping white women, or being a jungle savage . . . or being on welfare—the list goes on and on" (Lubiano, 1997, p. 111). The relationship between authenticity and essentialism must always be made problematic.[4]

Sixth, in making a claim for presenting it as it is, the realistic filmmaker also makes a counterclaim: reality is this way, and not this way. In its silence about alternative representations, the film asserts its own hegemonic power over its situated version of the real. Thus, for example, many of the hood films take up the topic of AIDS and its victims among black men. Yet no hood filmmaker presents a positive view of gay men and the gay black community. Nor do these filmmakers take up the nurturing responses to AIDS's victims by the black church and the black family. As a consequence, only black homophobia is presented.

Realism and the Didactic Protest Film

This form of racial realism was used by black (and brown) filmmakers of the 1990s for didactic or moral purposes. Singleton, Olmos, the Hughes brothers, and Lee sent moral messages to white as well as black and brown America. Lee said he wanted to "force America to come to grips with the problem of racism" (quoted in Lubiano, 1997, p. 101). Within the framework of the older black aesthetic these were protest films (Neal, 1998,

p. 1450). They used the narrative and cinematic techniques of mainstream Hollywood cinema. They were protesting conditions in the ghetto and sending their message to white America. They spoke in terms of a white and black middle-class morality. These were wake-up calls to the larger culture to understand the problems in the black and brown community. And, in many cases, they blamed members of the racial community for these problems.

The new filmmakers embraced a protest art, an art that had been rejected by the members of the original Black Arts movement. They articulated a white aesthetic that was filtered through the formulations of the original Black Arts movement. Whereas the films of the 1970s attempted to establish a counteraesthetic, the films of the 1990s embodied a white social problems aesthetic. In this regard they were what Knight called protest art.

As protest art they enacted an essentializing social problems ideology (see Mills, 1963, p. 527). This ideology emphasized identity politics and the values of home and community. These films focused on the democratic values of American society, irrespective of race, including the myths of success and the values of family, home, romantic love, education, and hard work. They centered their visual imagery on the problems of community disorganization. These problems were caused by pathological, dope-using, gun-carrying unadjusted individuals: the young black or brown male in a gang. It is an understatement to say that they did not present violence, drugs, or gangs in a positive light.

These films borrowed the format of the Victorian melodrama, with narratives organized around the poles of good and evil. Heroes and heroines were placed in conflict with violence and evil. They overcame or escaped these evils, temptations, obstacles, and conflicts through luck or the help of family, friends, lovers, or police. They were rewarded, if they were lucky, by the love of a good man or good woman and a safe place in respectable, black or brown middle-class society.

In the hood movies a societal condition (violence, gangs and drugs in the hood), coincides with a personal problem (absent fathers), a character defect (attraction to violence), and a violent act (killing someone). These conditions function, in turn, as dramatic devices that allow the filmmaker to tell a story with a moral message. This message includes commentary on the individual, his or her problem, and the larger society that contains, creates, and reacts to the problem. Didacticism is the distinguishing feature of these films; they attempt to teach and inform an audience about a problem—drugs, violence and gangs in the hood—and its solution, or lack thereof (Roffman and Purdy, 1981, p. viii; Denzin, 1991, p. 13).

A tautology organizes these didactic texts. Racial violence, murder, and father absence are the central social problems in the hood. These problems create social disorganization and pathology. These pathologies are happening because of a deterioration in key values connected to family, hard work, and personal responsibility. Because of this deterioration, and because of these pathologies, the hood is a pathological community. It experiences its pathology and disorganization through the signifiers connected to the pathology: rap, hip-hop, and the drug-dealing culture. The pathological members of the community are maladjusted. These violent drug-dealing youth have not been successfully socialized into the Christian values of the local moral community.

The answer to the problem of social disorganziation is clear. And here the hood films, as protest art, side with white society. The police must help the community get rid of the dope and drug dealers. Greater state intervention by the police is necessary if order is to be restored. Fathers must come home to their children, and grandchildren must listen to their grandparents.

In their antiviolence these films do not take up the larger political and economic situations that produced the so-called disorganization in the first place. Documentary footage from the 1965 Los Angeles race riots and close-ups of posters showing Ronald Reagan smiling are not sufficiently political. Thus, at this level the hood films fail to realize their own political agenda. They only repeated an age-old social disorganization, social problems story: that is, "We have a problem here, come help us" (see Mills, 1963, p. 542). And in so doing they confirmed the prophecy that protest art in the racial arena is doomed if it speaks from only a white political and moral aesthetic.

An Aesthetic of Color and Critical Race Theory

Back to the present. Baker (1997), commenting on the legacies of the Black Arts movement, observed that the

> creative and critical dreams of new black artistic forms were endorsed by emergent literatures and critical traditions around the world. In the United States alone, Native American, Chicano, and Chicana, and gay and lesbian writers, critics and scholars acknowledged . . . their enormous debt to the strategies, authors and works of the Black Arts movement. . . . [T]he Black Aesthetic . . . continues to enrich artistic traditions, and critical debate that will enliven the twenty-first century. (p. 1806)

Thus is hooks's call for a counterhegemonic cinema of race and Patricia Hill Collins's (1991, 1998) dream of an Afrocentric feminist agenda for the 1990s advanced into the next decade. Artists, filmmakers, activists, theorists, and practitioners enact a standpoint epistemology that sees the world and resistances to it from the point of view of oppressed persons of color, especially women.

Ethics and an Antiaesthetic

With hooks (1990, p. 110), who borrows from H. Foster (1983), I seek a discourse on aesthetics that is not trapped by the modernist agenda.[5] This agenda locates aesthetics outside of, or apart from history. Thus Foster calls for an antiaesthetic, or postmodern aesthetic that is "cross-disciplinary in nature, that is sensitive to cultural forms in a politic (e.g., feminist art), or rooted in a vernacular—that is, to forms that deny the idea of a privileged aesthetic realm" (p. xv). This antiaesthetic is subversive and utopian. It creates a space for the filmmaking and artistic representational practices of previously marginalized groups. It empowers members of such groups to break with naturalism and realism as the standard ways of representing reality. It suggests that that there are multiple artistic audiences for such work. It contends that there are multiple aesthetic measures of a work's value. It values transgressive and oppositional representations.

This a political and ethical aesthetic. It erases modernist distinctions between and among epistemology, ontology, aesthetics, and ethics. In a feminist, communitarian sense, this aesthetic contends that ways of knowing (epistemology) are always moral and ethical. They always involve conceptions of who the human being is (ontology), including how matters of difference, oppression, and injustice are socially organized. The ways in which these relationships are represented involve interpretive practices that answer to a political and epistemological aesthetic, what is good, true, and beautiful.

For the antiaesthetic, all aesthetics and standards of judgment are based on particular moral standpoints. There is no objective, morally neutral standpoint. Hence, an Afrocentric feminist aesthetic (and epistemology) stresses the importance of truth, knowledge, and beauty. Such claims are based on a concept of storytelling and a notion of wisdom that is experiential and shared. Storytellers, including filmmakers, take what they tell from experience, passing along the truths of this experience to others. In the telling, this experience becomes an experience for those who are watching and listening to the story being told, and therein lies the truth of the story (Benjamin, 1968, p. 87; L. McMurtry, 1999, p. 14).

Wisdom so conceived is derived from local, lived experience, and expresses lore, folktale, and myth. This is a dialogical epistemology and aesthetic. It enacts an ethic of care, and an ethic of personal and communal responsibility (P. Collins, 1991, p. 214). Politically, this aesthetic imagines how a truly democratic society might look, including one free of race prejudice and oppression (Feagin, 2000, pp. 270–271). This aesthetic values beauty and artistry, movement, rhythm, color, and texture in everyday life. It celebrates difference and the sounds of many different voices. It expresses an ethic of love, fellowship, and mutual empowerment,

This ethic presumes a moral community that is ontologically prior to the person. This community has shared moral values, including the concepts of care, shared governance, neighborliness, love, kindness and the moral good (Christians, 2000, pp. 144–149). This ethic embodies a sacred, existential epistemology that locates persons in a noncompetitive, nonhierarchical relationship to the larger moral universe. This ethic declares that all persons deserve dignity and a sacred status in the world. It stresses the value of human life, truth telling and nonviolence (p. 147).

This ethical aesthetic is dialogical and enabling. In generating social criticism, it also engenders resistance. It empowers persons to action (Christians, 2000, p. 147). It helps them imagine how things could be different in the everyday world. It imagines new forms of human transformation and emancipation. It enacts these transformations through dialogue. If necessary, it sanctions nonviolent forms of civil disobediance (p. 148). This aesthetic imagines and locates the downtrodden and the oppressed in the construction of new and liberating cultural formations. It opposes a culture of silence. It resists political programs that are led by those currently in power. It offers new forms of representation that create the space for new forms of critical race consciousness. It shows the oppressed how to find a voice in the spaces of oppression.

Thus theorists and filmmakers alike critically engage and interrogate the anti–civil rights agendas of the New Right (see Jordan, 1998). But this is not a protest or integrationist initiative aimed solely at informing a white audience of racial injustice. It dismisses these narrow agendas. In so doing it rejects classical Eurocentric and postpositivist standards for evaluating literary, artistic, and research work.

Thus are sought emancipatory, utopian cinematic texts grounded in the distinctive styles, rhythms, idioms, and personal identities of local folk and vernacular culture. These films record the history of injustices experienced by the members of an oppressed group. They show how members of a local group have struggled to find places of dignity and respect in a violent, racist, and sexist civil society. These films are sites of resistance. They are places where meanings, politics, and identities are negotiated. They transform and challenge all forms of cultural representation, white, black.

Antiaesthetics and Cinematic Practices

Within the contemporary black and Chicana/o film communities, a specific set of film practices is associated with this counterhegemonic, antiaesthetic project.[6] These practices inform and shape the narrative and visual content of these experimental texts. They include:

- Experiments with narrative forms, including jazz, blues, folk ballads, and *corridos* that honor long-standing African American and Chicano discourse traditions (Noriega, 1992a, pp. 152–153; Fregoso, 1993, pp. 70–76);
- The use of improvisation, mise-en-scene, and montage to fill the screen with multiracial images and to manipulate and deconstruct bicultural visual and linguistic codes;
- The use of personal testimonials, life stories, folktales, cultural myth, voice-overs and offscreen narration to provide overall narrative unity to a text (Noriega, 1992a, pp. 156–159).
- A celebration of key elements in African American and Chicano cultures, especially the themes of resistance, maintenance, affirmation, and neoindi-

genism, or *mestizaje* (Noriega, 1992a, p. 150), thereby challenging assimilation and melting pot narratives;

- Production of texts that deconstruct machismo, the masculine identity, and the celebration of works that give the black woman and Chicana subject an active part in the text, while criticizing such timeworn stereotypes as the virgin, whore, supportive wife, or home-girl (Fregoso, 1993, pp. 29, 93–94).
- A rejection of essentializing approaches to identity; an emphasis on a processual, gendered, performance view of self, and the location of identity within, not outside, systems of cultural and media representation.
- A refusal to accept the official race-relations narrative of the culture that privileges the ideology of assimilation, while contending that black and Hispanic youth pose grave threats for white society (Fregoso, 1993, p. 29).

Many of these cinematic practices are displayed in films made in the last decade by directors of color, including Bill Duke's *Rage in Harlem* (1991), Charles Burnett's *To Sleep with Anger* (1990), Mira Nair's *Mississippi Masala* (1991), Spike Lee's *Crooklyn* (1994), John Singleton's *Higher Learning* (1995), and *Rosewood* (1997), Gregory Nava's *Mi Familia* (1995), and Ang Lee's *Eat, Drink, Man, Woman* (1994).

These films articulate an aesthetic of production that celebrates ethnic culture while interrogating racial and gender stereotypes. They challenge assimiliation narratives. They emphasize community, family, and family solidarity. They experiment with narrative and visual form, use personal testimonials, voice-overs, and offscreen narration. They refuse the social-problems, didactic form of discourse; indeed, they refuse to locate pathology in the ethnic community. They do not invoke the state as the agency of salvation for the blighted, violent, drug-using minority community. They do not connect the signifiers of race with rap music, hip-hop culture, and youth violence. They work from within ethnic culture to present a cinema of pride and cultural resistance. Thus these films stand in bold contrast to the hood films of the last decade.

Implementing the Antiaesthetic

Throughout the twentieth century a series of structural commonalities shaped Hollywood's cinematic racial order. These commonalities included nineteenth- and twentieth-century racist ideologies, a racist popular culture, a racist performance vocabulary; gender-specific, cinematic racial stereotypes, a segregated society, a racist studio production system, the appearance of theaters in racial ghettos, minority actors, actresses, directors, and an expanding minority film audience; the civil rights and women's movements of the 1960s and 1970s; and a tradition of producing realistic, social-problems films.

Few of these factors have changed. The various civil rights movements are fighting for their lives. Another generation of conservatives attempts to undo the gains of the last quarter century. Cinematic and everyday racism is still present. The Hollywood studio system promotes a narrow range of race-based films, those that will entertain within an action, cop-buddy, or comedy format. So although the minority audience gets larger and Magic Johnson Theatres are now open in Harlem, these multiplexes can only show the films Hollywood makes. And while Spike Lee's film *Bamboozled* (2000) may mock the minstrel tradition of blackface, the film speaks to a larger truth about the culture's unwillingness to face up to its own racist past.

Valerie Smith (1997, p. 1) observes that African Americans still live with the legacies of D. W. Griffith's *Birth of a Nation*, the film that many claim is the "inaugural moment of African American cinema" (p. 1). Its all here: realistic cinema, a cinema that would tell the truth about America's post–Civil War racial history. Everything is present: the prejudices, the stereotypes, the use of parallel editing, cuts back and forth between action sequences, close-ups of actors in blackface. The images of blacks found in this film have been reproduced "throughout the history of U.S. cinema" (V. Smith, 1997, p. 1). Smith is clear. These images are racist, and they "threaten the lives of 'real' black people" (p. 1).

The new aesthetic of racial difference begins by challenging these representations. It searches for alternative representations that are neither racist or sexist. Paraphrasing Smith (V. Smith, 1997, p. 1), this black (and ethnic) cinema can be read as a search for new and different representations of black and brown subjects. It is understood that there is no longer any single representation that can any coded as more or less authentic. This search moves in two directions at the same time: the production of positive images that will replace negative representations; and the desire to criticize and recode negative images.

The first impulse can be seen in the films by Burnett, Duke, and Nair (noted above), as well as Kasi Lemmons's *Eve's Bayou* (1997) and Maya Angelou's *Down in the Delta* (1998) contemporary films about black women and their families. Carl Franklin's *Devil in a Blue Dress* and Julia Dash's *Daughters of the Dust* can also be included in this category. In contrast, Bill Duke's *Rage in Harlem* like Lee's *Bamboozled* deconstruct previous racist stereotypes about black community life in America, turning the negative into a series of jokes.

However, it is no longer sufficient to offer examples of good and bad films, including inventories of negative images. It is time to move away from the search for an essentialist (and good) black or brown subject, time to refuse cultural and biological essentialisms (Hall, 1996, p. 472).[7]

Two Case Studies

Consider Zeinabu irene Davis's 1999 film *Compensation*, which was entered in the 2000 Sundance Film Festival. This is a black-and-white silent film, set in two time periods, turn-of-the-century Chicago and present-day Chicago. It tells the story of two deaf African American women (Malindy, Malaika) women, and their relationships with two hearing African American men, Arthur and Nico. The film uses a simple Scott Joplin–like piano as its musical soundtrack.

Davis dedicates the film to Paul Laurence Dunbar, "America's Negro Poet Laureate" 1872–1906.[8] The film opens with a series of photographs, dated Chicago, early 1900s. These are seldom-seen slices of African-American history. They are images of turn-of-the-century middle-class blacks comfortably at home in an urban black public sphere. The screen informs the viewer that "Colored population of Chicago doubles— 1900–1910." Onscreen the streets fill with shots of middle-class blacks in expensive suits and dresses. The next storyboard informs the viewer that "W. E. B. Du Bois publishes *Souls of Black Folks*, 1903." The next storyboards state that "*The Chicago Defender* begins publication, 1905" and "Scott Joplin's classic Negro opera Treemonisha published, 1911."

Davis cleverly uses the methods of silent film to tell a story about the two deaf women. Both women write their messages on chalkboards, just as a silent film uses a printed text to convey story line. The film uses a cinematic language and a form of montage that brings the rhythms of deaf and hearing African American culture dramatically and vividly alive. Indeed, Davis's use of the hearing/deaf dichotomy can be read as a metaphor for black and white relationships. Each woman repeatedly questions her ability to have a relationship with a hearing man. Malaika's sister tells her, "Deaf and hearing relationships don't work. . . . Hearing people just don't understand our struggles for civil rights."

The film moves back and forth between the stories of the two couples, and the two time periods. In pairing the two deaf women with hearing men. Davis privileges language and literacy. Arthur cannot read, while Nico is a librarian, a man of books. Both couples fall in love, and each relationship confronts the epidemics of its time period: tuberculosis for Arthur,[9] who works in the meat plants in the stockyards; HIV for Malaika.

Compensation is a powerful film. It is boldly experimental. Illness and death are presented as forces that persons cannot control. The death of a loved one is blunted by the gift of love itself. That gift compensates for life's losses. In showing this, Davis's film brings great dignity and respect to the situations of African American women and men. At the same time her film honors African American culture and history.

This is not a protest film. It is not angry. It is quietly spiritual and empowering, as it quietly presents these women and their silent voices. Like the films of Charles Burnett and Julia Dash, this film lifts Du Bois's veil. It anchors its story firmly and proudly within the everyday worlds of African Americans and their lives.

In the language of the Black Arts movement, this is film art that is functional, collective and committed. This film is for deaf and hearing black woman. It is democratic: it celebrates diversity and personal freedom. It shows Chicago's racial ghettos as internal colonies, cut off from white society. This version of the black aesthetic stands in stark contrast to the hood movies of the last decade.

Now Carl Franklin's overlooked 1995 film *Devil in a Blue Dress*. This film is based on the novel by Walter Mosley (1990) of the same name. The opening credit sequence is framed with vivid nighttime colors of black, purple, blue, and red. A blues singer croons, "I got a west side baby. She lives way cross town." Stylized, cutout images of African American men and women in evening dress dance across the screen. Orange and yellow light streams from upstairs windows above a corner bar. Couples embrace and dance below a streetlight. Women in tight dresses cross their legs and smile at men. Men gossip with one another and lean against expensive limousines. The blues signer continues, "She sets my soul on fire." The back of a naked women appears in the upstairs window. "Ya, I got a west side baby. She lives clear cross town. And when I'm with my baby, I don't want a soul around. Now Monday mornin' early, someone knocked at my door. I know it wasn't my baby, cause she never knocked before."

The camera pulls back, revealing the larger street scene, which is filled with black city nightlife. This scene segues into the summer of 1948; real cars honk and come down the street. The blues singer continues singing. We cut to an upstairs bar. Denzel Washington as Easy Rawlins begins to narrate, "It was summer 1948, and I needed money." Thus does the film begin, a story of racism, violence, and oppression in post–World War II Los Angeles.

Franklin's film, like Davis's, illuminates and honors seldom seen slices of African American community life. Mosley's Easy Rawlins mysteries celebrate black art, religion, and music. Mosley tells stories about the struggles of black Americans attempting to create their own cultural, political, and economic spaces in midcentury Southern California. Franklin's film brings Mosley's world alive, a Raymond Chandler world of corruption, betrayal, double-crosses, femme fatales, race prejudice, and macho men beating up one another. Like *Compensation*, this is film art that is functional, collective, and committed. It gives a black man the power of the white private eye. It shows how black immigrants from the South created their own moral community in urban Los Angeles, a community of care, love, and mutual empowerment.

Franklin and Mosley turn a gentle eye on the eccentrics and odd persons who inhabit this space. They fold the music of jazz and blues into the nightlife. They expose the economic underside of racial discrimination. They tell a story with profound human implications; that is the lived side of midcentury racism for middle-class blacks.

These two films embody a version of a new aesthetic of color, an aesthetic that reconnects to the Black Arts movement of the 1970s. These films quietly present their version of a critical cinema of racial difference. They avoid violence. They celebrate cultural differences. They honor the art, rituals, myths, and religions of black culture. They ask how cinema can help create critical race consciousness. This is a black aesthetic that works for this century.

In Conclusion

Popular culture, Stuart Hall reminds us, is mythic, a theater of desires, a space of popular fantasies. "It is where we go to discover who we are" (1996, p. 474; see also Giroux, 2000a, p. 4). And in answering this existential question, we find that our gendered conceptions of self and Other are grounded always in misplaced notions of racial difference, of whiteness and privilege. We must always be on guard concerning what we learn about ourselves. And we must ask, after Pinar, what is the "historical character of 'whiteness' that renders it so aggressive, to tortured, so interested in subjugation?" (2001, p. 19).[10]

In his review of *Bamboozled*, MacGregor (2000) describes what he has learned about blacks in America by watching film and television:

> Black people are frightening. Black people are criminals. Black people are violent. Black people are athletic. Black people are successful members of the professional class. Black people are drug addicts. Black people are great entertainers. Black people are loving members of big families. Black people are musical. Black people are funny. Black people are loud. Black people are angry. Black people are churchgoers. Black people are always in trouble. Black people are frightening.
>
> This is what television has taught me about race in my own country. I am a 42-year-old American male and I am white and this is what I have learned from a lifetime of situation comedies, and one-hour cop dramas and commercials and those earnest documentaries. (pp. A11, A34)

And what can we say of white people? It is not enough to turn the tables, to ask of all persons of color what they have learned from a lifetime of watching whites on television and on the movie screen.

But even more is at issue. Ralph Ellison, Richard Wright, and James Baldwin framed the questions a half-century ago, and Walter Mosley, Z. I. Davis, bell hooks, and June Jordan rephrase them today. Paraphrasing Pinar (2001, p. 1), race and violence conflate in a crisis: "How can we use art, cinema and literature to communicate across our barriers of race and religion, class, color and region?" (Ellison, 1952, p. xxii). "How can we share in our common humanity, while valuing our differences?" "How can the interests of democracy and art converge?" "How can we use our literature, cinema and critical social science to advance the goals of this democratic society?" (Ellison, 1952, p. 11). "How can we overcome the structures of racism and sexism that are so deeply engrained in the marrow of this democracy?" (Feagin, 2000, p. 270; McCarthy, 2001, p. 105).

The cultural spaces of racial difference, Hall (1996, p. 474) tells us, are profoundly dialogic, always tangled in complex, interconnecting ways. Someday those who wore blackface out of choice will find that those who are really black or brown have painted their faces white. And now the white masks are black, and the black and brown masks are multicolored—a million off-white hues, mahogany, golden, dusky, tan and muddy brown, black, and satin. And in this colorful carnival-like space, a space that Bakhtin (1968) would take delight in, a new cinematic racial order is born. This is a racial order that truly honors racial difference. In its celebrations of difference, it unmasks and frees everyone. Here at the end, stealing a line from Ralph Ellison and Louis Armstrong, persons of color will no longer have to ask, "What Did I Do to be so Black and Blue" (Ellison, 1952, p. 8).

Thus from the violence of the hood movies of the 1990s, a new cinematic culture of gendered nonviolence is imagined. In this new space we begin to undo a hundred years of racism and violence and injury, a hundred years of a racist cinematic order. Farewell D. W. Griffith.

8

Troubling Heroes: Of Rosa Parks, Multicultural Education, and Critical Pedagogy

Dennis Carlson

In a provocative book on Sojourner Truth, the nineteenth-century aboli-
tionist and women's rights advocate, the historian Nell Irwin Painter
(1996) concludes that there is no "real" Truth only a series of representations by various authors who turned Truth into a legendary hero that they
could use to support their own cultural politics. Unmoored to any verifi-
able facts or any account from Truth herself, Painter writes, "the idea of
Sojourner Truth has been available for several purposes and been put to a
multiplicity of uses" (p. 263). The legend, symbol, and myth of Sojourner
Truth has taken on a life of its own, and it continues to take on new meaning. White, liberal biographers of Truth in the post–Civil War era saw the
"essence" of Truth in her famous meeting with President Lincoln. In this
myth of Truth, she is an Enlightenment thinker, a Europeanized African
American woman dedicated to the universal moral principles of human
freedom and equality before the law; and she comes to the White House to
thank the Great Emancipator for freeing the slaves. In the twentieth century, black biographers represented Truth more militantly, as a defiant,
angry woman, speaking before primarily black audiences, pressuring the
government to issue the Emancipation Proclamation. In the 1970s and
1980s, Truth was rediscovered and reappropriated by black women's studies scholars in the academy such as bell hooks (1981). The phrase attributed to Truth—"Ain't I a woman?"—was used to critique the primarily
white, middle class orientation of the women's movement. In the face of all
of this, Painter finds that the "truth" about Truth is that she lives an
"invented" life, a life "consumed as a signifier." She floats outside history,
"a symbol without a life" (p. 263).

I begin with this reference to one of America's great progressive heroes
because it points, in an ironic way, to both the trouble with heroic narratives and their promise as well. Heroes are always our own creation, which
is to say the creation of those who would use them to change the present
in some way. They represent and embody certain ideals, certain virtues,
certain ways of acting and being-in-the-world that support one set of inter-

ests or another. This means that there is no such thing as progressive or radical democratic heroes as such. Even those whose words and deeds represented a radical challenge to the dominant or hegemonic social order can be, and have been, incorporated within conservative narratives of national identity and progress. This is troubling to the extent that it means that even if progressives have succeeded in making the curriculum more inclusive, with a more multicultural cast of American heroes, there is no guarantee that these heroes will continue to serve progressive purposes once they are reworked within the dominant narratives of American history, which continue to be classist, Eurocentric, and patriarchal. If the meaning of the hero is battled over and contested, however, it does open up the possibility and the promise that heroes can be given new meaning to open up new democratic possibilities, to serve as metaphors and icons in the present that are not limited by past meanings. The promise is that heroes can be understood or appreciated for what they are, as useful icons and characters used to advance democratic projects in ways they themselves could not envision.

This leads me to the subject of multicultural education, and to the revision of the American history curriculum in recent years to make it more multicultural and inclusive, and to acknowledge struggles over social justice. Part of this revision of American history, as laid out in the *National Standards for United States History* (1994), a federally funded report published by the National Center for History in Schools at UCLA with the backing of the American Federation of Teachers and the National Council of Social Studies, calls for the construction of an "inclusive history," one that acknowledges the achievements of blacks, Native Americans, and women in particular, who have been ignored or marginalized in the past. Much of this is to be done by including the stories of prominent leaders of struggles for social justice. This is a significant victory for progressives, and one of the few such victories at a time in which school reform has been dominated by a corporate state discourse of standards, accountability, and high-stakes testing. Conservatives were quick to react to the report's recommendations and paint it as leading America toward what *Time* magazine characterized as "disproportionate revisionism." Lynne Cheney, who chaired the National Endowment for the Humanities when the grant was originally funded in the 1980s, was quoted in the article as saying that if the report's recommendations were followed, American students soon would be receiving "a warped view of American history," and that its criteria for including important historical persons and events was "politically correct to a fare-thee-well" (Elson, 1994).

Though progressives may have won a battle, we may be losing a larger battle over how history gets narrated, what stories it tells, and how national heroes get represented. Painter's biography of Sojourner Truth should give us cause to question what happens to progressive heroes, and indeed, what makes a hero progressive. It is not enough to make the curriculum more inclusive and multicultural. We must ask how the new cast of multicultural American heroes are integrated within various narratives of American history and contemporary culture. Which brings me, finally, to the subject of this essay—Rosa Parks—and to the question of how she has been represented in the curriculum and popular culture. There is reason to be concerned about what is happening to Parks, along with Martin Luther King Jr., as "floating signifiers." Michael Dyson (2000) has observed of King that political conservatives have, more than their liberal progressive counterparts, "appropriated King's image, identity, and ideology" (p. 6). They have turned him into a universalistic symbol of nonviolence and a defender of a minimalist interpretation of civil rights as strict equality before a color-blind law. If this is happening to King, what is happening to Parks, who has been elevated over the past decade or so to the status of the "mother" of the civil rights movement? Is Parks's story open to conservative tellings and interpretations? The fact that conservative social critic and educator William Bennett includes Parks as a universal symbol of courage in his *Book of Virtues* (1993) suggests that her story too is rapidly being rewritten as a story that is hardly progressive. If this is the case, it means that progressives need to engage in a protracted battle over the meaning of the civil rights movement and other great progressive social movements and individuals. Their meaning is never settled once and for all. And if that is the case, progressives will need to become more self-reflexive, more aware of their own beliefs and values, their own stories of history and progress. What distinguishes progressive tellings or interpretations of Parks's story from ones that serve conservative cultural politics? That is not an easy question to answer, and indeed it can have no unified or fixed answer. At best, I want to point to contingent, partial, multifaceted answers.

I also want to frame my remarks within the general domain of "critical pedagogy," as that term has taken on meaning over the past several decades as an emergent critical discourse and practice. In its various forms, critical pedagogy has been associated with approaches to education that emphasize critical literacy, the capacity to decode, demystify, and deconstruct the taken-for-granted narratives, symbols, metaphors, and tropes that guide the production of truth within texts. At the same time, critical pedagogy must also engage young people in the creative reworking and retelling of heroic narratives in American history, and in the production of new heroic texts that open up democratic possibilities in the present. In developing such a critical pedagogy, I want to explore the relevance of distinctions made by Friedrich Nietzsche and by Michel Foucault, who was so heavily influenced by Nietzsche, between different types of history, or different attitudes toward the reading of history. By drawing upon Nietzsche, the prophet of postmodernism, and Foucault, who is closely identified with the postmodern turn in the academy, I also mean to draw critical pedagogy in a postmodern direction—without at the same time falling victim to the worst excesses of postmodernism, including a tendency to deconstruct all foundations under our feet, resist any talk of a united front progressivism, and privilege popular culture as a site of cultural struggle.

Monumentalist History and Parks as a "Founding Mother"

The dominant narrative of Rosa Parks turns her into what I will call a "monumentalist" hero, following Nietzsche's use of that term (in *Untimely Meditations*). Nietzsche associated conservative and rightist cultural politics in late-nineteenth-century Europe with the active production of monumentalistic histories, narratives of the past that focus their gaze upon a few great individuals in order to derive comfort and inspiration from that fact that at least a few are capable of greatness (Kaufmann, 1974, p. 144). These heroic individuals carry the burden of cultural progress and development on their backs and speak of cultural origins and defining ideals. History is represented as either the progressive development of these "original" ideals, or as a story of decline and fall—with the hope that the nation, or Western culture, may recapture its previous glory by returning to these "founding" ideals. Though Foucault does not use the term "monumentalist," he does view dominant constructions of history as involved in the production of origin myths and firm foundations. We tend to think, Foucault observes, that this origin is the moment of a culture's "greatest perfections," when it "emerged dazzling from the hands of a creator or in the shadowless light of a first morning" (1992, p. 143). All great moments in cultural development are represented as recapitulations of these original or defining moments. They moments and the heroes associated with them speak of cultural "heights" and "purest individualities" (p. 155). Thus, Parks's refusal to give up her seat on the bus on December 1, 1955, often is represented as the symbolic origin of the civil rights movement and also its defining moment.

Bennett provides perhaps the best example of someone who seeks to turn Parks into a monumentalist hero, in his *Book of Virtues*. That book, targeted at an audience of parents, young people, and educators, was one of the most popular nonfiction books of the '90s. It spawned a whole cottage industry of lesson plan books and curriculum materials designed to teach character education, and it became the subject of a PBS miniseries. The *Book of Virtues* is a good example of how effective conservative commentators and social critics have been in tapping into commonsense public beliefs and sentiments concerning the need to return to the teaching of "traditional" values and moral virtues in schools and homes. In one sense, Bennett presents Parks as a real historical figure, and he sticks to the facts of her arrest and the subsequent bus boycott, even if important facts get left out. In another sense, Bennett removes Parks from history almost completely by situating her story within the company of Aesop's Fables, Grimm's Fairy Tales, and other morality tales in Western culture. The story of Parks's arrest is included in the chapter on the virtue of courage, right alongside stories of Chicken Little, David and Goliath, Jack and the Beanstalk, Hansel and Gretel, Ulysses and the Cyclops, and the defense of the Alamo. That is, real historical events, such as the defense of the Alamo and Parks's arrest, are grouped alongside stories from the Bible, European folklore, and Greek mythology. Furthermore, by lumping together the defense of the Alamo and Parks's defense of her civil rights, Bennett effectively incorporates Parks's story within an American narrative of expansionism that has participated in disenfranchising Mexican-Americans.

One way to translate Parks's story into a morality play, one that understands history as the culmination of a series of individual and isolated acts of moral courage, is to focus on the events immediately surrounding her arrest. So Bennett focuses upon the events of two days. He begins with her leaving work on December 1, 1955. "Rosa Parks was tired," he writes, "after a full day of stitching and ironing shirts" at a Montgomery department store (p. 489). He recounts her boarding the bus, sitting in the rear section reserved for colored people, except when there were not enough seats for whites. When whites had filled all the seats in the front of the bus, blacks in the rear section were required to give up their seats to whites. This is what Parks and several other black passengers were asked to do that day. Three other passengers got up to move, but Parks stood her ground. "In a firm but quiet voice," she told the driver she was not moving (p. 490). Throughout her arrest she is the model of self-discipline, and Bennett implies that she shamed the officer arresting her, so that he was confused and could say only, "I'm obeying the law" (p. 491).

Bennett then flashes forward to the morning of December 5, the day of her trial. As she and her husband got out of bed she rushed to the window to see if the bus across the road was empty. It was, and she was "filled with happiness." The boycott was a success. Later, as she was driven up to the courthouse, she was met by a crown of about five hundred black supporters. Bennett writes that while Parks was inside, "the crowd was getting restless. Some of them were carrying sawed-off shotguns, and the policemen were beginning to look worried" (p. 492). Here we have the fantasy image of white fear and resentment, the impulsive, violence-prone black mob, armed and ready to riot, to storm the courthouse. It is a particularly ironic image, for the reality was that blacks had much more to fear from organized white mobs than vice versa. Nevertheless, the black crowd remains a powerful symbol of nihilistic and destructive rage in the dominant culture, and Bennett uses it effectively in his account. Parks, like King, is represented as one of the "good" black leaders who helped calm the crowd, who was able to steer black protest and anger in a "positive" direction. She represents a morally literate voice in a community defined primarily in terms of morally illiteracy. Still, her arrest is represented as a "spark" that ignited the black community of Montgomery, as if that community were a bomb just waiting to explode, so that Parks is depicted as both igniting and calming an explosive black community.

Monumentalist narratives of Parks's life also play into the presumption that change, and thus social progress, occur in America when people make legalistic or juridical claims—for example, when they stand up for their rights to be treated equitably before the law. This is used by Bennett and other conservatives to suggest that affirmative action and other "special rights" legislation (including "hate crime" legislation) represent a sign of decline and fall from the ideals of the civil rights movement. It also is used to suggest that the mobilization of political power and militant action is not necessary in order to make the system respond to legitimate grievances. Thus, the U.S. Supreme Court is represented as the final savior of Parks, in striking down segregation laws in the South. Ironically, the same court system that found slavery constitutional throughout most of the nineteenth century, and that ruled that "separate but equal" public schools were constitutional in *Plessy v. Ferguson*, (1896), now assumes a saving and protective role toward African Americans.

The association between the civil rights movement and legalistic or juridical claims to equal access to public facilities establishes a very narrow framework for understanding social justice, one that does not leave us with anything to do at this point but celebrate how much progress we have made in overcoming inequities and resist efforts to expand the meaning of equality or the rights of democratic citizens. In this regard, the bus upon which Parks' staged her heroic act plays an important role. The public bus assumes an important symbolic value in a particular mythology of democratic public life in America, and it is perhaps not coincidental that public buses have assumed such a central role in the integration of public schools. Both public school classrooms and public buses have been represented in similar ways, as desegregated public spaces, spaces (ideally) of equity and tolerance, of civility and respect for difference. In Bennett's account, the bus assumes an important role in the story and is as much an actor in the drama as Parks is. We learn, for example, that Rosa and her husband wake each morning to "the familiar sound of a City Lines bus pulling up to a stop across the road." The green-and-white bus stands at the stop for over a minute, "puffing exhaust smoke into the cold December air," as black and white workers climb on board and prepare for their day's labor. The public bus takes them to work and back each day, so that the right to a seat on the public bus is associated with being able to hold down a job and thus be a responsible and productive member of the community. After the boycott begins, Bennett writes, "empty buses bounced around for everyone to see" (p. 491). They are a visible symbol of the disruption of public life.

As a progressive symbol of the public, the bus certainly has some value. When Atlanta baseball player John Rocker recently commented that he did not take the subway when he played in New York City because he did not want to sit next to gay people with AIDS or pregnant welfare mothers, he was pointing to the fact that public buses and subways can be very diverse and thus democratic sites. People uncomfortable with diversity avoid subways and public buses. The public bus is a space in which people acknowledge one another's rights to sit next to each other, to treat each other as equals in determining who will sit where. Everyone ostensibly has equal rights, and rich and poor, black and white, gay and straight can sit next to one another with civility and tolerance. Nevertheless, as a symbol of a democratic public space and public life, the public bus has taken on a very limited meaning. People may sit next to each other on a public bus, but they have no other commitments to one another other than tolerance and peaceful coexistence. Passengers may choose to ignore each other completely or even harbor hostility toward one another so long as it is kept repressed. In the intimate environment of the bus, the public often has a very impersonal, legalistic meaning. In his classic study *Life in Classrooms* (1968), Philip Jackson observed that public school classrooms are like public buses and movie theaters—"densely populated settings," places of "social intimacy" in which people for the most part ignore each other (p. 6). By representing Parks's story in terms of the legalistic rights of citizens to use public facilities, the meaning of public education, democratic citizenship, and communities of difference gets narrowed and restricted, and the meaning of the civil rights movement gets anchored in a conservative cultural politics.

This narrowing and restriction of the meaning of civil rights is furthered by another feature of monumentalist histories. In Bennett's account, as in many other stories about Parks, there is an implicit association between citizenship rights and performing a "normal" self-presentation and identity (Foucault, 1979). Parks is represented as a symbol of the normal, in Foucault's sense of that term. She conforms in particular to the norms established for self-presentation among African Americans in the dominant culture, and in doing so she marks the boundaries between acceptable and unacceptable behavior. The presumption is that because she is "normal"— a good wife, responsible and hardworking worker, and physically non-threatening—she deserves her rights, which can be used to imply that those who are not quite so "normal" do not deserve their rights. A year before Parks's arrest, an unwed, pregnant, teenage girl was arrested for refusing to give up her seat on a Montgomery bus, but the local NAACP decided not to use her as a test case in challenging the segregation laws. Parks writes in her autobiography, *My Story* (1992), "She wasn't married, and so that was the end of that case." The young woman, Parks observes, would surely be labeled "a bad girl, and her case wouldn't have a chance" (p. 112). The NAACP leadership in Montgomery decided that the best plaintiff to challenge the segregated bus laws would be a woman, "because a woman would get more sympathy than a man." But this woman would have to be "above reproach, have a good reputation, and have done nothing wrong but refuse to give up her seat" (1992, pp. 110–111). A few pages later Parks says of herself: "I had no police record, I'd worked all my life, I wasn't pregnant with an illegitimate child. The white people couldn't point to me and say that there was anything I had done to deserve such treatment except to be born black" (p. 125).

Though it may have made strategic sense for the NAACP leadership to look for a symbol of the normal to test the segregation laws in Montgomery, the result has been to affirm a "normal/abnormal" binary that historically has been used to separate "deserving" minorities from "undeserving" ones, "good" blacks from "bad" blacks. The implication, as I said, may be that African American and other marginalized youth only need to act "normal" and be "good" in order to succeed. In Parks's more recently published books for young people, this would seem to be her primary message. *Dear Mrs. Parks* (1996) is a series of inspirational letters written by Parks, supposedly in response to letters sent to her by concerned youth. The letters are organized around themes of Courage and Hope, The Power of Knowledge and Education, Living With God, Pathways to Freedom, and Making a Difference. Her short volume of memories and thoughts, *Quiet Strength*(1994) is much the same, with chapters on: Fear, Defiance, Injustice, Pain, Character, Role Models, Faith, Values, Quiet Strength, and Determination. There is nothing wrong with these virtues, as such. At the same time, the effect is to turn her story into a test of character, to imply (wittingly or not) that young, inner-city African American youth can succeed if they just think "positive," avoid "bad" influences, and become more self-disciplined. The burden is clearly on black youth to shape-up and become more self-disciplined. Her response begins to sound very similar to that of Bennett, a return to character education and the teaching of traditional moral virtues. But Parks, to her credit, reveals elsewhere a resentment of the fact that African American youth and adults have to act so "well-behaved" in public, so "normal." She understands it as a case of strategic necessity rather than a moral virtue. In her autobiography, for example, she writes that she never quite forgave southern whites for a racial order in which black people "had to be smiling and polite no matter how rudely you were treated" (1992, p. 107). Although she has become a symbol and advocate of good manners and self-discipline for African American youth, of never "losing your cool," she also decries the fact that black people have to assume such a heavy burden of politeness, of smiling when they are treated rudely, to keep out of trouble.

Critical Histories: Setting the Record Straight

Most tellings of Parks's story are monumentalist in at least some ways, and some—like Bennett's—almost seem to be ideal typical examples. One alternative to monumentalist history takes the form of what Foucault, following Nietzsche, calls critical history. "Critical" is a term that has a long history of meaning, but suffice it to say that it is used here to refer to the modernist critique of ideology or the worldview of the dominant culture, to reveal how ideology distorts and falsifies the past in the interests of power. The Marxian tradition in social theory, and particularly as it found expression in the twentieth century in the critical theory of the Frankfurt School, provided the primary grounding for critical educational scholarship in the last three decades of the twentieth century and also for what came to called "critical pedagogy"—based on Paulo Freire's groundbreaking work. Critical history, as Foucault uses that term, is, first of all, a way of reading monumentalist histories to reveal how they ideologically distort reality and, second, a way of retelling the past, of writing new histories that set the record straight (Kaufmann, 1974, pp. 144–145). But critical histories do more than this. They uphold an emancipatory project that understands history as formed out of the dialectic of struggle between "the oppressed" and their oppressors. Because of this dialectic, critical histories have a teleology or directionality. They demystify the liberal myth of a steady, evolutionary progress. However, they still hold out the hope (and even promise) of transformational progress, leading us through a series of revolutionary shifts in human consciousness toward the "good society" and the reconciliation of self and Other (Dean, 1994, pp. 3–4).

We live in an era when this critical epistemology and story of history is being questioned, and Foucault is among those most associated with the critique of critical theory and history. One of the problems with critical histories is that they typically take for granted a rather simplistic true/false binary opposition that merely seeks to replace falsehoods and distortions with the "real" truth about history or about historical heroes such as Rosa Parks. Granted, there are some "hard" historical facts that need to be revealed, and ideological distortions need to be demystified. But there is no place of autonomous, critical reason that cuts through all distortions. The story of history, as I have already argued, is a narrative production, and as a narrative it inevitably does more than demystify. It also frames the past to tell particular stories of the present. So it is impossible to merely set the record straight about Rosa Parks. A second problem with critical histories has to do with their use of the Enlightenment language of emancipation, social justice, and human freedom. These are very important and useful themes in critical pedagogy, and they should continue to guide and give meaning to progressivism in American education and cultural politics. But they need to be troubled in ways that they typically are not in critical histories. For example, critical histories tend to overunify "the oppressed" and hold out unification of all oppositions as the "happy ending" to history. The civil rights movement thus may be mythologized as a story about the need for blacks and whites to come together around a broader struggle, such as class. Critical histories of this form fail to interrogate their own Eurocentrism and class reductionism. They also privilege unification and the reconciliation of all oppositions in a way that is hard to sustain in an age of the "politics of difference." Neither Nietzsche nor Foucault meant to disparage critical histories completely. They are still important in helping people reflect on their commonsense beliefs about the past, and the present, even if we must now acknowledge that critical reason is not some autonomous light that reveals the world simply as it is, but in fact is intimately involved in constructing that world. Similarly, it is still important to affirm the radical democratic enlightenment language of social justice, human freedom, equity, community, and emancipation, even if this language must be understood as having only a pragmatic, strategic, situated meaning.

Herbert Kohl provides a good example of a critical telling of Park's story, in a 1991 article in the *Journal of Education*, in which he challenges the "myths" that have grown up around Parks in children's literature and the public school curriculum. Kohl's first book, *36 Children* (1968), was a national best-seller, one of a genre of books published in the late 1960s and early 1970s, including Jonathan Kozol's *Death at an Early Age* (1985), by young, white, middle class, male teachers. These authors describe their lives working in inner-city schools, helping poor black kids to build community in the classroom and to affirm a positive self-concept and sense that they can achieve, in spite of the odds against them. These books are, for all their merit, salvation texts, in the sense that they suggest that young white teachers save poor, inner-city black youth. But they are also critical to the extent that they cut through the lies being told about equality of opportunity in schools and society to reveal the truth about urban schools as institutions of domination and the "killing" of young minds. They are also critical in the sense that they affirm social justice as a guiding principle for guiding curriculum and pedagogy in public schools and attempt to move beyond the dominant "blame the victim" ideology of the era. They are based on acts of solidarity with the poor and the oppressed in America, and they hold out hope that blacks and whites can work together, side by side, in support of civil rights and equality.

In the late 1980s, Kohl was an associate at the Coastal Ridge Research and Education Center in Point Arena, California, where he continued to write about American public education from a populist political stance, mixing a Marxist-inspired class analysis with a civil rights movement–inspired commitment to struggles for racial justice. In his *Journal of Education* article Kohl describes a visit he had made at that time to a fourth-grade classroom in a Southern California public school in which the children were performing a dramatic version of Parks's arrest in celebration of Black History Month. Kohl stands transfixed as the girl who plays Parks takes a seat at the front of a pretend bus—assembled out of chairs and cardboard props. The girl acts visibly tired and is "dressed in shabby clothes." She carries two shopping bags which seem to weigh her down, and it appears she is trying to act elderly. After she refuses to give up her seat on the bus, the scene ends. The next scene begins as a group of students, both black and white, march around the classroom carrying signs that say, "Don't Ride the Buses," "We Shall Overcome," and "Blacks and Whites Together." The play ends, according to Kohl, "with a narrator pointing out that the bus problem in Montgomery was solved by people coming together to protest peacefully for justice" (p. 36).

When the class was over, Kohl attempted to point out to the teacher that the dramatization misrepresented what actually occurred on several counts. Parks was not particularly tired or old (she was forty-two years old at the time of her arrest), she did not take a seat at the front of the bus, and the Montgomery Bus Boycott was not a spontaneous and unplanned action. But Kohl's most important point is that the elementary school drama misrepresented the Montgomery Bus Boycott as a struggle in which whites and blacks worked together to end segregation. In reality, the boycott was organized and led by the African American community, and according to Kohl, "to represent it as an interracial struggle was to take the power and credit away from that community." The teachers' response, according to Kohl, was to agree that the play "took some liberty with history." However, the teacher defended these liberties, noting that since his class was interracial it worked out better when the play was presented as a joint struggle that brought whites and blacks together. According to Kohl, the teacher feared that if he presented the play as blacks against whites, it "might lead to racial strife in the classroom." Kohl disagreed, pointing out that by dramatizing the Montgomery Bus Boycott as an organized movement by the African American community, "it might lead all of the children to recognize and appreciate the strength oppressed people can show when confronting their oppressors." The play had left everyone with a sense of unity, but with "no sense of the risk and courage of the African American people." In effect, Kohl concludes, the teacher was constructing a mythological Parks, one which "exists on the level of a national cultural icon" (p. 37).

Though Kohl refutes the liberal myth that a significant number of whites joined with blacks in the Montgomery Bus Boycott, he does hold out hope that various groups, disempowered and disenfranchised by class, ethnicity, and race, can see that they have common interests. Here, I want to turn to another text by Kohl. He worked with Myles Horton, founder of the Highlander Academy, in writing Horton's autobiography, *The Long Haul* (1990), and while the words are attributed to Horton, they ring true to Kohl's own political commitments and beliefs. In one chapter of that autobiography we learn more about Parks's participation in a workshop/ retreat at Highlander in the summer of 1955, along with Dr. King, and representatives of workers' unions and white Appalachian community activists. Parks is depicted as increasingly convinced that the struggle was against power and privilege rather than white folks as such, and that poor whites and blacks shared common interests as economically exploited groups. The book quotes Parks's autobiography, in which she observes: "At Highlander I found out for the first time in my adult life that this could be a unified society. . . . I gained there the strength to persevere in my work for freedom, not just for blacks, but for all oppressed people" (pp. 149–150). One chapter in *The Long Haul*, titled "One Battle, Many Fronts," suggests that organized labor, rural poor Appalachians, and southern blacks all worked together at Highlander to provide important support for civil rights struggles. If the common bonds developed at Highlander were often not maintained back in the "real world," the book holds out hope that various oppressed groups can coalesce into something like "the oppressed" so that they may fight against a common source of social and economic exploitation and domination.

One further theme that Kohl develops in his discussion of the myth of Rosa Parks I have already hinted at in introducing the idea of monumentalist histories. That is the theme of the individualization of history. The myth of Rosa Parks contends that her arrest was a "spark" that ignited a movement. But as Kohl writes, "the boycott had been planned and organized before Rosa Parks was arrested. It was an event waiting to take place and that is why it could be mobilized so quickly" (p. 45). In fact, Parks was secretary of the Montgomery NAACP and involved in planning a test case against the segregated bus laws. She was the anointed one, the perfect test case; and if the exact time and place of her arrest was not determined in advance, her arrest was no accident. Her actions need to be understood within the context of a battle that had been waged for over several decades in Montgomery that was part of a broader historic struggle against racial oppression in America. Her victory would not have been possible without this history and the organization of civil rights movements. When Parks was arrested, the NAACP was ready to mobilize the community overnight and begin a bus boycott. She was not a "spark" that ignited a sleeping black community, but rather the signal that it was time to begin the boycott. Critical histories are histories of the collective struggles of peoples against oppression and domination, struggles that are located within a long historical context. Individuals do not make history as mere individuals, but as participants in a collective "becoming," as part of social movements engaged in struggles over social justice.

This is the attitude Parks takes in her autobiography. In some ways, as I already have indicated, Parks has contributed to the mythologizing of her life in ways that might be considered hegemonic. But particularly in her autobiography, she becomes the critical historian, setting the record straight about her life, and locating her own actions within the context of a long struggle for freedom. She refutes, for example, the image of her as a tired, frail, elderly woman when she was arrested, an object of pity. "I was not tired physically," she writes. "No, the only tired I was, was tired of giving in" (p. 116). Parks also suggests that she was a player in a much bigger drama, and that her part was relatively small. Only one chapter in the twelve-chapter volume is devoted to her arrest. She focuses on the mobilization of the black community and an incipient civil rights movement in the 1940s and early 1950s. At the same time, she situates the Montgomery boycott within a broader African American struggle against a hegemonic racist white culture and (simultaneously) a struggle by disenfranchised blacks and whites, with the support of good-willed people in places of power, around a common progressive vision of social justice and human freedom. Of the boycott, Parks recalls that, "ordinary black people contributed, and so did some important white people in Montgomery" (1992, p. 144). One of her earliest memories is of a white man who treated her "like a regular little girl, not a little black girl" (p. 2). The man was a soldier from the North, and he had patted her on the head and said she was "a cute little girl" (p. 3). This white man who treated her with respect, demonstrated to her that not all white people are "bad"—even if other childhood experiences taught her a quite different lesson, the kind of lesson lynchings taught all black people in the South. Hers is, in the final analysis, a hopeful story, although clearly this is a hope that Parks has had to work hard at keeping alive, as the promises of the civil rights era have not yet been met.

Effective History: Rosa Parks the Floating Signifier

What lies beyond critical history? How else can the story of Rosa Parks be narrated? To adequately address these questions we have to venture into the postmodern and understand "truth" not as something already out there, waiting to be revealed by the light of a critical reason, but truth as a production of discourse, or language in use, and truth as a production of power. From such a standpoint, the truth about Rosa Parks or Sojourner Truth is the meaning attached to the telling of their stories, and the interests that lie behind the telling, within popular culture and the school curriculum. Our interest is in how Parks has served as a "floating signifier"—a sign open to diverse usages, available to be inscribed with multiple and even contradictory meanings, and thus a sign whose meaning is contested and open rather than fixed and determined.

This is the terrain opened up by what Foucault, again following Nietzsche, called "effective" history—"effective" in the Aristotelian sense, as that causation associated with what Nietzsche called the "will to power." We can thus ask of an historical text, or a new cultural hero, what "will to power" brought this text or hero into existence, and what will to power is it involved in organizing and advancing in the present? The truth about the past is understood to be produced, and so one becomes an archaeologist of knowledge, a genealogist of truth production, tracing dominant "truths" back through various discourses and practices to reveal the interests that lie behind their production and enunciation, the power relations they have been involved in organizing. Effective history reveals historical heroes as fictions of sorts, as mythological characters more than "real" people, and it thus troubles all efforts to get to the final answers about history and historical figures. It is critical to the extent that it challenges "the taken-for-granted components of our reality and the 'official' accounts of how they came to be the way they are" (Dean, 1994, p. 4). However, it does not seek to reveal an "undistorted" truth behind the ideological representations of the past. Rather, it seeks to trouble the truth/falsehood binary opposition that governs modern histories. The trouble with effective history is that it leaves us without any platforms under our feet, without any heroes to look to as guides, without any ideals worth committing to. The effective historical attitude, like postmodernism more generally, may be associated with a sense that "nothing is worthy of passion or commitment because everything solid dissolves upon one's approach" (G. Smith, 1996, p. 10).

Nietzsche attempts to resolve this problem with another attitude toward history, the "suprahistorical." This attitude is associated with living in the present rather than the past, and thus approaching history merely as a reservoir of useful heroes, metaphors, symbols, and analogies that may be modified, revised, and reassembled in creative ways to serve a purpose at hand. From a suprahistorical attitude it is less important to get all the facts straight than it is to use historical events and stories in new ways, adapting them to a situation at hand, rummaging through the past for useful heroes and tropes, playing with history in creative ways rather than approaching it as a sacred text. Heroes can still serve democratic and progressive purposes from such a perspective, but only when they are explicitly understood as useful heroes, that is, as mythological figures who can be used to tell a new story. One might say that we are entering a suprahistorical age, one in which heroes become brand-name icons when Hollywood fictionalizes history. When the suprahistorical attitude dominates, it may lead to an ignorance of history that is dangerous; and this may indeed be the situation we face today. Consequently, Nietzsche presents the suprahistorical attitude as a complement to critical and effective histories rather than as their replacement, or as sufficient unto itself. But without suprahistorical histories, Nietzsche suggests, a culture is locked into the past, unable to reimagine what could be, to give new meaning to mythological heroes of history.

This is how Michael Eric Dyson approaches Rosa Parks in his popular book *I May Not Get There with You: The True Martin Luther King, Jr.* (2000). The suggestion that Dyson will reveal the "true" King beneath or behind the distortions makes this book a critical history, and explicitly so. Yet Dyson clearly means to play with the word "true." He is, in the end, far more interested in how a truth about King has been produced than he is about setting the record straight. Even the "real" King, the actual historical person, according to Dyson, was "produced" by the civil rights movement. He was an expression of a narrative of human freedom and social justice that gave him "a vision and a vehicle to realize his desire to serve" (p. 304). There is a reality about King's life, Dyson argues, but it always has been a socially constructed reality. The civil rights movement produced King rather than the other way around. King's relevance today, as a national hero, is that he continues to represent "our moral possibilities" and our "deepest wishes." He and other civil rights leaders are still useful heroes to Dyson because they suggest we can make a difference when we stand up for our rights, fight oppression, resist injustice, march, and in other ways put our bodies on the line and make our voices heard.

Dyson warns, however, that progressives will have to do battle over heroes such as King and Parks, for conservatives are always looking for ways of retelling their stories to support their own narratives of American history, including the notion that the civil rights movement was about a color-blind law, that it sought (and presumably was successful in gaining) in erasing race as a meaningful axis of struggle by making everyone equal before the law, and that affirmative action and hate crimes legislation constitute "special rights" and thus a subversion of civil rights movement ideals. If conservatives seem, in a way, to be desecrating the memories of heroic struggle expressed in the stories of both King and Parks, Dyson wonders whether progressives are engaged in their own desecration of civil rights. The occasion for this questioning of what progressives are doing to progressive heroes is the recent lawsuit, involving big-name lawyer Johnny Cochran, that Parks filed against the rap group Outkast because, she claims, the group's song "Rosa Parks" is commercially exploitive and personally degrading. The song appears on the group's 1999 album *Aquemini* and has sold more than two million copies. Parks is not mentioned directly in the song, but the phrase "back of the bus" is used in the refrain to show disrespect to rival rap groups, a way of telling them to go to the back of the bus and make room for Outkast up front. The lyrics include profanity and the use of the "N" word. Cochran is quoted in a newspaper report to the effect that the song has made Parks the focal point of a national ad campaign in a way that commercialized the civil rights movement and trivialized what she stands for, namely "the proposition that everyone has the right to sit in the front of the bus" (Horn, 2001, p. B9).

There seems to be merit to this argument, until one learns, as Dyson observes, that Outkast is among the most progressive rap groups and that the group claimed to be paying homage to Parks as a role model. Perhaps the song "Rosa Parks" is meant, he writes, to be "a cautionary tale against an uninformed obsession with the past," a dwelling in the past rather than the present (p. 308). Rosa Parks, in other words, represents a phase in the struggle of African Americans that now needs to be superceded by a new generation of self-affirming black youth. They give meaning to her story by relating it to the empowerment struggles of inner-city poor black youth, and it speaks to them in a language that they can understand. By interpreting Outkast's song literally, Dyson claims, Parks failed to see that she has become a "metaphor for social change," failed to understand "her symbolic importance to some of today's black youth" (pp. 308–309). In hip-hop groups such as Outkast, Dyson sees many of the same qualities that Parks had—including a commitment to the forgotten black poor and to social justice. He concludes that if Parks's legacy is to survive and prove useful in a rapidly changing world, "it will have to be adapted, translated, and reinterpreted by a new generation," a generation whose words may seem angry and crude at times. What Outkast did in its song "Rosa Parks" was to turn her into a "useful hero, a working icon, a meaningful metaphor" (pp. 310–311).

But the suprahistorical attitude is not necessarily and always progressive. It may manifest itself in the characteristic postmodernist playing with history and culture, combining and juxtaposing pieces of heroic texts together in a pastiche. It may indeed be consistent with a highly commercialized and commodified popular culture that "mines" the past for useful heroes to market, that turns them into marketable symbols, metaphors, and icons. Dyson's tendency to look to hip-hop culture as a site of a potentially quite politicized and radical critique of the dominant culture needs to be weighed against the deeply commercialized character of mass-market rap music and hip-hop culture. Indeed, the commercial producers of Out-kast's music may have stripped Parks of much meaning as a progressive hero, turning a civil rights story into a story about male self-assertion and competitiveness. So which is the real truth about Outkast's use of Parks as a metaphor and symbol? Or must we choose one truth over another? Is it possible that Parks's legacy is being commercialized and commodified, and also that it is being "read" or interpreted by many urban youth in ways that are potentially quite subversive and progressive? If we work outside the reigning logic of the truth/falsehood binary, then we must at least open ourselves to the possibility that commercialized popular culture can be a site of counterhegemonic or progressive struggle. We also have to open ourselves to the very real possibilities that the commercialization and com-modification process strips progressive forms of rap music and hip hop culture of much of their progressive potential.

Conclusion

Where does this leave us? It leaves us, I believe, with a critical pedagogy that "troubles" and questions all historical heroes. How are heroes forma-tive in shaping how people think about the world and interact with each other? How do heroes reinforce or challenge dominant representations of class, race, gender, sexual, and other identities? Where do heroes come from—which is to say, what is their genealogy in various cultural myths and texts? How are they circulated, and what interests do they support? How has the meaning attached to heroes changed over time and been con-tested? Finally, how can heroic myths be rescripted, subversively renarra-tive, and imaginatively reworked in ways that open up democratic possibilities? Progressives still need heroes. Any education that seeks to move beyond what has been, and is directed toward what could be, is in some way a variation on the mythological journey of the hero outward, beyond the safe harbors of home (Carlson, 2002). Progressive heroes like Parks confront great risks, trials, and tribulations, but what makes their journeys progressive is that they always face forward with renewed hope and vision, although not with a naive idealism or utopianism. Unlike Odysseus's journey, the journey of progressive heroes cannot lead back home, to some place of stable origins and foundations. Progressivism, like progressive heroes, must be reconstructed again and again, and given new relevance for each new generation. In this sense, we can say that progres-sive heroes, as myths, take on a life of their own. Any attempt to pin them down, to make them represent one thing alone, or to stop them from changing and taking on new meaning, is both futile and nonprogressive. Any attempt to turn them into foundational figures, expressions of a pure cultural essence, must be resisted.

At the same time, we have to be careful with our heroes. For while we may use the heroic form to tell radical democratic stories of empowerment and social justice, this narrative form cannot be totally or easily separated from its history of usage in the West. Some feminists argue, for example, that it is a contradiction in terms to even refer to a woman as a hero, since the hero is such a thoroughly masculinized character in Western mythology (Irigaray, 1991). The hero has agency, while others wait passively for heroes to act and speak for them. The hero is on a journey, like Parks on the bus, in which "he" faces great dangers and affirms high ideals. Meanwhile, women wait at home, like Penelope for Odysseus. Is Parks masculinized by our turning her into a hero? Or can we work outside of the binary oppositional logic that makes the hero a masculine category as well as a "white" category? My sense, and hope, is that we can come to think of heroes in new ways that will render the category more inclusive. Heroes are still needed as symbolic characters in an historical drama and as useful metaphors in forging a new radical democratic cultural politics. Barbara Finkelstein (1992) observes: "Through the recovery of the past, historians can sow seeds of hope and/or despair, encourage and/or discourage particular courses of action, sound political or moral calls, or otherwise shape the forms that future imagining can take" (p. 256). It is thus worth doing battle over the heroes like Rosa Parks, and contesting the conservative appropriation of her legacy. But our object must not be to appropriate her as the patron saint of progressivism either, only as a useful symbol and metaphor that releases the democratic imagination.

9

The Symbolic Curriculum: Reading the Confederate Flag as a Southern Heritage Text

Susan L. Schramm-Pate and Dennis Carlson

James West, a seventh-grader at a Derby, Kansas middle school, was in math class one day in 1998 when he decided to pass the time before his next class by doing some sketching rather than homework. He began drawing a flag he'd seen on the television show *The Dukes of Hazzard*, a flag that appeared in each episode on the roof of the "General Lee," a 1968 Dodge Charger that was one of the stars of that show. When his math teacher caught him sketching the flag, he immediately confiscated the piece of paper and sent James to the office. The boy was subsequently suspended for three days for violating the school's "racial harassment and intimidation" policy, a policy that banned students from possessing "any written material, either printed or in their own handwriting, that is racially divisive or creates ill will or hatred." The policy had been adopted in 1995 after a series of racial disturbances in the schools and the community. In order to ensure that such disturbances did not occur in the future any "symbolic expression" that might provoke conflict was banned from school property. West's parents filed suit against the school district, claiming that it was violating their son's First Amendment right to freedom of expression. James, for his part, maintained, "I didn't even know what it meant. I don't see it as being racial."

A school official argued in defense of the policy that, "You don't display a Confederate flag. You don't display a swastika. You don't write a racial slur on the front of your notebook." However, the school did acknowledge that the Confederate flag could be used in an "appropriate" context. For example, "it would be appropriate to study or draw a Confederate flag in the context of a history class." Interestingly, the president of the Wichita, Kansas chapter of the National Association for the Advancement of Colored People (NAACP) sided with the student, arguing that while children need to be informed about racism and slavery, the non-malicious act of drawing the Confederate flag did not warrant suspension. "If you start running from history," he told reporters, "and you don't know why you're running from history, then you have tunnel vision." A federal trial judge and the Tenth U.S. Circuit Court of Appeals ruled in favor of the school district. But it was a complicated decision that reemphasized the importance of understanding the specific context of usage. In this case, testimony revealed that West had previously been suspended for calling a student "blackie" and had been reminded of the harassment and intimidation policy at that time. The appeals court wrote in its decision that the school district "had reason to believe that a student's display of the Confederate flag might cause disruption and interfere with the rights of other students to be secure and let alone" (U.S. Government Information/Resources, 2000).

Whether young James West had or had not, consciously or unconsciously, been influenced by a racist ideology of "whiteness," we can't help but wonder how things might have turned out differently if his teacher had used the Confederate flag drawing instead as a context for beginning a class dialogue on race and identity. Such a dialogue would no doubt be unsettling and conflictual at times, but then perhaps—just perhaps—the role of the progressive educator is to unsettle what has become taken for granted, to acknowledge conflict as positive rather than as something that must be suppressed in order to maintain order, to make room for diverse voices that do not come together in any unified, consensual truth. In a public education system that too often is guided by discourses and practices of control and surveillance, there is precious little room for conflict and the "messiness" of dialogue across differences. Yet this is precisely what democratic education requires, and what students increasingly are demanding. Public education, if it is to live up to its promise of preparing young people for democratic citizenry, must be a "safe space" for democratic dialogue and the clash of opposing viewpoints, a space in which important issues are not silenced for fear they cause "control problems," a space in which freedom of expression—including symbolic expression—is respected and in which censorship (of dress or speech) is rare. Within such a space, the educator's role, like that of the public intellectual, is to raise troubling questions that resist easy, unified answers. Our fear is that because many young people are not learning to think about the Confederate flag, or other icons they use to perform their "identity work," in a reflexive, self-conscious manner, that they may more easily fall prey to the symbolic politics of the right, with its appeals to a return to a romanticized past, a past that serves as a supposedly firm foundation upon which an essentialistic sense of self and Other is constructed.

We live in an age of iconic identity, in which youth construct a sense of self in relation to others through the icons they wear, icons that represent lifestyles and values. Through iconic or symbolic labor, young people learn to construct and perform identity. In an information age, these icons increasingly are produced and distributed by global capital in the form of brand logos. Different brand logos and icons correspond to different representations of class, race, gender, sexual, and other markers of difference and identity. The Confederate flag has become commercialized in its own way, with brand-name apparel in the South using it on their logos, and with websites busy selling Confederate flag paraphernalia to customers around the world: flags, key chains, patches, flag charts, mini banners, parking signs, coffee mugs, fridge magnets, T-shirts, sweatshirts and hats. Dixie Outfitters produces clothing featuring the Confederate flag as part of larger hunting, fishing, trucking, and farming motifs in its advertising. The Confederate flag also is part of the iconography of *Dukes of Hazzard* and NASCAR culture in both the North and the South, a lifestyle organized around the images of the "redneck," the "macho male," and the "rebel." Finally, it is part of an assertion of southern pride and identity in relation to northern cultural, political, and economic hegemony. Thus, NuSouth Apparel, an apparel firm owned by two black men, uses a "Mandelized" Confederate flag in green, red, and black as a logo, as a symbol that both black and white southerners now rally behind. This all complicates the meaning of the Confederate flag, and points again to the importance of understanding context. What do people signify by plastering a Confederate flag on the bumper of their pickup trucks, or across the back window with the gun rack? What image are people seeking to convey when they wear clothing embossed with Confederate flags? What is being signified when the flag is flown from a state capitol dome?

In what follows, we want to explore the basis for a pedagogy that takes the Confederate flag seriously as an iconic identity text around which young people are learning to construct a sense of self in relation to others— particularly a white identity in relation to "blackness." We focus upon an analysis of the Confederate flag controversy in South Carolina and how that controversy was made part of the curriculum in one high school social studies class. We begin by locating that controversy within an historical context and mapping out some of the perspectives taken by different groups to the demand by the NAACP that the flag be removed from a place of "sovereignty" on the capitol dome. The attempt here is to provide an example of how citizenship education may be reconceptualized around the study of symbolic battles occurring in popular culture and public life. This is followed by a discussion of some of the data from a qualitative study of teaching about the Confederate flag and "southern heritage" in one class-room in South Carolina, a class that was organized around dialogue on the flag controversy. The case study suggests the importance of critical peda-gogy that carves out space for young people to engage in reflection and dia-logue across their differences. As white northerners brought up to believe in northern narratives that represent the South as a site of backwardness and bigotry, we (the coauthors) have been led to question some of our own taken-for-granted biases and prejudices. This questioning has been encour-aged by geography. One of us (Schramm-Pate) is on the faculty of the Uni-versity of South Carolina, a Yankee in the cradle of the former Confederacy; and the other (Carlson) is on the faculty at Miami University in southwestern Ohio, near the symbolic and "real" cultural borderland between the North and the South. We write within this landscape, and out of a commitment to the articulation of a new progressivism that is capable of significantly rethinking and advancing historic battles over civil rights and social justice in America.

The Confederate Flag and the Battle over Southern Heritage

One way to contextualize the current battle over the Confederate flag in South Carolina is to trace its genealogy, to follow the path of development that led to and produced the present. One of the characteristics of genealogy, as Michel Foucault has remarked, is that it teaches us "to laugh at the solemnities of the origin" (1992, p. 143). The genealogist learns that controversies and ideas have no stable origins, that their rhizomes and roots do not reveal a single or even original place at which one can say, Here is where it all began, this is the bedrock upon which this history can be written. So there is no unified or stable origin to the idea of southern heritage in America. Indeed, as we will see, the "South" is really a European construct and cannot even be said to find its first meaning on American soil. Still, the Confederate flag does have something close to an original usage, and it is one of relevance in the current controversy. Thus, the controversy largely has been framed by progressives in terms of the questions: Can the Confederate flag be detached from this original context of usage? How has its historic and contemporary usage implied a connection with that original usage?

The "original" Confederate flag approved by the provisional Confederate Congress, it turns out, was not the flag we associate with the Confederacy today, but rather the "Stars and Bars," a flag consisting of three horizontal stripes, alternating red and white, with a canton of blue emblazoned with a circle of stars corresponding to the number of Confederate states. In September 1861, a flag specifically for battle was requested by Confederate General Beauregard because his troops had confused the "Stars and Bars" with the U.S. flag and mistakenly fired upon each other (Dedmondt, 2000). Senator William Porcher Miles of South Carolina designed the new banner to purposely look different from the U.S. flag. Miles' design had a rectangular red field transversed by a blue St. Andrew's cross which bore seven white stars to represent the states of the Confederacy. Although the "Stars and Bars" remained the Confederacy's national flag until 1863, the battle flag was used by Confederate soldiers beginning in November 1861 (Coski, 2000). The battle flag went through several revisions before the St. Andrew's cross—adapted from a banner that was used at sea from 1863 onward called the "Confederate Navy Jack"—became the generally recognized symbol of the Confederacy. This Confederate flag, also commonly known as the Rebel flag and the Army of Northern Virginia banner, has a design composed of a blue St. Andrew's cross (also known as the Southern cross) with thirteen white stars emblazoned on a red rectan-

gular background. For contemporary Americans, this version is most rec-
ognizable as the Confederate flag.

The current controversy is thus partially about this original context of
usage, but perhaps more directly about the appropriation of the Confederate flag a century later to commemorate the centennial of the Confederacy
and to signify white resistance to the black civil rights movement. In the
late 1950s the South Carolina Senate ordered the Confederate flag placed
behind the rostrum of the Senate chamber. At the same time, the General
Assembly created the Confederate War Centennial commission to plan
South Carolina's participation in the upcoming celebration of the centennial of the Confederacy. A legacy of the centennial observance, which
included parades, battle reenactments, and marker dedications to Confederate veterans, was a concurrent resolution in the state legislature in February 1962, that authorized the flying of the Confederate flag atop the
capitol dome in Columbia. As a defiant gesture of white power in the face
of rising black discontent in the state, the flying of the flag symbolized to
many that the civil rights movement had not won after all, even as the
North had not won a century earlier, that things would not fundamentally
change. One might say that taking on the flag was thus unfinished business for the NAACP, a way of letting the New Right know that it had not
and would not win.

Although the NAACP has, since the 1960s, opposed flying the flag on
the capitol dome, it was not until the 1990s that civil rights leaders began
to seriously lobby state legislatures to do something. Twice in the mid-
1990s lawmakers considered bills to remove the flag, but each time the
issue proved too politically volatile to get very far. In 1996, Republican
Governor David Beasley called from the removal of the flag. Although six
former governors, many of the state's major religious leaders, and the
South Carolina Chamber of Commerce joined Beasley, the House rejected
the proposal. Furthermore, Governor Beasley's efforts to remove the flag
from the capitol dome alienated those on the right and was widely cred-
ited with costing him reelection. He was replaced by a Democrat, Governor Jim Hodges, who was less politically vulnerable, so the NAACP stepped
up its demands. In July 1999, the NAACP called for the removal and relocation of the Confederate flag to a place of "historical rather than sovereign context" (cited in Warthen, 2000, p. D2). This time the NAACP backed
up its demand by calling for a national tourism boycott of the state until its
primary goal of removing the flag from atop the capitol dome was
achieved. More immediately, civil rights progressives, like their counterparts on the New Right, mobilized efforts to sway public opinion. As the
South Carolina General Assembly convened in the year 2000, forty-six
thousand anti-flag marchers surged through Columbia, where they were
met with six thousand pro-flag marchers, many in Confederate regalia and
waving Confederate flags.

On January 19, 2000, in his state of the state address, Governor Hodges called for the removal of the Confederate flag from the state capitol dome. He asked both sides to "take a deep breath and talk," and immediately launched a series of meetings with business leaders to work out a compromise. The plan they worked out was to keep the flag on the state house grounds but fly it on a thirty-foot pole behind a monument to Confederate General Wade Hampton. The South Carolina Senate voted 36–7 in April 2000 to remove the flag from the capitol dome, and the House of Representatives followed suit in May 2000. On July 1, 2000, thirty-eight years after it was raised, the Confederate flag was finally lowered from the capitol dome.

We want to turn now to a more detailed analysis of the battle over the Confederate flag in South Carolina, as reported and represented in the popular press. Newspaper coverage, of course, is not neutral, and one of the points we want to make later on is that editorials in major newspapers in the state generally endorsed the "compromise" worked out through the leadership of the business community. Nevertheless, it is also possible to make out the broad outlines and fine detail of a public debate in news stories, editorial page columns, and letters to the editor. Here we focus on the broad outlines rather than the fine detail of that public discourse, mapping out three identifiable "voices" in the discourse and linking these voices to identity politics: a conservative and New Right voice of Southern heritage linked to a cultural politics of whiteness; a progressive voice of social justice linked closely to the black civil rights movement; and a hegemonic state and corporate voice of compromise, consensus, and the integration of the South in the new global economy.

The New Right Discourse of "Whiteness"

In the post–civil rights era a New Right power bloc formed in the South around several social movements. This power bloc includes small-town businesses hurt by the "invasion" of northern corporations, as well as elements of the white middle class, particularly in small rural communities. It also includes a growing number of white, working-class, deunionized men threatened by gains made by blacks and women who feel that nobody cares about them—the constituency of the David Duke right, dedicated to the restoration of an overtly racist and white supremacist South. Finally, the New Right power bloc in the South includes Christian fundamentalists, for whom the African American civil rights movement, the women's movement, and the gay and lesbian movement together are taken to be signs of the decline and fall of a South that used to be God-fearing, "civilized," and morally upright.

Those who identify with the New Right in a more overt sense are increasingly mobilized via the internet and magazines targeted to a New Right market. The *Southern Partisan*, for example, is a self-proclaimed neo-Confederate magazine. A recent issue targeted at youth featured a cover article titled "Boy Heroes of the Confederacy." The subscription coupons show a Confederate army with the second national Confederate flag. A full-page subscription ad has a picture of Robert E. Lee and his personal Confederate flag. Many of the articles focus on the Confederacy and remembrance activities. *Southern Partisan* enjoys a wide publication and hand-to-hand circulation and is considered "respectable" by many politicians. The magazine's masthead lists Patrick Buchanan as a senior advisor, and he is a regular or irregular contributor to a column titled, "Dividing Line."

A sign of just how much the Confederate flag has become a national signifier of New Right identity can be seen in the broad appeal of the Council of Conservative Citizens (CofCC), perhaps the major neo-Confederate organization in the country. Though the organization is based in St. Louis, Missouri, much of its work in now done over the Internet, and its audience is increasingly global. The main speaker at a recent convention organized by the group around the theme of southern heritage was well-known writer Michael Andrew Grissom, author of *Southern by the Grace of God, The Last Rebel Yell,* and *When the South Was Southern.* In a survey of its membership in 1994, 96.9 percent said no to the question "Should Confederate flags, statues, memorials and other Southern heritage symbols be removed?" Both Pat Buchanan and U.S. Senator Trent Lott of Mississippi have published columns in the Citizen Informer, the organization's magazine. This and other organizations and their publications helped make the battle over the Confederate flag in South Carolina a national battle, one in which even northerners could claim an honorary southern heritage; more to the point, it was a battle in which the New Right could count on support from around the nation and the world. This means that the Confederacy is no longer tied to geography as much as to a fantasy, a state of mind, a lifestyle, a cultural politics—represented by the flag and by the idea of "southern heritage."

This notion of southern heritage turned out to be the central code used by those on the right to narrate the South Carolina Confederate flag controversy. South Carolina State Senator Glenn McConnell was widely quoted in the press in 1996 as saying: "For us to surrender at the dome is to eventually surrender across South Carolina, where we will not be free to exhibit our heritage for the fear of condemnation" (CNN, November 27, 2000). Here, "our heritage" is a racially coded phrase. It serves as a form of collective white memory, or collective fantasy we might say, for the construction of a stable sense of identity in an unsettling age. William Pinar has observed of the South that emerged from the devastation of the Civil War: "More than ever before, fantasy, not reality, came to characterize (white) Southern history and culture" (2001, p. 264). The narrative of southern heritage is thus one that promises a return to a nostalgic time and place of lost innocence, a lost golden age of southern pride and nobility. Southern heritage represents itself in the image of fully formed and foundational space of rural landscapes interrupted by great plantations built in neoclassical style, suggesting that they are the fulfillment of a culture that began in ancient Greece. Indeed, the attempt to link southern culture to ancient Greece (witness, for example, the replica of the Parthenon in Tennessee), may derive—on an implicit and taken-for-granted level—from the common heritage of slavery shared by both the South and "classical" Athenian society.

Since slaves were not viewed as fully human in Athenian society, it was only "natural" that they should be denied human rights and citizen rights, as it was only "natural" that slaves should be denied human rights in the South. The myth of black intellectual inferiority is thus a central theme in Southern heritage narratives, and one that was a subtext in New Right discourse throughout the South. As the Senator Arthur Ravenel of the so-called Charleston aristocracy proclaimed, "Can you believe, can you believe, can you believe, can you believe that there's those who think that the General Assembly in South Carolina is going to pull its wool, knuckle under, grovel and do the bidding of that corrupt organization known as the National Association for Retarded People?" (cited in Stroud, 2000, p. A1). To add insult to injury, when asked to apologize, Ravenel said he wanted to apologize to retarded people for mistakenly associating them with the NAACP. Here we see the all-too-familiar face of Eurocentric racism, the rank ordering of people according to natural or God-given intelligence, from the "normal" white, to the "retarded" white, to the black.

This "natural order" also has been given meaning in religious terms. Thus the infamous (but also popular) South Carolina restaurateur and crusading white supremacist Maurice Bessinger can proclaim that "God gave slaves to whites." For whites to continue to occupy their position of superiority in the "natural order," however, they supposedly must maintain a pure blood. "You are WHITE because your ancestors believed in SEGREGATION," reads a tract distributed by a group of which Bessinger is a past president—the National Association for the Preservation of White People (Monk, 2000, p. B5). Southern heritage thus is linked to a cultural politics of establishing bloodlines and "purifying" the white race, to return it to its "original" essence.

This concern with bloodlines also is related to a European aristocratic mythology that was well established in the antebellum South. The ideal of the plantation owner and master as cavalier aristocrat, however, was adopted from popular fiction more than from reality. Plantation owners on the Pee Dee River in South Carolina borrowed names such as "Arundel," "Annandale," and "Dirleton" for their estates from the mythological Scottish and English castles in Sir Walter Scott's "Lady of the Lakes," *The Bride of Lammermoor*, and *Ivanhoe*. Within this pastoral past, slavery was supposedly not oppressive. This paternalistic, aristocratic myth is, in turn, overlaid with another and related myth, that of the happy patriarchal family. The intellectual progenitor of the Confederacy, South Carolinian John C. Calhoun (1782–1850), argued that southern plantations were not only small communities, but also family units with a male master and head of household (Edgar, 1998). To attack slavery was to attack this family structure. By locating slaves within the "family" overseen by the master, this mythology suggests that slaves were not dehumanized. As recently as 1993, longtime U.S. senator Strom Thurmond of South Carolina informed his colleagues in the United State Senate that, "They [slave owners] treated the slaves well" (cited in Leifermann, 1998, p. 104). Slavery, he maintained, was a basically benign institution.

At the same time that Senator Thurmond defended the "peculiar institution" of slavery as benign, he observed that "southerners didn't bring them [slaves] here. Northerners brought them here. Slave traders in Boston." This is a telling comment, and one that leads to another dominant code in the discourse of southern heritage, one that understands southern identity as constructed in relation to a northern other. In deconstructing the southern heritage mythology, we must simultaneously deconstruct northern heritage mythology. To understand southern identity, we must understand northern identity, for both historically have been involved in constituting each other. From the beginning, the South has not been an autonomous space, with its own history and culture, but rather a space constructed in battle. The South is the creation of a double consciousness in the sense that the "double" of the South (the North) is always a visible or invisible presence in southern heritage narratives.

The construction of a national identity in America historically has occurred by bifurcating Americans into two identity groups, one northern and one southern, one hegemonic and the other subordinate. In order for northern industrial culture to establish its hegemony over the American character, it required its Other, its alterity, always interrupting and slowing down the inexorable march of progress. So the South has been made to assume this role in American public life and public consciousness. It has been unable to establish its own identity apart from its controlling alter ego, the North. The South has been made to represent the origins of racism in America, from which it supposedly spread like an infection to the North. Racism has been represented as the result of a deficiency in Southern character, one of many. This hegemonic representation of southern character, which has been used to place the North on a moral and cultural high ground, is actually a variation on one of the great themes of Eurocentric culture, a theme that pits northern Europeans against southern Europeans, and even divides peoples within one country. Take, for example, the situation in Italy. In his 1920s essay "On the Southern Question," Antonio Gramsci writes that to northern Italians, "The southerners are biologically inferior beings, semi-barbarians or complete barbarians by natural destiny; if the south is backward, the fault is not to be found in the capitalist system or in any other historical cause, but is the fault of nature which has made the southerner lazy, incapable, criminal, barbarous" (quoted in Holub, 1992, p. 158). What is interesting here is the degree to which the colonizer-colonized binary operates at so many different levels in European culture, even relegating some of its own to the status of the colonial Other. In America, this colonial discourse is, of course, deeply implicated in the representation of "blackness." But it is also, and in an ironic way, deeply implicated in the representation of the southern white. Under the gaze of the hegemonic, colonial discourse on national identity, whites and blacks in the South are reintegrated, together assuming the role of the uncivilized, "backward" Other that impedes the economic, cultural, and moral development of the nation. In the popular mythology of the Old South we also find a dominant image of climate-induced lassitude with veranda sitting and life that moved at a slow pace (Kirby, 1978, p. 79).

Resentment of the northern Other and of hegemonic representations of southern culture and identity has been articulated with New Right agendas in a number of ways. For example, it takes the form of resistance to "outside agitators" from the North, such as the freedom riders in the 1960s. In the South Carolina Confederate flag controversy, this resentment was tapped into by presidential candidate George W. Bush during the presidential primary in that state. While campaigning in the state, Bush was asked where he stood on the controversy and the boycott. He remarked, "I think the good people of south Carolina can settle the issue." He was dismissive of NAACP plans for a national tourism boycott, declaring that "my advice is for people who don't live in South Carolina to butt out of the issue. The people of South Carolina can make that decision" (cited in Strope, 1999). Bush's statement was widely popular in the state, which he carried by a landslide in the subsequent presidential election. This resentment of northern "outsiders" finds expression in a popular bumper sticker that reads "We don't care how you do it up North." While much can be read into this bumper sticker, it is ambiguous enough in its meaning to appeal to a broad spectrum of whites and some blacks. Less ambiguous is the message of the group called "No Votes for Turncoats," which held its first meeting in Bessinger's Columbia barbeque restaurant, "Piggy Park," on September 20, 2000, to mount a campaign against legislators the group viewed as turncoats and "Benedict Arnolds." According to one of the organizers, it did not matter where the candidates endorsed by the group stood on various issues: "What matters is that the candidates are running against turncoats" (cited in Bauerlein, 2000, p. B1).

This resentment of the North, and this attitude of doing battle against the North, also becomes easily commodified and commercialized in the redneck and rebel images and lifestyles. Though rednecks can be found in every state and corner of the nation, it is a representation of the Other that has been painted with southern features. In the Deep South, one supposedly can find the redneck in its natural habitat. The redneck is, in this sense, a creation of the white middle class, and more particularly white, northern middle class, that seeks to distance itself from racism (and sexism and homophobia) by locating the source of these prejudicial beliefs and practices in the psyche of the southerner redneck. Of course, racism, sexism, and homophobia do exist among poor and working-class males in the South, and one form of reactionary southern cultural politics consists of proudly proclaiming one's redneck identity, of becoming the narrow-minded bigot represented in popular culture, consistently opposing all "politically correct" ways of thinking. Others embrace redneck identity more as a commodified lifestyle than as a political identity, although the two may overlap and become interconnected. To become a redneck, people must perform a good deal of "identity work," to use Philip Wexler's (1992) phrase. They must wear clothing that projects the right image, and they must drive a pickup. Across the rear window of the pickup a Confederate flag may be draped, which forms a backdrop to a window gun rack. This is almost a Village People–type stereotype of the redneck, and certainly one can pass as redneck on any given occasion with less than this assemblage of stitched-together signifiers.

If the redneck image signifies resistance to politically correct thinking, it also may signify resistance to cultural domination and the struggle to be free. Albert Camus, in his study of the mythology of the rebel in Western cultural history, writes that "rebellion cannot exist without the feeling that, somewhere and somehow, one is right." The rebel is the slave in revolt, the one who confronts an oppressive order of things with the insistence of a right to not be oppressed (1956, p. 13). This means that the rebel identity in the South is not necessarily "bad" or antiprogressive, even if it has been steered in rightist directions. As a form of resistance to northern hegemony, it needs to be taken seriously. Still, the rebel image largely has been stripped of its progressive potential through commercialization and through linking it to the redneck image and a southern heritage mythology. For example, the commodification of the rebel image has been key to the success of NASCAR in the South. Stock-car racing has a long heritage in the South, and NASCAR increasingly serves as a producer and marketer of southern rebel identity. In the 1960s, Chrysler Corporation invested heavily in stock-car racing in order to sell to a southern market, and it began to associate its cars, particularly Dodge cars, with the rebel image. In 1968, when Dodge came out with its new Charger model, versions of which ran on the stock car circuit, its advertising slogan was, "The Dodge rebellion wants you!" As a national ad campaign, the Dodge rebellion was designed to sell the rebel image to the nation. When the popular television show *The Dukes of Hazzard*, was looking for a symbol of southern rebellion, Chrysler Corporation offered the Charger, a car rather than a person. Perhaps not coincidentally, the Dodge Charger that was leading the Dodge rebellion in television commercials was named General Lee in *The Dukes of Hazzard* television show and was adorned with a Confederate flag. Far from complaining, Chrysler clearly participated in linking its cars to this southern white male, rebel identity, and the Confederate flag represented this identity better than anything else could.

In the face of rising opposition to the Confederate flag, some of the more moderate supporters of the mythology of southern heritage have sought to distance themselves from those on the right, to view the flag more as a marker of lifestyle than politics (as in its use in NASCAR culture) or as a symbol that can be detached from racism. One popular T-shirt reads: "Fly me with dignity not bigotry," over a Confederate flag background. The T-shirt also contains in smaller print the following statement: "I was not designed as a hate object, although many people look at me this way today. I was not born to represent white sheets and shaved heads. I was designed to support states rights and soldiers who wore grey." Here the effort is made to transform the Civil War into a battle over states rights, and to defuse its racially coded meaning. Similarly, one flag supporter was quoted in a press story as saying, "In the history of the battle flag, it really has very little do with racism and too many people have a perception that it does" (cited in Willingham, 2000, p. A10). In spite of these efforts to make support for keeping the Confederate flag on the capitol dome respectable, to detach it from a racialized discourse on southern heritage and identity, the New Right has been a powerful force in rearticulating the flag with such a racialized discourse, from which it historically has never been detached. The mythology of southern heritage makes the Confederate flag part of a nostalgic narrative of a past that was oppressive to many, and deconstructing that narrative must be a major priority in the progressive reconstruction of historical memory, in a national dialogue that is about coming to grips with the past and its continuing legacy.

The Progressive Response:
From Critique to Reappropriation of the Confederate Flag

The controversy over the Confederate flag was initiated by the NAACP in order to raise critical questions about the flag and the heritage it represents, and thus to reframe the public dialogue on civil rights in the South. In more overtly political terms, the NAACP and progressives more generally in the state hoped they could win the flag dispute, thereby delivering a major political defeat to the growing New Right movement in the state. The NAACP resolution adopting economic sanctions against South Carolina (July 12, 1999) represented the issues in a form that would be used over and over again in various news reports, press, releases, and public addresses. Consequently, we want to focus much of what we have to say on how that resolution framed the issues. The resolution begins by acknowledging some facts conveniently ignored or glossed over in dominant narratives of southern heritage. The origins of the Confederate flag, for example, cannot be separated from "an economic system based on slave labor." In these ways, the resolution calls upon South Carolinians to face the facts of history and not to be deluded by the romanticized mythology that conservatives were selling. These facts also helped contextualize the flag controversy. For example, there is the fact that the flag was placed over the dome as part of the celebration of the centennial of the Confederacy and that in such a context it symbolized "resistance to the battle for civil rights and equality" in the 1960s. It is also a fact, according to the resolution, that the Confederate flag is linked to "numerous modern-day groups advocating white supremacy." The effort here is to locate the state's usage of the Confederate flag within a history that is not yet totally in the past, but rather constitutes a living history of state-sponsored white supremacy.

Then the NAACP resolution shifts to the issue of "sovereignty," the issue of who the Confederate flag speaks for when it flies above the capitol dome. The state, as Michel Foucault (1979) has observed, wrapped itself in the powers and discourses of sovereignty in the early modern era, claiming to speak for and represent the "public interest" and the "public good." This sovereignty of the state is not questioned by the NAACP, but what is called into question is whether the state of South Carolina is acting like a democratic sovereign, representing the interests of all of its citizens. Flying the flag over the capitol dome also implies, according to the resolution "allegiance to a non-existent nation." To call upon African Americans in particular to swear allegiance to the Confederacy is a clear violation of their rights and "an affront to the sensibilities and dignity of a majority of African Americans in the state of South Carolina." The resolution ends with a call for the removal and relocation of the flag "to a place of historical rather than sovereign context." It decries the compromise of moving the flag to the front of the capital grounds on a twenty-foot pole, noting that this is still a position of sovereignty, and that it is also a slap in the face to those citizens of South Carolina "who do not accept or revere the supposed heritage represented by the flag" (see South Carolina NAACP website for the entire resolution).

In a general sense, the approach taken by the NAACP was deconstructive and critical. Progressives devoted much of their effort to demystifying the southern heritage discourse of flag supporters to reveal it as a discourse of white privilege. This is an absolutely central element, in our view, of a progressive public pedagogy. It will be useless to construct a new southern identity without first thoroughly deconstructing the mythology of the old South. Too often, however, progressive pedagogy stops at deconstructionism. In place of the mythology of an original Eden, a pure southern essence, implicit in southern heritage texts, progressives in South Carolina had little in the way of a new narrative of southern heritage to offer.

Within the public, the Confederate flag also began to be demonized by many African Americans and some whites in a way that failed to distinguish between various contexts of usage. In letters to the editor and comments on websites, opponents of the flag made it clear that to them the Confederate flag was similar to the German swastika, a symbol of evil and hate, one for which a museum is the only proper context for exhibition. This position was articulated in a less essentialist form by those who argued that the time is not yet right when the Confederate flag can be exhibited in public without promoting fear and intimidation. Like the swastika in Germany, the Confederate flag in the South is a symbol which may yet be too provocative, too much of an invitation to relive the past, too much of an instigator of white racism and black rage. Our sense, however, is that progressives are better off understanding the Confederate flag in all its complexity of usage, even staying open to some subversive reappropriations of the flag.

How are we to interpret, for example, the emergence and popularity—among African Americans in the South—of the so-called Mandela Confederate flag? This variation on a theme appears on all the clothing of NuSouth Apparel, which is based in Charleston, South Carolina. Hip, young, progressive Southerners, primarily African American but also a growing number of whites, have embraced the flag, which incorporates the colors that are often associated with African liberation. The background is blood red, the stars are green, and the St. Andrew's cross is black. Here we have a very postmodern approach to the Confederate flag, one that parodies and subverts its "normal" exhibition, that affirms southern heritage and identity even as it links that heritage with Africa and Europe simultaneously and inseparably. NuSouth Apparel is popular with entertainers like "Boyz II Men," who have helped popularize the line and its logo in stores as far north as Massachusetts. According to the NuSouth website, the uniquely colored flag is a symbol of the firm's commitment to "tackle the age-old issue of racism in America. The firm's slogan is, "For the sons and daughters of former slaves. For the sons and daughters of former slave owners." This certainly represents a commercialization and commodification of a southern identity icon. As Judith Butler has observed, subversive performances and representations run the risk of becoming clichés through repetition, and particularly "through their repetition within commodity culture where 'subversion' carries market value" (1990, p. xxi). At the same time, the popularity of this parody of the Confederate flag reflects a growing sentiment among young people in the South that they can assemble a southern identity by stitching together various pieces to form a hybrid, that they can reappropriate and play with the Confederate flag, like other icons of southern heritage, to make them carry new, even contradictory meaning, to make them say something new.

If progressives have been limited in their response and less able to declare victory than they had hoped at the outset, it may be because progressives generally have been content to read the Confederate flag only as a racial text, one which had to do with relations between blacks and whites. The trade unions and the women's and the gay and lesbian rights movements all supported the tourism boycott, yet questions remain as to how much this translated into support among the rank-and-file membership of these groups. Boycott organizers did little to link the Confederate flag to socioeconomic injustice, sexism, and homophobia. Though the Confederate flag is, first and foremost, symbolic of a history of oppression of African Americans, particularly in the South, the southern heritage it is made to represent needs to be deconstructed as oppressive to more than African Americans as a group. By failing to develop linkages between battles over social justice across lines of class, race, gender, and sexual orientation, progressives were left with a narrower issue, and one many whites had a hard time identifying with. So long as various progressive social movements and discourses are understood to be relatively autonomous rather than interrelated, it becomes difficult to organize a broader democratic movement and discourse around the construction of a "New South."

The Corporate and State Discourse of the "New South"

Although most corporate leaders in South Carolina would probably describe themselves as conservatives, they tend to align themselves with "reformist" elements in state government and politics, which includes a loose coalition of Republican and Democratic leaders drawn together by a common or unifying vision of a New South. This coalition of interests in the corporate world and the state has become hegemonic in the post–Civil Rights era in the sense that it tends to set the terms of the public debate on most issues, and their framing of the issues tends to prevail. The hegemonic power bloc seeks to appease and co-opt both progressive and New Right constituencies as it advances their number one priority—the economic reorganization of the South to better integrate it within the new global economy. The New South is to be built on economic revival, according to this corporate discourse, which means attracting more multinationals. Multinational corporations do not like to get embroiled in racial and other disputes, and they like all of their employees to work together cooperatively. Most have nondiscrimination policies with regard to race or ethnicity, national origin, gender, religion, and (increasingly) sexual orientation. The new global workforce is to be multicultural in the sense that people of diverse racial and ethnic identities increasingly are being drawn together as the labor force is being reconstituted. Corporations are also self-interested in reducing prospects of public censure and economic boycotts. It is not surprising, for example, that BMW and Michelin, two multinational corporations with a sizable presence in South Carolina who took the lead in pressuring legislators and the governor to remove the Confederate flag from the capitol dome, did so only after the NAACP threatened to expand the tourism boycott to include products made in South Carolina.

From that point on, business leaders took over much of the leadership in forging a coalition to support a compromise; and indeed, "compromise" was a governing theme in corporate discourse on the flag controversy. Thus, the compromise proposed by the governor and accepted by the legislature was largely crafted by the business community. The *New York Times*, in its coverage, noted: "Standing with the governor when he announced the plan were business and community leaders who are concerned with the impact of the dispute on the state" (Ayres, 2000, p. 13). Noticeably absent from the picture were civil rights leaders. The fact that the NAACP did not accept the compromise, along with many supporters of the flag, meant that it was a compromise in name only. By asserting that a compromise or settlement had been reached, business and political leadership hoped the public (both nationally and in South Carolina) would view the dispute as effectively settled. The governor, with the support of the major newspapers in the state, then implied that it was everyone's responsibility to support the compromise. That translated, in effect, into an effort to stifle continuing public dialogue on the issue, a dialogue that is much needed in the state and the nation. As in the James West case, the state was associated with defusing and controlling controversy. The hegemonic power bloc viewed controversy as something to be managed and suppressed when possible. Controversy is, after all, a form of dialogic conflict, and conflict can upset the established order. That, indeed, is part of the democratic promise of public dialogue.

Teaching the Confederate Flag Controversy

Linda McNeil (2000) observes that the quest for control in the classroom is contradictory in that it leads to forms of curriculum and pedagogy that only exacerbate the problem. Dialogue causes conflict, and so the curriculum gets reduced to a teacher-delivered, depoliticized discourse that is much more about controlling students than empowering them, more about preparing them for the rituals of standardized testing than preparing them to be democratic citizens. But this is a contradictory strategy in that it only produces more student resistance and disengagement. And so a vicious cycle of control is initiated that effectively drives dialogue out of the classroom, relegating it to the halls and corridors.

If McNeil is right, then it would seem reasonable to presume that the Confederate flag controversy would be banished from the curriculum in South Carolina, or at least not made an explicit focus of student study and discussion. In the spring of 2000, Schramm-Pate informally interviewed either in person or by e-mail correspondence twenty-five high school social studies teachers in South Carolina regarding whether and/or how they handled the flag controversy and other issues of southern heritage in their classrooms. Although most of the teachers had strong personal opinions about the flag controversy, most said they shied away from a discussion of sensitive issues in their classrooms because they either feared repercussions from district administrators, parents, and the community or did not feel "comfortable" addressing the issues. Teaching in what we might call the "comfort zone" involved, for these teachers, not raising issues that would make them or some of their students uncomfortable. But what is "uncomfortable"? The teachers tended to represent anything that would divide students or make them more aware of their differences as uncomfortable. In practice, this meant that most teachers avoided discussions about gender, class, and sexual orientation as well as race. Issues of identity in a general sense were represented as leading instruction into a danger zone, and open dialogue on identity was particularly taboo. Consequently, any conversations these teachers may have had with students regarding the flag controversy was informal in nature, usually occurring in the hallway before

classes or in the cafeteria. Although many expressed a belief in the importance of empowering students to become critical thinkers and to debate
important social issues openly in class, all but one teacher expressed concerns about actually teaching for critical literacy in their own classes.

This one exception was a man we will call Richard, a white, full-time
social studies teacher in a rural community. Richard also, and not coincidentally, was a doctoral student in curriculum and instruction at the University of South Carolina, where he had become conversant in the
discourses of critical literacy, critical pedagogy, and democratic dialogue. At
the same time, he had become more and more concerned about the dis-
junction between the critical discourses of the university and the "real
world of the school." It was in this context that he decided to undertake, in
collaboration with Schramm-Pate, an action research project involving the
teaching of a unit on southern heritage for his "Advanced Placement
American Government & Politics" class, using the flag controversy as an
organizing theme.

The high school was small, like the community, with an enrollment of
approximately 240 students in grades 7–12. The student population was
68 percent white, 30 percent African American and 2 percent Hispanic,
Asian or bi-racial. The high school, like so many other small, wood frame,
schoolhouses dotting the "Upstate," was built with the participation of the
textile mills and historically has provided its students with a good general
education complemented by a full range of athletic and social activities.
Today as in the past, most graduates of the high school do not go on to college, and very few students come from homes in which the breadwinners
are professionals. The current curriculum has expanded to include two to
five advanced placement (AP) classes each year, three years of the same
foreign language (Spanish), and a minority studies course. Still, the culture
of the school is formed by a widespread perception that college-prepara-
tory programs are not necessary because most people do not frame "success" as leaving the town. From this perspective, some groundedness in
place and community is part of the promise of democratic public life.

The town, with a population of fifteen hundred, is essentially a mill
town in an age in which smokestack industries founded around the turn
of the twentieth century are in a terminal state of decline. In 2001, the
town's largest employer closed its mill, and the next-biggest employer,
which makes socks for Fruit of the Loom, declared bankruptcy. The increasing obsolescence of the town's industrial base, along with its isolation from
major interstate highways and urban areas, meant that it was being left
behind in the restructuring of the southern economy. This was associated
with a conservatism among many residents, who reminisced about the
"good old days." These "good old days" were a romanticized version of the
immediate post–World War II years, when the town's predominantly
Scottish-Irish population achieved a modest level of financial security. One
could see the influence of such a discourse of the "good old days," and of a
stable community bounded by tradition, in the social studies curriculum.

Its influence was also apparent in the visible absence of multicultural discourses and practices in the school. Even marginally multicultural activities such as Black History Month and Women's History Month were not observed in the high school for fear they would be divisive. In fact, a celebration of Kwanzaa as part of the Winter Assembly in 2000 was contested by white students and Christian conservatives, and this only reinforced the sense among administrators and much of the faculty that race relations were too sensitive an issue to be raised in the curriculum.

Sixteen students signed up for Richard's AP government class in the spring of 2001: one biracial (white and African American) female, eight African Americans (three females and five males), one Hispanic female, and six whites (two females and four males). Richard began the unit on southern heritage in March, announcing to the class that he wanted do something different. Instead of the usual textbook readings, the class was to undertake a study of the battle currently being waged over the Confederate flag as a symbol of southern heritage. What was all the fuss about? What were the various positions in the battle, and who was taking what position? What did the controversy have to do with the historic construction of "whiteness" and "blackness," white identity and black identity? How might the current battle be resolved? These are the questions he raised with students. Finally, he suggested that blacks and whites tend to see things from different positions or standpoints, and that only through dialogue can they begin to see things from the Other's perspective, even if this may not always lead to agreement. Thus, he proposed that the unit be based on dialogue rather than lecturing. This led to a discussion of some ground rules for engaging in "dialogue across differences," rules such as making sure that all voices are heard, that everyone is respected, that language is used as clearly as possible, that "truth claims" are backed up with facts, examples, or logical arguments, and that a genuine effort is made to understand and appreciate the perspective of others (Burbules and Rice, 1991). Much of the class time each day would thus be devoted to a discussion of a series of articles and opinion pieces appearing in major state newspapers, and on websites, that took a position in some way on the flag controversy.

To help students understand the importance of their own, taken-for-granted way of "seeing" the world, Richard also introduced students to Afrocentric discourse and asked them to think about things from an Afrocentric perspective. Most white students found this to be a threatening activity, and at this point Richard faced some resistance. As he distributed some readings on Afrocentrism, he heard grumbling from a few white students about the emphasis on "black stuff." One student asked Richard when he was going to "start talking about white people and the problems they have." In contrast, the black students were almost uniformly supportive of learning about Afrocentrism, although on several occasions black students did express concerns about "white backlash," hinting that Richard (perhaps particularly as a white man) was "asking for trouble" by teaching Afrocentric "stuff."

With all the messiness and potential for conflict raised by this introduction to the unit on southern heritage left unresolved, Richard shifted discussion to the Confederate flag controversy in South Carolina. In this case, discussions were organized around the reading of editorials and opinion pieces in major state newspapers that dealt with the controversy in one way or another. One of the first of these readings was a column in the *State* newspaper by an African American writer, who sought to counter the argument of flag supporters that the civil rights movement is over and that it is inappropriate to think of this use of the flag as an issue involving civil rights. The author of the essay noted that, indeed, civil rights struggles continued in South Carolina, and used as an example the fact that there are a disproportionate number of African Americans on death row in South Carolina. He questioned whether black males were not being "railroaded" into prison so that the police could claim they had solved crimes that remain unsolved. This opened up a heated discussion. Several black students argued that racial prejudice was still prevalent, that black people still did not have full civil rights and that black people were not treated fairly in the courts, although they acknowledged that some things were getting better. Generally, black students demonstrated a capacity to see the present as part of a long struggle for freedom, and they viewed the civil rights movement as an uncompleted project.

White students did not engage the controversy or stake out a defensive "white" position. Most remained silent during the discussion, except for the two white females, who positioned themselves as speaking for whites generally. One complained that Richard's presentation of class material was too gloomy, too "negative." Another complained that "everything is black in this class"—a rather telling comment that suggests the student felt "blackness" had taken over and driven out "whiteness," that by introducing black perspectives, the perspectives of white students were being silenced. This resentment, as Richard explained, was similar in some ways to the resentment that black students must experience every day when all they get is white history and white perspectives on the news. So if nothing else, white students had learned a valuable lesson about how it feels to be marginalized, if only briefly. Dianna, a voluble and articulate African American female who was also valedictorian of the senior class, agreed, saying that in her twelve years of schooling she had learned only about white people and their history, nothing about herself. Leonard, an African American male, echoed this sentiment later in a follow-up class by urging whites to study African American history, saying he had been forced to study whiteness his entire life.

Each week during the term, the class watched a videotaped segment of the PBS series *Eyes on the Prize*. Several black students regularly hummed along with the chorus soundtrack that opens each episode—"if it's one thing we did right, it's the day we started to fight. Keep your eyes on the prize, hold on!" Pam, a white female student, usually made a deliberate show of sleeping through segments of *Eyes on the Prize* while Samantha, the other white female, sat with her arms folded and with an angry expression on her face. They were a bit more responsive to the History Channel's presentation of *The Unfinished Civil War*, a video on Civil War reenactment and reenactors that includes an extensive presentation of the Confederate flag controversy in South Carolina. After viewing the video the class read and discussed some of the press reaction to the broadcasting of the program in the state for the first time in February 2001. Some of those who are part of the reenactment culture and lifestyle were particularly angry, claiming that they had been portrayed as a "bunch of idiotic racists" (see *The State*, online, March 14, 2001, paragraph 2). Samantha and Pam agreed. Pam told all of the black students in the class who were still "whining" to "get over it!" because the flag was not, in her view, ever coming down from behind the Confederate monument nor should it ever have been taken off the dome in the first place. On another occasion she exclaimed, "Move to another country if you don't like it!"

One of the first changes in Samantha's attitude was acceptance of the idea that positionality did matter, that whites see things from one position and blacks from another. However, this at least provided her with a new way of defending her position without coming across as having the one, correct truth. She could now acknowledge that if she were black she might indeed see things differently. Thus, she said one day during discussion that she was often unfairly stereotyped as a racist for her beliefs, but that she really was not. Because she was white, she thought the way she did. How could it be otherwise? Didn't blacks view the Confederate flag from their own perspective? Samantha's awareness of the decisive importance of the master narrative of whiteness in constructing her own identity allowed her to acknowledge the partiality of all knowledge, including her own. "Whiteness" had become for her one way of knowing among several possible, of which one was "blackness." The limitations of this new awareness is that it treated blacks and whites as having two completely separate and autonomous worldviews, as equally valid. In reality, blackness and whiteness, or black and white identity, historically have been constructed in relation to one another, and in relations of privilege and domination.

As the term continued Pam and Samantha moved more in the direction of arguing that the Confederate flag has no fixed meaning, and that it could mean many different things to different people and groups. Thus, they avoided a direct confrontation with black students over the privileging of their own truths. They also modified and revised their own thinking about the flag controversy. They could now acknowledge that some groups were rallying around the flag for the "wrong reasons," and they maintained that the "right reason" for flying the Confederate flag on the capitol grounds should be to honor the war dead. However, for Dianna, this "compromising" position on the part of Pam and Samantha was unacceptable. With a steady but emotion-laden voice, she said: "The Confederate flag will always mean slavery, Jim Crow, segregation, and generations of suffering. It's the heritage that makes me hate it." Referring to the slogan of some pro-flag supporters, "Heritage not Hate," Dianna argued: "The facts aren't going to change. The ability of southerners to own slaves was their heritage." Jennifer, another African American female, added that honoring ancestors who fought for secession and states' rights to allow slavery was also honoring the cause of slavery.

Chris, a quiet, white male student of working-class background, played a particularly important role in resisting the framing of the discussion in terms of a unified white heritage. Once, as Samantha made a comment about white people's heritage, he calmly turned to her and remarked, "Samantha, I hope you don't include all of us whites when you talk about your heritage." He said that in his view the Confederate flag stood for slavery and it could never separate itself from that past. So whites needed to "get over it." This led Pam to at least concede that for African Americans, the Confederate flag would always be a reminder of slavery, and that was unfortunate. Kaitlyn, from a mixed black/white family, as might be expected, spoke of the need for compromise, although she did not support the compromise that had been reached by the legislature. Perhaps some other compromise could be reached, she hoped. Dianna said that in her view the best compromise would be to place the Confederate flag in a museum to the war dead, but nowhere else. To Pam, this was hardly a compromise. She urged those who might be offended by the current placement of the flag behind the war memorial on the capitol lawn to "use a different street" when they went to the capitol so they could avoid seeing it. Samantha asked, "What more do you want us to do?" For Dianna, that "more" was complete removal of the Confederate flag from the State House grounds.

The unit on southern heritage and the Confederate flag controversy ended with Richard asking students to write reflective essays on what they had learned in the unit. Pam, who had always advanced a conservative argument in dialogue, perhaps because she was friends with Samantha and did not want to stake out a separate position, wrote an essay in which she was critical of some of the "macho male" posturing of those who "got into" dressing up in Confederate uniforms, waving Confederate flags, and reliving the "glories" of battle. She had begun to question, she wrote, whether women were not also oppressed during slavery. As for whether the Confederate flag could ever be made to stand for a proud southern heritage, she wrote that "the flag is seen as a racial sword to blacks. . . . So how can we really revere our 'heritage' if our heritage was hatred to begin with?" Leonard, an African American male wrote an essay that was about reconciliation and "talking it out." Among his points: "There will always be pressure between the co-existences of different U.S. history stories because there will forever be people who disagree with it one way and talk about it in another. It's probable for non-compromised viewpoints to dialogue across their differences. Just because you don't like something doesn't mean that you can't talk it out."

There were no neat and tidy conclusions to this study of southern heritage and the Confederate flag controversy, just as there was no way to neatly separate public controversy over the rewriting of American history from the private lives of students. But these were not the aims of the teacher. Rather than understanding a unit of study in linear terms, as a movement toward a final destination, a final, culminating truth about the topic under study, Richard approached the unit as a journey, an opening of a conversation, an opportunity to "trouble" the idea that there is a unified, culminating truth about southern heritage or about identity.

Conclusion

The battle over the Confederate flag wages on in South Carolina, as it does in other states. In April 2000, the Jackson, Mississippi, City Council voted to condemn the flying of the Confederate flag in any sovereign place. In Alabama, where the Confederate flag is flown every April 26 for the state's Confederate Memorial Day, the legislature has proposed replacing the Confederate battle flag with the first national flag of the Confederacy as a compromise. Supporters hope that flag, with its similarities to the American flag, will evoke less acrimony. In Georgia, where the state flag also incorporates the battle flag, protesters at the Super Bowl in 2000 demanded that the flag be brought down. Meanwhile, in Virginia, the state is taking an opposite tack, seeking to block the use of the Confederate flag on the state's new personalized license plates. It is being sued by the Virginia Sons of the Confederacy for its actions. These symbolic battles being waged over the icons of southern and American heritage point to a new form of cultural politics, one in which the battles are being waged in popular culture over the representation of identity and heritage. As cultural politics moves into an age of symbolic battle, progressivism in education will need to change in very far-reaching ways.

The approach to the Confederate flag controversy explored in this essay implies a number of things pedagogically, and we want to close by highlighting and reiterating some of what it implies. To begin with, it implies looking at classrooms, other school spaces, and various sites in the public as what Lois Weis and Michelle Fine (2000) call "safe spaces," educational sites in which young people can feel safe to express their beliefs and feelings openly in dialogue with others. Of course, as Weis and Fine maintain, it is important that we not romanticize spaces in schools, classrooms, and the public as ever "innocent, uncontaminated, or 'free'" (p. xii). They are, at best, sites in which privilege can be questioned even as it continues to shape discourse, in which identity can be affirmed even as it is troubled and reconstructed, in which it is possible to engage in new social realignments even if these realignments are constantly undermined in the broader culture.

Second, and as Henry Giroux has aptly observed, "a critical pedagogy for democracy does not begin with test scores but with questions" (1997,

p. 74). These questions, furthermore, cannot be of the variety that require "yes" or "no" answers, or that have a "correct" answer. Rather, they must be questions that open dialogue and establish some of the parameters for discourse. Of course, teachers and other educators have an important role to play in helping guide and direct this dialogue. It is important, for example, that the dialogue address issues of social justice, equity, and the meaning of democratic public life. But progressives also need to resist a doctrinaire "politically correct" form of pedagogy that would, for example, censor all uses of the flag. That, we believe, would only foster more resistance and resentment. By shifting toward dialogic pedagogy, the teacher is decentered as the keeper of an objective, final, authoritative truth and young people are made much more active subjects in the production of truth, values, and identity. Dialogic pedagogy thus creates the conditions for the development of the discursive virtues and ethics associated with democratic public life, and for this reason it is subversive. In the dominant discourse of citizenship education the emphasis is on "normalizing" young people to fit into the dominant social order, and this has resulted in a deemphasis upon dialogue, with its openness and polyvocality.

This leads us to a third element of a progressive pedagogy, the organization of dialogue around the critical reading, deconstruction, and reconstruction of various popular culture "texts." Cultural studies leads us to approach the Confederate flag as a signifier around which symbolic battle is being waged, a "floating signifier" tied to diverse political projects and open to re-articulation and reappropriation. It is an icon around which an essential southern heritage is stitched together, through which "whiteness" is performed and deployed. In viewing the flag as a socially constructed and contested sign, we are able to break through the reification of signs such as the flag, in which they appear as objects with an already-given meaning. This is consistent, we believe, with a genealogical method of study, as Foucault has used that term, a method of tracing back the contemporary usage of a term, or an icon, through its various rhizomes of development, revealing all the time the power relations and interests organized around it, the aims behind its deployment within discourse, the ways it produces and regulates difference, and so on. Such a pedagogy cannot offer an "undistorted" or unified truth about the Confederate flag. But it can offer the hope that young people will become critical readers of their own identity work, and become more skeptical of heritage narratives that promise a return to a pure, essential, foundational sense of self.

10

Urban Education, Broadcast News, and Multicultural Spectatorship

Suellyn M. Henke

A whip of fear broke through the heart chambers as soon as you saw a Negro's face in a paper, since the face was not there because the person had a healthy baby, or outran a street mob. Nor was it there because the person had been killed, or maimed or caught or burned or jailed or whipped or evicted or stomped or raped or cheated, since that could hardly qualify as news.... It would have to be something out of the ordinary—something white people [*sic*] would find interesting, truly different, worth a few minutes of teeth sucking if not gasps. And it must have been hard to find news about Negroes worth the breath catch of a white citizen of Cincinnati.

—Toni Morrison, *Beloved*

I can't breathe. I can't breathe.

—Pharon Crosby, as he is held down and Maced, 1995.

The commitment is always to be able to adapt our methods as the new historical realities we engage keep also moving on down the road.

—Jennifer Slack, "The Theory and Method of Articulation"

This chapter will focus on the violent videotaped arrest in 1995 of Pharon Crosby, an African American teenager, in Cincinnati. The setting for this text analysis of the 1995 violent, broadcast arrest of Pharon Crosby, an African American teenager, is the cityscape of Cincinnati. The racially defined history of this city penetrates deep in the American psyche. Cincinnati resident Harriet Beecher Stowe wrote of Eliza's escape to freedom on the ice floes of the Ohio River, and in Tony Morrison's *Beloved* readers are steeped in a painful reminder of how far our society can be from fully enacting communities of equality and justice. "Cincinnati's a microcosm, the belly of the whale," Kweisi Mfume, national president of the NAACP, described the city (quoted by Clines, 2001b). Recently Cincinnati became the site of national attention as media images of police firing rubber bullets and spraying tear gas at protesters were circulated throughout the country. Discourses of race, gender, social class, and police distrust commingled to create a media frenzy, after Timothy Thomas—nineteen years old, unarmed, and African American—was shot and killed by a white police officer. Thomas had fourteen outstanding warrants and was fleeing police at the time of the shooting. Many of the warrants were for traffic violations, five of them for not wearing a seatbelt. This is not a story without history. In May of 2001 a coalition of black civil rights groups and the ACLU of Ohio filed suit in federal court in Cleveland accusing Cincinnati of a "30-year pattern of racial profiling" (Clines, 2001a). The story of what is "acceptable" policing of African American youth has wider implications for urban secondary education, as the 1995 video footage of the Pharon Crosby arrest illustrates. Public narratives about controlling teenage bodies are always potentially narratives about schooling.

Perhaps even before the 1955 film *Blackboard Jungle* first showed Mr. Dadier stepping off the bus to teach at a New York City public high school, it has been clear that public, urban education plays a role in the popular imaginary about place, race, ethnicity, social class, youth, and democratic possibility. When the beating and arrest of Pharon Crosby were first broadcast they did not receive national attention on the same scale as the recent uprisings and protests around the Thomas shooting, but because the arrest itself was caught on videotape, its immediacy and violence became a lightning rod for far-reaching community attention. Repetitive airing of the video footage forced the community of Cincinnati to pay attention, in essence to become a captive audience. An audience cannot be perceived merely as "subjects" duped by the ideological content of media, nor as purely active, embodied viewers capable of eliciting counterhegemonic readings at will (Mayne, 1993). The complexity of spectatorship of realist tales, such as nightly broadcast news, and their impact upon urban education is codified and read in unique ways by raced, gendered, classed, culturally diverse bodies. In order to understand how meanings were operationalized around this text, I collected archival information and conducted thirty-two open-ended interviews with students, teachers, administrators, and journalists.[1] Analysis focused upon three registers of multicultural spectatorship as described by Shohat and Stam (1994): the spectator as fashioned by the text itself; the spectator as fashioned by the institutional contexts of spectatorship; and the spectator as fashioned by diverse and evolving technological apparatuses.[2] Questions that guided this inquiry are: How is the story of urban education framed? What are the institutional parameters of news media? And how does the "there as it happens" videotaping of reality help construct the story?

In the week after the arrest was broadcast a dominant reading of the incident began to emerge in the press. The arrest was transformed into a public "spectacle" and inscribed within a commonsense discourse on the "problem of urban youth." The media understood the incident in terms of youth being unsupervised and in a space where they did not belong—the central business district. This discourse of youth supervision linked with discourses about race and social class that placed urban students in the center of meaning making, despite the absence of schools and schooling from the dominant frame of the story. Although the incident opened up a space for multiple readings upon which community members could discuss race and injustice, the media story ultimately advanced a tighter linkage between the police and public schools and represented both in terms of their overlapping surveillance over youth.

Storey, paraphrasing Dahgren (1992), writes that there are two different

> modes of knowing and making sense of the world. The analytic which is marked by referential information and logic . . . [and] the storytelling mode which is marked by the narratological configurations which provide coherence via enplotment. The official aim of journalism is to present information about the world and is thus a commitment to the analytic mode. However, in practice, it is the storytelling mode which is most often brought into play. (1996, p. 75)

News is storytelling. And all stories must sell. They must engage and move product through advertisement, or there is little to no room for them in this moment of advanced capitalism. Despite the appearance of discovering and creating stories, news media are bound by popular narratives already in circulation. As Pedelty (1995) puts this point: "While the rules of objective journalism prohibit reporters from making subjective interpretations, their task demands it. A 'fact,' itself a cultural construct, can only be communicated through placement in a system of meaning, shared by reporter and reader" (p. 7).

A narrative that situates urban schools as sites of "pathology" (Giroux, 1996) lying outside the range of "the normal" (Popkewitz, 1998) undergirds the possible ways in which the arrest story is told, at the same time the story itself appears to advance new levels of meaning about urban schools. What follows is a critical textual analysis of the conditions of production of a particular news story and its implications for meaning making about urban education[3]. Analysis of this intense, localized text is aimed at shedding more insight into the contradictory tensions within the relationship of news media and urban public education.

Fashioned by the Text Itself: How Is the Story Framed?

The violent afternoon arrest of Crosby, then eighteen years old, was videotaped by a news crew. The video shows Crosby being requested by a police officer to place his hands behind his back. After this a scuffle occurs, and the officer appears to pull Crosby down to the ground, behind a taxicab and out of view of the camera. A police car rushes to the scene, and several other police officers run out and subdue Crosby with physical force and Mace. The film crew captures a close-up of Crosby as his face is sprayed with Mace, screaming that he can't breathe, and follows the action as he is carried to the back seat of the police car. There is a cut to another officer chasing a young man down the sidewalk. The final image of the arrest segment is a silhouette of Crosby's head framed in the rear window of the police car.

Apparently the police action was precipitated by a 911 phone call from a female office worker in the downtown area. According to a police transcript of the call, the woman said, "There are a whole bunch of teen-agers out front blocking the door. I had to say, 'Excuse me' like, 10 times, and, like, pretty much scream it in order for them to move for myself to get out. And then they start cussing me out. I just wanted you to know that" (quoted in Weintraub, 1995d, p. A8). The time of the call was 2:56 P.M., and within four minutes police converged on the scene (p. A1). As was repeatedly reported by the news, "Local businesses have complained about the loitering teens for years, and despite recent efforts by Cincinnati Public School (CPS) to route their students around downtown 700–2000 of them still pass through the area daily" (Weintraub, 1995a, p. A4). After the arrest, nine different civil rights organizations formed a coalition and voiced their displeasure at the physical restraint of Crosby, which they believed was both excessive and racially motivated. The coalition linked the violent arrest historically to images of black males being beaten, a particularly strong image in the wake of Rodney King's videotaped beating in California. One man compared it to the violence that civil rights protesters met in 1963 Alabama: "The only thing you didn't see was the [police] dogs" (Weintraub, 1995a, p. A1). A contrasting view was articulated by the wife of one of the police officers involved: "This is not about race, it's about law and order. It's about hoodlums" (Goldberg, 1995a). A civilian committee and the police internal investigation section, investigated the struggle to determine whether inappropriate force was exerted by the police. Despite the existence of video footage and testimony from witnesses, the investigations yielded completely different findings (Weintraub, 1995b, p. B1). The police internal affairs division exonerated the officers, and the civilian committee recommended suspensions and/or retraining for three of the officers. The city manager was called upon to mediate between the two reports. Approximately six months after the arrest, Crosby was tried on several counts: assault on a police officer, disorderly conduct, inducing panic, and resisting arrest. Crosby was assigned to a halfway house and put on probation. Later he filed a civil suit against the police and was awarded $32,000. Although this story was framed dominantly by the media as a case of race and police-community relations, these discourses overlap and intersect with discourses relevant to urban secondary schools. By examining closely how the Crosby arrest story is told and in what ways schools are implicated in the public imaginary, I hope to shed light on power and representation in relation to schooling.

The continual airing of the videotape WLWT-TV news created a contradictory public space. On the one hand it reified negative imagery about African American males and the police force; on the other hand its presence as a videotape sanctioned as "news" also opened up a space to question power inequity. Although spectatorship is always a negotiation, and there are multiple possibilities for readings, not all readings are as readily available. A useful concept to understand this is Goffman's idea of frames as ways in which story organizes reality. "Frames are persistent patterns of cognition, interpretation, and presentation, of selection, emphasis and exclusion by which symbol handlers routinely organize discourse, whether verbal or visual" (Gitlin, 1980, pp. 6–7, paraphrased from Pedelty, 1995, p. 7). The first news broadcast of the video constructed three sides from which to view the story. Television reporters interviewed a police administrator who supported the actions of the officers, a teenage friend who supported the innocence of Crosby, and a local office worker who blamed the school system for "dumping kids downtown with nothing to do but get in trouble." In subsequent stories, mention of the school system was dropped, and police and race became the dominant signifiers of the story. Schools were not part of the dominant frame. If the schools were mentioned directly, it was usually in a dismissive tone, as illustrated by this newspaper report:

> "The problem is that the only place where most routes come together is downtown," said Sallie Hilvers, spokeswoman for Metro. Cincinnati Public Schools use Metro for transportation of middle and high school students. The cash-strapped district, already making $31 million in cuts, would have to pay even more to add more special student routes that stay out of downtown. (Weintraub, 1995b, p. B4)

Even though schools are not part of the dominant news media frame, they never leave the picture; they are always present. The dominant question posed by the media was Did the police exert too much force? The school district is continually implicated in the answering of this question by the placement of teenage students in the replays of the video footage, discussion of bus routes creating a heavy "incident area," constant identification of Crosby with the school he attends, and questions about what type of student he was and whether he had a "promising path." The schools were also implicated in discussion of Crosby's truancy, discipline referrals, and statements from teachers that were gathered in attempts to shed light on his character.

The question of punishment, of appropriate force, is inextricably part of a larger system of effects of power (Foucault, 1977) that (particularly in the case of a teenage student) unavoidably involves issues of schooling. Schooling is enacted upon bodies. Repeated videotape footage of Crosby's arrest can be viewed as a microcosmic "theater of punishment" (Foucault, 1977, p. 106) in which the representation of crime comes to speak for more than its corporeal reality; it comes to speak as a "representation of public morality" (p. 110). The line between the body and state-sanctioned official power is visually represented by this display. As the city manager stated, "What we all need to understand . . . is that our society has sanctioned police to use force when necessary. There will be times when that use of force will not be pleasant for anyone" (Incident need not have occurred, *Cincinnati Enquirer* 1995, June 7, A5). The question becomes, under what conditions does the use of force legitimately apply? What control does the state have over the bodies of citizens, especially youthful citizens? "The question . . . treats the regulation of force, its constitution and performance in terms of an ethics of dosage" (Ronell, 1995, 115).

Although the dominant frame posed the question in terms of whether the beating was police brutality or justified action, at stake through understanding the gradations of force was: "How does society treat urban (in this city primarily) African American youth?" Other important school stories reported at the time were about: racial discrepancy in discipline records, teenage curfews, intense budget cuts, police community sweeps for truant students, day care for students, linking the privilege of a driver's license to grades. All these stories signified the contested space for urban education, urban students. Many of these "school" stories existed side by side with stories about the Crosby case. Some examples can be found by glancing through Cincinnati's most widely distributed newspaper, the *Cincinnati Enquirer*. Situated directly above the article "Arrest Outcry Unabated" (Weintraub, 1995b, B1) was the article "No Contracts for 150 More in Public Schools (Skertic, 1995a) which described budget cuts that reduced librarians, counselors, and teachers for the coming school year. Later, the story "Officer's Defenders Chide City for Lack of Support" (Goldberg, 1995a, p. A1) is next to "High School Academic Standards in Jeopardy" (Skertic, 1995c, p. A1), a story about the possible loss of accreditation by schools because of budget cuts. Still later, "Questions Still Not Answered: Shirey Asks More About Crosby" (Goldberg, 1995b, p. C1) is placed adjacent to "Doors Close on Hopes" (Skertic, 1995d, p. C1) a story about the closing of a day-care center for children of student mothers at the alternative school for overage students. A photograph of an eighteen-year-old African American mother placing shoes on her four-month old son, lying prone between the bars of a baby crib, is the central visual of the page. These are only a few examples that illustrate the narrowing sense of public space for urban students. The fact that the viewer of the Crosby arrest tape was placed in the position to speculate on his deservedness or lack of deservedness to be beaten, that this was a hot topic for the city of Cincinnati to debate, has important implications for schooling at the secondary level. A strong discourse of "adolescence as deviance to be controlled" (Acland, 1995, p. 27) or even more strongly put, a discourse of bodies that are uncared for and unvalued in society runs through these cultural debates.

When the city manager was called upon to mediate between the two reports of the Crosby beating, one by civilians and the other by police, he saw the ultimate goal as developing a stronger relationship between the police and the community. In his own words he sought to "bridge the gaps that exist between police and citizens, youth and adults, black and white" (Incident need not have occurred, 1995, June 7, A5). A complex combination of training, rewards, discipline, psychological counseling, and increased visibility of police policies and practices to community members were advised by the city manager. Through the process of the city manager's mediation, police reforms were aimed at creating a stronger connection between police and urban youth. This further legitimized the presence of police in schools as part of the common sense of schooling. Suggestions that police officers become better versed in "methods of dealing with and understanding youth"; that officers should be paired with "School Resource Officers who have been able to establish excellent rapport with youth"; and that the police chief's apprenticeship program should be expanded "each year to recruit police officers from Cincinnati schools with an emphasis on African American individuals" (Incident need not have occurred, 1995, June 7, A5) helped further cement the indirect connection between the school and the police. The city manager's direct comment about the schools was somewhat ambiguous:

> As many have pointed out, there have been problems at the bus stop at Sixth Street and Vine for many years. The Police Division has pointed out that a disproportionately high number of incidents occur at that location. While steps were taken last year to reduce the number of youth who have to use the stop as a transfer point the fact remains that about 700 young people transfer there each school day. I understand the situation is being reviewed, and I am calling on officials at Metro and Cincinnati Public Schools to find creative ways to reduce the number again. (Incident need not have occurred, 1995, June 7, A5)

The term "creative" suggests that the program may have been underfunded, whereas funds for training, increased psychological counseling, and police reform in general do not, in this quote, appear to be qualified in this way. That a public bus stop, structurally related to urban schools, is contested as public space is an issue that is ignored.

The city manager's comment that the large number of students at the bus stop is the cause of "a disproportionately high number of incidents" there, and that these might well abate if students were rerouted, clearly identifies the problem as the students themselves. As a friend of Crosby's stated, "[T]hey tried to make it seem like it was his fault for being downtown catching a bus" (Steele, interview with author, Oct. 23, 1998). Questions about students' need to be mobile, social, and independent are left unasked. A former administrator of the school system sums up Crosby's videotaped arrest this way:

> I know that the end result is that he was another kid who happened to also attend Cincinnati Public Schools, who while downtown was very, very

rowdy, and it was an example of the kinds of rowdiness that the merchants in that community were fed up with because it was drawing their business away. And if we could make them go away, then maybe our problems would be solved. (Lewis, interview with author, Nov. 30, 1998)

The city manager suggests that the community should "commit to working together to repair those underlying basic flaws in our system which allow such incidents to ever occur" (Incident need not have occurred, 1995, June 7, A5). Indeed, through his reform suggestions, the system becomes more tightly woven creating a more intricate and indelible web between police relations with youth. Public schooling is the absent presence that promotes this relationship. Although urban schools are not foregrounded in the narratives evolving from the videotaped arrest, an understanding of schools and the students who attend them is at the center of the story. Rather than filling the gaps between police and youth with schooling initiatives, schooling becomes the gap that is filled with policing initiatives.

Fashioned by Institutional Contexts:
What Are the Parameters of News Media?

Somewhere after Crosby's initial point of bodily noncompliance, the arrest became a spectacle beyond its immediate audience, transformed into "news." Purely by chance, on that particular day, veteran television news reporter Barry Smith (pseudonym) and videographer Charles Laud (pseudonym), turned their news van onto Sixth Street. It was not their intention to find news there; they were on their way back to the station from a story but, "because there was either construction or a slow moving truck" (Smith, e-mail, Jan. 22, 1999) their regular route had been abandoned. Instead, they turned on Sixth Street, and this turn made all the difference.

News is a socially constructed reality (Tuchman, 1978) and usually it is constructed from official sources and operates as an "ally of legitimated institutions" (p. 4). The "city hall, court house, police and fire dispatches" (p. 20) are all mainstay sources of American television news. Though news crews often listen to police scanners for potential stories, according to Smith, being on Sixth Street at that moment of the day was only a "bizarre coincidence" (field note, Oct. 9, 1998). News is constructed by professionals who work within specific institutional contexts in order to put stories together. Often the labor conditions of news production are overlooked and it is taken for granted that the news is an objective, continuous "record of everything that is fit to be published" (Curran, 1996, p. 120). "It's funny," Barry Smith says after being recognized at a restaurant, " people are always surprised to see me out on the street. There is a perception that I work *all the time*. I basically have a nine-to-six job. I log in my story and go home after work, just like everybody else" (fieldnote Dec. 30, 1998). "Important events" do not unfold in an uninterrupted flow, but are sedimented in specific conditions of a job. According to Tuchman (1978) "few reporters are available to cover stories before 10 A.M. or after 7 P.M. on weekdays, and even fewer of those times on the weekend (42) . . . TV news was potentially limited to occurrences happening between ten and four P.M." (43). Violence on the streets is not uncommon; in the words of a local protester, the story was "unique, only because it was captured on tape" (Skertic, 1995b, p. A1). Although arrests and community police interactions occur on a daily basis in urban centers, the video footage of Pharon Crosby's arrest was not an average news story because of its spontaneity.

In contrast to most large, mainstream newspapers, which might have education reporters for the metropolitan area as well as the surrounding suburbs, most broadcast news shows do not assign a specific "education beat." There are certain "mandatory" stories that are covered such as first week of school and test scores, but for the most part education is an "elective," and elective stories are generated by the personal interest of the individual journalist or specific circumstances at hand (Smith, interview with author Dec. 17, 2000). Although newspapers generally delve more in depth in their stories, they do not have the power to construct an image burnished into the memory synapses of the brain in the same way that the televisual image does (Jameson, 1992). Broadcast news has one major yardstick to decide whether a story is worth covering. In the words of a broadcast news editor, "Our philosophy is NEWS IS WHAT PEOPLE ARE TALK-ING ABOUT [emphasis his]. So we do a lot of watercooler stories and stories that don't require a lot of depth to cover" (Manta, e-mail Aug. 23, 1999). During my fieldwork I had an opportunity to witness a typical "morning meeting" in which story ideas were put forth by reporters and editors; the question "What are people talking about?" was repeated every few minutes as a way to focus the fast-paced discussions (fieldnote Oct. 9, 1998). Broadcast news consistently tries to gauge possible public interest. This can create a circular effect between venues of storytelling. According to a broadcast news editor,

> Like most people, we get "what people are talking about" from listening to radio, reading papers, magazines and hearing what co-workers and others are talking about. There are a number of "hot buttons"—if the conversations refer to children, celebrities, entertainment and/or animals, it usually is top of mind. And then, of course, there is the weather . . . on most people's mind. And we always look for conflict, which makes a good story. So if it meets any of those criteria, we take it to a talking stage and see if the story can be turned around within a day. Then it's up to reporters to find the players and make it even more interesting. (Manta, e-mail, Sept. 3, 1999)

When asked whether broadcast news creates public interest or only reacts to it, this editor replied:

> Both. We create more interest in some issues that get buried or little play because of other news of the day. We also react. Sometimes we'll expand on

a story the news paper might have broken that morning, or a radio station. Or a competitor. Besides, how does one measure public interest. We do what we think has people's interest or will get their interest. After all, we are the public too. (Manta e-mail, Sept. 3, 1999)

According to a newspaper reporter, only "[o]ccasionally do the TV news beat us on something, which they usually don't; they usually follow our lead" (Jackson, interview with author Dec. 8, 1998). With the airing of the footage of the broadcast arrest of Crosby, broadcast news definitely took the lead and became definer of "what people are talking about."

As Smith and Laud pulled onto Sixth Street on April 25, they saw a police car and a crowd of people. Laud hopped out of the car and "just began rolling film. We didn't even know for sure what was happening" (Smith, field note, Oct. 9, 1998) Channel 5's news team proceeded to capture the subsequent physical struggle and arrest of Crosby on film. "I had no idea, *no idea*, at the time that it would become such a big story," Smith said (fieldnote, Oct. 9, 1998). A "big story" is one that captures the public's imagination, that raises interest to a fever pitch; a big story is one that draws viewers to the television because they want to see, have to see, have to know. Like Fiske's (1994) analysis of the news story of Rodney King, a "big story" becomes its own media event. "A media event is hypervisual, for besides its condensation of social antagonisms, it is technologically distributed and thus inserted in to our unpredictably different social contexts. Its mediation gives it a different social reality from an event that is confined to the immediate conditions of its occurrence" (Fiske, 1994, p. 128). The videotape of the arrest of Crosby became a "media event" for Cincinnati in 1995. Documented to live beyond its own time, the arrest symbolized many things to many different people. Channel 5 confined the video footage to its own exclusive coverage, turning down requests from a twenty-four hour national news network, as well as many national, international, and local programs. "The station manager didn't want to give it to anyone. Those 15, 20 seconds out of context, we were afraid, out of context, there would be a riot" (Smith, field note, Sept. 14, 1998). Despite the decision not to share the news footage with other media outlets, the story did gain some national coverage. For example *NBC Nightly News* aired the story (Weintraub, 1995a, B1) and *Inside Edition* interviewed Crosby (Skertic, 1995, April 13, A13).

In regard to news, the national and the local are never completely separate. Regardless of its purposefully contained localness, the arrest video of Crosby shares much in common with the nationally viewed homemade video of Rodney King of 1992. Both are inscribed through race, violence, masculinity, police-community relations, and the sheer energy of bearing witness, of being there as it happens. They visually tap into a historical narrative of "official" authority being marshaled brutally against African Americans. Rodney King, a black man, is shown being kicked and hit by the Los Angeles police. Crosby, a black teenager, is shown struggling with a single police officer and then as other police officers arrive on the scene he is hit, kicked, and Maced. Although Cincinnati's police chief Snowden, a distinguished-looking white man, was, told WLWT-TV on April 26, the day after the arrest, "It's not a Rodney King situation, and I don't think those comparisons are fair" his assertion only lends credence to the fact that the beating of Rodney King could never be separated from a public understanding of what became branded by the news as the "Sixth Street Melee" or "Scuffle on Sixth and Vine." During Crosby's trial, in an effort to uncover bias, the prosecution was allowed to cross-examine a witness by inquiring about her attitude toward the Rodney King case (Delguzzi, 1995f, B6).[4] In the United States, Rodney King is a consensus image, without a consensus understanding. By this I mean that the public consents (not always with conscious will) to internalize an image of "the beating of Rodney King" even at the same time individuals strain with all their faculties to draw their own understanding of what this image might or might not mean. The "arrest" of Pharon Crosby became a consensus image, without a consensus understanding for the city of Cincinnati. People vehemently disagreed about what they saw happen, yet inevitably the event became woven into their diverse social contexts.[5]

In discussion of this story, I focus primarily on television coverage because "[t]elevision is the most important source of news in our society. It has now far outstripped the press as the main source of information" (Eldridge, 1982, p. 1). It has been suggested that "[t]he 'average' American will spend in excess of seven years watching television' (Storey, 1998, p. 9). Although print journalism, news radio, and other forms of media helped construct the story, the arrest of Crosby became a media event only because it was videotaped. Without its televisual qualities, this incident most likely would have remained unexamined, possibly as a small blurb in the newspaper, if it even progressed that far.

Tuchman (1978) utilized the concept of frame in his study of how news constructs reality. He listed several ways in which news apparently operated on reality, in its function as a "window on the world."

"[T]he news aims to tell us what we want to know, need to know, and should know (1) . . . News imparts to occurrences their *public character*, as it transforms mere happenings into publicly discussable events . . . (3) [N]ews coordinates activities within a complex society by making otherwise inaccessible information available to all. (paraphrase Lasswell, 1948, p. 4)

Television news acts as a frame legitimizing a story as important for public consumption. In the case of Crosby's arrest, all viewers of the newscast in were provided with the same image of violence, thus in some sense, giving the city a feeling of being a connected landscape. "Mass communication helps people to visualize society, feel connected to it, and make sense of its processes through a shared set of understandings" (Curran, 1996, p. 127). However, it is important to note that in the same moment the image constructs a communal landscape, it also fractures the idea of a total community understanding. Through news coverage of the investigations and through the professional media practice of "showing both sides," the notion of wholly consensual meaning is collapsed through divergent axes of black and white, police and civilians, youth and adult.[6] In the Crosby case the media both fed off these divisions and attempted to "heal" them, by calling their very nature to the attention of viewers.

Also, the news has a unique public/private character not unlike the nature of public education. Both school and television operate on the individuals within their own private space (home, body), as windows and doorways to larger public space. As stated by Dahlgren (1995),

Television is a part of our daily lived reality, penetrating into the microcosms of our social world. It also serves to organize and structure that world, both in terms of daily schedule and interaction within the household . . . and in offering frameworks of collective perception: television links the everyday world to the larger symbolic orders of social and political life. (p. 39)

The word "schooling" could be substituted for the word "television" in the above quote and it would still make sense. Both schooling and television work to socialize individuals. I raise the idea here to point out that the public-private nature of schools and television news overlaps, particularly in large urban school districts. Public schools and broadcast news have, at their hearts, conceptions of a relationship between the individual and society, and conceptions of public citizenry. The primary rationale for the press in the United States, according to Seibert, Peterson, and Schramm (1963) is to "assume an obligation for social responsibility" (p. 7). The "chief purpose" of the media is "to inform, entertain, sell, but chiefly to raise conflict to the plane of discussion" (p. 7). Conceptions of public character are not static, but change through time. For example, both television news and public schooling are currently being reshaped through market-driven policies. Strong ties to advertising and the advent of cable television in the 1980s have led television shows to increase "target" marketing (Turow, 1997). Instead of envisioning a "mass market," the audience is conceived based on categories of income, gender, age, race, and ethnicity (Turow, 1997). The target demographic of most local broadcast news is a female consumer between the ages of 18 and 49 or 25 and 54 (Smith, interview with author, Dec. 30, 1998). Private schools, voucher systems, charter school programs, and an emphasis on "school choice" illustrate a changing notion of "the public" in schooling as well. The public in both instances is becoming increasingly articulated through the lens of consumer identity. The most obvious way in which broadcast and educational conceptions of the public interest intersect is when schools or images of schools and students are portrayed on television news. However, the Crosby arrest story, while not making a strong visible link between schooling and news, still speaks to the space in the community that is constructed for urban secondary students. Having the video footage of Crosby's arrest on television news provided it with a certain legitimization and publicity that it otherwise would not have been afforded. News has an authority to interpose frames for organizing experience on a large scale.[7]

Fashioned by Technology:
How Does the Videotape Construct the Story?

In her reading of the Rodney King video Ronell (1995) suggests that television produces narratives that compulsively turn around crimes, that in effect, "name an unreadable relation to the incomprehensibility of survival in relation to the law" (p. 109). Videos, such as the beating of Rodney King (and in this case, the beating of Crosby) "act as an ethical scream" forcing on TV an interrogation "about its own textual performance in the production of force" (p. 116). This reflects several of what Dahlgren (1995) suggests are postmodern characteristics in televisual discourses that undermine the mimetic: "self disclosure, self reflexivity . . . and acknowledgement of and commentary about the media's status as constructed artifice" (p. 36). A certain amount of self-consciousness appeared in the broadcast television news about the Crosby case. After issuing its initial claim to "capture the entire incident on tape," all the succeeding stories worked to rescind this notion. Repeatedly Barry Smith, the television reporter, warned in broadcasts, "This is not the whole story. It would be a big mistake to draw conclusions based just what was seen on the videotape." He emphatically reminded the audience that "things happened *before* videographer Charles Laud and I got on the scene, and things also happened out of camera range while Charles was shooting," emphasizing to the viewers that there were "eight seconds behind the cruiser" when the camera could not see Crosby and Hall. The video footage places the news in the position of reporting on the incompleteness of its narrative conventions and, at the same time, subtly suggesting that if the camera had only more access, more reality would be uncovered.

Another way in which the media text worked to question itself is by showing the unedited version of the film footage. In this film footage, the camera can be seen turning to and fro, slightly staggering, as it combs the street for the site of action, the site of the story. This draws attention to the constructed nature of the visual and how the spectator's attention is focalized.[8] Also, the plot is changed. Rather than showing the second young man being chased by police at the end of the story, the viewer learns it happened simultaneously at the beginning of Crosby's arrest. In fact Officer Traine, who chased the young man instead of remaining and helping Officer Hall, was recommended to receive counseling and possible additional training in the city manager's report because of his lack of judgment (Incident need not have occurred, 1995, June 7. A5). How much does this transposition alter the meaning of the text? Viewers were introduced to the story through the edited version. If the audience perceived during the first edited versions, that there were two officers at the scene of arrest, before the physical struggle with Crosby escalated, would this have put more emphasis on the responsibility and actions of the police?

Finally, this broadcast story focused self-consciously on the issue of race. Race as a signifier was used to deconstruct race as a signifier in the case. Racial injustice could not be separated from what was perceived to be happening on the screen, and yet essentialized notions of race seemed to be deconstructed through the very medium whose portrayal seemed to reify racial difference. The broadcast news devoted a segment on April 27 to deconstructing obvious racial codings of the police officers. That Crosby was black was never disputed, but that the police represented monolithic whiteness was. This wasn't a black teenager being beaten by four white cops. Officer Hall was Japanese American and American Indian. One officer was African American; three were Anglo Americans (one being female). In an evening news segment on April 27, Officer Hall's sister sentimentally spoke of Hall's mixed heritage, emphasizing his identity as an American of color who had himself been subjected to racist terms such as "Jap" and "Chink." Officer Smith, the officer who the OCCI reports suggested "did not act reasonably when he Maced Mr. Crosby while Mr. Crosby was held on the cruiser" (Curnutte, Weintraub and Goldberg, 1995, May 25, p. A6), was African American. This was a black teenager being beaten/disciplined, to some extent, by a multicultural police force. However, Crosby's status as essentialized "black subject" was never openly interrogated from mainstream media; only the identities of the police officers were destabilized. In the words of Angela Davis (1999),

> [T]he most insidious effect of reality-based shows is that the myth of rampant crime is reinforced, and the repetitions of "criminals" that flash across the television screen become symbolic objects in the viewers' minds and then translate into fearful and racist responses to certain types of people of color, who are criminalized by these representations. (p. 200)

The tactic of destabilizing the race of the officers and leaving Crosby's representation to stand did not open up the cyclic connection between criminality and race that Davis critiques.

Essentialism is always a project of power, but its ends are not always hegemonic. Spivak (1993) discusses the "risk of essentialism" as moments when cultural groups essentialize aspects of identity in order to form strategic coalitions. Although "[s]pectatorial positions are multi-form, fissured, even schizophrenic" (Shohat and Stam, 1994, p. 350), it was Crosby's essentialized "blackness" which helped mobilize many members of the African American community to protest the force used against him. However, as Stuart Hall (1996) reminds us, there is no essential black subject. "Race cannot be represented without reference to the dimensions of class, gender, sexuality, ethnicity" (p. 443). During the interview for *Inside Edition* the week after the arrest, Crosby said, "I just don't think that race is really important. I think that it is much more important that police used excessive force regardless of my race" (Hopkins, 1995, p. A4). Later, Crosby, through his lawyers, publicly stated that he "thought police actions were motivated by race." In contrast to the Rodney King beating, in some ways race is less simple, less direct to discuss. Yet, race as a concept appears inescapably necessary to make meaning of this video footage. Crosby's blackness is merged with the concept of inner-city schooling. Adolescence, social geography, his black knit cap, the taxi, the metro bus, the band of yelling students, the anchor's opening comments the night of the arrest of "trouble, wild, scary" swirl together, and Crosby becomes representative of urban high school students. Crosby's identity cannot be completely separated from his identity as student in one of "those schools." Urban schools, urban teenagers, they are the problem contained in the phrase "inner-city school," and a negative reading is already provided in plentiful supply.

The happenstance videotaping of the arrest interrupted news as usual. When I asked informants whether or not that they thought the existence of the videotape was positive or negative, responses varied along a fairly narrow continuum. As one former CPS student explained: "It keeps things in perspective for me. That's how I feel. You know that everybody knows what's going on. You know you could judge for yourself if it was wrong, if it was right. I think that was a good thing. Made the police look bad, but you know, that's life" (Kenner, interview with author, Nov. 23, 1998). Another student, a friend of Crosby's suggested,

> Yeah, I think it [videotaping the arrest] was good just to let people know how come because, believe it or not, a lot of people become educated off the media. They won't believe a story until it is on the news. And whatever slant is put on that story is how they will believe. And I'd rather it was caught on videotape for people . . . to see what happened. And I'm glad they were able to see what happened, because if it wasn't put on videotape it might have been a little bit worse than what it was. Or you know, if it wasn't put on videotape it'd been Pharon Crosby arrested because of this and they could've added anything else, and if we didn't see it and we weren't there, then it would be everybody else's word against the few students' words who were there during the time that it happened. (Steele, interview with author, Oct. 23, 1998)

However, all the people I talked with, regardless of their personal feelings about whether the police or Crosby were more "right," spoke against the over-playing of the video. As a school administrator phrased it: "My personal view of this incident is that it was a travesty. It seemed to be a ploy to boost ratings for Channel 5 and their news dep't. You could not turn on that station for any length of time without them showing that footage between one commercial or show" (Drey e-mail, Oct. 12, 1998). Interestingly, the

skepticism about the overinsertion of the violent videotape across the air-
waves did not translate into a compulsion not to watch. The desire to see
was still compelling despite a cynical knowledge that it was a ratings
booster.

As a media event, the videotaped arrest operates in a contradictory fashion. It helps create the spectacle of broadcast news while also causing the
news to discuss its own limitations in storytelling. It reifies a connection
between African American males and criminality at the same moment it
opens up a space to contest these power relations by prompting the coalition of nine civil rights groups (Curnutte, 1995) and providing a platform
to address issues of race, youth, and police publicly. And finally, the video
is "the testimonial that cannot speak with referential assurance but does
assert the truth of what it says" (Ronell, 1995, p. 116).

Conclusion

This study raises questions about moral attribution, spectatorship, and
urban education. Moral investments in mediated productions of urban
youth are a fertile ground for investigation. As Hall et al. (1978) illustrated
in *Policing the Crisis*, media images are utilized to convey a larger sense of
societal panic, often along identity axes such as race, class, and gender.
However, aside from its role in otherizing there is also the possibility that
the media can construct solidarity. Rorty (1989) suggests that solidarity
persists through media communication. He posits that differences in
culture can be transcended by seeing someone else as "one of us." Rorty
states, "This is a task not for theory but for genres such as ethnography, the
journalists' report, the comic book, the docudrama, and, especially the
novel" (xvi; quoted in Tester, 1994, p. 92). Tester (1994) suggests that
although news media have the possibility of connecting people through a
moral thread, what they actually do is a different story. Because of institutional parameters, for example the abundance of visual assaults within
even the same broadcast news show, all that results is a "moral boredom
and dullness" (p. 105). Tester quotes Baudrillard to make his point: "The
large systems of information relieve the masses of the responsibility of
having to know, to understand, to be informed, to be up on things" (Baudrillard, 1993, p. 114 quoted in Tester, 1994, p. 123). The Crosby arrest
story illustrates this tension well. As a readily available spectacle, much like
the Rodney King video and the protests over the death of Timothy Thomas,
it mobilized, paralyzed, fragmented, and united different aspects of the
community all at the same time. These stories are ultimately undergirded
by moral narratives. The representing individuals are viewed as more than
themselves; they stand in for broader beliefs about societal relations. They
become popular memories floating across time. "Within postmodern
culture, the media not only set agendas and frame debates, but also inflect
desire, memory, fantasy. By controlling popular memory, they can contain
or simulate popular dynamism" (Shohat and Stam, 1994, p. 359). One

consequence of the spectacle of the Crosby arrest was that it further entrenched surveillance in urban schooling. But it must be acknowledged that the brutal videotaped imagery also created a space in the community to openly discuss issues of injustice and inequity. The news media framed the Crosby arrest story, shaping its potential in specific ways; however, the image of the violent arrest also leaves open other possible readings and uses through time. Its memory is always capable of being recalled to stimulate public action. For example, popular media memories can and do fuel coalitions to form and address questions of inequity.

Those of us interested in public education and democratic possibilities cannot dismiss the power of media representations. Contemporary media stories are bringing race to the forefront of conscious discussions. But, if readings of these discussions result in solutions that use public schools as sites to increase police surveillance of urban youth, this is a shortsighted compromise to the historically ingrained racism that plagues our communities. The possibility that schools can be sites of empowerment and opportunity for urban youth erodes severely with such compromises. Other community mechanisms to ensure "safety" without further overt policing need to be developed. Urban youth must be conceived of as part of the "public good" not as outliers on a border outside of the community. Readings that envision urban youth not as "problems" but as members of society who warrant public space that is inclusive and nurturing need to be highlighted in order to realize the democratic potential of public schools.

11

"They Need Someone to Show Them Discipline": Preservice Teachers' Understandings and Expectations of Student (Re)presentations in *Dangerous Minds*

Debra Freedman

As a supervisor of preservice teachers I have overheard numerous conversations among them extolling the virtues of teacher characterizations within media culture. One particular teacher (re)presentation[1] stands out for me—ex-U.S. Marine turned high school English teacher LouAnne Johnson from the movie and television series *Dangerous Minds*. In their conversations pre-service teachers usually talk about LouAnne Johnson's tough management style and her ready-for-anything attitude. The premise of the *Dangerous Minds* story, however, is no different than other media representations within this hero teacher genre (e.g., *Stand and Deliver*, *The White Shadow*, *Lean on Me*, *Blackboard Jungle*)—each dramatization retells the story of the lone teacher who sacrifices everything to connect with and transform a small group of angry, undisciplined students.

These familiar narrative conventions are built upon sight, sound, and spectacle and have the ability to seduce audiences into identifying with certain views, attitudes, feelings, and positions (A. Cole and Knowles, 1993; Kellner, 1995; Freedman, 1999). Throughout each television episode of *Dangerous Minds*, for example, the narrative represents students of color as being out of control, violent, socially unacceptable, sexually promiscuous. And though LouAnne Johnson's class has a handful of white students, the narrative predominantly focuses on the students of color. White youth have temporary problems, growing pains that become part and parcel of reaching adulthood and maturity, while black and Hispanic youth are viewed as problem, menace, Other—dangerous minds that must be kept in check through strict discipline and severe boundaries. Thinking back to the preservice teachers that I have worked with, I wonder how they might decode these student representations. More specifically, how do media representations of students influence the perceptions preservice teachers have of their emergent teaching identity and of education? In this essay I examine student representations within the *Dangerous Minds* television show (1996–97) and explore the ways preservice teachers make sense of these representations. I begin with an explanation of my methodology—a multiperspectival analysis, followed by an analysis of student representations in the *Dangerous Minds* television show, data analysis and interpretation of preservice teachers' responses to the *Dangerous Minds* television show, and finally, some concluding thoughts and recommendations.

A Multiperspectival Analysis

As Kellner (1995) argues, a cultural studies approach to reading media texts should involve a multiperspectival analysis: (1) an understanding of political culture (text production, formula and convention), (2) textual analysis (analyzing discourse/narrative structure, understanding ideological positions, image construction, and effects), and (3) audience reception (How do people actually read these cultural texts? How do these texts affect everyday life?). According to Kellner use of this multiperspectival analysis enables a researcher to question and to analyze relationships among texts, audiences, media industries, politics, and historical context.

This type of multiperspectival analysis guides my study. First, I look at the political culture, or rather the history behind LouAnne Johnson's story and the subsequent making of the *Dangerous Minds* television series. I then analyze five specific episodes of the television series. These five episodes are particularly good examples of the themes inherent to this formulaic narrative representation and exemplify the themes found within the complete television series: heroic teacher, teacher-student interactions, and angry and out-of-control adolescents. Finally, I inquire into preservice teachers'[2] understandings, interpretations, and wonderings of/about the five *Dangerous Minds* television series episodes.

This way of enacting a multiperspectival analysis generates discussions of social power and struggle as well as an understanding of the ways media culture shapes our understandings of the world, public opinion, values, and behaviors. Pedagogically, this analysis aligns with a critical cultural practice: challenging dominant perspectives, moving toward social change, troubling interpretations, questioning taken-for-granted norms, and recognizing the role that the broader media culture plays in our every daylives (Giroux, 1997a; Hytten, 1999; Kellner, 1995).

Representations of Students in *Dangerous Minds*

Kellner (1995) notes that "[t]he more perspectives one focuses on a text to do ideological analysis and critique—genre, semiological, structural, formal, feminist, psychoanalytic, and so on—the better one can grasp the full range of a text's ideological dimensions and ramifications" (p. 98). With this in mind, in this section I combine a history of the production of the *Dangerous Minds* television series with a critical textual analysis of student representations found in five episodes of the *Dangerous Minds* television series. This combined, layered analysis provides for a complex inquiry into this particular media culture event. In particular I will discuss the ways in which the plot structure of the *Dangerous Minds* television series forces students to deny their identities in order to conform to the dominant discourse; I will explain how the narrative eliminates black male youth who do not conform; and I will explore the representation of gender in relation to academic achievement and presented sexuality.

Dangerous Minds: Production History

The real-life LouAnne Johnson began teaching during the 1988–89 school year. In 1992 she published her story, under the title *My Posse Don't Do Homework*. In this book, Johnson, a former U.S. Marine, chronicled her experiences teaching English in the Academy, an academic program designed to empower students who score well on tests yet show little motivation to succeed in school. Written as a series of "snapshots," Johnson described her teaching experience, focusing on her understanding of students' lives, explaining her views on the educational system, and characterizing her style of working outside of the norm.

In 1995, Don Simpson and Jerry Bruckheimer (producers of such films as *Flashdance, Beverly Hills Cop, Top Gun,* and *The Rock*) had LouAnne Johnson's stories transformed by Ronald Bass (screenwriter of such films as *Rain Man, The Joy Luck Club,* and *Snow Falling on Cedars*) into the screenplay for the movie *Dangerous Minds.* The stories collapsed in upon themselves—often embellished or completely changed from Johnson's original "snapshots." The movie further modified Johnson's story by condensing her seven-year teaching career into a one-year experience. To further entice viewers, the producers cast Michelle Pfeiffer (*The Witches of Eastwick, Grease 2, Batman Returns*) as LouAnne Johnson and produced a hip-hop soundtrack complete with a few music videos.

Capitalizing on the crossover appeal, Don Simpson and Jerry Bruckheimer altered the story further and produced a television show based on the movie, based on the book, for the 1996–97 television season(the final piece to the *Dangerous Minds* collection. For sixteen weeks a new episode appeared every Monday night. And though the producers used a new group of actors—for example, Annie Potts (*Designing Women*) was now cast in the role of LouAnne Johnson—each week the story lines reproduced the taken-for-granted characterizations found within this genre: a fearless teacher who saves angry, out-of-control students.

Dangerous Minds:
Textual Analysis—Representations of Students

Each episode of the television series *Dangerous Minds* displays black and Hispanic students fighting, involved in gang violence, mixed up in criminal acts (stealing, in jail, vandalism), or struggling with family concerns. The representations of these students are cliched—African American teenage mother, Hispanic gang member, African American with no parental support, students of color who endure violent lives—yet interestingly they mirror the feelings that American society has about youth in general, as Giroux (1997a) points out:

> American society at present exudes both a deep rooted hostility and chilling indifference toward youth, reinforcing the dismal conditions under which young people are increasingly living. . . . fueled by a degrading visual depiction of youth as criminal, sexually decadent, drug crazed, and illiterate. In short, youth are viewed as a growing threat to the public order. (p. 31)

Though the narrative of *Dangerous Minds* presents students as being a threat, it also provides a space for students to change—that is, as long as they deny their identities, conform to the dominant discourse, and follow the appropriate codes. For example, when students enter the Academy program, they sign a contract that states they will stay out of gangs, will stay off drugs, will stay out of fights. For the character Gusmaro, however, these rules require semantic manipulation—Gusmaro is a member of the 23rd Street Gang. So that he can enter the Academy, he struck a deal with his homies, his *familia*: no "bangin'." This delicate balance between being a member of a gang and following the rules of the Academy changes when Gusmaro is the target of a drive-by shooting. His two worlds collide, his gang membership suddenly public, the tattoos that delineate his gang alignment called into question. However LouAnne Johnson has difficulty understanding Gusmaro's motives—Gusmaro is being rebellious, he is not conforming to the prescribed rules. The character of Mr. Griffin, the gang counselor, an African American and a former gang member, is called in to interpret the situation for LouAnne Johnson. Mr. Griffin is held up as a role model: his gang background allows him to connect with students, and his intellect, interpretation skills, and articulate presentation provide credibility for teachers. For Gusmaro, Mr. Griffin becomes a guide, leading him, teaching him about social conformity and the dominant codes. And although Mr. Griffin is aware of issues of respect with regard to the gang life, it is Mr. Griffin who takes Gusmaro to get his tattoos removed.

There is no recognition within the narrative of the emotional loss, the cultural struggle that Gusmaro is going through. By removing his tattoos, Gusmaro is losing his gang, his *familia*, his homeboys—he is conforming. Yet instead of interrogating these issues within the story line, Gusmaro's choice to leave the gang is reduced to the physical pain, the group beating that jumping out of a gang incurs. By conforming to dominant codes, the characterization of Gusmaro erases or rather transcends the caricature of the Chicano. Fregoso (1993) explains that "one of the major ways Chicanos become visible in public discourse is as "social problems." From greasers to bandidos to gangs, dominant culture characterizes Chicanos and Chicanas as "culturally deficient," "inherently violent," and "sexually and morally pathological" (p. 29).

Yet in the series *Dangerous Minds*, Gusmaro is the only Hispanic male to transcend these caricatures—evidence, perhaps, of his being saved by LouAnne Johnson. His homeboys, the bad kids on the street, do not follow Gusmaro's lead. And as a result of not acquiescing to the dominant codes, the narrative reduces them to a pack of wild animals—fighting, killing, rebelling.

This caricature of the Hispanic male student is similar to the portrayals of African American male students. The plot of *Dangerous Minds* eliminates black male youth who do not conform, who do not become like Mr. Griffin (Giroux, 1996). This process of elimination becomes a site of tension between African American students in the Academy program and those in regular classes as the narrative structure plays upon the division between African American Academy students and African American non-Academy students.

For example, three African American non-Academy students jump James, an African American Academy student, because James would not complete their homework for them. Afraid of repercussions, however, James refuses to identify his attackers. LouAnne Johnson and another African American student, Cornelius, decide to uncover James's attackers. Cornelius runs cover for LouAnne Johnson—"I got your back," he tells her. His black skin allows access to the non-Academy world, a world LouAnne Johnson cannot enter or understand. And like Mr. Griffin, Cornelius has learned the dominant codes and his ability to conform provides credibility.

James's attackers, the non-Academy students are hyper aware of the differences between themselves and the Academy students. They know that they are the dangerous minds that the dominant culture fears. When caught and confronted by LouAnne Johnson, the three non-Academy students explain that James did not do the homework they asked of him. One of them says in a menacing tone: "Your little house nigger got a attitude problem, seems he thinks he's better than everybody—him and your Academy program." He goes on, "Like he's some kind a braniac. What do you think he's white?" A look of fear, or horror, or shock crosses LouAnne Johnson's face—these non-Academy students seem to know the score. And because they will not conform to the dominant codes, they are taken away by police—the power structures must remain intact, the hegemony secure.

Ogbu (1992) maintains that African American students often have to choose between "acting white" and "acting black." He defines "acting white" as the adoption of "attitudes and behaviors or school rules and standard practices that enhance academic success but that are perceived and interpreted by the minorities as typical of White Americans" (p. 10). This choosing process plays out in the relationship between Academy and non-Academy students. Non-Academy students resist the adoption of white codes for success. Furthermore, they challenge Academy students' alignment with white codes, citing disloyalty to the black community and Uncle Tomism.

Non-Academy students' challenging attitudes—their choosing to "act black"—and non-conformity with white codes are seen as menacing. Their image becomes more terrifying for the spectator when compared with the conforming Academy student. Cornelius, for example, now completely aligned with the white codes, has become the infantryman in LouAnne Johnson's Marine Corps; Johnson commands, her obedient soldier follows orders. In the end, it is Cornelius who finds the videotape that James's attackers made during the beating and gives it to Johnson, and it is Cornelius who encourages James and a another student who witnessed the attack to come forward, "to do the right thing, quick! Or I will!" Because the narrative, places this conflict within the structures of a white peer pressure, Academy students pressure one another to maintain the "white" structures that allow them access yet deny those who do not conform. Initially James is conflicted. Despite the conflict, James concedes to doing the "right thing." He turns in his attackers, he gives in to the white codes, and he separates himself from the Black community.

Doing the right thing, however, means more than just coming forward with information. In the process of playing detective, LouAnne Johnson gets threats from James's attackers, and her house is vandalized. The dutiful students must now protect their beloved teacher from any (real or imagined) attackers—the fear of Others entrenched deeply in LouAnne Johnson's mind, her tough, Marine Corps exterior cracked by taken-for-granted notions of the menacing African American. And so, organized by the role model, Cornelius, the students sign up for guard duty, keeping watch over LouAnne Johnson's house: LouAnne Johnson sleeps while her obedient, docile, compliant, African American students, James and Cornelius, "do the right thing"—they protect LouAnne Johnson from possible attack while completing homework happily underneath streetlights.

And while much of the action relates to curbing aggression and hostility in order to conform to the dominant culture, a great deal of focus concerns male students' academic achievement (Sadker and Sadker, 1995). LouAnne Johnson substitutes for students at their part-time jobs, for example she mows lawns so that Gusmaro can study for an exam. LouAnne Johnson relates a lesson to Cornelius's interest in trains. LouAnne Johnson takes the class on a field trip to Alcatraz because the male students idolize gangsters. Moreover, during scenes in which teaching is central, LouAnne Johnson concentrates on male students, asking them questions, focusing the content on their particular needs and interests. This focus on male student achievement, however, relegates the female students of color into an alternative position within the narrative and results in a characterization of the girls that emphasizes sexuality and their relationships with others (Brown and Gilligan, 1993; Cardenas, 1994; Gilligan, 1982).

Focusing on these gendered positions, the narrative tends to display the young female students as sexually knowing. For the character Blanca, sexual awareness is presented in her actions, her clothing, her body. Wearing tight-fitting jeans, miniskirts, half-shirts, Blanca dances, flirts, and plays with the camera. The camera focuses usually on her belly, her smile, her hips, her hair. Her brown skin is displayed, her Hispanic identity sexualized. Blanca's overt sexual presence, however, is in direct contradiction to Callie's identity characterization. Unlike the overt display of Blanca's sexuality, Callie's sexual experience, her prowess, is invoked in a more subtle manner. Callie is a sixteen-year-old African American mother—and seems in the context of the show to be symbolic of all African American adolescent girls. Callie's dress is unassuming, her presentation is serious. Yet Callie has a three-year-old daughter. Callie's sexual history—her promiscuity since the age of thirteen—is undeniable, always present, forever taken for granted.

This subtle yet explicit exhibition of adolescent female sexuality plays out in many questionable ways. Take, for example, the hair war. In response to funding cuts, LouAnne Johnson's students propose having a hair war to raise money. A hair war, as explained by students, is a competition in which girls get their hair done by local salons and compete for the best hairstyle. And not just any hairstyle: this is "big hair, get-out-of-my-way hair"—teased, sprayed, and adorned with accessories such as Christmas lights or extensions. Figuring an admission charge of $10 per person, students believe they will obtain the necessary funds for the Academy. LouAnne Johnson goes along with the idea, excited to see students working together and raising money for the school.

Problems arise, however, when Amanda Bardales, the principal, will not let the students use the school auditorium for the hair war. In response, a local club owner, a family friend of a student in LouAnne Johnson's class, offers his club—a strip club—for the show. Yet the show must go on. And despite the troubling representations that a strip club engenders, there is only perfunctory hesitation by LouAnne Johnson: "I just think that some people might consider a place like this to be inappropriate for a school fund-raiser." The use of the word "inappropriate" is ambiguous. For LouAnne Johnson's concern is not about the sexualized position in which this places her adolescent female students; her concern centers on the funding relationship with the school board, as she goes on to say: "In our enthusiasm, let us not bring down the wrath of the school board gods. Remember, they are the ones that guard the checkbook." Placing funding as the main issue dismisses any and all discussion of the underlying societal taboos, the sexualization of adolescent girls, or the strip club locale. And despite some minor setbacks—the local newspaper publishing a story about the strip club connection, the school board offering to give 60 percent of the funding back if the show is canceled—the hair war takes place.

At the hair war, the girls are introduced as they walk down the catwalk. The neon words "PLEASURE" can be seen in the background. Dressed scantily in sheer lingerie-type clothing or tight fitting ensembles, the girls smile to the crowd, spin around the pole—the girls on display, sexually objectified. The audience of students, teachers, and administrators claps and cheers. Male students sit near the stage hooting and hollering at the girls; Bud Bartkus, the computer teacher, asks a boy to sit down because he cannot see the stage. The images are disturbing, the meanings clear. These adolescent girls are destined for a life of objectification. Guided by the male gaze, they walk, they strut, they expose themselves. Their bodies are on display; their presentation is of utmost importance.

This normalization of the sexually mature adolescent girl manipulates the spectator into accepting a variety of socially constructed stereotypes in relation to female roles. In particular, the depiction of relationship maintenance and interaction becomes a central theme for girls within the narrative. Blanca, for instance, serves as emotional support for Gusmaro throughout the series. She takes him dancing; she listens to him. When Gusmaro is arrested for a crime he did not commit, Blanca appeals to the perpetrator to turn himself in to police. Her role is as helpmate, friend, supporter (Brown and Gilligan, 1993; Gilligan, 1982). Blanca's academic goals are not known, never discussed. At one point during the first episode, Callie's academic goals are discussed briefly, but this is the only moment of consideration. The narrative gives way to the overwhelming relational concerns in her life: her daughter, her mother, and LouAnne Johnson.

Seen only in terms of their sexuality or their ability to deal with relational concerns, the adolescent girls tend to evoke traditional gender representations. Though there are rare moments when the girls rebel against these roles—for example, Alveena brawls with another student—the moments regress to traditional representations. In the case of Alveena, the focus is not necessarily on the fight or Alveena's traditional tough ghetto attitude, but on the fact that Alveena lied to LouAnne Johnson about settling a dispute with another student that resulted in a fight. LouAnne Johnson became angry with Alveena for lying and not talking out the problem. However, while the adolescent boys of color get expelled from the environment for not following the rules, Alveena's punishment is just a cold shoulder—the relationship between Alveena and LouAnne Johnson placed in jeopardy (Belenky et al., 1986; Gilligan, 1982). LouAnne Johnson's actions cause Alveena to reestablish their relationship, thus restoring the relational balance. In a sense, LouAnne Johnson's actions remind Alveena of the consequences of not maintaining this important relationship, which in the case of the adolescent girls is not having access to the dominant codes that a relationship with LouAnne Johnson provides.

Presented as colonized subjects, the students of color in the series *Dangerous Minds* must conform in order to succeed. And in the process of conforming to the dominant ideology, students lose their voices: they abandon their language and their culture and submit to traditional gender stereotypes. For them, whiteness and accepted gender roles are the norms by which they are judged (McLaren, 1995). Forced to abandon everything they know in order to assimilate within the dominant culture, the student characters of *Dangerous Minds* are not allowed or given access to a critical understanding of the educational environments, the circumstances they struggle with and endure every day.

Focus Group Responses

Usually a cultural study of a media text ends with an understanding of the text's production and a textual analysis. However, Kellner (1995) reminds that an awareness of audience perceptions is key to reading and making sense of a media culture event. The addition of audience interpretation to the analysis complicates the reading and enables a researcher to explore the various ways viewers resist and/or appropriate images. Wanting to make sense of the ways preservice teachers viewed, understood and identified with these student representations, I organized two focus groups of preservice teachers (focus group #1 and focus group #2).[3] Each focus group consisted of five members. Focus group #1 had four women and one man, ranging in age from twenty-one to thirty-five: Donna, Nicholas, Emma, Annie, and Marlene.[4] Focus group #2 was composed of all women, ranging in age from twenty-one to twenty-six: Daisy, Rose, Lauren, Holly, and Ginger. Participants were predominately white. Two participants identified themselves as other than white: Nicholas identified himself as racially mixed, and Lauren identified herself as Hispanic.

Each focus group met six times and followed a similar format. For five of the meetings, the viewing of an episode of *Dangerous Minds* prompted discussions.[5] The final meeting was designated as a debriefing session. My role within each focus group was as group moderator. However, as Morgan (1988) recognizes, there is a continuum for moderator involvement: "At the low end, moderators play only a small role in the ongoing group discussion and attempt to keep their comments as nondirective as possible; at the high end, moderators control both the set of topics that are discussed and the dynamics of the group discussion" (p. 48). During focus group #1, I remained at the low end of the continuum of moderator involvement; I remained nondirective. At the conclusion of each episode I would turn off the television, turn on the tape recorder, and ask what the participants thought about the episode.

Conversely, I approached focus group #2 as a more involved directive moderator. I believed that by using a more directive emancipatory stance, as a teacher educator I could guide participants in critically reflecting upon and interrogating preconceptions and misconceptions about teaching identities in relation to representations of students in *Dangerous Minds*. As a result, focus group #2 participants would challenge the varied layers and multiple interpretations that proliferate in media representations of education in a more open, different, and activist manner than focus group #1. And in turn, they would make sense of their teaching identities in relation to these texts. As such, I made specific, overt pedagogical choices with focus group #2: I asked focused questions, I contradicted participants' statements, and I stated my opinions.

In addition to focus group interactions, I had individual connection with each participant (in both focus group #1 and focus group #2) through email dialogue exchanges (McIntyre and Tlusty, 1995; Ojanen, 1993; Tella,

1992). These exchanges allowed me to interact with each preservice teacher to access individual experiences throughout the research process.

What follows is an exploration of the themes that emerged from both focus group conversations and e-mail exchanges: acceptance and alignment with hegemonic understandings of inner-city students, and misconception and inexperience with people from backgrounds that were different from their own. I will end this section with a discussion of the renegotiation, rereading, and rearticulation process that seemed to occur after focus group meetings ended.

Acceptance and Alignment

Connecting to other films and television shows of this genre, the participants identified with the representation of the rough, tough students in a very matter-of-fact manner. For example, focus group #1 participants saw disciplinary actions and control tactics as normal, taken-for-granted, everyday strategies that must be employed in the inner-city school. Marlene, a participant in focus group #1, explained her understanding:

> I remember *Lean on Me* because I was living in New Jersey and I know the school and I know the area. And I know when it was in the news and everything and what happened. And that neighborhood is really like that. And . . . I have read studies that have shown that violence on TV does promote, does encourage violence in society. The thing is when you are talking about teaching, and teachers have to go into these schools and they have to deal with the problem of violence. You know, from what I have seen from these movies and these shows that I have seen, it seems that what works is a tough attitude. A) Because [students] respect that, and B) because [students] don't have discipline in their lives so they need someone to show them discipline and to expect discipline from them. And the only way to get that is not by asking nicely, it's by demanding it. That is the only way . . . that seems to work as far as from the movies I have seen, and they are based on reality so I am thinking that it does work. (focus group p1–meeting 1)

Marlene constructed her hypotheses based on her prior awareness of the story behind *Lean on Me* and her reading of research that connects violence to TV viewing. Marlene accepted these understandings. She did not interrogate or critically challenge the meanings behind the representations she saw on the news or the findings within the research articles because the images and findings fit with her conception of how to work with students. In a sense, Marlene's comments correspond with Memmi's (1965) discussion of the concept of depersonalization. Interrogating the roles of the colonizer and the colonized, Memmi explains that the colonizer sees the colonized as impulsive, strange, disturbing: "They are unpredictable!" "With them, you never know!" (p. 85). Marlene's expertise, her way of knowing, reflected these stereotyped notions that students of color or students of lower socioeconomic status respect tough attitudes and do not have control in their lives and therefore need strict discipline—an overreliance on coercion, force, and compliance with the status quo (Haberman, 1995; Kagan, 1992).

Moreover, this understanding of the Other is layered with "the mark of the plural." Memmi clarifies that "[t]he colonized is never characterized in an individual manner; he is entitled only to drown in an anonymous collectivity" (1965, p. 85). Marlene's comments of "these schools," "students don't have discipline," "they need someone to show them discipline and to expect discipline from them" serve as examples of this anonymous collectivity. These comments place the teacher/school into the role of colonizer. Students become the colonized—their individual nature lost in this search for classroom and institutional control.

As a result of this pluralizing discourse, participants' conversations were replete with stereotypical perceptions of students of color and students of lower socioeconomic status as being "at risk." Labeled as "at risk," students were seen as less than, not up to par, questionable. Haberman (1995) writes:

Blaming the victim is an active pastime of schools and educators. It is an occupational disease. In former times we used terms such as culturally deprived, socially deprived, culturally disadvantaged, academically disadvantaged, underdeveloped, disaffected, difficult to serve, hard to read, alienated, and a host of others. All of these terms, including the present "at risk," are labels used for the same purpose: to attribute the causes of low achievement and school failure to the child and family, but to do so in a manner that implies the labeler is not prejudiced and is sincerely trying to help. There is no way to provide a hopeful or an equal education to a child that one perceives and labels as basically inadequate. (p. 51)

Focus group participants used this terminology to talk about student representations. For example during the first meeting of focus group #2, Lauren used the term to describe the students' behavior: "[These students] are amazingly well behaved for an at risk group" (fg2–1). The term "at risk" seemed to cover a broad range for participants: from low socioeconomic status, to minority, to not becoming contributing members of society, to disabled, to having behavior problems. Moreover, their language placed responsibility for this "at risk" behavior on students. At one moment during the first meeting of focus group #2, however, Holly tried to reframe the terminology:

I was talking to my sister about [the "at risk" issue], and she is getting her master's in social work, and they [work with] at risk kids, but they have changed the term to "at promise." Which at first I thought was kind of cheesy. But then when you think about it, the word you associate with different things can really change your opinion on it. And if you start thinking of these kids as "at promise" kids it would, I think, kind of change your motivation. And a lot of the at risk programs expect too little from the kids because they are at risk so they don't challenge them enough. (fg2–1)

Holly's reframing only served to rename the same concept. Saturated ideas were left unexamined, unchanged. Whether the term was "at risk" or "at promise," there was an unspoken yet expected compliance with dominant codes. Meanings and messages of the dominant code became the taken-for-granted norm with either wording—both labels normalizing a deficit model and aligning with taken-for-granted representations of students in the *Dangerous Minds* television series.

Misconception and Inexperience

Participants' comments seemed to be based on misunderstanding and fear stemming from misconception and inexperience with people from backgrounds that were different from their own. For example, participants seemed to deemphasize the issue of whiteness and conformity, even when focus group #1 was confronted with Nicholas's personal experience. Marlene began this portion of a focus group #1 conversation with the reminder that the non-Academy students had called James "white."

MARLENE: Yeah, and one of the kids said [that James] was trying to be white or something. I think that happens a lot.
DONNA: Uh huh, it does.
NICHOLAS: Yeah, I got a lot of that in school.
DONNA: Did you really?
NICHOLAS: Yeah . . . You know, I never really . . . it was always said jokingly. And I just kinda . . .
DONNA: Blew it off?
NICHOLAS: Yeah, but the black guys in school called me whitey . . .
DONNA: Were you popular?
NICHOLAS: Yeah, I was kinda popular in high school.
DONNA: I mean that changes part of it. You know what I mean? If you weren't it probably would have bothered you a lot more, but if you are accepted for other reasons—you [were] a good athlete?
NICHOLAS: I was good in sports.
DONNA: Then I am sure it makes some of the teasing a little easier than it would have been if maybe you weren't so good in some other things.
NICHOLAS: It is a pretty vivid memory, though.
DONNA: I would think so. (fg1–4)

Donna's response to Nicholas's disclosure was one of shock and surprise: "Did you really?" Perhaps, Donna did not want to believe that something like this could actually happen. And as evidenced by her responses, Donna wanted to cheer Nicholas up, find alternative, more acceptable constructions: Nicholas was able to blow off the comments; Nicholas was popular so the teasing was easier to manage. Participants evaded conversation that interrogated hegemonic discourses. In addition, Nicholas did not want to expand on this "vivid memory"—when asked to elaborate on these issues in an e-mail dialogue he sidestepped the subject and ended this line of inquiry. Nicholas did not respond to drafts during the member checking process.

In contrast to focus group #1, during the second meeting of focus group #2, participants discussed their desire to be critical and active with regard to questioning dominant cultural attitudes within school systems. Concentrating on her classroom environment, Ginger explained, "someone might disagree with me, but I think that [talking about it] is always best, to be open about things" (fg2–2).

And Daisy responded: "especially if you introduce it . . . in a non-belligerent way. Just say, 'Okay, I know this sucks, but this is the way the world is. But, that's not the end of it. There are ways in which you can subvert it, you can work within the system . . . [and] not just accept the world the way it is.' I think you can be critical not apathetic" (fg2–2).

Building upon the ideas brought forth during this conversation, I asked participants in focus group #2 to read for the third meeting "The Silenced Dialogue: Power and Pedagogy in Educating Other People's Children," a chapter from Delpit's book *Other People's Children*. Delpit illustrates how school systems maintain a culture of power through exploration of the debates over skills versus process approaches to education and learning. In the chapter, she outlined five basic premises:

1. Issues of power are enacted in classrooms.
2. There are codes or rules for participating in power; that is, there is a "culture of power."
3. The rules of the culture of power are a reflection of the rules of the culture of those who have power.
4. If you are not already a participant in the culture of power, being told explicitly the rules of that culture makes acquiring power easier.
5. Those with power are frequently least aware of—or least willing to acknowledge—its existence. Those with less power are often most aware of its existence. (p. 24)

Calling for a balanced approach to teaching, Delpit argued that the culture of power denies access and thus silences students of lower socioeconomic status and students of color. I chose this article so that we could specifically build upon their conversations and together interrogate issues of power within schools and the role that teachers play within this process.

Participants in focus group #2, however, responded much differently than I anticipated. For example, Daisy's comments were in direct contrast to statements made during the second meeting:

[Delpit] is like, "We need to teach these students, don't let them lose their culture. . . . But at the same time we need to teach them that [the white power structure] is there." And it seems that by recognizing that [the white power structure] is there, almost kind of enforces it to me. . . . Like you [would] say, "Look there is this power structure, that unfortunately you have no control over." Which if you are going to be honest with the kids, this is what you have to say. You have to say, "You have no control over it." Okay, right there, you have probably lost half of those students. They are going to say, "Well, shit, I can't do anything about that, screw that structure." . . . It seems dichotomous to me. You can't have both sides to such an extent. It is not possible. If you teach them, you know, the ways of the world as we see them, which is a white power structure, then you are teaching them how to survive in a white power structure but you are not teaching them how to survive with their culture. You are teaching them how to survive under a system they have no control over. (fg2–3)

Contradicting her earlier statement, Daisy believed that if she talked about these issues then reinforcement of the dominant structure occurred. In addition, she assumed a rigid, unmoving structure that students would never be able to challenge: "You are teaching them how to survive under a system they have no control over." Ginger echoed a similar sentiment during this third meeting: "And teaching them how to make it in the white man's world is teaching them the white man's way" (fg2–3).

As I said, the reactions to Delpit's work surprised me. I had expected the conversation to draw from the *Dangerous Minds* episode to focus broadly on issues of power in education and more practically on the importance of direct explanation and heightened awareness of these issues with regard to their teaching practice. Similar to focus group #1, however, focus groups #2 did not question these issues during the meetings. Moreover, focus group #2 participants' understandings seemed to retreat toward a dominant-hegemonic discourse (Hall, 1993).

Renegotiation, Rereading, and Rearticulation

Participants' initial readings, however, are not the complete picture and deny the complexity of renegotiation, rereading, and rearticulation that they accomplished after the viewing of *Dangerous Minds*. It appears that participants were involved in an ongoing transformational process. For example, at the conclusion of focus group #1 participant Donna's student teaching experience she wrote this comment within her final e-mail dialogue exchange:

I was noticing that having been asked to consider how media affects my perception of education has gotten me to look at the possibilities of where my underlying definitions of education and teachers lie. Just like coming into consciousness about feminism and women's issues, or racism, or any other

"ism," until you are faced with the challenge of breaking down the stereotypes and perceptions you may not realize why or even what you feel or like
about a given situation. Being part of the discussion group helped me to take
a close look at how the media portrays education and then break the stereotypes down. [Participating in the study] helped me to make more substantial and thoughtful decisions concerning my perception of education. Until
meeting with the group I hadn't ever considered why people feel that teachers can save the children, or even should. I too had the belief that some how,
some way teachers are portrayed as and expected to have the gift to reach
out and change even the toughest students in order to save the future.
(fg1–Jan. 7, 1999)

Donna was making sense of her initial classroom experiences in relation
to media portrayals and further connected with the dialogical process that
emerged within the nondirective focus group experience: "[Participating
in the study] helped me to make more substantial and thoughtful decisions
concerning my perception of education." Donna's initial decodings within
focus groups maintained dominant-hegemonic positionings. As exemplified by her comments, however, she was moving toward a more negotiated decoding of these media texts. It appears that growing experience and
interaction within dialogic spaces complicates the decoding of televisual
images.

Concluding Thoughts

Lawrence Grossberg (1997) reminds that the objective media cultural
studies is more than simply to describe how people's everyday lives are
rearticulated and reshaped by media and the broader social culture. Media
cultural studies is about the "possibilities of transforming people's lived
realities and the relations of power and about the absolutely vital contribution of intellectual work to the imagination and realization of such possibilities" (pp. 4–5).

However, transformation with regard to teacher education is not simple.
Research on preservice teachers points to the constancy and steadfastness
with which preservice teachers retain their prior beliefs and understandings of teaching and educational practices (A. Cole and Knowles, 1993;
Kagan, 1992; Tabachnick and Zeichner, 1984). For example, Tabachnick
and Zeichner (1984) found that despite an introduction to alternative
understandings of teaching and education practices the "dominant trend
was for teaching perspectives to develop and grow in a direction consistent
with the 'latent culture' that students brought to the experience" (p. 33).
The appropriation and adherence to dominant-hegemonic understandings
of media culture student representations by preservice teachers in my
study further support these insights. Participants did not question their
fears concerning students. Participants did not question the ways in which
schools sort and track students. Participants did not question the forced

assimilation and conformity that Academy students dealt with. And participants seemed to deemphasize issues of whiteness and their own consequent privileged standpoint. Moreover, between and within both focus groups, discussions were saturated with "the mark of the plural" and a tenor of depersonalization (Memmi, 1965).

Yet what of Donna's transformational experience? Weedon (1987) explains:

> Every act of reading is a new production of meaning. Positions from which to read and the new discourses with which to read are in principle infinite and constantly changing. At any particular historical moment, however, there is a finite number of discourses in circulation, discourses which are in competition for meaning. It is the conflict between these discourses which creates the possibility of new ways of thinking and new forms of subjectivity. (pp. 134–135)

And so, I wonder about the possibilities for transformation, for rereading, within teacher education and in relation to media representations of education. I wonder how we, as teacher educators, begin the process of "skeptical re-thinking" (Dittmar, 1997)—how do we develop pedagogical strategies that enable preservice teachers to question and deconstruct media culture (re)presentations of students to recognize "the rhetorical effects of their visual, acoustic, and verbal 'languages'" (Dittmar, 1997)? What would it look like if teacher educators discussed theories of power in preservice teachers' methods courses? How would preservice teachers talk if teacher educators provided the necessary support so that preservice teachers could critically interrogate their positionality, their standpoint, their alignment and/or privilege within the dominant culture? And, what if teacher educators asked preservice teachers to make sense of their teaching practice before the beginning of the student teaching experience?

I believe that teacher educators must begin the process of developing methods for helping preservice teachers to become aware of the ways in which media culture representations of education influence prior beliefs and assumptions about educational practices. Teacher educators need to provide opportunities for preservice teachers to challenge their understanding of and complicity with or subjugation to the dominant culture. They must call into question preservice teachers' positionality, their standpoint, their alignment and/or privilege within the dominant culture and preservice teachers' perceptions of students of color and students of lower socioeconomic status. Concurrently, preservice teachers need to be involved in understanding the hegemonic influences of media texts in order to reflect upon and dismantle preconceived assumptions about what it means to teach (Britzman, 1991; Brunner, 1991; Kellner, 1995). Take for example, focus group participants' acceptance of dominant-hegemonic representations of students as the norm. One possible strategy a teacher educator could enact would be the organization of class sessions and activities via discussions and readings relating to the social construction of norms within society. Instead of speaking broadly about multiculturalism and diversity, the interrogation of such topics as whiteness, patriarchy, ability, heterosexuality, and the middle class would take precedence. Another possible strategy would be the incorporation of a critical multiculturalist perspective (McLaren, 1995b; Kincheloe and Steinberg, 1997) to encourage preservice teachers to question and reflect upon their personal lived experiences, media representations of education, and their complicity with or subjugation to the dominant culture in relation to their emergent teaching practice.

The above thoughts are offered only as possibilities. Moreover, they are put forward to begin a conversation—a conversation that can build from a multiperspectival analysis, a conversation that will challenge teacher educators to develop a repertoire of pedagogical strategies that challenge preservice teachers' prior beliefs, media culture representations of students, and teacher education practices.

Afterword
Schooling in Capitalist America: Theater of the Oppressor or the Oppressed?

Carlos Alberto Torres

Cast of Characters

ARRACHERA, MARÍA: 17, born and raised in East Palo Alto, in Northern California, her family moved to Venice, Los Angeles, five years ago. She has no siblings, and her parents work for a transnational corporation as clerks. She aspires to be a Latino fashion model.

ARROYO, MARTÍN: a jock, 17, and at 6 feet 6 inches, a physically imposing young man. Captain of the soccer and football teams, as quarterback, he has a good future in professional sports. Born in Los Angeles of Spanish parents who went into bankruptcy two years ago with their small corner store in Venice. He is being courted by most California universities, especially USC and UCLA, to attend on an athletic scholarship.

CAMPS, PRISCILLA: 31, a high school teacher of social sciences at Venezia High School. Educated in Connecticut, she attended the University of Notre Dame. She moved to Los Angeles to be with her partner, Juliette Mushimushi.

CORTINAS, SANDRA REGINA: 16, born in Mexico and crossed into the United States illegally when she was three, accompanying her family. The oldest of her six siblings, she works in a supermarket in the afternoon as a stocker. At home she cooks when her mother is away and takes care of her siblings, all brothers. Her mother is a maid and her father held temporary jobs though he is currently unemployed.

JOHNSON, SANDAL: in his early fifties, an Anglo male. He was born and educated in Mississippi, obtained a teaching credential in Waco, Texas, and worked as a teacher in Texas until he obtained from the University of Florida a Ph.D. in Lusófona literature. Former Professor of Portuguese at the University of California at Los Alamitos, when the department was closed as a result of the fiscal crisis of 1991–1995, he sought and obtained a job as principal of Venezia High School in 1995. Married, he has no children. He has sizable stock options in the movie industry and writes regularly as a movie critic for several local newspapers in Los Angeles County, work for which he also receives secret compensation from the industry. With this side income, he plays the stock market regularly and is an active member of the Republican Party (Grand Old Party).

SINNOMBRE, JOSÉ: a union activist in the Janitors' movement and member of the Trotskyist party of the United States. Of unknown education, he is a self-taught graphic designer, single father of two teenagers who attend Venezia High School. He is employed as a janitor in a high-rise building in Westwood. He was born in Los Angeles of illegal immigrant parents, one of them deported twice to Mexico.

MARTINEZ, ANGIE: born and educated in Los Angeles, a 29-year-old Latina, single. She has never considered any profession other than teaching, and obtained a teaching credential and master's degree from California State University, Dominguez Hills. She is a member of the Educators for Social Justice Network in Southern California, a member of the NEA union, and a member of the Green Party.

MORTON, DR. LARRY AND MRS. MARY ANN: in their early sixties, of English descent. Born and raised in Cambridge, Massachusetts, both attended Harvard University, as did their fathers and grandfathers. They met when they were undergraduate business majors there. They moved west in 1962, after Dr. Morton accepted an offer from UCLA. They bought a beautiful estate on Malibu beach. Doctor Morton has an endowed professorship at UCLA, and is chair of the UCLA Committee on Diversity for West Los Angeles. Mrs. Morton, a homemaker, is known for her contribution to the Women's League for the promotion of golf among women, and for her work in promoting the opening of oil exploration of the Alaskan wilderness to solve the energy crisis in California.

MUSHIMUSHI, JULIETTE: a college professor, a single mother, and an ardent feminist, working in diverse women's organization in West Los Angeles. She is the head of the PTA of Venezia High School and a member of the lesbian parents association of West LA. She recently moved in with Priscilla Camps.

PAVEL, ERNESTO: 17 years of age, born in El Salvador and immigrated illegally to the United States in 1984 with the rest of the family. He is a member of the Latino Gang of Venice. Heroin addict, with a genius IQ and a photographic memory that allows him to be a successful bridge and poker player, packs a gun at school for protection against the Bloods. Once completing his high school education, he plans to try his hand in the professional poker circles of Los Angeles and Las Vegas.

RAMIREZ, PABLO: 28 years of age, born in Guatemala. His parents, both university professors from Antigua, Guatemala, moved to Los Angeles as political refugees after a death squad declared them enemies of the country in the middle of the Guatemalan civil war. Tall, slim, elegant, with long, shining black hair, an infectious smile, and quick wit, he dresses very informally. A philosopher by training at the University of California-Berkeley, obtained a remedial credential in Los Angeles School District five years ago. He lives with his parents in the suburbs, is a member of the teachers union, and is planning to run for office next year or return to school to pursue a Ph.D. in journalism.

ROBINSON, MOSES AND ELLIE: in their mid-fifties, African American workers from Mississippi. They have settled in Los Angeles to seek a better life for their seven children—three sons and four daughters. They met almost forty years ago as militants in the civil rights movement in Mississippi. Both work in the nearby Garment Industries, Inc. corporation. Activists in the garment union, they are also activists in the PTA of Venezia High School, which their children attend.

MELISSA, YAÑEZ: 16 years of age, intelligent but lacking confidence in herself and intellectual drive. She is the only daughter of a single Chicana parent, who works as a bus driver in the public transportation system of Santa Monica.

The Place: West Los Angeles; The Time: Winter 2001

Getting to Know Some of the Characters
Romantic music from the Nueva Trova Cubana plays on the radio of a beat-up '67 Ford Mustang parked in the parking lot of Venezia High School in West Los Angeles. Martín Arroyo passionately kisses Maria Arrachera. Their hands travel over each other's bodies, caressing, exploring every inch of flesh. In the urban silence they swear to each other perpetual love, breathing heavily in ecstasy while they make love inspired by a few drinks and a couple of joints. The moon, hidden between the clouds, pretends to spy on the lovers who take command of the night.

"Te amaré te amaré en lo profundo, te amaré como pueda, te amaré aunque no sea paz . . . amaré si estoy muerto."

In a warm winter Los Angeles evening, Silvio Rodriguez and Anabel López fill up with their love song the emptiness of the soul.

In the black house across the street Ernesto Pavel drinks his last beer, listens to the music and plays with the tattoo of the Virgen de Guadalupe on his forehead. A hypodermic needle tied to his arm dances like a wolf in empty tundra. Filled with the passion and pleasure of the white powder, Ernesto smiles and closes his eyes. A feeling of nothingness and peace begins to comfort him until he can no longer listen to the music emanating from the high school parking lot.

It is 10 P.M. *Sandra Regina Cortinas* is walking home from the supermarket where she worked all afternoon. It doesn't bother her that her homework is once again incomplete; what bothers her is the likelihood her father will once again drink too much will rape her in the early hours of the morning, after beating her mom. Sandra's dream is very simple: to sleep in her own house for one night without fear.

In the Faculty Lounge

It is 7:10 A.M., and maestro Pablo Ramirez is sipping his coffee with sleep in his eyes. He couldn't take his shower that morning, having overslept, rushing with his gray Ford Focus, hacking through the jungle of the freeway, to get to his classroom on time. For almost five years he has been negotiating sixty minutes of freeway driving from his parents' house, where he still lives to save money. Five years have elapsed since he started teaching high school on an emergency credential, fresh out of UC-Berkeley, with a degree in analytical philosophy. More than 28 years have passed since his birth in Antigua, Guatemala, and the immigration he had to endure when his parents, both university professors, fled the repression of the Guatemalan military. Yet his anguish is still there as it was on his first day of teaching, facing his students in a high school classroom. "Why I am here?" is his perennial question. "What difference do I make in the lives of my beloved Latino students?" Smoking his cigarette outside the door of the faculty lounge, he addresses his closest friend, Maestra Angie Martinez, a graduate of Cal State Dominguez Hills and a native-born Los Angelena.

PABLO: Angie, why are we doing this?

ANGIE: What, Pablo, smoking before class begins?

PABLO: No, idiot, I mean teaching. Why are we coming early in the morning, with immense stress after driving hours on the damn freeway with our classes barely prepared, taking away time from our sleep, to find our students beaten up, drugged, drunk, raped, living a life of what Nietzsche, if he had known of it most likely would have called a "splendid lived nihilism"? Why the hell are we doing this? Dealing with the bureaucracy of the school district, the sleepy, greedy principal we have, who is a policeman not an intellectual or spiritual leader, and the corrupt teachers union, which only seeks financial advantage for the senior teachers, leaving the rest of us behind?

ANGIE: Pablo, you know—we have discussed this before—that teaching is a noble profession. It is perhaps the oldest profession on Earth. All of us have spent a great deal of our professional lives trying to serve children, youth and adults with our teaching, seeking the improvement of school systems, teaching and learning, engaging in passionate public debates about education and culture—criticizing and celebrating at the same time. You don't have the right to quit . . .

PABLO: Don't give me that academic shit, Angie! You know that I know the answers, but I also know all the stories, the *cuentos*. Let me say to you,

Angie, paraphrasing the Spanish poet León Felipe, *no me cuentes un cuento, yo que me sé todos los cuentos* [don't tell me another story, I who know all the stories].

ANGIE: My dear Pablo, calm down. I don't understand your reaction! You are a philosopher at heart. You know that a committed, decent teacher should be an advocate for an educational system of quality and relevance in the lives of people. We also know that we want to expand the frontiers of knowledge because we believe that knowledge could be made a powerful democratic tool, an instrument for social transformation, for revolution. Pablo, we are here because we need to start the revolution. Knowledge is power, Pablo . . .

PABLO: (with a face mockingly showing respect) Yup, Angie, you are always so politically correct and passionate. But passion for the truth doesn't necessarily find the truth. Reality, Angie, is a social construction. Never forget that. Reality is a social construction. You make of reality whatever you want to make to please your senses, to feed your own convictions, to satisfy your ego, to justify your ideology. We human beings have an incredible capacity to deceive ourselves. Your revolution is simply another social construction, as good as the next one. As good as the social construction of Mr. Sandal Johnson, who seeks only more power and money for himself. He has sacrificed all and every one of the principles that might have guided his beginnings as a teacher, to become a principal, which he did when he lost his university job, not out of conviction. He is nothing but a dangerous, despicable educational bureaucrat, and you and I are at his mercy. Yes, I know that every day, everywhere in the world, the educational adventure is being re-created by devoted teachers like you and me who are eager to help children, youth, and adults to get educated even in the most adverse conditions. Mr. Johnson, however, is neither an aberration nor the norm. Yet we don't even make a dent in the problem, and you and I will waste our lives if we choose to continue in this profession, asking ourselves the same question that you, so eloquently but I am afraid so cavalierly, have answered just now with un cuento, just *un cuento*. . . . Like those cuentos that we heard in our training as young teachers. They took advantage of our innocence, our enthusiasm to change the world . . .

ANGIE: The bell is ringing, Pablo. Forget our philosophizing, and let us go to our classroom, and do whatever we have to do . . . do what you can to get through the day. Don't let your depression get you down . . .

In Pablo's Classroom

PABLO: Good morning. Today, in social sciences, we are supposed to discuss our lives as students. I want to discuss with you the importance of schooling. What difference does schooling make in our lives, in your lives as young Latinos in Southern California?

[The room shows that people were not prepared to work that day. Students just lean against their chairs as if their own bodies were empty bags, without any shape, just lying there without purpose. Their eyes are pursuing dreams, strange lands nobody else can know. Their hands are playing with pieces of paper, poking rhythmically with a pen their desks, or shifting through the pages of popular magazines.]

> MARTÍN ARROYO: (jumps into the conversation) Hey, dude, *La escuela* is good!
> PABLO: Martín, I told you countless times, you should address me as Mr. Ramirez or Teacher or Maestro, not "dude."
> MARTÍN: Anyhow, dude. The school gives us opportunity to meet other people, to make love to nice chicks like *la* María Arrachera. Oh boy, was she really good yesterday in the back of my Mustang!

Furious, María, seated two rows behind Martín, jumps on him, yelling "You are a sonofabitch!" Skillfully, she manages to slice his right eye using her nails as pair of sharp scissors. Martín, struggling to get free from her hands and enraged by the aggression, retaliates with an upper cross that hits María in the chest, knocking her between desks. The desks fall all over the classroom with squeaking sounds. María starts crying while Martín shouts, with blood all over his face, and points his finger at her. "Bitch, get away from me!" Maestro Pablo and a few other students intervene to calm the situation, separating the lovers. More blood is dripping from a deep cut on the upper corner of Martín's right eye, and he is sent to the infirmary for treatment. Maria, hysterical, is taken out of the classroom by her girlfriend Melissa, and Maestro Pablo indicates that they should come back when she is feeling better. The students comment laughingly about the episode.

"Pessimism of the intelligence, optimism of the will" muses Maestro Pablo, remembering Gramsci's motto while trying to resume his Socratic dialogue with his students; a dialogue taking place not in the streets of Athens, but in the hard-core reality of urban poor America, asking himself, "What is the point in continuing the conversation after what happened?"

[However, the students respect him. Young, tall, with long black shiny hair, a provocative look in his face, an infectious smile, and a quick wit displaying his intelligence and years of reading, thinking and writing philosophical pieces and personal vignettes, just for himself, Maestro Pablo is one of those urban intellectuals who have chosen teaching as their profession, committed in his daily encounter with the lives of people of color like himself. Among his students and peers he is known as a knowledgeable, affectionate, and effective teacher, who knows exactly—most of the time—what his Latino students need or want. With his ability to deal with his students, he has been able to keep a reasonable level of discipline in his high school classroom, the envy of his peers. He is known because he doesn't give up trying to teach his students, despite days like this.]

MAESTRO PABLO: "What is the purpose of schooling, of education?" was my question.

SANDRA: (still upset by the previous scene, and feeling angry toward men, shouts defiantly): "Maestro, you don't really know what school is for us. You come here from your nice suburban neighborhood. Your father or any member of your family has never abused you. You studied in one of the best universities in the United States because you attended a good suburban high school, and you *are un hombre, un macho,* not affected by patriarchy or the violence of the *macho* to women. See, Maestro, you ask about schooling to us as if this could be explained from some theory. You need to come to school every day as I do, tired and beaten up after working all afternoon in the *Supermercado,* and worried that this day you will ask me another question I will not be able to answer. Worried about tomorrow, Maestro, you know. I don't know if I will have a tomorrow, or what it will bring to me. But you see Maestro, I don't get beaten up or raped in the school. The school is a place where I feel safe. The school is better than the street. What option do I have, the school or the gang?

ERNESTO PAVEL (with distorted pupils and trembling hands): You may feel safe in the school, bitch, but schools are another latrine. Schooling justifies and reproduces inequalities in America. The rich go to the good schools, and the poor come here. What security are you talking about? Don't give me that security shit! Don't you see the racist behavior we experience daily in our schools? Don't you realize that in the good schools there is an elite creating their own networking and advancing their own positions in society, sanctioning with an educational degree the advantages that they already have? This elite is now trying to bring down the only welfare system in America: Public Schools! If they cannot shoot down the schools because of their lack of quality, you know what they will do, what they all do, and make quality even worse. Don't you realize that disciplinary sanctions, lack of honor courses, separating the "bright always white" folks from us in the advanced courses, are just different ways to dominate us, to break our will, rather than educate us? Don't you realize, Sandra, the lack of relevance our "studies", that pompous word, have for our lives? Shit, I'll take the needle any day over your romantic notion of school as a safe haven. Give me a break!

Calmly and meticulously, Maestro Pablo picks up Ernesto Pavel's argument and seems to concur: "Ernesto is mostly right in his criticism of schooling. Yet we should not deny that for some people, and Sandra is a good example, the school is a safe place where they come because they find a haven for their lives, a haven that allows them to get away from oppressive realities. However, in terms of the educational purpose of schools, I would like to add a few other critical commentaries to what Ernesto has, so eloquently, said. If you study, as I did to get my teaching credential, you will learn a theory, something called school tracking, according to which students are separated apparently by differential ability, but they are in fact segregated by class, race, and ethnicity. You will also learn that there is inefficient resource allocation, with suburban schools receiving plenty of resources from rich parents and school districts and schools in the barrio remaining perpetually underfunded. You will also hear about the lack of efficacy of schooling as measured in the high drop out and repetition rates or the irrelevant pro forma learning.

> SANDRA: Don't take me wrong, Maestro. We have several times discussed how the school reproduces authoritarian behavior, how there are a bunch of classist, racist, homophobic and patriarchal people in American schools and society. So don't take me wrong. Even so, I feel safe: this is a house where I can come and spend my time without fear.

Maestro Pablo feels the need to light up a cigarette but refrains. He is feeling slightly tense with the exchange, and can feel the adrenaline rushing through his veins. He never imagined that his students would engage in such sharp criticism of their own educational experience. He adds his views to Sandra's analysis.

> MAESTRO PABLO: What Sandra seems to imply is that those features of schools are the result of the authoritarianism of administrators and school bureaucrats, like Mr. Sandal Johnson, and are compounded by the authoritarianism of parents, and the authoritarianism of knowledge production, distribution, exchange, consumption. *Aun más*, schools can be a place where inferior teachers moonlight, or simply kill time, sacrificing the education of their students. But schools are also a place where there is knowledge. Indeed, knowledge is not in and by itself democratic but it could be placed at the service of a democratic project. Remember that, if you have knowledge, if you have a college degree, you may be able to be someone in this capitalist society. Without knowledge, or without a degree you are nobody: *Como te ven, te tratan . . .* They see you looking Latino or Latina, they treat you like a Latino or Latina.

[The bell cuts the conversation short. The students go out on their break, and Maestro Pablo goes back to the faculty lounge, where the conversation with Maestra Angie continues.]

> MAESTRO PABLO: Angie, I have been thinking of what you said this morning. I just had an incredible exchange with my students. Let me say to you boldly that, if I follow their comments, education and schooling are not means to bring about a social revolution in contemporary societies as you want. As Émile Durkheim reminds us, these systems are always conservative in nature. Yet a number of contemporary factors contribute to make the situation even worse. There is a slowdown of social movements. After the fall of socialism, capitalism seems to have triumphed all over the world. With the triumph of capitalism, individualism as a philosophy of

life has triumphed. Individualism has triumphed because with the decline in the welfare state, any form of organized solidarity has also been damaged, perhaps beyond repair. With the destruction of organized solidarity, competition, not collaboration, has emerged as the key goal in educational institutions and elsewhere in civil society. Life is a jungle, Angelica, just a jungle.

ANGIE: Pablo, seriously, I will concur with one of your favorite sayings: 'Schooling and knowledge commodify social relationships.' School culture creates nothing but a culture of consumption. Even in the radical camps there is a culture of consumption prevailing. There is a cottage industry of Paulo Freire's thought. Remember that conference we went to, and we saw those regal peacocks walking in leaps and bounds with their Versacci black shirts and preaching revolution and cultural studies in their obscure language? Yes, there is a cottage industry of radicals promoting models of social transformation that only advance their individual careers. There are those invoking Dewey because he is a fashionable author. These liberals just want to get teaching credential programs to thrive in mainstream America but with a *patina*, a varnish of social justice. They are all sellouts, even though they may not know it; even though they may believe they are doing the right thing. There is a large number of intellectuals, many of whom you and I know, who previously advocated social transformation but now act as a new class of managers in capitalist societies—more so in universities in capitalist societies. This new intellectual bourgeoisie cut across all races, ethnicity, sexual orientation, gender, religion, and the like. So there is no guarantee that a Latino brother or sister will behave like one of us. There is powerful sense of a whitening cultural melting pot, where everybody becomes white. I am with you Pablo, we have to avoid essentialisms!

MAESTRO PABLO: Yes, Angie, I agree. That is the reason some radical educators, including some following the Freirean tradition, at some point in their struggle for liberation have left school settings with the intention to change the systems of public education from the outside. This has allowed the right to take progressively more control of the available "spaces" within academic institutions. Have you read Michael Apple's new book, what is its title? . . . Something like *Educating the Right Way*. This positioning has been helped by the logic of administrative and technical control, which challenges—allow me to speak as a philosopher now— through instrumental knowledge any form of reflexive knowledge (á la Habermas), and creates new conditions for the manipulation of consciousness rather than consciousness raising. So you see, we have here a great dilemma. We either struggle in the middle of schooling as a social site of contestation, or give it up to the neoconservative movements, the movement for testing, the newborn Christians, and the marketers . . .

ANGIE: Let me see, Pablo. Are you saying that school cannot help the revolution because it is pure social reproduction? And, as such, it is losing ground to the mass media as a socialization device?

MAESTRO PABLO: I don't understand what is going on. Are you saying, Angie, that even as social reproduction the schools are losing relevance?

ANGIE: Precisely, Pablo. They are. But not only are schools losing relevance. The written word is losing relevance to the culture of images: one image is more powerful than a thousand concepts. Even the curriculum as official knowledge is losing relevance given the hidden curriculum of the mass media. There is a growing sense of fragmentation and isolation in terms of learning and knowledge. There is a kind of solipsism, which may in the end result in the political apathy, nihilism, and social disorganization we are beginning to experience in America. There is an increased power of unconventional relationships taking over the experience of the common people. What other explanation can you give to the proliferation of gang behavior we observe among our students?

MAESTRO PABLO: Come on, Angie, don't give me the conservative cry about democratic failure! You are buying the neoconservative argument that there is a breakdown in family relationships, in the connections between youth culture and adult cultures, in the connections between teachers and pupils, in the structured mechanisms of social control, in the rule of the law, and in community intimacy . . .

ANGIE: *Sí*, Pablo, *sí*. That part of the story is true. My argument is that while schooling may be pure social reproduction, and mass media appear as a more powerful means of social reproduction than schooling, what is being reproduced are not even the traditional, conservative cultures or traditional themes of schooling but desegregated communities, fragmented selves, isolated individuals, nihilism, and the utopia of the apocalypse as reflected in the several school shootings that have been experienced recently in the United States. The shooting at Columbine High School is a deadly example of this nihilism.

MAESTRO PABLO: If that is true then schooling and educational expenditures are just a waste of money for society. Schools are nothing but a breeding ground for nihilism, opportunism, and pedantry. My student Ernesto who only believes in the needle, is right...

ANGIE: Don't be an *iluso*, Pablo. It seems that you have forgotten your readings of Nietzsche. When one wants to be a teacher, even the wildest criticism of Western reason is forgotten. But Nietzsche was right—modernism is the complete failure of reason. Schooling is more valuable as a parking lot for children and youth, helping their parents forget about taking care of them for a few hours. Schools are more like holding pens than learning places, and you and I are prison guards rather than agents of the Enlightenment.

MAESTRO PABLO: I know that our schools have lost the edge as state instruments acting *in loco parentis*, helping children and youth to become socialized in morality, and cultivated in the disciplines of the spirit and the body. But I am not certain that the most meaningful cultural creation of the nineteenth century and modernism has become totally irrelevant in the twenty-first century.

ANGIE: Pablo, why hold on to the perception that there is a promise to keep in public education in America? That's nonsense! I'm reading a book about globalization, and this business is serious. The lack of relevance of schooling is now augmented by the phenomena of globalization. The dialectics of the global and the local show that the school, rather than being a space for emancipation, is a space for authoritarianism, control, social reproduction, and disciplinary behavior. The dynamics of the global are demolishing the dynamics of local control of educational establishments and posing challenges that the educational establishment is unable or unwilling to meet. What you and I do makes absolutely no difference. If we really think carefully about our own lives, we should get the hell out of here, and use our modest savings to play the stock market rather than playing Russian roulette in this high school. Or someday we may end up with a *balazo*, a bullet in our backs!

The principal, Mr. Sandal Johnson enters the lounge. He shows his ample smile framed by spectacles resembling the bottom of an old green wine bottle. According to Pablo's recollection of his first impression when he met the principal, Mr. Johnson's glasses make his face resemble the smile of a Polynesian pig.

The principal greets the two teachers with his proverbial admonition: "Teachers, you must be so relaxed here, chatting in the lounge, because your plans for classroom activities are fully completed, and I will be able to inspect them on demand, if I choose to observe your classrooms today, right? Is that the truth?"

Dumping the remainder of his fifth coffee in the trash can, Pablo looks at Mr. Sandal Johnson on his way out and asks him: "Mr. Principal, what is truth?" And so, another pedagogical day in Southern California continues . . .

After the Play: Critical Commentaries

José Sinnombre a Latino activist, enraged after seeing the play, argues with a neighbor: "This Theater of the Oppressed is nothing but a bunch of bologna to further desempower the Latinos in Southern California. This is a racist piece depicting Latinos only as people in despair. Where are the César Chavezes who lead by example and spirituality, and have dozens of public places and university centers named after them? Where are the thousands of men and women who work hard every day to produce in industries, services, gardening, the fields? We Latinos, with just half the education of the playwright of this obscene piece, are more productive, bringing more value to our society, feeding and clothing their families. For God's sake, we should boycott this play, and denounce it as an anti-Latino, anti-immigrant ploy! They want to deny education to the Latinos, that is what they want!"

"We are all multiculturalists now, my dear!" Dr. Morton smiles at his wife while chewing his medium rare steak at *Spago*. "You see, they claim that they have something special, and we should be careful because they do. They have the numbers. They are going up demographically in Southern California, because they reproduce like rabbits. They could use their numerical power if they ever got organized. But that is going to take a long time, it will not be in the generation of our grandchildren, or our children's grandchildren. Gosh, I hope it never happens. They have, we all know, low IQs—given the way they were raised in families that are exposed to so many diseases, without good food, unable to speak English and little or no education. They need education. We know that in the university, my dear. We have seen the declining test scores when more minorities were allowed to enter UCLA under affirmative action programs. I hate affirmative action. The way I see it, my dear, diversity should be used to advance the cause of white women, not of these miscegenated wetbacks who now claim a new privilege . . ."

Mrs. Morton: "Sweetie, please pass the salt. I really liked this piece of Theater of the Oppressed. We should sponsor more of these pieces. They should be on our charity list. You see, my dear, while you and I enjoy the best music, the best food, the best view of the ocean from our property in Malibu, this idiotic playwright, who thinks that he has done a masterful work of social consciousness for. . . . What is that despicable term they use to describe themselves? Oh, I know: LA RAZZA. In fact, he is playing to our hand. They need to talk race. Let them do that. They need to complain about the system. Let them do it. By the time they realize these plays are only a kind of therapeutically induced catharsis or clinical tool for their own fears, they will be so sad about their own lives that they will do what this piece does, bring up just plain despair, sadness, nihilism. Don't you think, sweetie pie, that a minority child, with a low IQ and access to drugs and alcohol will put work and perseverance before progress in education after seeing this play? If that doesn't work, we still have the control of this affirmative action–diversity thing, particularly because many people think that it is simply a black versus white problem, easier to solve than with a bunch of Latinos . . ."

Mr. Morton looks at his wife intensely, with the love that they have shared for so many years, and asks the question that was really bothering him: What do you think my dear of this Chateau Moline Rouge, 1983? Outstanding bouquet, hasn't it? Nothing like a good French Cabernet Sauvignon for a nice steak. We Californians claim that we have the best wines in the world, but nothing compares with the old country, nothing . . ."

Priscilla Camps is furious, talking to her partner, Juliette, after watching the show in the high school where she teaches.

"Juliette, this piece of Theater of the Oppressed is a boring patriarchal piece of shit. Did you notice how women are represented? As sex symbols and hyperhysterical? Don't they appear simply in need of security and protection by the *macho*? In this piece women are portrayed, as in most of the media, on a second plane, as if we don't really exist! They rarely speak. They silence us, they make us invisible. God, I hate men!

> JULIETTE: "That's right, Priscilla, these people of Pedagogy of the Oppressed are nothing but a bunch of sexist headshrinkers who cannot understand the needs of feminism or women. I tell you, this Latino culture is totally *macho*, as the playwright himself has shown. We should get the Feminist Club to boycott the exhibition of this piece and denounce it, and do the same with the PTA."

After the play in the school where their children attend, Moses and Ellie Robinson walk home with a sense of unhappiness, and they try to understand why. Mrs. Robinson breaks the silence.

"They don't get it, Moses, do they? The issue is not race or gender, it's class. These social consciousness pieces are all the same. They want to show the roots of oppression, but you and I know, after so many years of working in the factory, that the capitalist slave owners are ripping off the profits, and we the workers just like our captive ancestors, are living a meager life of subsistence. Children should be exposed to serious knowledge, not to this stupid lament about schooling. We fought in the union for years to get better public education. Now the teachers unions are fighting against a voucher system they want to implant to privatize California schools while these know-nothing intellectuals are just discovering oppression in the schools! They come to tell us that it is all a ruse, that education is a ruse, in which minorities cannot progress, in which they only get more alienated.

> MOSES: "Yes, Ellie, these people sound like the people of the Second International but without a revolutionary subject, because they have no faith in class struggle, they don't even know what it is. Let me tell you, they pretend to do a school play that uses multiculturalism to challenge power, but we know better. There is no culture other than money. There is no power other than money. We are not poor because we are blacks. We are poor because we are workers. One day, our Latino brothers will learn this truth as well. I hope it is not too late."

Notes

1: The Globalization of Capitalism and the New Imperialism

Sections of this essay have appeared in the following journals: P. McLaren and R. Farahmandpur, "Educational Policy and the Socialist Imagination: Revolutionary Citizenship as a Pedagogy of Resistance," *Educational Policy* 15, 3 (2001): 343–378; "Teaching against Globalization and the New Imperialism: Towards a Revolutionary Pedagogy," *Journal of Teacher Education* 52, 2 (2001): 136–150; "Class, Cultism, and Multiculturalism: A Notebook on Forging a Revolutionary Multiculturalism," *Multicultural Education* 8, 3 (2001): 2–14; "Reconsidering Marx in Post-Marxist Times: A Requiem for Postmodernism?" *Educational Researcher* 25, 3 (2000): 25–33; and "Freire, Marx, and the New Imperialism: Toward a Revolutionary Praxis," in *The Freirean Legacy: Educating for Social Justice*, edited by J. J. Slater. New York: Peter Lang.

1. John McMurtry (1998) makes the case that the freedoms that accompany the free market are masked in deceit and constitute little more than a swindle of fulfillment. He notes, for instance, that the range of freedoms in this day and age is staggering. There is, for example, greater freedom to purchase a "gold-plated toilet priced at $100,000" or a greater freedom to be rejected under the rules of the free market because one does not have the hundred dollars it takes to pay for a well to provide water for an entire village in the developing world. The first freedom has to do with choice, the second has to do with necessity or what the capitalist prefers to call "dependent want." The poor are free to stop living or they are free to die. This is the market doctrine's "ethic of life." It all boils down to freedom for the rich, and increasing enslavement for the poor. This is a theme McMurtry has developed so powerfully throughout his corpus of writings and exercised cogently in his *The Cancer Stage of Capitalism* (1998).

2. The globalization of capital has new features that some argue constitutes a new stage of capitalist formation. These include but are not limited to the following internally related developments: the rise in influence of financial capital; a glamorous new role for banks and treasury ministries; a massive increase in personal debt that serves as a catapult for increased consumption; a restructuring and downsizing of the labor force and a fluid relocation of industries to developing countries in order to secure lower labor costs; the weakening of independent organs of the working class; the rapid flows of advertising, public relations and infotainment; the replacement of real goods as the main targets of investment with "financial instruments," such as national currencies, insurance, debts, and commodity futures; an increase in outsourcing and contract labor following the replacement of full-time jobs with temporary and part-time jobs; the privatization of public institutions and attacks on economic welfare and security reforms of the past century (Ollman, 2001).

3. Distributional socialists or social democrats assume the state is a semiautonomous democratic institution and can be used to legislate an equal distribution of wealth. Within this group there are calls for supranational and international modes of governance at regional and international levels. By contrast, transformational or revolutionary socialists do not see the state as semiautonomous or neutral. Rather, the modern nation-state is viewed as organizationally and functionally advantageous to the reproduction of capitalist society since the logic of capitalism linked to the state is what sets the limits to the debate over socialist policy. Within this group, there are those who believe that the nation-states have been weakened and transcended by a transnational capitalist class (Robinson) and those that believe the nation-state is needed (Wood) in order to facilitate capitalist transactions. According to Wood, a new capitalist class has not been created, but the globalization of capital has aided the class fraction that is already involved in international finance. We do not wish to resolve these different perspectives here, only to point out that the key to approach this debate involves exploring and analyzing the competitive struggle among various capitals in the context of the tension between labor and capital and the link between horizontal intercapitalist relations and vertical class relations and class conflict (Allman, 2001).

4. It has become impermissible to promote any criticism of capital's internally determining law of maximizing, by any vehicle available, the ratio of its owners' money-demand increases to money-demand inputs. The corporate media select only for those messages that do not contradict the money-sequence organization of social bodies. The regulating code of this growth sequence has resulted in the enslavement and genocide of entire societies. Anything that gets in the way of this decoupled or delinked growth is life-depredated, and gets eaten up.

5. That the United States has fared better than western European countries in terms of unemployment cannot be attributed to the less flexible labor markets of the latter, nor on the information technologies revolution. In the case of Japan and Korea, their periods of fast economic growth, poverty reduction, and rises in the standard of living were under managed trade and capital controls, not laissez-faire evangelism. When Korea, Malaysia, and Indonesia, for example, liberalized their external capital flows they suffered economic meltdowns (Singh, 2000). As Kagarlitsky notes, conscientiously following the neoliberal prescriptions has not made a single country richer. Moldova, Russia, and Kyrgyzstan religiously followed the recipes of the International Monetary Fund, but their economies failed, whereas Slovenia has refused to privatize and enjoys the highest standard of living in the region (Kagarlitsky, 2001, p. 57).

6. Free-market reforms—such as privatizing state-run businesses, lowering government payrolls, and inviting foreign investment—have recently led to energy rationing and a sinking currency in Brazil, a debt crisis in Argentina, the threat of a state of emergency in Venezuela, and worsening economic prospects in Chile, Columbia and Peru. Some people blame the failure if free market reforms on the cyclical downturns that are hurting capital flows and prices of commodities on which Latin American economies depend, and others are convinced that Latin American economies haven't become as efficient, modern, and competitive as they could be. Of course, these perspectives are common to bourgeois economists. Argentina is in the midst of a three-year recession during which tax collections have fallen 9 percent. Brazil President Fernando Henrique Cardoso is rationing electricity in order to cut consumption by 20 percent. Chile is facing mounting unemployment, Columbia is suffering from a stagnant economy and rising unemployment.

7. As Kim Moody (1997) has noted, most production still occurs in the North and most foreign direct investment is still controlled by the North. In fact, 80 percent of this investment is invested in the North itself. Though northern industries are moving to the South to take advantage of cheaper labor markets, the North merely modernizes its economic base while making it more technologically sophisticated. The state hasn't dramatically withered away under the Silicon Valley onslaught of an information economy or the derealized character of information-based capital. In fact, he and other socialist adult educators argue that, if anything, we have witnessed not the diminution of state power but rather its augmentation. We have not seen a qualitative rupture in capitalist relations of production since World War II. We still live within monopoly capitalism or late capitalism and internationally the struggle between capital and labor as part of the practice of imperialism has not recorded any seismic shift that warrants world-historical reconsideration. Consequently the privileged agent for fundamental social change must remain the working class, with the state still serving as the central target of the revolutionary struggle. This is because the state is still the main agent of globalization, continues to maintain the conditions of accumulation, undertakes a rigid disciplining of the labor force, flexibly enhances the mobility of capital while ruthlessly suppressing the mobility of labor, and serves as a vehicle for viciously repressing social movements through the state apparatuses of the police, the military, the judicial system, and so on. That the state is still the major target of working-class struggle is evidenced by the recent mass political strikes in France, South Korea, Italy, Belgium, Canada, Panama, South Africa, Brazil, Argentina, Paraguay, Bolivia, Greece, Spain, Venezuela, Haiti, Columbia, Ecuador, Britain, Germany, Taiwan, Indonesia, Nigeria, and elsewhere.

Contrary to the opinion of many mainstream social and political theorists, who support the globalization thesis, the power and influence of the state in regulating the capitalist economy has not diminished or rendered the state an appendage of transnational capital. Though the role of the state in providing basic social services for the working poor, children, women, and the elderly has been noticeably curtailed by capital, the state continues to play a number of fundamental functions in maintaining capitalist social relations of exploitation. For example, the state continues to be the guardian of property rights. It also regulates and overlooks currency exchange rates and oversees international economic trade agreements. In short, it provides a base for the legitimate operation of multinational corporations and friction-free operation of capital accumulation.

8. Marx's value theory of labor does not attempt to reduce labor to an economic category alone but is illustrative of how labor as value form constitutes our very social universe, one that has been underwritten by the logic of capital. Value is not some hollow formality, neutral precinct, or barren hinterland emptied of power and politics but the very matter and antimatter of capitalism's social universe. It is important to keep in mind that the production of value is not the same as the production of wealth. The production of value is historically specific and emerges whenever labor assumes its dual character. This is most clearly explicated in Marx's discussion of the contradictory nature of the commodity form and the expansive capacity of the commodity known as labor power. For Marx, the commodity is highly unstable and nonidentical. Its concrete particularity (use value) is subsumed by its existence as value-in-motion or by what we have come to know as "capital" (value is always in motion because of the increase in capital's productivity that is required to maintain expansion). The issue here is not simply that workers are exploited for their surplus value but that all forms of human sociability are constituted by the logic of capitalist work. Labor, therefore, cannot be seen as the negation of capital or the antithesis of capital but the human form through and against which capitalist work exists (Rikowski, 2000). Capitalist relations of production become hegemonic precisely when the process of the production of abstraction conquers the concrete processes of production, resulting in the expansion of the logic of capitalist work. Class struggle has now been displaced to the realm of the totality of human relations, as abstract social structures such as labor now exists as the transsubstantiation of human life as capital (Neary, 2000). So when we look at the issue of education reform, it is important to address the issue of teachers' work within capitalist society as a form of alienated labor, that is, as the specific production of the value form of labor that culminates in the production of social agents as transhuman, capitalized as subjectivity.

This becomes clearer when we begin to understand that one of the fundamental functions of schooling is to traffic in labor power, in the engineering and enhancement of the capacity to labor so that such labor power can be harnessed in the interests of capital. Glenn Rikowski has put forward an important argument on the topic of schooling and the production of value. In a capitalist society we are inescapably embedded in the social universe of capital. The substance of our social universe of capital is value. Value in this sense operates as a social energy field. The fluid movements of capital in its various forms and the social relations between capital and labor mediate the social forces of this energy field.

This value, or social energy, is always in motion and is variously transformed into forms of capital. They key term for Rikowski in this process is "labor-power." Labor power—the capacity to labor rests upon the energy, skills, knowledge, and physical and personal qualities that we as laborers possess—constitutes what Rikowski calls the "cell form" of value or "the primordial form of social energy within capital's social universe." Labor power is transformed into labor in the act of laboring (i.e., through living labor) and this process powers social life as we know it. While value is the substance of capital's social universe, labor power (expended as abstract labor or living labor) is the substance of value.

Labor power is always expended in a dual mode as both concrete and abstract labor. But since value's substance is labor power and since labor power is a living commodity labor power constitutes capital's *weakest link*. Why? Because labor power has to be manipulated or coerced into action as workers must be forced to produce more value than that which covers their subsistence (i.e., socially necessary labor time). Labor power is purchased as a capacity for generating and creating value. Labor-power expenditure can create value over and above its own value. From this perspective critical educators are in a unique position to play in struggles over the privatization and business takeover of education—and ultimately in the struggle for a socialist future. Since teachers are involved in the reduction of humanity to a capital as they socially produce the human as capital, human capital, they need to develop pedagogical approaches that can resist the capitalization of human subjectivity. Labor power—capital's weakest link—needs to be channeled into non- and anticapitalist social forms. ·

9. We have borrowed the concept of "revolutionary critical pedagogy" from Paula Allman (2001).

10. See also Giroux and McLaren (1997).

2: Civil Society and Educational Publics

This essay is a revised version of "Civil Society as a Site for Building Educational Publics: Possibilities and Limitations," *Educational Studies* 31, 4 (winter 2000): 375–393. I would like to thank Richard Quantz and Kathy Hytten for their constructive criticism of earlier drafts of this essay.

1. For a more complete comparison between the theories of Habermas and Fraser on these points, see Knight Abowitz 2001, pp. 152–159.
2. Benjamin Barber (1996) argues that "the politically alienated public, equally uncomfortable with what it understands to be a rapacious and unsympathetic government and a fragmented and self-absorbed private sector, finds itself homeless" (p. 270).
3. "Liberal" here refers to political liberalism. John Rawls (1993) provides a defense of the welfare state based upon political liberalism.
4. Rather than being direct "consumers" of education, they are investors, and apply "a criterion to the support of education for other people's children that is both stingier than that arising from the consumer perspective and loaded down with an array of contingencies that make support dependent on the demonstrated effectiveness of education in meeting strict economic criteria . . ." (Labaree 1997, p. 62).
5. See the research of Tom Loveless (1997), who provides empirical evidence that public support for public schools is strong though cyclical in nature. Also, see the annual Phi Delta Kappan/Gallup polls on public attitudes toward public schools, which in recent years have reported strong support for public schooling (Rose and Gallup, 2001)
6. David Mathews (1996), president of the Kettering Foundation, finds that there is a deteriorating relationship between the public and its schools:

    A breakdown of the contract between the public and the public schools may be one reason for the more obvious problems—dissatisfaction with the performance of the schools, difficulties in communication between administrators and the public, and lack of citizen participation. While these are all serious, a deterioration of the commitment to public education would call for more than improving test scores, doing a better job of communicating, and what is usually implied by "engaging the public." (p. 3)
7. In their book *Dismantling Desegration*, Orfield and Eaton write:

    For the first time since the Supreme Court overturned segregation laws in 1954, southern public schools returned to greater segregation. Southern segregation grew significantly from 1988 to 1991 and segregation of African American students across the United States also increased. Latino students remained in an unbroken pattern of increasing segregation dating to the time national data was first collected in the late 1960s. (p. 53)

8. This does not consider the situations in which for-profit companies are starting charter schools to serve low-income communities of color. Whether or not educational publics initiate the formation of these for-profit charter schools is one key question to ask about these marriages of market and the goods pursued by an educational public. Later in this essay, I more fully consider the context of an aggressive educational market as an influencing factor on educational publics.
9. Zollers and Ramanathan (1998), for example, in a study of Massachusetts charter schools, found evidence of charter school representatives "counseling out" students with disabilities prior to enrollment. Cobb and Glass (1999), in a study of Arizona charters, found that "the charters that we have a majority of ethnic minority students enrolled in them tend to be either voc-ed secondary schools that do not lead to college or schools of last resort for students being expelled from the traditional public school system."
10. Michael Walzer (1999) makes a similar argument that "democratic politics requires vigorous associations, but it must also cope with the inequalities that arise within the associational world" (p. 67).

3: Extraordinary Conversations in Public Schools

We thank Carlton Jordan for this title. We also thank the Spencer Foundation and Carnegie Foundation for their support of these projects.

1. Doris Carbonell-Medina, Esq. has her J.D. from the SUNY Buffalo Faculty of Law and Jurisprudence and is licensed to practice law in New York state. She runs most of the workshops for Womanfocus and now practices law on a referred basis only.
2. My Bottom Line, like most sex education programs in schools currently, is an *abstinence-based* program. Unlike *abstinence-only* programs, which receive federal funding under

the Family Adolescent Life Act (AFLA, Title XX of the Republic Health Act) and the Personal Responsibility and Work Reconciliation Act of 1996 (otherwise known as "welfare reform"), abstinence-based programs offer information about safer sex techniques and contraception in the event that adolescents do not "choose" abstinence.

4: A Talk to Teachers

1. This chapter draws on work first elaborated upon in the following: G. Dimitriadis and C. McCarthy (2000). "Stranger in the Village: James Baldwin, Popular Culture, and the Ties that Bind." *Qualitative Inquiry* 6, 2 (2000): 171–187; G. Dimitriadis and C. McCarthy (2001). *Reading and Teaching the Postcolonial: From Baldwin to Basquiat and Beyond.* (New York: Teachers College Press, 2001).

6: Stan Douglas and the Aesthetic Critique of Urban Decline

1. This chapter originated as a paper presentation at American studies in the World/The World in American Studies, American Studies Association conference in Detroit, Michigan, October 2000. I would like to thank Kass Banning for her insightful criticisms and contributions to this revised chaper. Much appreciation to Stan Douglas and David Zwirner Gallery for permission to reprint photographs from the *Le Detroit* project.
2. Drawing from his interview with Douglas, Okwui Enwezor (2000), adjunct curator of Contemporary art at the Art Institute of Chicago, notes: "The most common police car models in the United States and Canada are the Chevrolet Caprice and the Ford Crown Victoria and that an unmarked police car [as the type of car seen in the film resembles] is called a 'ghost car'."
3. Though not addressed here, I suggest that Douglas's work may be further explored through notions of cultural haunting and remembering so complexly articulated in Toni Morrison's *Beloved* (1987). Also see Kathleen Brogan *Cultural Haunting: Ghosts and Ethnicity in Recent American Literature*; and Sharon Patricia Holland, *Raising the Dead: Reading of Death and (Black) Subjectivity*.
4. For an account of the bull-dozing of Africville in the 1960s and the dislocation of its population see D. Clairmont and D. McGrill (1999a).
5. The idea of the open work is drawn from Umberto Eco (1971) Also see W. Crichlow (March 2000).
6. Here note a parallel with Samuel R. Delaney's work in *Time Square Red, Time Square Blue*.
7. As American as recent preoccupations in Hollywood cinema. Note, for example, *American Beauty, The Sixth Sense, What Lies Beneath,* and *Fatal Attraction*.
8. Thomas Sugrue's *The Origins of the Urban Crisis: Race and Inequality in Detroit* is a valuable recent study of these extreme events. Grace Boggs's political memoir, *Living for Change: An Autobiography* provides a brilliant personal account of her and her husband's lives on the black left and of left labor radicalism in Detroit from the 1950s to present-day efforts to rebuild communities through engaged grass-roots radicalism. Susan E. Smith, *Dancing in the Street: Motown and the Cultural History of Detroit*, provides a rich cultural history of Detroit as a major industrial city and of the music created in its black communities in the 1960s.
9. The French explorers probably derived the term from one of the many aboriginal groups whose villages populated the region. For example, one indigenous name for the present day area of Windsor-Detroit was *Karontaen*, or "coast of the straits." See Woodford and Woodford (1969).

7: Screening Race

1. This essay elaborates arguments in Denzin 2001, chapter 8.
2. These films include *Lethal Weapon I, II, III, IV* (1987, 1989, 1992, 1998), *Colors* (1988), *Do the Right Thing* (1989), *Grand Canyon* (1991), *New Jack City* (1991), *Boyz N the Hood* (1991), *A Rage In Harlem* (1991), *Straight Out of Brooklyn* (1991), *Juice* (1992), *Deep Cover* (1992), *Passion Fish* (1992), *White Men Can't Jump* (1992), (1995), *Menace II Society* (1993), *Just Another Girl on the IRT* (1993), *Die Hard with a Vengeance* (1995), *Dangerous Minds* (1995), *Clockers* (1995), *Zoot Suit* (1981), *American Me* (1992), *Bound by Honor (Blood In, Blood Out,* 1993), *My Family/Mi Familia* (1995), *My Crazy Live/Mi Vida Loco* (1995), *Set It Off* (1996).
3. I am mindful of the criticisms of the movement (see Baker 1997 for a review).

4. Hall after Spivak (1990), addresses the notion of strategic essentialism, indicating that in certain historical moments a form of strategic essentialism has been necessary. But strategic essentialism can essentialize, naturalize, and dehistoricize differences in problematic ways (Hall, 1996, p. 472; see also Lott, 1997, p. 93).

5. Extending Dewey (1934), this agenda views aesthetics as that branch of philosophy dealing with the politics of the aesthetic experience, including concepts of beauty and standards of value in judging artistic expressions. It builds on Benjamin's (1968, p. 243) call for a political, revolutionary aesthetic that supports democracy, while avoiding the turn to state-sponsored war and fascism.

6. The New Communicators Program, which was started in 1968 at the University of Southern California and the University of California at Los Angeles, produced first and second-generation minority filmmakers and were called by some the black and brown Los Angeles Schools (see Diawara, 1993; Masilea, 1993; Noriega, 1992a, p. 142). According to Masilela (1993, p. 107) the post–civil rights movement filmmakers implemented their version of critical race theory, especially the arguments of Fanon.

7. It is perhaps also time to move away from revisionist stories about the civil rights movement told from the white point of view. Films which do this include *Mississipi Burning* (1988), *A Time to Kill* (1996), *The Chamber* (1996), *Ghosts of Mississippi* (1996). I would also include A. Banderas's *Crazy in Alabama* (1999) in this category, but not Singleton's *Rosewood* (1997).

8. "Compensation" is the title of a Dunbar poem (see Barksdale and Kinnoman, 1972b, p. 361). Dunbar was known for his dialect poetry. which celebrated the contributions of blacks in the Civil War and in the building of America (see T. Harris, 1998, p. 602; Barkesdale and Kinoman, 1972, pp. 357–358).

9. Dunbar also died of tuberculosis.

10. Pinar (2001) uses a radical, multicultural queer theory of politics to answer his own question, showing how violent racial politics in America have always been gendered and structured by the homophobic fears of white males.

10: Urban Education, Broadcast News, and Multicultural Spectatorship

1. I write this chapter from the standpoint of a middle-class white woman. The Pharon Crosby arrest first drew my attention while I was teaching English in a Cincinnati public high school. I never knew Pharon, but the image of his arrest haunted me. First, the fact that the violence against a teenager had been commited sickened and saddened me. Second, one of his friends who had been interviewed by the nightly news had been one of my students, making it even easier for me to make connections between my own work as a teacher concerned with justice issues and the harsh realities of daily living that many of my students faced. Third, I found my own response to watching the tape puzzling. The tape simultaneously repulsed me and compelled me to look. On one level, I clung to my belief that more advocacy is needed for youth, particularly urban youth, and that the entire incident was wrong. He was subdued with undue force, and placing it on TV would only further criminalize black male youths in some minds. But there was another, more subtle part of me, a part that perked up and listened intently in the school lounge anytime teachers who had taught Pharon uttered a detail or insight about him. With embarrassment, I realized that this part of me secretly wanted to gain enough evidence to make a judgment with certitude in my own mind about what the "truth" of the incident was. Such is the dangerous power of representation it subtley makes us feel we can and do know the truth. Finally, the arrest footage made me abruptly aware of how often my students and many other urban high school students were focus on in nightly news stories (not always negatively). It occurred to me that I had started watching the local nightly news only after I had begun teaching, because suddenly the local news seemed extremely relevant. When I quit teaching and became a full-time graduate student I decided to go back to these questions that I somehow never felt capable of thinking through during the immediacy of teaching adolescents. The result is this study. Throughout this work I have been confronted painfully by my own racist, sexist, classist assumptions. There is no neutral place from which to write.

2. Realizing that although "media can 'otherize' cultures . . . they can also promote multicultural coalitions" (Shohat and Stam, 1994, p. 7), Shohat and Stam suggest that a "comprehensive ethnography of spectatorship must distinguish multiple registers" in order to attend to multiple and contradictory possibilities of media reception:

1. The spectator as fashioned by the text itself (focalization, point of view conventions, narrative . . .)
2. The spectator as fashioned by the diverse and evolving technological apparatuses
3. The spectator as fashioned by the institutional contexts of spectatorship
4. The spectator as constituted by ambient discourses and ideologies
5. The actual spectator as embodied, raced, gendered and historically situated. (p. 350).

3. Information was gathered from media artifacts as well as through interviews with educators, journalists, students, and members of the business community. Since it is a matter of public record, I use the actual name of the student who was arrested, members of the police, and those who participated in the trial. However, I use pseudonyms for the rest of my informants, even those who may be members of the public media.

4. From Delguzzi's account: "Another tense moment came when Tieger [prosecutor], through his question, implied that a separate defense witness was motivated to testify on Crosby's behalf because of her feelings about the police beating of Rodney King in Los Angeles. His question came during the cross examination of Eloise Flowers, who watched Crosby's arrest from a third-floor balcony at the Cincinnati Commerce Center. Flowers, who was in Los Angeles during the 1991 beating of King, testified that Crosby was complying with Hall's orders and never was abusive to the officer, whom she said was responsible for starting the scuffle. Tieger's question about the King incident brought Keys and his cocounsel William Al-Uqdah [defense attorneys] to their feet. "Objection!" both shouted at the same time. "Now the state's playing the race card, your honor," Keys said. Tieger said he posed the question to reveal a potential bias. Nurre [judge] overruled the objection, and Flowers acknowledged that she thought the officers were wrong to beat King. But she said that incident had no bearing on her testimony, even though she began writing down the identifying numbers on the police cars as soon as they arrived and kept track of the activity of each officer. "It was going to be a mess, and I knew it,' she said. 'I wanted to make sure I had the details right.'"

5. During Pharon Crosby's trial, out of a jury pool of fifty, only five individuals had not seen the video footage. Most of the potential jurors reported seeing it five times or more. (Delguzzi, 1995, October 18, B1) Everyone I interviewed remembered the Pharon Crosby news story and video, although it had happened three years prior to our discussion.

6. "According to the Commission on Freedom of the Press" one of the five major things that a contemporary society should require of its press is "a representative picture of the consistent groups in society . . . this requirement would have the press accurately portray the social groups" (Siebert, Peterson, and Schramm, 1963, p. 91). Gannett, which owns seventy-five newspapers around the country has mandated a practice it refers to as "mainstreaming," in which minority voices are sought for stories "that are not necessarily about race" (Greenstein, 1999, p. 82) This practice highlights the inherent tension of showing all sides (e.g., "The constant search for minorities means that if you live in Greenville, and you've got an appropriately 'ethnic' last name, chances are you've heard from a *News* reporter. Consider Yuri Tsuzuki . . . [who] was quoted three times in 13 days. . . . On September 14, she weighed in on the popularity of a local jogging path: 'It's inspiring to me.' On September 19, she appeared in the 'Lifestyle' section, expounding on the virtues of changing an area rug each season: 'It's very important to respect the seasons.' A week later, her comments on an upcoming Elton John concert made the front page: 'I think it's a good follow-up after Janet Jackson.' Never mind that Tsuzuki isn't an Elton John fan, and doesn't have any particular expertise on jogging or rugs" (Greenstein, 1999, pp. 83–84). On the one hand this practice creates a vision of a more inclusive society, however, an emphasis on superficial responses does not delve into the real issues of representation in a culturally diverse society. The overarching narratives remain the same, making the counterhegemonic inclusion of difference unlikely.

7. However, it is important to note various community groups often apply alternate readings and discourses to mainstream texts. Spectatorship is negotiated. Media spectatorship forms a trialog between texts, reading, and communities. (Shohat and Stam, 1994, p. 347) Meaning is multivoiced and thus embedded within certain cultural arrangements. Therefore, "the consciousness or experience of a particular audience [can] generate a counter-pressure to dominant representations" (Shohat and Stam, 1994, 347). A frame is not all encompassing.

8. Shohat and Stam (1994) utilize the concept of "focalization" instead of point of view. Point of view suggest the perspective of a character in a story that the audience/reader

is allowed to perceive events through. Audiences can be positioned in specific ideological ways despite the point of view. "Focalization" is a broader term referring the way in which the spectator is brought with the point of view of character. It refers to how the ideology of the film and the ideology of the spectator meet to organize the affective and cognitive investment of the viewer. In "Los Angeles: A Tale of Three Videos" Fiske (1994) utilizes three videos: the arrest and beating of Rodney King, a black man, by white police officers; the beating of Reginald Denny, a white man, by black youths; and the shooting of Latasha Harlins, a black teenager, by Soon Ja Du, a woman of Korean heritage, in order to analyze the way meanings are constructed and deployed to ascribe social power, primarily around the signifier of "race." Although it was acknowledged that violent events really happened in which people were affected bodily, the videos were not presented as clips of reality. Instead the technology itself was questioned for the types of viewer access it engaged. In the case of Rodney King, certain instances of the video were retechnologized by being frozen or inscribed with explanatory arrows and circles (p. 127). The store camera that viewed the shooting of Latasha Harlins already positioned the spectator from behind and thus in favor of he clerk (p. 159). Fiske refers to the original videos as the "videolows" and retechnologized versions as "videohighs" (p.127). By creating a "videohigh" and framing it through various commentaries (such as Rush Limbaugh's "looping" over and over of the first few seconds of the Rodney King video to highlight a logic for the officers response [p. 131]), a fairly "straightforward" videotape can be made to tell many different stories, moving away from its original focalizations.

11: "They Need Someone to Show Them Discipline"

1. I have placed parentheses around the prefix "re-" to emphasize the reconstructed characteristics and partial production of media culture presentations of education. For ease of reading, however, throughout this chapter I use the word "representation" without parentheses.
2. All participants were English language arts preservice teachers enrolled in an undergraduate teacher education program at a university in the southern United States.
3. I organized participants according to their student teaching schedules. Participants in focus group #1 began student teaching during the fall semester, and participants in focus group #2 began student teaching in the spring semester.
4. Participants chose pseudonyms to maintain anonymity and confidentiality.
5. The episodes viewed by participants were the same five episodes used for the textual analysis.

Afterword

1. I would like to thank my advisee Peter Lowds, who read the paper carefully, and provided much needed editing as well as technical suggestions. As a professional actor and editor, scholar and adult educator, Peter has been a superb contributor to any of the favorable qualities that this piece might have. I would like to also thank students of the Research Apprenticeship Course that I teach at UCLA. Many of the CATS, as they like to call themselves, not only read and commented upon the document but also represented the different characters in theatrical fashion, to assess the quality of the dialogues. Indeed, I am grateful to Aly Juma, Octavio Augusto Pescador, Carmen Laura Lopez Torres, Saul Duarte, Chitra Goldestani, Tomomi Kurokawa, Andrea Brewster, Peter Lowds, and Salva Sorbille.

    Several bibliographical sources inspired the analysis. For those who would like to pursue the theoretical issues involved here, I would like to recommend Raymond A. Morrow and Carlos Alberto Torres, *Social Theory and Education. A Critique of Theories of Social and Cultural Reproduction* (New York: Suny Press, 1995), and Fernando J. García Selgas and José B. Monleón (eds.) *Retos de la Postmodernidad. Ciencias Sociales y Humanas* (Madrid, Editorial Trotta, 1999).

    This work draws from my chapter entitled "Lois tesis diabolicas" in Antonio Teodoro (organizer) Educar, Promovar, Emancipar: Os contributos de Paulo Freire e Rui Grácio para uma pedagogia emacipatoria. Lisbon, Universidade Lusófona de Humanidades e Tecnologias. I thank Antonio Teodoro for his insightful critical comments to the thesis that inspired this work of fiction. All characters in this play are fictitious.

References

Acland, C. *Youth, murder, spectacle: The cultural politics of "youth in crisis."* San Franciso: Westview Press, 1995.

Adorno, T. *The culture industry: Selected essays on mass culture.* New York: Routledge, 1991.

Adorno, T., and M. Horkheimer. *Dialectic of Enlightenment.* New York: Continuum, 1998.

Alcoff, L. "The problem of speaking for others." In *Who can speak?* ed. J. Roof and R. Wiegman. Urbana: University of Illinois Press, 1995.

Alexander, J. "The mass media in systematic, historical and comparative perspective." In *Mass media and social change,* ed. E. Katz and T. Szecsko. Beverly Hills, CA: Sage, 1981.

Allman, P. *Critical education against global capital: Karl Marx and revolutionary critical education.* Westport, CT: Bergin & Garvey, 2001.

Althusser, L. *Lenin and philosophy,* trans. B. Brewster. London: New Left Books, 1971

Amin, S. "Imperialism and globalization." *Monthly Review* 53, 2 (2001): 6–24.

Anyon, J. "Workers, labor, and economic history, and textbook content." In *Ideology and practice in schools,* ed. M. Apple and L. Weis. Philadelphia: Temple, 1983, 37–60.

———. *Ghetto schooling.* New York: Teachers College Press, 1998.

Anzaldúa, G. *Borderlands.* San Francisco: Spinsters/Aunt Lute, 1987.

Apple, M. *Education and power.* Boston: Routledge, 1982.

———. *Official knowledge: Democratic education in a conservative age.* New York: Routledge, 1993.

Archer, J. "Research: Unexplored territory." *Education Week on the Web, 1999* [cited April 4, 2000]. Available at www.edweek.org/ew/ewstory.cfm?slug=15home.h19.

Arrighi, G., I. Hopkins, and I. Wallerstein. "1989: The continuation of 1968." In *After the fall: 1989 and the future of freedom,* ed. G. Katsiaficas. New York: Routledge, 2001, 35–51.

Art Gallery of Windsor. *Stan Douglas: Le Detroit.* Windsor, Ontario, Canada, 1999.

Augaitis, D. (Ed.). *Stan Douglas.* Vancouver, British Columbia, Canada, 1999.

Ayres, B. D. Jr. "NAACP opposes compromise on flag." *New York Times* (February 20, 2000): 13.

Azad, A. *Heroic struggle! Bitter defeat—Factors contributing to the dismantling of the socialist state in the USSR.* New York: International, 2000.

"A Zapatista reading list." *The Nation* 273, 1 (July 2, 2001): 36–37.

Baker, H., Jr. "The black arts movement." In *The Norton anthology of African American literature,* ed. H. L. Gates, Jr., and N. Y. McKay. New York: W. W. Norton, 1997, 1791–1806.

Bakhtin, M. *Rabelais and his world.* Cambridge: MIT Press, 1968.

———. *The dialogic imagination: Four essays.* Austin: University of Texas Press, 1994.

Baldwin, J. *Notes of a native son.* Boston: Beacon Press, 1955.

———. *The fire next time.* New York: Vintage, 1963.

———. *No name in the street.* New York: Dell, 1972.

———. *The devil finds work.* New York: Dial Press, 1976.

———. "A talk to teachers." In *The graywolf annual: Multi-cultural literacy,* ed. R. Simonson and S. Walker. St. Paul, MN: Graywolf, 1988, 3–12.

———. *Early novels and stories.* New York: Library of America, 1998.

Baraka, A. "Spike Lee at the movies." In *Black American cinema,* ed. M. Diawara. New York: Routledge, 1993, 145–153.

Barber, B. R. "An American civic forum: Civil society between market individuals and the political community." *Social Philosophy and Policy* 13, 1 (1996): 269–283.

———. *A Place for us: How to make society civil and democracy strong.* New York: Hill & Wang, 1998.

Barksdale, R., and K. Kinnamon. "Reconstruction and reaction, 1865–1915: Paul Dunbar." In *Black writers of America: A comprehensive anthology,* ed. R. Barksdale and K. Kinnamon. Englewood Cliffs, NJ: Prentice-Hall, 1972a, 349–352.

———— (Eds.). *Black writers of America: A comprehensive anthology.* Englewood Cliffs, NJ: Prentice-Hall, 1972b.

Barry, R. "Sheltered children: Gay, lesbian, and bisexual youth." In *Construction Sites,* ed. M. Fine and L. Weis. New York: Teachers College Press, 2000.

Baudrillard, J., with M. Gane. *Baudrillard live: Selected interviews.* London: Routledge, 1993.

————. *America.* Verso Press, 1988.

Bauerlein, V. "Pro-flag group campaigns to oust legislators it calls turncoats." *The State* (October 1, 2000): B1.

Bauman, Z. *Community: Seeking safety in an insecure world.* London: Polity Press, 2001.

Belenky, M. F., B. Clinchy, N. Goldberger, J. Tarule. *Women's ways of knowing.* New York: Basic Books, 1986.

Benhabib, S. "Models of public space: Hannah Arendt, the liberal tradition, and Jürgen Habermas." In *Habermas and the public sphere,* ed. C. Calhoun. Cambridge: MIT Press, 1992a.

Benhabib, S. *Situating the self: Gender, Community and postmodernism in contemporary ethics.* New York: Routledge, 1992b.

Benjamin, W. *Illuminations.* Edited by H. Arendt. New York: Harcourt, Brace & World, 1968.

Bennett, W. *The book of virtues: A Treasury of great moral stories.* New York: Simon & Schuster, 1993.

Bertram, C., M. Fine, L. Weis, and J. Maruzza. "Where the girls (and women) are." *Journal of Community Psychology* 28, 5 (2000): 731–755.

Bhabha, H. "DissemiNation: Time, narrative, and the margins of the modern nation." In *Nation and narration,* ed. H. K. Bhabha. New York: Routledge, 1990, 291–322.

Boggs, G. *Living for change: An autobiography.* Minneapolis: University of Minnesota Press, 1998.

Bonacich, E., and R. P. Appelbaum. *Behind the label: Inequality in the Los Angeles apparel industry.* Berkeley: University of California Press, 2000.

Borgmann, A. *Crossing the postmodern divide.* Chicago: University of Chicago Press, 1992.

Borowski, J. F. "Schools with a slant." *New York Times* (August 21, 1999): A23.

Bourdieu, P. *Acts of resistance.* New York: New Press, 1998.

Bourdieu, P., and John Passeron. *Reproduction in education, society, and culture.* Beverly Hills: Sage, 1977.

Bowles, S., and H. Gintis. *Schooling in capitalist America.* New York: Basic Books, 1976.

Bowman, D. H. "Charters hit by facilities funding woes," November 8, 2000. *Education Week on the Web* [cited June 20, 2001]. Available at http://www.edweek.org/ew/ewstory.cfm?slug=10facilities.h20.

Boyd, T. *Am I black enough for you? Popular culture from the 'hood' and beyond.* Bloomington: Indiana University Press, 1997.

Boyles, D. *American education and corporations: The free market goes to school.* New York: Garland, 1998.

Bradley, A. "Divided We Stand." *Education Week* (November 6, 1996): 31–35.

Britzman, D. *Practice makes practice.* New York: State University of New York Press, 1991.

Brogan, K. *Cultural haunting: Ghosts and ethnicity in recent American literature.* Charlottesville: University Press of Virginia. 1998.

Brookhart, S. M., and D. J. Freeman. "Characteristics of entering teacher candidates." *Review of Educational Research* 62 (1992): 37–60.

Brosio, R. A. "The role of the state in contemporary capitalist and democratic societies: Ramifications for education." *Educational Foundations* 7, 1 (1993): 27–50.

Brown, L. M., and C. Gilligan. "Meeting at the crossroads: Women's psychology and girls' development." *Feminism & Psychology* 3, 1 (1993): 11–35.

Brunner, D. D. *Stories of schooling in films and television: A cultural studies approach to teacher education.* Paper presented at the 1991 annual meeting of the American Education Research Association, Chicago (ERIC Document Reproduction Service No. ED 335 330).

Burbules, N., and S. Rice. "Dialogue across differences: Continuing the conversation." *Harvard Education Review* 61, 4 (1991): 393–415.

Butler, J. *Gender trouble: Feminism and the subversion of identity.* New York: Routledge, 1990.

————. *Subjects of desire: Hegelian reflections in twentieth-century France.* New York: Columbia University Press, 1999.

Calhoun, C. Introduction to *Habermas and the public sphere,* ed. C. Calhoun. Cambridge: MIT Press, 1992a.

—— (Ed.). *Habermas and the public sphere.* Cambridge: MIT Press, 1992b.

Camus, A. *The rebel.* New York: Vintage, 1956.

Cardenas, J. A. *IDRA Newsletter* 21, 3 (March 16, 1994): 3–4.

Carey, J. *Communication as culture.* London: Routledge, 1992.

Carleheden, M. and R. Gabriels. "An interview with Jürgen Habermas." *Theory, culture & society* 13,3 (1996): 1–17.

Carlson, D. *Making progress: Education and culture in new times.* New York: Teachers College Press, 1997.

——. *Leaving safe harbors: Toward a new progressivism in American education and public life.* New York: RoutledgeFalmer, 2002.

Carlson, D., and M. Apple. (Eds.). *Power/knowledge/pedagogy: The meaning of democratic education in unsettling times.* Boulder, CO: Westview, 1998.

Center for a New American Dream. *Kids and commericialism* [cited February 22, 2000]. Available at http://www.newdream.org/campaign/kids/facts.html.

Center for Commercial-Free Public Education [cited February 21, 2000]. Available at http://www.commericalfree.org/commercialism.html.

Christians, C. "Ethics and politics in qualitative research." In *Handbook of qualitative research.* 2nd ed. Edited by N. K. Denzin and Y. S. Lincoln. Thousand Oaks, CA: Sage, 2000, 133–155.

Churchill, W., and J. J. Vander Wall. *Cages of steel: The politics of imprisonment in the United States.* Washington, D.C.: Maisonneuve Press, 1992.

Claiborne, W. "Zero tolerance punishes blacks, study suggests." *Plain Dealer* (December 18, 1999): A10.

Clairmont, D. and D. McGrill. *Africville: The life and death of a Canadian black community.* Toronto: Canadian Scholar Press, 1994.

Cleaver, E. *Soul on fire.* New York: McGraw-Hill, 1968.

Clines, F. "Appeals for peace in Ohio after two days of protests." *New York Times* (April 11, 2001a).

——. "Cincinnati mayor imposes curfew to quell violence." *New York Times* (April 12, 2001).

——. "Blacks in Cincinnati hear echoes amid the violence." *New York Times.* (April 13, 2001).

Cloud, J., and J. Morse. "Home sweet school." *Time* 158 (August 27, 2001): 46–54.

Cobb, C. D., and G. V. Glass. "Ethnic segregation in Arizona charter schools," January 14, 1999. *Educational Policy Analysis Archives* 7, 1 [cited September 4, 2001]. Available at http://olam.ed.asu.edu/epaa/v7n1/

Cochran-Smith, M. "Learning to teach against the grain." *Harvard Educational Review* 61 (1991): 279–310.

—— and S. L. Lytle. *Inside/outside: Teacher research and knowledge.* New York: Teachers College Press, 1992.

Cole, A. L., and J. G. Knowles. "Shattered images: Understanding expectations and realities of field experiences." *Teaching and Teacher Education* 9 (1993): 457–471.

Cole, M. "Globalization, modernisation and competitiveness: A critique of the new labour project in education." *International Studies in Sociology of Education* 8, 3 (1998): 315–332.

Collins, C. and F. Yeskel. *Economic apartheid in America: A primer on economic inequality and security.* New York: New Press, 2000.

Collins, P. H. *Black feminist thought: Knowledge, consciousness, and the politics of empowerment.* New York: Routledge, 1991.

——. *Fighting words: Black women and the search for justice.* Minneapolis: University of Minnesota Press, 1998.

Comolli, J. L., and J. Narboni. "Cinema/ideology/criticism." In *Movies and methods: An anthology*, vol. 1, ed. B. Nichols. Berkeley: University of California Press, 1971/1976, 22–30.

Cornbleth, C. *Curriculum in context.* New York: Routledge, 1990.

Corporate Watch. [Cited February 21, 2000]. Available at http://www.igc.org/trac/feature/education/industry/fact.html

Coski, J. "The Confederate battle flag in historical perspective." In *Confederate symbols in the contemporary South*, ed. M. Martinez, W. Richardson, and R. McNinch-Su. Gainesville: University of Florida Press, 2000, 89–129.

Crichlow, W. "That slippery element of chance: Stan Douglas." *Literary Review of Canada* (1999).

————. *Hors-champs: The poetics of seeing double (for Stan Douglas)*. Paper presented at the University of Western Australia, Department of Art History, March 2000.

Curnette, M. "Shirey praised for 'healing the wounds.'" *Cincinnati Enquirer* (June 7, 1995): A4.

Curnette, M., and J. Hopkins. "Blacks to demand change today: 'This is a racist city' some say after arrest." *Cincinnati Enquirer* (May 6, 1995): A1, A3.

Curnette, M., A. Weintraub, and L. Goldberg. "Split verdict in the police scuffle." *Cincinnati Enquirer* (May 25, 1995): A1, A6.

Curran, J. "Rethinking mass communications." In *Cultural studies and communications*, ed. J. Curran, D. Morley, and V. Walkerdine. London: Arnold, 1996.

Curran, J., D. Morley, and V. Walkerdine. (Eds.). *Cultural studies and communications*. London: Arnold, 1996.

Dahlgren, P. *Television and the public sphere: Citizenship, democracy, and the media*. London: Sage, 1995.

Dahlgren, P., and C. Sparks. (Eds.). *Journalism and popular culture*. London: Sage, 1992.

Daspit, T., and J. A. Weaver. *Popular Culture and Critical Pedagogy*. New York: Routledge, 2000.

Davis, A. "Prison abolition." In *Black genius: African American solutions to African American problems*, ed. W. Mosley, M. Diawara, C. Taylor, R. Austin. New York: W. W. Norton, 1999, 196–214.

Dean, M. *Critical and effective histories: Foucault's methods and historical sociology*. New York: Routledge, 1994.

De Angelis, M. "Enclosure and integration." *Workers' Liberty* 63 (July 2000): 9–10.

Dedmondt, G. *The flags of civil war South Carolina*. Gretna, LA: Pelican, 2000.

Delaney, S. R. *Times Square red, Times Square blue*. New York: NYU Press, 1999.

Delguzzi, K. "Student faces felony charges of assault on officer." *Cincinnati Enquirer* (June 7, 1995a): A1, A5.

————. "Officer testifies Crosby's arrest warranted." *Cincinnati Enquirer* (August 19, 1995a): B1.

————. "Crosby refused change of venue: Judge says defense can winnow jurors." *Cincinnati Enquirer* (October 7, 1995): B2.

————. "Crosby defense to point finger at police." *Cincinnati Enquirer* (October 16, 1995d): A1, A4.

————. "Crosby defense rebuts reports." *Cincinnati Enquirer* (October 24, 1995e): B1, B6.

————. "Crosby trial tensions grow." *Cincinnati Enquirer* (October 25, 1995f): B1, B6.

————. "Crosby jurors to get case today." *Cincinnati Enquirer* (October 27, 1995g): C1.

Delpit, L. "The silenced dialogue." *Harvard Educational Review* 58, 3 (August 1988): 280–298.

————. "The silenced dialogue: Power and pedagogy in educating other people's children." In *Other people's children: Cultural conflict in the classroom*, ed. L. Delpit. New York: New Press, 1995, 21–47.

————. (ed.). *Other people's children: Cultural conflict in the classroom*. New York: New Press, 1995.

Denzin, N. K. *Hollywood shot by shot: Alcoholism in American cinema*. New York: Aldine De Gruyter, 1991.

————. *The cinematic society: The voyeur's gaze*. London: Sage, 1995.

————. "Editor's introduction." *Cultural Studies/Critical Methodologies*, 1,1 (2000b): 3–4.

————. *Reading race: Hollywood and the cinema of racial violence*. London: Sage, 2001.

Denzin, N., & Lincoln, Y. Eds. *Handbook of qualitative research*. Thousand Oaks, CA: Sage, 1994.

Dewey, J. *Art as experience*. New York: G. P. Putnam, 1934.

————. *Democracy and education*. New York: Free Press, 1916

Diawara, M. "Black American cinema: The new realism." In *Black American cinema*, ed. M. Diawara. New York: Routledge, 1993, 3–25.

DiFilippo, D. "Private schools see applications soar." *Cincinnati Enquirer* (February 7, 2000): A1.

Dimitriadis, G. *Performing identity/performing culture: Hip hop as text, pedagogy, and lied practice*. New York: Peter Lang, 2001a.

————. "Pedagogy and performance in black popular culture." *Cultural Studies— Critical Methodologies* 1 (2001b): 24–35.

Dimitriadis, G., and C. McCarthy. "Stranger in the village: James Baldwin, popular culture, and the ties that bind." *Qualitative Inquiry* 6, 2 (2000): 171–187.

————. *Reading and teaching the postcolonial: From Baldwin to Basquiat and beyond.* New York: Teachers College Press, 2001.

Dinerstein, A. "The violence of stability: Argentina in the 1990s." In *Global humanization: Studies in the manufacture of labor*, ed. M. Neary. New York: Mansell, 1999, 47–76.

Dittmar, L. "Introduction." *Radical Teacher* 50 (1997): 2–6.

Dolby, N. "Changing selves: Multicultural education and the challenge of new identities." *Teachers College Record*, 102,5 (2000): 898–912.

————. *Constructing race: Youth, identity, and popular culture in South Africa.* Albany: SUNY Press, 2001.

Douglas, S. "Artist statement." *Flash Art* 32, 206 (1999): 68.

Doyle, D. "Education and the press: Ignorance is bliss." In *Imaging education: The media and schools in America*, ed. G. Maeroff. New York: Teachers College Press, 1998, 46–58.

DuBois, P. *Centaurs and amazons: Women and the pre-history of the great chain of being.* Ann Arbor: University of Michigan Press, 1982.

Du Bois, W. E. B. *The souls of black folk: Essays and sketches.* New York: Bantam, 1903/1989.

Dyson, M. *I may not get there with you: The true Martin Luther King Jr.* New York: The Free Press, 2000.

Eagleton, T. *Marx.* New York: Routledge, 1999.

Ebert, T. "Globalization, internationalism, and the class politics of cynical reason." *Nature, Society, and Thought* 12, 4 (2001): 389–410.

Eco, U. *The poetics of an open work.* Cambridge, MA: Harvard University Press, 1971.

Edgar, W. *South Carolina: A history.* Columbia: University of South Carolina Press, 1998.

Eldridge, J. (Ed.). *Getting the message: News, truth, and power.* London: Routledge, 1993.

Elliott, C. *Crime and punishment in America.* New York: Henry Holt, 1998.

Ellison, R. *Invisible man.* New York: Random House, 1952.

Ellsworth, E. "Why doesn't this feel empowering? Working through the repressive myths of critical pedagogy." *Harvard Educational Review* 59 (1989): 297–324.

Elshtain, J. B. "A call to civil society." *Society* 36, 5 (1999): 11–19.

Elson, J. "History, the sequel." *Time* (November 7, 1994): 64.

Emerson, R. M., R. I. Fretz, and L. L. Shaw. *Writing ethnographic fieldnotes.* Chicago: University of Chicago Press, 1995.

Engel, M. *The struggle for control of public education: Market ideology vs. democratic values.* Philadelphia: Temple University Press, 2000.

Enwezor, O. *Stan Douglas: Le Detroit.* Chicago: Art Institute of Chicago, 2000.

Evans, S., and H. Boyte. *Free spaces.* Chicago: University of Chicago Press, 1992.

Feagin, J. R. *Racist America.* New York: Routledge, 2000.

Fine, M. "Sexuality, schooling, and adolescent females: The missing discourse of desire." *Harvard Educational Review* 58 (1988): 29–53.

————. *Framing Dropouts.* Albany: State University of New York Press, 1993.

Fine, M., and L. Weis. *The unknown city.* Boston: Beacon Press, 1998.

————. (Eds.). *Construction sites: Excavating class, race, sexuality and gender.* New York: Teachers College Press, 2000.

Fine, M., L. Weis, C. Centrie, and R. Roberts. "Educating beyond the borders of schooling." *Anthropology and Education Quarterly.* 31, 2 (2000): 131–151.

Fine, M., L. Weis, and L. Powell. "Communities of difference." *Harvard Educational Review* 67, 2 (1997): 247–284.

Finkelstein, B. "Education historians as mythmakers." *Review of Research in Education*, 18 (1992): 255–297. Washington, D.C.: American Educational Research Association.

Fischman, G., and P. McLaren. "Schooling for democracy: Towards a critical utopianism." *Contemporary Society* 29, 1 (2000): 168–179.

Fiske, J. "Los Angeles: A tale of three videos." *Media matters: Everyday culture and political change.* Minneapolis: University of Minnesota Press, 1994.

Floden, R. "Confrontation of teachers' entering beliefs." *ATE Newsletter* 28, 6 (1995): 1.

Forgacs, D. (Ed.). *The Antonio Gramsci reader: Selected writings 1916–1935.* New York: New York University Press, 2000.

Forrester, V. *The economic horror.* Malden, MA: Blackwell, 1999.

Foster, H. "Postmodernism: A preface." In *The anti-aesthetic: Essays on postmodern culture*, ed. H. Foster. Port Townsend, WA: Bay Press, 1983), ix–xvi.

Foster, J. "It's not a postcapitalist world, nor is it a post-Marxist one." *Monthly Review*, 54, 5 (2002): 42–47.

Foster, M. *Black teachers on teaching.* New York: New Press, 1997.

Foucault, M. *Discipline and punish; The birth of the prison.* Trans. A. Sheridan. New York: Vintage Books, 1977.

———. *The history of sexuality.* New York: Pantheon Books, 1978.

———. "Nietzsche, geneology, history." In *Language, counter-memory, practice: Selected essays and interviews by Michel Foucault,* ed. D. F. Bouchard. Ithaca, NY: Cornell University Press, 1992, 139–164.

Fraser, N. "Rethinking the public sphere." In *The phantom public sphere,* ed. B. Robbins. Minneapolis: University of Minneapolis Press, 1993.

———. *Justice interruptus: Critical reflections on the "postsocialist" condition.* New York: Routledge, 1997.

Freedman, D. "Images of the teacher in popular culture: Pre-Service teachers' critical interpretations of dangerous minds." *Journal of Curriculum Theorizing* 15 (1999): 71–84.

Fregoso, R. L. *The bronze screen: Chicana and Chicano film culture.* Minneapolis: University of Minnesota Press, 1993.

Freire, P. *Pedagogy of the oppressed.* New York: Seabury Press, 1970.

Friend, R. "Choices not closets: Heterosexism and homophobia in schools." In *Beyond silenced voices,* ed. L. Weis and M. Fine. Albany: State University of New York Press, 1993, 209–236.

Fukuyama, F. *The end of history and the last man.* New York: Free Press, 1992.

Fuller, H. "Towards a black aesthetic." In *The Norton anthology of African American literature,* ed. H. L. Gates, Jr. and N. Y. McKay. New York: W. W. Norton, 1997, 1810–1816.

Gans, H. J. *The war against the poor: The underclass and antipoverty policy.* New York, NY: Basic Books, 1995.

Gaonkar, D., and C. Nelson. *Disciplinarity and dissent in cultural studies.* New York: Routledge, 1999.

Gaskell, J. *Gender matters from school to work.* Philadelphia: Open University Press, 1992.

Gayle, A., Jr. Introduction to *The black aesthetic,* ed. A. Gayle, Jr. New York: Doubleday, 1971, xv–xxiv.

———. "The black aesthetic." In *The Norton anthology of African American literature,* ed. H. L. Gates, Jr., and N. Y. McKay. New York: W. W. Norton, 1997, 1870–1877.

Gibbs, J. T. "Black adolescents and youth: An update on an endangered species." In *Black adolescents,* ed. R. L. Jones. Berkeley, CA: Cobb & Henry, 1989, 3–28.

Gilbert, S. "The four 'commonplaces of teaching': Prospective teachers beliefs about teaching in urban schools." *Urban Review* 29 (1997): 81–96.

Gilligan, C. *In a different voice.* Cambridge, MA: Harvard University Press, 1982.

Ginsberg, M. *Contradictions in Teacher Education and Society: A Critical Analysis.* New York: Flamer Press, 1988.

Giroux, H. *Ideology, culture, and the process of schooling.* Philadelphia, PA: Temple University Press, 1981.

———. "Theories of reproduction and resistance in the new sociology of education." *Harvard Educational Review* 53, 3 (August 1983a): 257–293.

———. *Theory and resistance in education: A pedagogy for the opposition.* South Hadley, MA: Bergin & Garvey, 1983b.

———. *Teachers as intellectuals: Towards a critical pedagogy of learning.* South Hadley, MA: Bergin & Garvey, 1988.

———. *Border crossings.* New York: Routledge, 1991.

———. "Is there a place for cultural studies in colleges of education?" In *Counternarratives: Cultural studies and critical pedagogies in postmodern spaces,* ed. H.A. Giroux, C. Lankshear, P. McLaren, M. Peters. New York: Routledge, 1995, 41–58.

———. *Fugitive cultures: Race, violence, and youth.* New York: Routledge, 1996.

———. "Hollywood, race, and the demonization of youth: The 'kids' are not 'alright.'" *Educational Researcher* 25 (1997a): 31–35.

———. "Race, pedagogy, and whiteness in *Dangerous Minds.*" *Cineaste* 22, 4 (1997b).

———. *The mouse that roared: Disney and the end of innocence.* Lanham: Rowman & Littlefield Publishers, 1999.

———. *Stealing innocence: Youth, corporate power, and the politics of culture.* New York: St. Martin's Press, 2000a.

———. *Impure acts: The practical politics of cultural studies.* New York: Routledge, 2000b.

———. "Zero tolerance: Creating a generation of suspects." *Tikkun* 16, 2 (2001): 29–32, 58–59.

Giroux, H., and P. McLaren. "Teacher education and the politics of engagement: The case for democratic schooling." *Harvard Educational Review* 56 (1986): 213–238.

————. "Paulo Freire, postmodernism and the utopian imagination: A Blochian reading." In *Not yet: Reconsidering Ernst Bloch*, ed. J.O. Daniel and T. Moylan. London: Verso, 1997, 138–162.

Gitlin, T. *The whole world is watching: Mass media in the making and unmaking of the new left.* Berkeley: University of California Press, 1980.

Glesne, C., and A. Peshkin. *Becoming qualitative researchers.* New York: Longman, 1992.

Goffman, E. *Frame analysis: An essay on the organization of experience.* New York: Harper & Row, 1974.

Goforth, C. "Response on the street largely muted." *Cincinnati Enquirer* (June 7, 1995): A4.

Goldberg, L. "Officers' defenders chide city for lack of support." *Cincinnati Enquirer* (May 17, 1995a): A1, A6.

————. "Questions still not answered." *Cincinnati Enquirer.* (May 31, 1995b): C1, C4.

Goldberg, L., A. Weintraub, and M. Curnette. "Shirey orders suspensions for 2 cops; crosby indicted: City manager calls for reviews of police training." *Cincinnati Enquirer* (June 7, 1995): A1, A5.

Goldhaber, D. D. "School choice: An examination of the empirical evidence on achievement, parental decision making, and equity." *Educational Researcher* 28, 9 (1999): 16–25.

Gramsci, A. *The prison notebooks: Selections.* Trans. Q. Hoare, G. N. Smith. New York: International, 1971.

Greene, M. *Releasing the imagination.* New York: John Wiley, & Sons, 1999.

Greenstein, J. "Just add color." *Brill's Content* (March 1999): 82–85.

Greider, W. "Time to rein in global finance." *Nation* 270, 16 (2000): 13–20.

Griggs, F. "Grim truth: Preventing a paducah impossible," *The Cincinnati Post*, July 14, 1998. Available at http://www.cincypost.com:80/news/ secure120397.html

————. "Keeping guns out of school: Searches detectors working," *Cincinnati Post*, July 14, 1998. Available at http://www.cincypost.com:80/news/ guns071498.html

Grossberg, L. "Can cultural studies find true happiness in communication?" *Journal of Communication* 43, 4 (1993): 89–97.

————. "On postmodernism and articulation: An interview with Stuart Hall." In *Stuart Hall: Critical dialogues in cultural studies*, ed. D. Morley and K. Chen. New York: Routledge, 1996, 131–150.

————. *Bringing it all back home.* Durham, NC: Duke University Press, 1997.

Grossberg, L., C. Nelson, and P. A. Treichler (Eds.). *Cultural studies.* New York: Routledge, 1992.

Grossberg, L., E. Wartella, and D. C. Whitney. *Mediamaking: mass media in a popular culture.* Thousand Oaks, CA: Sage, 1998.

Haberman, M. "Preparing teachers for the real world of urban schools." *Educational Forum* 58 (1994): 162–168.

————. *Star teachers of children in poverty.* West Lafayette, IN: Kappa Delta Pi, 1995.

Haberman, M., and L. Post. "Does direct experience change education students' perceptions of low-income, minority children?" *Midwestern Education Researcher* 5, 2 (1992): 29–31.

Habermas, J. "Further reflections on the public sphere," In *Habermas and the public sphere*, ed, C. Calhoun. Cambridge: MIT Press, 421–461.

Habermas, J. "Three normative models of democracy." In *Democracy and difference: Contesting the boundaries of the political*, ed. S. Benhabib. Princeton, NJ: Princeton University Press, 1996.

Hainsworth, G. "Tinsel town teachers." *Rethinking Schools* 13 (1998): 19.

Hall, S. "Ethnicity, Identity and Difference." *Radical America* 3 (1991): 9–22.

————. "Encoding, decoding." In *The cultural studies reader*, ed. S. During. New York: Routledge, 1993, 90–103.

————. "Cultural identity and diaspora." In *Contemporary postcolonial theory: A reader*, ed. P. Mongia. New York: Arnold, 1996, 110–121.

————. "What is this 'black' in black popular culture?" In *Stuart Hall: Critical dialogues in cultural studies*, ed. D. Morley and K. H. Chen. London: Routledge, 1996, 465–475.

Hall, S., C. Chricters, and T. Jefferson. *Policing the crisis: Mugging, the state and law and orders.* London: Macmillan, 1978.

Hall, S., D. Morley, and K. H. Chen. (Eds.). *Stuart Hall: Critical dialogues in cultural studies.* New York: Routledge, 1996.

Hamilton, D. "Review of high school high—*Dangerous Minds* spoof." *Atlanta Constitution* (October 25, 1996): 18.

Hamlin, M. C. W. *Legends of le Dâetroit*. Detroit, MI: Omnigraphics, Inc. (reprint edition), 1996.

Haney, W. "Testing and minorities." In *Beyond silenced voices*, ed. L. Weis and M. Fine. Albany: SUNY Press, 1993, 45–74.

Haraway, D. *Simians, cyborgs, and women*. London: Routledge, 1991.

Hardt, M., and A. Negri. *Empire*. Cambridge, MA: Harvard University Press, 2000.

Harris, T. "'No more shall they in bondage toll': African American history and culture, 1865–1915: Paul Laurence Dunbar." In *Call and response: The Riverside anthology of the African American literary tradition*, ed. P. L. Hill. New York: Houghton Mifflin, 1998, 600–604.

Harris, W. J. "'Cross Roads Blues': African American history and culture, 1865–1915: Paul Laurence Dunbar." In *Call & response: The Riverside anthology of the African American literary tradition*, ed. P. L. Hill. New York: Houghton Mifflin, 1998, 1343–1385.

Harvey, D. *The condition of postmodernity*. Oxford: Basil Blackwell, 1989.

———. "Reinventing geography." *New Left Review* 4, second series (2000): 75–97.

Hawkes, D. *Ideology*. New York: Routledge, 1996.

Hawkins, D. F., and N. E. Jones. "Black adolescents and the criminal justice system." In *Black adolescents*, ed. R. E. Jones. Berkeley: Cobb & Henry, 1989, 403–423.

Henig, J. R., and S. D. Sugarman. "The nature and extent of school choice." In *School choice and social controversy: Politics, policy, and law*, ed. S. D. Sugarman and F. R. Kemerer. Washington, D.C.: Brookings Institution Press, 1999, 13–35.

Hill, D. "State theory and the neo-liberal reconstruction of schooling and teacher education: A structuralist neo-Marxist critique of postmodernist, quasi-postmodernist, and culturalist neo-Marxist theory." *British Journal of Sociology of Education*, forthcoming.

Hill, D., and M. Cole. "Social class." In *Schooling and equality: Fact, concept and policy*, ed. D. Hill and M. Cole. London: Kogan Page, 2001.

Hill, D., P. McLaren, M. Cole, and G. R. Kikowski. (Eds.). *Marxism Against postmodernism in educational theory*. Lanham, MD: Lexington Books, 2002.

Hoggart, R. *The uses of literacy: Changing patterns in English mass culture*. Boston: Beacon Press, 1961.

Holland, D. C. *Educated in romance: Women, achievement, and college culture*. Chicago: University of Chicago Press, 1990.

Holland, S. P. *Raising the dead: Reading of death and (black) subjectivity*. Durham, NC: Duke University Press, 2000.

Holloway, J. "The freeing of Marx." *Common Sense: Journal of Edinburgh Conference of Socialist Economics* 14 (October 1993): 14–21.

Holloway, J. "The relevance of Marxism today." *Common Sense: Journal of Edinburgh Conference of Socialist Economics* 15 (April 1994): 38–42.

Holst, J. *Social movements, civil society, and radical adult education*. Westport, CT: Bergin & Garvey, in press.

Holub, R. *Antonio Gramsci: Beyond Marxism and postmodernism*. London: Routledge, 1992.

Home Schooling. *Education Week on the Web*, March 3, 2000. Available at http://www.edweek.org.we/vol-15/38home.h15

hooks, b. *Yearning: Race, gender, and cultural politics*. Boston: South End, 1990.

Hopkins, J. "Race unimportant, teen tells 'Inside Edition.'" *Cincinnati Enquirer* (May 2, 1995): A4.

Horn, D. "Rosa Parks argues vs. rap." *Cincinnati Enquirer* (May 5, 2001): B1.

Horton, M. *The long haul* (with Judith and Herbert Kohl). New York: Doubleday, 1990.

House, E. R. *Schools for sale: Why free market policies won't improve America's schools, and what will*. New York: Teachers College Press, 1998.

Hytten, K. "The promise of cultural studies in education." *Educational Theory* 49, 4 (1999): 527–543.

Imam, H. "Global subjects: How did we get here?" *Women in Action* 3 (1997): 12–15.

Irigaray, L. *Marine lover: Of Friedrich Nietzsche*. Translated by Gillian C. Gill. New York: Columbia University Press, 1991.

Irwin, J. "Marchers want all 3 cops fired: 13 recommendations given to Shirey." *Cincinnati Enquirer* (May 14, 1995): A1, A12.

Jackson, P. *Life in classrooms*. New York: Teachers College Press, 1968.

Jackson, S. *The haunting of hill house*. New York: Viking Press, 1984.

Jameson, F. *The political unconscious: Narrative as a socially symbolic act*. Ithaca: Cornell University Press, 1981.

———. *Signatures of the visible*. London: Routledge, Chapman, & Hall, 1992.

Jordan, J. *Affirmative acts*. Garden City, NY: Anchor, 1998.

Kaestle, C. *Pillars of the republic: Common schools and American society, 1780–1860*. New York: Hill & Wang, 1983.

Kagan, D. M. "Professional growth among preservice and beginning teachers." *Review of Educational Research* 62 (1992): 129–169.

Kagarlitsky, B. "The road to consumption." In *After the fall: 1989 and the future of freedom*, ed. G. Katsiaficas. New York: Routledge, 2001, 52–66.

Karenga, M. "Black art: Mute matter given force and function." In *The Norton anthology of African American literature*, ed. H. L. Gates, Jr., and N. Y. McKay. New York: W. W. Norton, 1997, 1973–1977.

Katz, C. "The expeditions of conjurers." In *Feminist Dilemmas in Fieldwork*, ed. P. Wolf. Boulder, CO: Westview Press, 1996, 170–184.

Kaufman, B. "City asks court to toss out suit: Pharon Crosby alleges police violated rights." *Cincinnati Enquirer* (January 2, 1998).

Kaufmann, W. *Nietzsche: Philosopher, psychologist, Antichrist*. Princeton, NJ: Princeton University Press, 1974.

Keane, J. "Despotism and democracy: The origins and development of the distinction between civil society and the state 1750–1850." In *Civil Society and the state: New European perspectives*, ed. J. Keane. New York: Verso, 1988.

Keither, M., and S. Pile. *Place and the politics of identity*. London: Routledge, 1993.

Kelley, R. *Race rebels: Culture, politics, and the black working class*. New York: Free Press, 1994.

Kellner, D. *Media culture*. New York: Routledge, 1995.

Kellner, D., Liebowitz, F., & Ryan, M. "Blade runner: A diagnostic critique." *Jump Cut* 2 (1984): 6–8.

Kelly, G., and A. Nihlen. "Schooling and the reproduction of patriarchy." In *Cultural and economic reproduction in education*, ed. M. Apple. Boston: Routledge and Kegan Paul, 1982, 162–180.

Kilbourne, J. *Deadly persuasion: Why women and girls must fight the addictive power of advertising*. New York: Free Press, 1999.

Kincheloe, J. *Towards a critical politics of teacher thinking: Mapping the postmodern*. Westport, CT: Bergin & Garvey, 1993.

———. *How do we tell the workers? The socioeconomic foundations of work and vocational education*. Boulder, CO: Westview, 1998.

———. *The sign of the burger: McDonald's and the culture of power* (Labor in crisis). Philadelphia, PA: Temple University Press, 2002.

Kincheloe, J. L., and S. R. Steinberg. *Changing multiculturalism*. Philadelphia: Open University Press, 1997.

King, J. "Dysconscious racism: Ideology, identity, and the miseducation of teachers." In *The education feminism reader*, ed. L. Stone. New York: Routledge, 1994, 336–348.

Kirby, J. T. *Media-made Dixie*. Baton Rouge: Louisiana State University Press, 1978.

Klein, N. *No logo: Taking aim at the brand bullies*. New York: Picador, 1999.

Knight Abowitz, K. "Charter schooling and social justice." *Educational Theory* 51, 2 (2001): 151–170.

Kohl, H. *Thirty-six children*. New York: Penguin, 1968.

Kohl, H. "The politics of children's literature: The story of Rosa Parks and the Montgomery bus boycott." *Journal of Education* 173, 1 (1991): 35–50.

Kozol, J. *Death at an early age*. New York: New American Library, 1985.

Kress, H. *Bracing for diversity: A study of white professional middle class, male and female identity in a United States suburban public school*. Unpublished Ph.D. dissertation. University at Buffalo, State University of New York, 1997.

Krupskaya, N. *On labour-oriented education and instruction*. Moscow: Progressive, 1985.

Labaree, D. F. "Public goods, private goods: The American struggle over educational goals." *American Educational Research Journal* 34, 1 (1997): 39–81.

Laclau, E., and C. Mouffe. *Hegemony and socialist strategy*. London: Verso Books. 1985.

Ladsen-Billings, G. *The dreamkeepers: Successful teachers of African-American children*. San Francisco: Jossey-Bass, 1994.

Larsen, N. "Dialectics and 'globalization': The problem of how (not) to think about a new internationalism." *Working Papers in Cultural Studies* 22 (2000): 6–16. Pullman: Department of Comparative American Cultures, Washington State University.

Lasn, K. *Culture jam: The uncooling of America*. New York: Eagle Brook, 1999.

———. "USA TM." *Adbusters* 28 (2000): 52–55.

Lasswell, H. "The structure and function of communication in society." In *The communica-*

tion of ideas, ed. L. Bryson. New York: Institute for Religious and Social Studies, 1948, 37–51.

Lather, P. *Getting smart: Feminist research and pedagogy with/in the postmodern.* New York: Routledge, 1991.

———. "Drawing the lines at angels: Working the ruins of feminist ethnography." *Qualitative Studies in Education* 10, 3 (1997): 285–304.

———. "Ten years later, yet again: Critical pedagogy and its complicities," in *Feminist engagements: Reading, resisting, and revisioning male theorists in education and cultural studies*, ed. K. Weiler. New York: Routledge, 2001, 183–195.

Lawrence, C. "The word and the river: Pedagogy as scholarship and struggle." In *Critical race theory: The key writings that formed the movement*, eds. K. Crenshaw, N. Gotanda, G. Peller, and K. Thomas. New York: New Press, 1995, 336–351.

Laycock. J. "In-between spaces: Not your typical postcard." *Windsor Star* (November 5, 1999): B1, B5.

Lee, M. "Relocating location: Cultural geography, the specificity of place and the city habitus." In *Cultural methodologies*, ed. J. McGuigan. London: Sage, 1997, 126–141.

Lee, S. *By any means necessary: The trials and tribulations of making* Malcolm X. New York: Hyperion, 1992.

Leeming, D. *James Baldwin: A biography.* New York: Knopf, 1994.

Leifermann, H. *South Carolina.* Oakland, CA: Compass American Guides, 1998.

Lenin, V. *Imperialism: The highest stage of capitalism.* Moscow: Foreign Language Publishing House, 1951.

Leonard, J. "Educating television." In *Imaging education: The media and schools in America*, ed. G. Maeroff. New York: Teachers College Press, 1998, 209–219.

Lipsitz, G. *The possessive investment in whiteness: How white people profit from identity politics.* Philadelphia: Temple University Press, 1998.

Liston, D. and K. Zeichner. *Culture and teaching. (Reflective teaching and the social conditions of schooling: A series for prospective and practicing teachers).* Mahwah, NJ: Lawrence Erlbaum, 1996.

Lortie, D. C. *Schoolteacher.* Chicago: University of Chicago Press, 1975.

Lott, T. L. "A no-theory of contemporary black cinema." In *Representing blackness: Issues in film and video*, ed. V. Smith. New Brunswick, NJ: Rutgers University Press, 1997, 83–96.

Loveless, T. "The structure of public confidence in education." *American Journal of Education* 105 (February 1997): 127–159.

Lubiano, W. "But compared to what? Reading realism, representation, and essentialism in *School Daze, Do the Right Thing*, and the Spike Lee discourse." In *Representing blackness: Issues in film and video*, ed. V. Smith. New Brunswick, NJ: Rutgers University Press, 1997, 97–122.

Luxemburg, R. *The crisis in German social democracy: The Junius pamphlet.* New York: Socialist Publication Society, 1919.

MacGregor, J. "TV, the movies' abused (and abusive) stepchild: Review of Spike Lee's *Bamboozled*." *New York Times*, Arts and Leisure (October 8, 2000): A-11, A-34.

MacIntyre, A. *Making meaning of whiteness: Exploring racial identity with white teachers.* Albany: State University of New York Press, 1997.

Maeroff, G. (Ed.). *Imaging education: The media and schools in America.* New York: Teachers College Press, 1998.

Marshall, S. "Rattling the global corporate suites." *Political Affairs* 79, 1 (2000): 6–12.

Marusza, J. *Canal Town Youth.* Albany: State University of New York Press, 2000.

Marx, K., and F. Engels. *Address of the Central Committee to the Communist League.* London, March 1850.

———. *Critique of the Gotha program.* New York: International, 1973.

———. *Capital: A critique of political economy.* Vol. 1. Translated B. Fowkes. New York: Vintage, 1977.

Masilela, N. "The Los Angeles school of black filmmakers." In *Black American cinema*, ed. M. Diawara. New York: Routledge, 1993, 107–117.

Massood, P. J. "Mapping the hood: The genealogy of city space in *Boyz N the Hood* and *Menace II Society*." *Cinema Journal* 35 (1996): 85–97.

Mathews, D. *Is there a public for public schools?* Dayton, OH: Kettering Foundation Press, 1996.

Matsuda, M. *Where is your body? And other essays on race, gender, and the law.* Boston: Beacon Press, 1997.

Mauer, M. "Americans behind bars: A comparison of international rates of incarceration." In *Cages of steel: The politics of imprisonment in the United States*, ed. W. Churchill and J. J. Vander Wall. Washington D.C.: Maisonneuve, 1992, 22–35.

Mayne, J. *Cinema and spectatorship*. London: Routledge, 1993.

McCarthy, C. *The uses of culture: Education and the limits of ethnic affiliation*. New York: Routledge, 1998.

———. "Mariners, renegades, and castaways: C. L. R. James and the radical postcolonial imagination." *Cultural Studies—Critical Methodologies* 1 (2001): 86–107.

McCarthy, C., and G. Dimitriadis. "Globalizing pedagogies: Power, resentment, and the renarration of difference." *World Studies in Education* 1, 1 (2000): 23–39.

McCarthy, C., and W. Crichlow. *Race, identity, and representation in education*. New York: Routledge, 1993.

McCarthy, C., et al., "Danger in the safety zone: Notes on race, resentment and the discourse of crime, violence, and suburban security." In *Power/knowledge/pedagogy: The meaning of democratic education in unsettling times*, ed. D. Carlson and M. Apple. Boulder, CO: Westview, 1998, 203–223.

McChesney, R. W. Introduction to *Profit over people: Neoliberalism and global order*, ed. N. Chomsky. New York: Seven Stories, 1999, 7–16.

McIntyre, S. R., and R. H. Tlusty. "Computer-mediated discourse: Electronic dialogue journaling and reflective practice." Paper presented at the 1995 annual meeting of the American Educational Research Association, San Francisco, CA. (ERIC Document Reproduction Service No. ED 385 232).

McLaren, P. *Critical pedagogy and predatory culture: Oppositional politics in a postmodern era*. London and New York: Routledge, 1995.

———. "White terror and oppositional agency: Towards a critical multiculturalism." In *Rethinking media literacy*, ed. P. McLaren, B. Hammer, D. Sholle, S. Reilly. New York: Peter Lang, 1995, 87–124.

———. *Revolutionary multiculturalism: Pedagogies of dissent for the new millennium*. Boulder, CO: Westview, 1997.

———. *Life in schools: An introduction to critical pedagogy in the foundations of education*. 3rd ed. New York: Longman, 1998a.

———. "Revolutionary pedagogy in post-revolutionary times: Rethinking the political economy of critical education." *Educational Theory* 48, 4 (1998b): 431–462.

———. *Che Guevara, Paulo Freire, and the pedagogy of revolution*. Boulder, CO: Rowman & Littlefield, 2000.

McLaren, P. and R. Farahmandpur. "Critical pedagogy, postmodernism, and the retreat from class: Towards a contraband pedagogy." *Theoria*, 93 (1999a): 83–115.

———. "Critical multiculturalism and globalization. Some Implications for a Politics of Resistance." *Journal of Curriculum Theorizing* 15, 3 (1999b): 27–46.

———. "Reconsidering Marx in post-Marxist times: A requiem for postmodernism?" *Educational Researcher* 29, 3 (2000): 25–33.

McMurtry, J. *Unequal freedoms: The global market as an ethical system*. West Hartford, CT: Kumarian Press, 1998.

———. *The cancer stage of capitalism*. London: Pluto Press, 1999.

———. "A failed global experiment: The truth about the US economic model." *Comer* 12, 7 (2000): 10–11.

———. *Value wars: The global market versus the life economy*. London: Pluto Press, 2002.

McMurtry, L. *Walter Benjamin at the Dairy Queen*. New York: Simon & Schuster, 1999.

McNally, D. "The present as history: Thoughts on capitalism at the millennium." *Monthly Review* 51, 3 (1999): 134–145.

McNeil, L. *Contradictions of Control*. Boston: Routledge, 1986.

———. *Contradictions of school reform: Educational costs of standardized testing*. New York: RoutledgeFalmer, 2000.

McQueen, A. "Charter schools increase 40%." *Cincinnati Enquirer* (2000): A8.

McRobbie, A. "Working class girls and the culture of femininity." In *Women take issue*, ed. Women's Study Group. London: Hutchinson, 1982, 96–108.

Mecklenburg, M. E., and P. G. Thompson. *The Adolescent Family Life Program as a Prevention Measure: Public Health Reports* 98 (1983): 21–29.

Melucci, A. *Nomads of the present: Social movements and individual needs in contemporary society*. Philadelphia: Temple University Press, 1989.

Memmi, A. *The colonizer and the colonized*. Boston: Beacon, 1965.

Mercer, K. "Diaspora culture and the dialogic imagination: The aesthetics of black independent film in Britain." In *Black frames: Critical perspectives on black independent cinema*, ed. M. B. Cham and C. Andrade-Watkins. Cambridge: MIT Press, 1988, 50–61.

Mészáros, I. *Beyond capital*. New York: Monthly Review Press, 1995.

———. "Marxism, the capital system, and social revolution: An interview with István Mészáros." *Science and Society* 63, 3 (1999): 338–361.

Miller, J. H. *Black holes. J. Hillis Miller; or Boustrophedonic reading*. Stanford, CA: Stanford University Press, 1999.

Mills, C. W. *The Sociological Imagination*. London: Oxford University Press, 1959.

———. *Power, politics, and people: The collected essays of C. Wright Mills*. Edited by I. L. Horowitz. New York: Ballantine, 1963.

———. *The racial contract*. Ithica, NY: Cornell University Press, 1997.

Monk, J. "God, barbecue, slavery mix at Maurice's." *State* (October 1, 2000): B1–B5.

Moody, K. *Workers in a lean world: Unions in the international economy*. London: Verso, 1997.

Moores, S. *Interpreting audiences*. Thousand Oaks, CA: Sage, 1993.

Morgan, D. L. *Focus groups as qualitative research*. Newbury Park, CA: Sage, 1988.

Morley, D., and K. Chen. (Eds.). *Stuart Hall: Critical dialogues in cultural studies*. New York: Routledge, 1996.

Morris, M. *Curriculum and the holocaust*. Mahwah, NJ: Lawrence Erlbaum Associates, 2001.

Morrison, T. *Beloved*. New York: Alfred A. Knopf, 1987.

Morton-Christmas, A. "An ethnographic study of an African American holiness church in the 1990s: An exploration in alternative education empowerment and free space." Ph.D. dissertation, State University of New York at Buffalo, Department of Educational Leadership Policy, 1999.

Mosley, W. *Devil in a blue dress*. New York: Pocket Books, 1990.

———. *Workin' on the chain gang: Shaking off the dead hand of history*. New York: Ballantine, 2000.

Mouffe, C. "Hegemony and new political subjects." In *Marxism and Interpretation of Cultures*, ed. C. Nelson and L. Grossberg. Urbana: University of Illinois Press, 1998.

Nathan, J. "Possibilities, problems, and progress: Early lessons from the charter school movement." *Phi Delta Kappan* 78, 1 (1996): 18–23.

Neal, L. *Visions of a liberated future*. New York: Thunder's Mouth Press, 1988.

———. "The black arts movement." In *Call and response: The Riverside anthology of the African American literary tradition*, ed. P. L. Hill. Boston: Houghton Mifflin, 1998, 1450–1448.

Neary, M. *Travels in Moishe Postone's social universe: A contribution to a critique of political cosmology*. Unpublished paper, 2000.

Nelson, C., P. Treichler, and L. Grossberg. (Eds.) "Cultural Studies: An Introduction." In *Cultural studies*. New York: Routledge, 1992, 1–16.

Niemark, M. K. "If it's so important, why won't they pay for it? Public higher education at the turn of the century." *Monthly Review* 51, 5 (1999): 20–31.

Noddings, N. *Caring, a feminine approach to ethics and moral education*. Berkeley, CA: University of California Press, 1984.

Noriega, C. A. "Review of *Lethal Weapon*." In *Magill's cinema annual: 1992: A survey of the films of 1981*, ed. F. N. Magill. Englewood Cliffs, NJ: Salem, 1988, 210–213.

———. "Between a weapon and a formula: Chicano cinema and its contexts." In *Chicanos and film: Representation and resistance*, ed. C. A. Noriega. Minneapolis: University of Minnesota Press, 1992a, 141–167.

———. Introduction to *Chicanos and film: Representation and resistance*, ed. C. A. Noriega. Minneapolis: University of Minnesota Press, 1992b, xi–xxvi.

———. "Imagined borders: Locating Chicano cinema in America/America." In *The ethnic eye: Latino media arts*, ed. C.A. Noriega and A. M. Lopez. Minneapolis: University of Minnesota Press, 1996, 3–21.

Ogbu, J. U. "Understanding cultural diversity and learning." *Educational Researcher* 21 (1992): 5–14, 24.

Oja, S. N., and L. Smulyan. *Collaborative action research: A developmental approach*. London: Falmer, 1989.

Ojanen, S. "A process in which personal pedagogical knowledge is created through the teacher education experience." Paper presented at the International Conference in Teacher Education, Tel-Aviv, Israel, 1993. (ERIC Document Reproduction Service No. ED 398 200).

Ollman, B. *How to take an exam and remake the world*. Montreal: Black Rose Books, 2001.

Orfield, G., and S. E. Eaton. *Dismantling desegregation: The quiet reversal of Brown v. Board of Education*. New York: New Press, 1996.

Painter, N. *Sojourner Truth: A life, a symbol.* New York: Norton, 1996.

Panitch, L., and S. Gindin. "Transcending pessimism: Rekindling socialist imagination." In *After the fall: 1989 and the future of freedom,* ed. G. Katsiaficas. London: Routledge, 2001, 175–199.

Parenti, M. "Rollback: Aftermath of the overthrow of communism." In *After the fall: 1989 and the future if freedom,* ed. G. Katsiaficas. London: Routledge, 2001, 153–158.

Parks, R. (with Jim Haskins), *Rosa Parks: My story.* New York: Dial Books, 1992.

Parks, R. *Quiet strength: The faith, hope, and the heart of a woman who changed a nation.* New York: Zondervan, 1994.

Parks, R. (with Gregory Reed), *Dear Mrs. Parks: A dialogue with today's youth.* New York: Lee & Low, 1996.

Pedelty, M. *War Stories: The culture of foreign correspondents.* New York: Routledge, 1995.

Peery, N. "The birth of a modern proletariat." In *Cutting edge: Technology, information, capitalism and social revolution,* ed. J. Davis, T. Hirschl, and M. Stack. New York: Verso, 1997, 297–302.

Perlstein, D. "Saying the unsaid: Girl killing and the curriculum." *Journal of Curriculum and Supervision* 14, 1 (1998): 88–104.

Perrucci, R., and E. Wysong. *The new class society.* Boulder, CO: Rowman & Littlefield, 1999.

Petras, J. "Globalization and citizenship: Social and political dimensions." *Working Papers in Cultural Studies* 22 (2000): 1–20. Pullman: Department of Comparative American Cultures, Washington State University.

Phillips, A. "Who needs civil society?" *Dissent* 46, 1 (1999): 56–61.

Pinar, W. F. *The gender of racial politics and violence in America.* New York: Peter Lang, 2001.

Plato. *The republic.* Trans. A. Bloom. New York: Basic Books, 1991.

Pohan, C. A. "Preservice teachers' beliefs about diversity: Uncovering factors leading to multicultural responsiveness." *Equity & Excellence in Education* 29 (1996): 62–69.

Popkewitz, T. *Struggling for the soul: The politics of schooling and the construction of the teacher.* New York: Teachers College Press, 1998.

Pratt, M. L. "Arts of the Contact Zone." *Profession '91* (New York: Modern Languages Association) (1991): 33–40.

Putnam, R. D. "Bowling alone: America's declining social capital." *Current* 373 (June 1995): 3–9.

Radel, T. "Councilman handcuffing the police." *Cincinnati Enquirer* (July 10, 1996).

Rawls, J. *Political Liberalism.* New York: Columbia University Press, 1993.

Reeves, J.L., and R. Campbell. *Cracked coverage: Television news, the anti-cocaine crusade, and the Reagan legacy.* Durham, N.C.: Duke University Press, 1994.

Reichart, M. "Disturbances of difference." In *Construction sites: Excavating class, race, sexuality and gender,* ed. L. Weis and M. Fine. New York: Teachers College Press, 2000.

Reid, M. A. *Postnegritude visual and literary culture.* Albany: State University of New York Press, 1997.

Reinarman, C., and H.G. Levine. "The crack attack: Politics and media in the crack scare." In *Crack in America: Demon drugs and social justice,* ed. C. Reinarman and H. G. Levine. Berkeley: University of California Press, 1997, 18–51.

Rikowski, G. *Messing with the explosive commodity: School improvement, educational research and labor-power in the era of global capitalism.* A paper prepared for the symposium "If We Aren't Pursuing Improvement, What Are We Doing?" held at the British Educational Research Association Conference, Cardiff University, Wales, September 7, 2000.

———. *After he manuscript broke off: Through on Marx, social class and education.* A paper prepared for the British Sociological Association, Education Study Group Meeting, King's College London, June 23, 2001a.

———. *The battle in Seattle: Its significance for education.* London: Tufnell, 2001b.

Robinson, T., and J. Ward. "A belief in self far greater than anyone's disbelief: Cultivating healthy resistance among African American female adolescents." In *Women, girls and psychotherapy: Reframing resistance,* ed. C. Gilligan, A. Rogers, and D. Tolman. Bimingtan, NY: Harrington Park, 1991, 87–103.

Robinson, W., and J. Harris. "Towards a global ruling class? Globalization and the transnational capitalist class." *Science & Society* 64, 1 (2000): 11–54.

Roediger, D. (Ed.). *Black on white: Black writers on what it means to be white.* New York: Schocken, 1998.

Roffman, P., and J. Purdy. *The Hollywood social problems film.* Bloomington: Indiana University Press, 1981.

Ronell, A. "Video/television/Rodney King: Twelve steps beyond the pleasure principle." In

Transmission toward a post television culture, 2nd ed., ed. P. d'Agostino and D. Tafler. Thousand Oaks, CA: Sage, 1995, 105–120.

Rorty, R. *Contingency, irony, and solidarity*. Cambridge: Cambridge University Press, 1989.

Rose, L. C., and A. M. Gallup. "The 33rd annual Phi Delta Kappan/Gallup poll of the public's attitudes toward the public schools." *Phi Delta Kappan* 83, 1 (2001): 41–58.

Ryan, W. *Equality*. New York: Pantheon, 1981.

Sadker, M., and D. Sadker. *Failing at fairness: How our schools cheat girls*. New York: Touchstone, 1995.

Said, E. *Orientalism*. New York: Vintage, 1978.

San Juan, Jr. "E. Raymond Williams and the idea of cultural revolution." *College Literature* 26, 2 (1999): 118–136.

Sapon-Shevin, M. "Gifted education and the protection of privilege." In *Beyond Silenced Voices*, ed. L. Weis and M. Fine. Albany: State University of New York Press, 1993, 25–44.

Saunders, F. S. *Who paid the piper: The CIA and the cultural cold war*. London: Granta, 1999.

Schnailberg, L. "Staying home from school." *Education Week on the Web, 1996* [cited April 4, 2000]. Available at www.edweek.org/we/vol-15/38home.h15

Schwab, J. *College curriculum and student protest*. Chicago: University of Chicago. 1969.

Scott, J. "Experience." In *Feminists theorize the political*, ed. J. Butler and J. Scott. New York: Routledge, 1992, 22–40.

Sedgwick, E. *The epistemology of the closet*. Berkeley: University of California Press, 1992.

Seibert, F., T. Peterson, and W. Schramm. *Four theories of the press*. Chicago: University of Illinois Press, 1963.

Seligman, A. B. *The idea of a civil society*. New York: The Free Press, 1992.

Shohat, E., and R. Stam. *Unthinking Eurocentrism: Multiculturalism and the media*. London: Routledge, 1994.

Singh, A. "Free trade and the 'starving child' defense: A forum." *Nation*, 270, 16 (2000): 24–26.

Skertic, M. "No contracts for 150 more in public schools." *Cincinnati Enquirer* (April 28, 1995a): B4.

———. "400 demand justice." *Cincinnati Enquirer* (April 30, 1995b): A1, A13.

———. High school academic standard . . . (May 17, 1995c): A1.

———. "Doors close on hopes: Student moms lose support as daycare center shuts down." *Cincinnati Enquirer* (May 31, 1995d): C1, C5.

Slack, J. "The theory and method of articulation." In *Stuart Hall: Critical dialogues in cultural studies*, ed. D. Morley and K. Chen. New York: Routledge, 1996, 112–127.

Smith, C. *Marx at the millennium*. Chicago: Pluto, 1996.

Smith, G. *Nietzsche, Heidegger, and the Transition to Postmodernity*. Chicago: University of Chicago Press, 1996.

Smith, S. E. *Dancing in the street: Motown and the cultural history of Detroit*. Cambridge, MA: Harvard University Press, 2001.

Smith, T. M. *The pocket condition of education 1997 (97–980)*. Washington D.C.: U.S. Department of Education, National Center for Education Statistics, 1997.

Smith, V. Introduction to *Representing blackness: Issues in film and video*, ed. V. Smith. New Brunswick, NJ: Rutgers University Press, 1997, 1–12.

Solomon, P. *Black resistance in school*. Albany: State University of New York Press, 1992.

Spivak, G. (with E. Rooney). "In a word." Interview. *Differences* 1, 2 (1990): 124–155.

Spivak, G. *Outside in the teaching machine*. New York: Routledge, 1993.

Stinger, E. T. *Action research: A handbook for practitioners*. Thousand Oaks, CA: Sage, 1996.

Storey, J. *Cultural studies and the study of popular culture: Theories and methods*. Athens: University of Georgia Press, 1996.

Stowe, H. B. *Uncle Tom's cabin: Or life among the lowly*. 1852.

Strope, L. *Bush dismissive of NAACP push on Confederate flag issue*, September 7, 1999 (cited February 10, 2002). Available at http://www.texnews.com/abilene2000/elec/flag0907.html" [cited February 10, 2002].

Stroud, J. "As legislators return, S.C. senator's 'insult' hardens flag debate." *State* (January 11, 2000): A1-A10.

Su, J. Z. X. "The study of the education of educators: A profile of teacher education students." *Journal of Research and Development in Education* 26, 3 (1993): 125–132.

Sugrue, T. *The origins of the urban crisis: Race and inequality in Detroit*. Princeton, NJ: Princeton University Press, 1998.

Tabachnick, B. R., and K. M. Zeichner. "The impact of the student teaching experience on the development of teacher perspectives." *Journal of Teacher Education* 35, 6 (1984): 28–36.

Tarcov, N. "The meaning of democracy." In *Democracy, education, and the schools*, ed. R. Soder, New York: Jossey-Bass, 1996, 1–36.

Taussig, M. *Defacement: Public secrecy and the labor of the negative*. Stanford, CA: Stanford University Press, 1999.

Teeple, G. *Globalization and the decline of social reform*. Atlantic Highlands, NJ: Humanities Press, 1995.

Tella, S. "Talking shop via e-mail: A thematic linguistic analysis of electronic mail communication." University of Helsinki, Department of Teacher Education, Helsinki, Finland, 1992. (ERIC Document Reproduction Service No. ED 352 015).

Terrill, M. M., and D.L.H. Mark. "The Role of Effective Mentors in Learning to Teach." *Journal of Teacher Education* 51 (2000): 149–155.

Tester, K. *Media culture and morality*. London: Routledge, 1994.

Thompson, E. P. *The making of the English working class*. New York: Vintage, 1963.

Thompson. W. *The left in history: Revolution and reform in twentieth-century politics*. London: Pluto, 1997.

Trend, D. *The crisis of meaning*. Minneapolis: University of Minnesota Press, 1995.

Trifonas, P. "Simulations of culture: Disney and the crafting of American popular culture." *Educational Researcher*, 30,1 (2001): 23–28.

Trinh, T. Min-Ha. *When the moon waxes red: Representation, gender, and cultural politics*. New York: Routledge, 1991.

Tuchman, G. *Making news: A study in the construction of reality*. New York: Free Press, 1978.

Turow, J. *Breaking up America: Advertisers and the new media world*. Chicago: University of Chicago Press, 1997.

Valli, L. *Becoming clerical workers*. Boston: Routledge Kegan & Paul, 1986.

Van Galen, J., and M. A. Pitman. *Home schooling: Political, historical, and pedagogical perspectives*. Norwood, NJ: Ablex, 1991.

Vrana, D. "Education's pied piper with a dark past." *Los Angeles Times* (September 7, 1998): A1.

Vygotsky, L. *Mind and society*. Cambridge, MA: Harvard University Press, 1978.

Wadsworth, D. "Do media shape public perceptions of America's schools?" In *Imaging education: The media and schools in America*, ed. G. Maeroff. New York: Teachers College Press, 1998, 59–68.

Walzer, M. "Rescuing Civil Society." *Dissent* 46, 1 (1999): 62–67.

Wathen, B. "Hodges steps out as leader with well-thought-out flag plan." *The State* (February 20, 2000): D2.

Watkins, S. C. *Representing: Hip hop culture and the production of black cinema*. Chicago: University of Chicago Press, 1998.

Watson, S. "Terminal city: Place, culture, and regional inflection." In *Vancouver art and artists: 1931–1983*. Vancouver, B.C., Canada: Vancouver Art Gallery, 1983.

Weatherby, W. J. *James Baldwin: Artist on fire*. New York: Donald I. Fine, 1989.

Weedon, C. *Feminist practice and poststructuralist theory*. Oxford: Basil Blackwell, 1987.

Weintraub, A. "Cop gets desk duty in taped arrest." *Cincinnati Enquirer* (April 27, 1995a): A1, A4.

———. "Arrest outcry unabated." *Cincinnati Enquirer* (April 28, 1995b): B1, B4.

———. "Police chief, councilmen tangle over arrest." *Cincinnati Enquirer* (May 2, 1995c): A1, A4.

———. "Police tape reveals chaos." *Cincinnati Enquirer* (May 4, 1995d): A1, A8.

Weintraub, A., and M. Curnette. "Both sides protested Crosby proposals." *Cincinnati Enquirer* (June 10, 1995): A1, A4.

Weis, L. *Between two worlds: Black students in an urban community college*. London: Routledge, 1985.

———. *Working class without work: High school students in a de-industrializing economy*. New York: Routledge, 1990.

Weis, L., and L. Fine (Eds.). *Beyond silenced voices*. Albany: State University of New York Press, 1993.

Weis, L., and M. Fine. "Narrating the 1980s and 1990s: Voices of poor and working class white and African American men." *Anthropology and Education Quarterly* 27, 4 (1996): 1–24.

Weis, L. and M. Fine (Eds.). *Construction Sites*. New York: Teachers College Press, 2000.

Weis, L., J. Marusza, and M. Fine. "Out of the cupboard: Kids, domestic violence, and schools." *British Journal of Sociology of Education*, 19, 1 (1998): 53–74.

Weis, L., A. Prowellor, and C. Centrie. In *Off-white*, ed. M. Fine, L. Weis, L. Powell, and L. Wong. New York: Routledge, 1997.

Weis, L., M. Fine, C. Bertram, A. Prowellon, and J. Marusza. "I've slept in clothes long enough: Excavating the sounds of domestic violence among women in the white working class." *Urban Review* 30, 1 (1998): 1–27.

Wells, A. S., and UCLA Research Associates. "Charter school reform in California: Does it meet expectations?" *Phi Delta Kappan* 80, 4 (1998): 305–311.

Wells, A. S., A. Lopez, J. Scott, and J. Holme. "Charter schools as postmodern paradox: Rethinking social stratification in an age of deregulated school choice." *Harvard Educational Review* 69, 2 (1999): 172–204.

Went, R. *Globalization: Neoliberal challenge, radical responses*. London and Sterling, VA: Pluto, 2000.

West, C. "On my intellectual vocation." In *The Cornel West reader*. New York: Perseus Books, 1999, 19–33.

Wexler, P. *Becoming somebody: Toward a social psychology of school*. London: Falmer, 1992.

Whatley, M. "Raging hormones and powerful cars: The construction of men's sexuality in school sex education and popular adolescent films." In *Postmodernism, feminism and cultural politics*, ed. H. Giroux. Albany: State University of New York Press, 1991, 119–143.

Whitty, G. *Sociology and school knowledge: Curriculum theory, research and politics*. London: Methuen, 1985.

Wilcox, B. "Sexual obsession: Public policy and adolescent girls." In *Beyond appearances: A new look at adolescent girls*, ed. N. Johnson, M. Roberts and J. Worrell. Washington, DC: APA, 1998.

Willard, D. J., and D. Oplinger. "School battle eludes voters, takes its cues from coalitions," December 15, 1999. *Akron Beacon Journal Online* [cited September 4, 2001]. Available at http://www.ohio.com/bj/projects/ whose_choice/docs/021598.htm

Williams, R. *The long revolution*. New York: Columbia University Press, 1961.

Willingham, B. "Community reactions divided on decision." *Greenville News* (May 19, 2000): A10.

Willis, P. *Learning to labor: How working class kids get working class jobs*. New York: Columbia University Press, 1977.

Witheford, N. "Cycles of circuits and struggles in high-technology capitalism." In *Cutting edge: Technology, information, capitalism and social revolution*, ed. J. Davis, T. Hirschil, and M. Stack. New York: Verso, 1997, 195–242.

Wood, E. M. "Identity crisis." *In These Times* (June 13, 1994): 28–29.

Woodford, F., and A. Woodford. *All our yesterdays: A brief history of Detroit*. Detroit, MI: Wayne State University Press, 1969.

Yon, D. *Elusive culture: Schooling, race, and identity in global times*. Albany: State University of New York Press, 2000.

Young, M. *The curriculum of the future: From the 'new sociology of education' to a critical theory of learning*. London: Falmer Press, 1998.

Žižek, S. *The ticklish subject: The absent center of political ontology*. London: Verso, 1999.

———. "Why we all love to hate Haider." *New Left Review* 2 (second series) (2000), 37–46.

———. *Did somebody say totalitarianism? Five interventions in the (mis)use of a notion*. London and New York: Verso, 2001a.

———. *Repeating Lenin*. Unpublished manuscript, 2001b.

———. "Have Michael Hardt and Antonio Negri rewritten the *Communist Manifesto* for the twenty-first century?" *Rethinking Marxism*, 13,3/4 (2001): 190–198.

———. "Seize the day: Lenin's legacy." *London Review of Books*, July 23, 2002. As cited in *Interactivist Info Exchange*, http://slash.autonomedia.org/article.pl?sid= 02/08/04/2214225&mode=nested, 1–26.

Zollers, N. J., and A. K. Ramanathan. "For-profit charter schools and students with disabilities." *Phi Delta Kappan* 80, 4 (1998): 297–303.

Contributors

Kathleen Knight Abowitz is Associate Professor of Educational Leadership at Miami University of Ohio. She is the author of *Making Meaning of Community in an American High School: A Feminist-Pragmatist Critique of the Liberal-Communitarian Debates*.

Dennis Carlson is Professor in the Department of Educational Leadership and Director of the Center for Education and Cultural Studies at Miami University. He is widely published in educational journals and is the author of *Teachers and Crisis, Making Progress,* and *Leaving Safe Harbors,* and is coeditor with Michael Apple, of *Power/Knowledge/Pedagogy,* and with Thomas Oldenski of *Educational Yearning*.

Warren Crichlow is Associate Professor in the Faculty of Education, York University, Toronto, Canada, where he teaches in the area of cultural studies and education. He is coeditor with Cameron McCarthy of *Race, Identity, and Representation in Education*.

Toby Daspit is Assistant Professor of Curriculum Studies at Western Michigan University. He is coeditor of *Popular Culture and Critical Pedagogy*.

Norman K. Denzin is Distinguished Professor of Communications, College of Communications Scholar, and Research Professor of Communications, Sociology, Cinema Studies, and Humanities at the University of Illinois at Urbana–Champaign. His publications include the *Handbook of Qualitative Inquiry* (edited with Yvonna Lincoln), *Images of Postmodern Society,* and *The Cinematic Society*.

Greg Dimitriadis is Assistant Professor of Sociology of Education in the Department of Educational Leadership and Policy at the University at Buffalo, SUNY. He is the author of *Performing Identity/Performing Culture: Hip Hop as Text, Pedagogy, and Lived Practice* and coauthor, along with Cameron McCarthy, of *Reading and Teaching the Postcolonial: From Baldwin to Basquiat and Beyond*. He has two books forthcoming from Teachers College Press: *Struggling Toward Success: Masculinity, Adulthood, and Friendship in Urban America Today* and *Qualitative Approaches to Language and Literacy Research* (coauthored with George Kamberelis).

Ramin Farahmandpur is an Assistant Professor in the Department of Educational Policy, Foundations, and Administrative Studies at Portland State University. A former middle school teacher in Los Angeles, he worked with UCLA's teacher education program. He was also a lecturer at the Charter School of Education at California State University, Los Angeles, before he accepted a position at Portland State University in 2002. Farahmandpur has coauthored a number of articles on a variety of topics and issues ranging from globalization, neoliberalism, critical pedagogy, and critical multiculturalism. Currently, he is completing a book with Peter McLaren, which is titled: *Globalization and the New Imperialism: Towards a Revolutionary Pedagogy*.

Michelle Fine is Professor of Social Psychology at the City University of New York Graduate Center. Her recent books include *The Unknown City* (with Lois

Weis), *Off White* (with Lois Weis, Linda Powell, and Mun Wong), and *Becoming Gentlemen* (with Lani Guinier).

Debra Freedman is Assistant Professor of Curriculum and Supervision in the Department of Curriculum and Instruction at Pennsylvania State University. Her research interests include teacher education, media cultural studies, and feminist theory/pedagogy. She teaches undergraduate courses in secondary education and graduate courses in curriculum, supervision, and research.

Suellyn M. Henke received her Ph.D. from Miami University of Ohio in 2000. She was an Assistant Professor of Education at the University of Hawaii–Hilo from 2000–2002. She now teaches at Albion College in Michigan.

Cameron McCarthy teaches cultural studies at the Institute of Communications Research at the University of Illinois at Urbana–Champaign.

Peter McLaren is a Professor in the Urban Schooling Division of the Graduate School of Education and Information Studies, University of California, Los Angeles. He is the author and editor of more than thirty-five books on a variety of topics, including the sociology of education, critical pedagogy, and critical ethnography. He is the recent recipient of the inaugural Paulo Freire Social Justice Award, presented by Chapman University. His most recent books are *Che Guevara, Paulo Freire, and the Pedagogy of Revolution* and (with Dave Hill, Mike Cole, and Glenn Rikowski) *Marxism against Postmodernism in Educational Theory*.

Susan L. Schramm-Pate is Assistant Professor in the College of Education at the University of South Carolina, specializing in curriculum history and theory. She received her Ph.D. in educational administration (curriculum) at Miami University of Ohio. Her books include *Transforming the Curriculum: Thinking Outside the Box* and *A Separate Sisterhood: Women Who Shaped Southern Education in the Progressive Era* (with Katherine Reynolds). Her research also appears in the *International Journal of Educational Research, Journal of Communications and Minority Issues*, and *Art Education Journal*.

Carlos Alberto Torres, a political sociologist of education, is Professor of Social Sciences and Comparative Education at UCLA and Director of the Latin American Center. His most recent book, with Raymond Morrow, is *Reading Freire and Habermas*.

John A. Weaver is an Associate Professor of Curriculum Studies at Georgia Southern University. His most recent book is *Under Suspicion: Essays on Popular Culture, "the Classics," and Academic Work*. He has edited three books, including *Popular Culture and Critical Pedagogy* with Toby Daspit. He is also the coeditor of two special journal issues: "Hip Hop Pedagogies" with Greg Dimitriadis and Toby Daspit in *Taboo* and "Popular Culture as Curriculum Theorizing" with Toby Daspit and Dianne Smith in the *Journal of Curriculum Theorizing*.

Lois Weis is Professor of Sociology of Education in the Department of Educational Leadership and Policy at the University at Buffalo, SUNY. She is the author and/or editor of numerous books and articles on social class, race, gender, and schooling. Her most recent books include *The Unknown City: The Lives of Poor and Working Class Young Adults* (coauthored with Michelle Fine) and *Construction Sites: Excavating Race, Class, and Gender among Urban Youth* (coedited with Michelle Fine).

Index